ESCHATOLOGY:
A Futurist View

L. Thomas Holdcroft

CeeTeC

CeeTeC Publishing
Abbotsford, Canada

The author wishes to express sincere thanks to the following who contributed most helpfully in preparing the manuscript for publication: Dr. Truett Bobo, Art Craddock, Debie Liva, Sylvia Quiring, Laurence Van Kleek, and Dr. Dwight Wilson.

ESCHATOLOGY: A Futurist View

Holdcroft, L. Thomas (Leslie Thomas)
    Eschatology: a futurist view /
    L. Thomas Holdcroft
    p. cm.
    Includes bibliographical references and index.
    ISBN 0-9680580-4-3 (pbk.)
    1. Eschatology. 2. Second Advent.
3. Tribulation (Christian eschatology)
4. Judgment Day. 5. Millennium
I. Title
BT821.H726 2001   236

Printed in the United States

PUBLISHED BY

CeeTeC Publishing   U.S. Address:
P.O. Box 466 Main   P.O. Box 1117
Abbotsford BC V2S 5Z5   Sumas WA 98295-1117
☎ (604) 853-5352 or (604) 807-5831

Table of Contents

Affectionately dedicated to all students of biblical eschatology who qualify for God's blessing promised in Revelation 1:3, whether or not they accept the views that this book defends.

Figures and Charts

Throughout this book, when Greek or Hebrew words are cited, their approximate pronunciation is shown phonetically. The syllable to be accented is printed in capital letters.

Traditionally, the names of eschatological events are capitalized (e.g., Rapture, Millennium). In deference to current styles, however, CeeTeC's editorial committee has elected to minimize capitalization. We trust this usage will be acceptable to our readers.

ONE

The Study of Biblical Eschatology

Eschatology is a theological study concerned with topics and events that are yet future in God's program. The Greek root *eschatos* (ES-khat-os) denotes "that which is most remote or uttermost," or "that which is last and after which there is nothing to follow." Topics included in the study of eschatology are the rapture, the second coming of Christ, the intermediate state, the tribulation, the resurrections, the millennium, the judgments, and the eternal state.

Since eschatology concerns the future, its basic sources are the prophetic portions of Scripture. The nonbiblical term "eschatology" (which came into the English language about 1845) is not identical with the biblical term "prophecy." In its primary definition, "prophecy" (Gk. *propheteia* [prof-ay-TIE-ah]) means "that which is divinely revealed and spoken by a prophet," and such messages may or may not concern the future. The bulk of the contents of the sixteen Old Testament books that scholars call the major and minor prophets is prophecy, but only some portions reveal the future. The expression "predictive prophecy" identifies that portion of prophecy that is also eschatology.

In many Christian circles, sermon topics popularly called "prophecy" are an application of eschatology. Serious students of Biblical eschatology would likely prefer to distance themselves from extreme speculative examples of this sort. As this book will seek to establish, however, a strong Biblical mandate exists for the legitimate study of eschatology or predictive prophecy. Note that Peter's address on the day of Pentecost (Acts 2:14-36), said to be "the first Christian sermon ever preached," was largely the citation of a series of Old Testament prophetic portions.

The Development of Biblical Eschatology

The church has been very slow in developing its eschatological understandings. Even to the present day, among the various topics of theology, eschatology tends to be the most incomplete and controversial. Christians have found many other demanding issues to resolve, and most circles have assigned eschatology a low priority.

The eschatology of the church Fathers

The Fathers who taught and wrote in the era immediately following the apostles generally settled for casual references to eschatological themes. A few of them can be noted as follows:

Clement of Rome (flourished first century) taught the literal and visible return of Christ and the bodily resurrection of the dead. He made no mention of the millennium.

Papias (c. 60-130) wrote of the fulfillment of Old Testament prophecies, the return of Christ, and a future millennium. His concept of the millennium, however, was imaginatively exaggerated.

Justin Martyr (c. 100-165) described the resurrection of the dead and the reign of Christ in Jerusalem for 1,000 years as foretold in the prophecies of Ezekiel and Isaiah.

Tertullian (c. 160-220) in *Against Marcion* spoke of the resurrection of the dead and of a future millennial kingdom ruled from Jerusalem.

Though the references are brief and nonsystematic, most scholars agree that the literature which survives from this early era indicates that millennialism, achieved through the return of Christ, was a commonly held belief. These fragmentary eschatological expressions comprise a rudimentary statement of literal futurism.

Some advance was evident in the second century. Irenaeus (c. 120-c. 202), of the city of Lyons, in his five-volume work *Against Heresies*, interpreted Scripture literally to develop a relatively coherent futurist eschatology. He wrote that in the last days of the sixth millennium (counting from creation and based on a year-day count), the Roman Empire would be divided into ten kingdoms. Antichrist would emerge within these kingdoms and rule for three and one-half years. At the conclusion of Antichrist's rule, Irenaeus saw the triumphant return of Christ, the resurrection of the righteous, the establishment of Christ's millennial kingdom of earth, the great white throne judgment, and the launching of the eternal state. Obviously, Irenaeus' account was the most complete expression of futurist premillennial eschatology thus far. Scholars debate whether Irenaeus suggested that the church would be raptured to avoid Antichrist's persecutions, and thus this aspect of his teaching remains inconclusive.

The Alexandrian school that included Clement of Alexandria (c. 150-215) and Origen (c. 185-254) rejected literal futurism. This school held that "all Scripture must be taught allegorically," and what scholars had thought to be future could well be a present spiritual event. In his commentary on Matthew Origin wrote, "There comes daily, to the soul of every believer, the second advent of the Word in the prophetic clouds, that is, in the writings of the prophets and apostles." He considered eschatology to be little more than a description of heaven and hell. Many apparent prophecies of future events on earth were in reality descriptions of the eternal struggle between good and evil.

In the field of eschatology, allegorism rapidly took hold. By the end of the third century it was well entrenched, and futurism was scarcely to be heard from again until the nineteenth century. As the church emerged from the era of persecution early in the fourth century, many Christians concluded that these political developments were the dawning of the millennium.

Aurelius Augustine (354-430), who otherwise championed biblical orthodoxy, became a spokesperson for the allegorical interpretation of prophecy. He held that, while Scripture overall should be interpreted literally, those portions concerning eschatology or prophecy should be interpreted figuratively. Augustine declared that belief in a literal future kingdom was "carnal," that biblical time designations (e.g., 1000 years) were figurative, and that the new birth was one's personal resurrection by which he entered the millennium. Such outlooks assured that the major church creeds beginning in this era supported only a vague amillennialism[1].

Medieval and early Reformation eschatology

Throughout the middle ages the Roman Catholic church maintained Augustine's allegorical view of eschatology, and it saw the church as embodying the kingdom of God. On the basis of tradition, however, the church expanded its beliefs to include the doctrine of purgatory. In the later medieval era, St. Thomas Aquinas (c. 1225-1274), in his *Summa Theologica*, compiled a systematic statement of the church's eschatological teaching. He described a future bodily resurrection, a general judgment, and the visible return of Jesus. Since he believed that the millennial kingdom was already present through the victories of the church, he made no mention of a future millennium and thus his view was amillennial. The *Summa Theologica* remains the basis of modern Roman Catholic theology.

During the medieval period, the occasional rare scholar who managed to see in his Latin manuscripts eschatological viewpoints that differed from those of Augustine or St. Thomas was either ignored, or denounced as a heretic. Any major change

---

1   Chapter 3 provides definitions of some of the terms used in discussing systems of eschatology.

in the situation awaited the day when thoughtful readers, independent of direct ecclesiastical control, could sit before an open Bible in their everyday national language and systematically research the eschatological texts.

The neglect of the serious study of eschatology continued into the era of the Protestant Reformation (1517). Martin Luther (1483-1546), for the most part, retained the overall eschatological beliefs of Catholicism, but he concluded that the coming of Christ was imminent. Also, he identified the papacy with the Antichrist, and thus he adopted a historicist interpretation of the Book of Revelation. In his view, the millennium had ended before his lifetime. John Calvin (1509-1564) seems to have said little about eschatology, but one of his associates, Martin Bucer (1491-1581) introduced an important insight. Bucer taught that in a future day the Jews would be converted to Christ. This claim marked a shift from traditional amillennialism to postmillennialism, and it found increasing acceptance in succeeding centuries.

An important outcome of the Reformation was that it led to Luther's German Bible (1522), and Tyndale's and Coverdale's English Bibles (1525 and 1535 respectively). The availability of these biblical texts in the vernacular provided new incentives for the development of eschatology. At least some scholars, such as Hugh Latimer (martyred 1555), were able to begin to explore the outcomes of a futuristic approach to eschatological Scriptures. Most scholars, however, continued to overlook eschatology, while splinter sects escalated it into radical extremes.

The statements of faith of the emerging Protestant denominations tended to reaffirm Roman Catholic allegorism and to maintain traditional amillennialism, though they rejected the non-Biblical doctrine of purgatory. Methodism's John Wesley (1703-1791) adopted the eschatology of postmillennialism, but in later centuries most believers who were committed to holiness (Methodism's primary emphasis) adopted Darby's futurist premillennialism.

Although the phenomenon was not new[2], the fallacy of setting a date for the return of Christ became a recurring ground for discrediting eschatology based on literal Scripture. Bible readers who rejected traditional ecclesiastical authority were especially vulnerable to this pitfall. The German peasants, who in the Münzer Revolt (1533-35) attempted through military action to establish that city as the millennial new Jerusalem,

---

2   One of the earliest predictions was by the church father Lactantius who taught that Christ would return in the year 200.

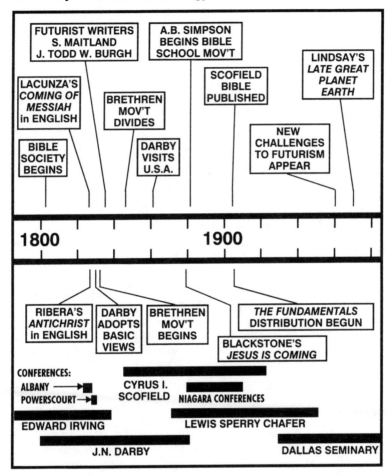

Fig. 1. Significant events and personalities in the nineteenth and twentieth centuries leading to the development of futurism with its view of Christ's two-stage return and a pretribulation rapture.

similarly confounded the development of biblically sound eschatology.

Precursors of modern futurist eschatology

Following the Reformation, two Catholic scholars wrote in support of futurist eschatology. Their motive in each case was to defend the Pope from critical attacks by Protestants. In 1580, the Jesuit scholar Francisco Ribera (1537-1591) published *Antichrist and the Scarlet Woman*. He argued that, contrary to charges that the Pope was the Antichrist, in fact the Antichrist would only come when future events were fulfilled, and at that time he would destroy the Pope. Cardinal Robert Bellarmine (1542-1621) endorsed Ribera's position and wrote in its defense. Bellarmine taught that Antichrist would rule for three and one-half years.

Among John Calvin's followers, Johann Alsted (1588-1638) adopted a futurist position. His scholarly volume *Beloved City* was clearly premillennial in its approach, but he seems not to have influenced mainstream Calvinism. In 1627 a contemporary in England, Joseph Mede, (or Mead), (1586-1638), under Church of England auspices, published *Clavis Apocalyptica* (The Key of the Revelation), a commentary on the Book of Revelation. He interpreted the book as portraying future events, including one thousand years of peace on earth. Mede held that 1 Thessalonians 4:13-18 taught the catching up of believers, and he called this event the "rapture." Ed Hindson, who tells of Mede's accomplishments, comments, "In many ways Mede was the forerunner of later dispensational eschatology."[3]

In the nineteenth century, a systematic eschatology based on literal Bible exegesis began to take shape. A notable milestone was the publication in 1812 of *The Coming of Messiah in Glory and Majesty* by Roman Catholic Jesuit Manuel Lacunza (1731-1801)[4]. From its completion in 1790 this manuscript, under the pseudonym J.J. Ben-Ezra, had circulated surreptitiously. In 1826, British revivalist Edward Irving (1792-1834) translated this work into English and promoted it within his circle. Also, in 1826, Ribera's futurist volume from the sixteenth century was published for English readers. Influential Protestants who drew on these materials and adopted a futurist eschatology included Samuel R. Maitland, James Todd, and William Burgh. Each of these men published works prior to 1835 defending futuristic beliefs. None of them, however, put forth a systematic two-stage eschatology with a church-wide pretribulation rapture.

Anglican clergyman Lewis Way's publication of *Letters* in 1816 was a further milestone in the development of futurist eschatology. Way interpreted Scripture as portraying an end time return of the Jews to Palestine and their national conversion before the return of Jesus Christ. He taught that when the Old Testament predicted future events for Israel, literal national or ethnic Israel was meant, and not the church. Way's ministry stressed evangelism among Jewish people, and

---

3   Ed Hindson, *Earth's Final Hour*. Eugene: Harvest House Publishers, 1999, p. 52.

4   To validate his credibility as a writer, Lacunza declared that he had read numerous "prophetical books." Apparently, many were studying and writing about prophecy in this era even though few works were notable enough to have been preserved.

the local success of his efforts confirmed to many his eschatological views.

One factor in the nineteenth century development of futurist eschatology was the uneventful passing of certain specified dates and times. Common chronologies counted the tribulation to have begun in 533 when Emperor Justinian asserted secular authority over the church. By reckoning Scripture's 1,260 days (cf. Rev. 11:3; 12:6) as years, the end of the tribulation and Christ's return was determined to be 1793. If 1,290 days (i.e., years) of Daniel 12:11 were counted, the period should have ended in 1823. An alternate system assigned the count's beginning to 457 B.C. when Artaxerxes decreed the restoration of Jerusalem and Israel's temple. Taking the 2,300 days of Daniel 8:14 as years placed the end of the period in 1844. When Christ failed to return on these predicted dates, it became evident that some other method of interpretation was needed.

A further factor in the nineteenth century was the founding of the British and Foreign Bible Society in 1804. At last personal Bibles were readily obtainable in the English-speaking world. The Bible was no longer restricted to the professional scholar who knew Latin, Greek and Hebrew. Even laymen were now equipped to discover what the Bible really said.

J.N. Darby and his successors

Out of such antecedents, many Christians began to pursue the study of futurist eschatology based on the literal interpretation of Scripture. They applied the same principle of interpretation of Scripture to eschatology that the reformers had applied to salvation. Their spokesman became John Nelson Darby (1800-1882). The degree, if any, to which Darby drew from his futurist predecessors has been the subject of a long-standing debate. It seems unnecessary, however, to require specific human origins, since it is simply what literal Scripture teaches. Darby explained matters, "The truths themselves were then revealed of God, through the action of His Spirit, by reading His word."[5] In his report, Tim LaHaye provides evidence that Darby's basic views were in place by 1827, and well before he was impacted either by Lacunza's work or the charismatic followers of Edward Irving. Further, LaHaye sees both these latter "sources" to have been committed to a partial rapture,[6] and therefore their views were not fully acceptable to Darby.

---

5 Cited by R.A. Huebner, *The Truth of the Pre-Tribulation Rapture Recovered.* Morganville: Present Truth Publishers, 1982, p. 35.

6 See Tim LaHaye, *No Fear of the Storm.* Sisters (OR): Multnomah Press, 1992, pp. 115-183; or in the reprinted and retitled edition of this same work see *Rapture Under Attack*, Sisters: Multnomah Press, 1998, pp. 119-176.

A vital contribution of Darby was his teaching of the two-stage return of Christ in the pretribulation rapture. This emphasis on the pretribulation rapture of the church has been called "the cornerstone of Darby's eschatology." In his extensive lifetime of prophetic teaching, Darby traveled widely—Europe, United States, Canada, West Indies, New Zealand—and he published fifty-two books. By these efforts he expanded and systematized futurist eschatology both in Britain and in North America. Also, Darby motivated a wide circle of speakers, writers, and teachers. He identified denominationally with the Brethren Movement.

By the late nineteenth century in North America, the interest in futurist eschatology led to the annual Niagara Bible Conferences which met in New York State on Lake Ontario. These summer conferences began in 1878 and continued to 1909. The overwhelming majority of participants were pretribulationists, and though some speakers and supporters held post or midtribulation views, virtually all were premillennial. Thus, the Niagara and similar conferences popularized premillennialism among North American Christians.

By the twentieth century, summer prophetic Bible conferences as centers for the development of futurist eschatology were largely replaced by the resident Bible college. The publication of the *Scofield Reference Bible* in 1909 placed study helps and references from a futurist standpoint in the hands of millions of Christians. Also in 1909, three million copies of the twelve volume publication *The Fundamentals* were circulated. One of the five themes was Christ's Resurrection and His Second Coming, and this event was described as personal, glorious, and imminent. Though the official eschatology of most mainline denominations remained untouched, futurism flourished widely in laymen's circles and at the undergraduate level in theological education. Futurism was often an aspect of dispensationalism, but in the latter half of the twentieth century the two outlooks tended to separate.

During the nineteenth and twentieth centuries, Darby's futurism with his two-stage return of Christ gained a vast worldwide following. Virtually all who adopted these views held the Scripture as God's Word to be accepted literally. Many were informed and capable scholars with skills to interpret Scripture and evaluate proposed interpretations. That in a few decades such a multitude of Christians became convinced of the truth of Darby's views is strong evidence of the validity of his teaching. When believers checked Darby's teaching with what they read in their Bibles, they concluded that they were in agreement.

Lewis Sperry Chafer's establishment in 1924 of Dallas Theological Seminary significantly boosted futurism. Chafer had been mentored by C.I. Scofield, and thus Scofield's views advanced to graduate level studies. Many who became Bible college teachers trained at Dallas. Chafer was succeeded by John F. Walvoord who became a major voice for pretribulational futurism.

The current scene

At this time, futurist eschatology has by no means won the day, although popular interest remains high. Among all publications in North America, Hal Lindsay's *The Late Great Planet Earth* (1970) became the number one nonfiction best seller for the decade of the 70's, with sales of more than 18 million copies. By 1990 the book was in its 108th printing, and by the beginning of the twenty-first century, sales were at the thirty million mark. Although Lindsay's writing style is unique, his message is that of more or less conventional futurist eschatology.

Eschatology remains a theological frontier, for Christians still differ extensively in the positions they hold and defend. The situation constitutes an exciting challenge and invites research, dialogue, and the pursuit of consensus.

Mandates for the Study of Biblical Eschatology

Though there are limits upon what humans can understand, God desires that His people be informed regarding His future plans. "When he, the Spirit of truth, comes, he will guide you into all truth . . . and he will tell you what is yet to come" (John 16:13).

Commonly recognized facts about the eschatological content of the Bible include the following:

1) about 165,000 words in the Bible when written were predictive prophecy (Wilbur Smith),

2) a total of 8,352 verses or 27% of the Bible is predictive material[7] (J. Barton Payne),

3) Matthew, Mark and Luke include a greater amount of prophetic material than that which is contained in the entire Book of Revelation (Wilbur Smith),

4) the prophetic verses of the Bible discuss 737 separate topics (J. Barton Payne),

5) at least 16 (some scholars count as high as 19) Bible books are classified as basically prophetic,

---

7   In his generation, Lewis Sperry Chafer estimated that one-fifth of the text of Scripture was prophetic when it was written.

6) the only Bible books with no predictions are Ruth, Song of Solomon, Philemon, and 3 John (J. Barton Payne),

7) a total of 1,527 Old Testament passages refer to the second coming; in the New Testament Jesus twenty-one times spoke of His return (Joe Jordan),

8) at least 641 Bible passages refer to the ministry of prophecy and prophesying,

9) approximately 225 Bible passages refer to a future divine kingdom,

10) in the New Testament the doctrine of the second coming of Christ is spoken of in 318 verses and this total is substantially greater than that of any other doctrine including the atoning blood and saving faith.

A goal of Daniel's vision of the seventy "sevens" (weeks or heptads) was "to seal up vision and prophecy" (Dan. 9:24). Scholars understand these words to refer to a time when all prophecy is fulfilled. Scripture plainly sets forth God's plans for humans, and His plans for national Israel. At the conclusion of his visions, Daniel was instructed, "close up and seal the words of the scroll until the time of the end" (Dan. 12:4). After a reference to Daniel's vision, however, Jesus commented, "let the reader understand" (Matt. 24:15). Evidently the divine plan is that God's people now understand what at one time was sealed—God wants Christians now to fathom Daniel's prophecies.

Peter had heard God's testimony of His Son on the occasion of Jesus' transfiguration (cf. Matt. 17:5). But for Peter, instruction in prophetic truth was even more certain.

> **We have the word of the prophets made more certain, and you will do well to pay attention to it, as to a light shining in a dark place, until the day dawns and the morning star rises in your hearts. Above all, you must understand that no prophecy of Scripture came about by the prophet's own interpretation. For prophecy never had its origin in the will of man, but men spoke from God as they were carried along by the Holy Spirit. (2 Pet. 1:19-21).**

The only book of the Bible which promises blessing upon those who read and respond is the basically eschatological Book of Revelation. "Blessed is the one who reads the words of this prophecy, and blessed are those who hear it and take to heart what is written in it, because the time is near" (Rev. 1:3). This theme is repeated in the Bible's final chapter, "Blessed is he who keeps the words of the prophecy of this book" (Rev. 22:7).

Understanding prophecy, and knowing Jesus Christ, go hand in hand. John wrote, "The testimony of Jesus is the spirit of prophecy" (Rev. 19:10). The Knox version renders these words, "It is the truth concerning Jesus which inspires all prophecy."

The Twentieth Century New Testament reads, "To bear testimony to Jesus needs the inspiration of the Prophets." A literal translation might be, "The essential role of prophecy is to give a clear witness on behalf of Jesus."

The conscientious student of the Bible must embrace what Paul described as "the whole will [counsel, purpose, plan] of God" (Acts 20:27), and that surely includes prophetic and eschatological truth. The same sound principles of biblical understanding that assure God's valid instruction for life's ongoing problems will also assure His truth in regard to the future. God says of Himself, "I am God, and there is none like me. I make known the end from the beginning, from ancient times, what is still to come" (Isa. 46:9-10).

Benefits from Studying Biblical Eschatology

The study and understanding of biblical eschatology will significantly enrich the believer's walk and his or her relationship with God.

1. It is an incentive to godly living

The believer's insight into God's eternal plan and His provision for the total future becomes a dynamic motivation to godly living and vigorous service. Knowledge of God's government and control in the moral and the physical universe confers comfort, peace, and assurance upon the believer. An understanding of eschatology illumines one's life in the present and enables one more clearly to recognize God's sovereign rule.

When the New Testament mentions the return of Jesus Christ, it almost always associates it with a message of personal everyday godliness. Notable texts illustrate this fact:

> **The grace of God ... teaches us ... to live self-controlled, upright and godly lives in this present age, while we wait for the blessed hope—the glorious appearing of our great God and Savior, Jesus Christ (Titus 2:11-13); "We know that when he appears, we shall be like him, for we shall see him as he is. Everyone who has this hope in him purifies himself, just as he is pure" (1 John. 3:2-3); "You ought to live holy and godly lives as you look forward to the day of God and speed its coming" (2 Pet. 3:11-12). (cf. also, Phil. 1:10; 1 Thess. 2:12, 5:4, 6, 8; James 5:7-9.)**

2. It especially reveals the Lord Jesus Christ

Much that God has revealed concerning His Son is contained in prophetic or eschatological Scriptures. Aspects of His career that are yet future continue to be prophecies. For every prophecy of Christ's first advent, one can find seven prophecies of the second advent. Prophecy honors Christ and Christ validates prophecy (cf. Rev. 19:10 cited above). After discussing His departure and future return, Jesus said to His disciples, "I have told you now before it happens, so that when it does happen you will believe" (John 14:28).

On the road to Emmaus, as Jesus sought to teach concerning Himself, He specifically included prophetic or eschatological Scripture. "And beginning with Moses and all the Prophets, he explained to them what was said in all the Scriptures concerning himself" (Lk. 24:27). Likewise, Peter heightened his presentation of Jesus of Nazareth to Cornelius' household by reporting, "All the prophets testify about him " (Acts 10:43).

3. It comprises a vital portion of revealed truth

Prophetic or eschatological truth constitutes a major area of God's revelation. God commonly reports events prior to their occurrence. "I the Lord will speak what I will, and it shall be fulfilled without delay" (Ezek. 12:25). He alone possesses the power to declare truth in advance, and this power is one of the basic proofs of His godliness. He says, "apart from me there is no God. Who then is like me? Let him proclaim it. Let him declare . . . what is yet to come—yes, let him foretell what will come" (Isa. 44:6-7). In many instances, what was predicted has now come to pass and the truth of the prophecy has been vindicated.

As previously noted, Scripture includes 641 references to prophets and prophesying. God used the prophets to speak, both for the present and for the future. "Surely the Sovereign Lord does nothing without revealing his plan to his servants the prophets" (Amos 3:7). In Jesus' account, the rich man's request for a resuscitated Lazarus to witness to his brothers was denied. "They have Moses and the Prophets; let them listen to them" (Luke. 16:29). God assures prophecy's validity: "For prophecy never had its origin in the will of man, but men spoke from God as they were carried along by the Holy Spirit" (2 Pet. 1:21).

4. It is essential to understand God's person

God's truth, and especially truth concerning His Person, is revealed through the prophetic word. "When a prophet of the Lord is among you, I reveal myself to him in visions, I speak to him in dreams" (Num. 12:6). Through prophetic announcement, God conveys insights into His glory, His power, and His omniscience. "I am the Lord. . . . I will not give my glory to another. . . . See, the former things have taken place, and new things I declare; before they spring into being I announce them to you" (Isa. 42:8-9). Because of prophecy's vital role in understanding and knowing God, as already noted, He promises a special blessing upon students of prophecy. "Blessed is the one who reads the words of this prophecy, and blessed are those who hear it and take to heart what is written in it" (Rev. 1:3).

Prophecy confirms God's provision of justifying righteousness. "But now a righteousness from God, apart from law, has been made known, to which the Law and the Prophets testify" (Rom. 3:21). In the vision of the splendor of the new Jerusalem, John saw God's future moral standard: "Nothing impure will ever enter it, nor will anyone who does what is shameful or deceitful" (Rev. 21:27). Paul noted that ignorance of prophecy had caused the Jews at Antioch to fail to recognize Christ. "Those who live in Jerusalem . . . recognizing neither Him nor the utterances of the prophets . . . fulfilled these by condemning Him" (Acts 13:27 NASB). Those not recognizing God's predicted plan of blessing became candidates for God's predicted judgment.

5. It is a necessary weapon against error

Biblical eschatology, in its multifaceted insights, will refute virtually all common false "isms." Jesus refuted both naturalism (materialism) and critical liberalism in a single eschatological verse. "Heaven and earth will pass away, but my words will never pass away" (Matt. 24:35). The end time exaltation of God the Father contradicts polytheism: "the Son himself will be made subject to him who put everything under him, so that God may be all in all" (1 Cor. 15:28). Since deity will dwell within, but exist distinctly apart from the substance of the new Jerusalem, pantheism is contradicted. "The throne of God and of the Lamb will be in the city " (Rev. 22:3).

To know of God's plan for human destinies and for this earth is to be armed against cults and wrong personal goals. The informed Christian will have no interest in self-acclaimed leaders calling for elaborate physical preparation for supposed forthcoming events. On the other hand, neither will the informed Christian struggle to build earthly monuments to his or her own memory. The person who knows God's revealed plans, and His values and realities, enjoys a wholesome perspective in living life today.

When the church neglects biblical eschatology, it often sees itself primarily as a political instrument for social reform. God's eschatological revelation, however, is not the reform of the world's system, but its total replacement by Jesus Christ the Conqueror. "Out of his mouth comes a sharp sword with which to strike down the nations. He will rule them with an iron scepter" (Rev. 19:15). Sound biblical eschatology will guide the church's attitudes and relationships, and guard it from meddling outside its proper sphere, or dissipating its energies on the trivial.

6. It can be an effective tool for outreach

Among humans there is widespread interest in knowing the future. Many have come to hear a prophetic message, but because the gospel was also presented, they have made a commitment to Christ. The solemnity of the earth's future as revealed in Scripture is a persuasive argument for people to prepare now by accepting Christ as their Savior.

The Christian who knows the future that God has projected for humankind has useful and accurate insights. The counsel that such people can offer stands to be particularly valuable. These Christians are equipped to reach out to others, not only spiritually, but in practical meaningful ways. The national leader who knows and acts upon Bible prophecy has a great advantage over one who does not.

Rules for Developing One's Eschatology

Some ground rules that should help in maintaining the validity of one's eschatology, and in assuring the most accurate understanding of Scriptural truth include the following:

1. Whenever possible accept Scripture literally

The first assumption, unless clear evidence indicates otherwise, should be that eschatological Scriptures mean just what they say. The words should be taken to mean what the dictionary says they mean, and to refer to the objects that they name in the normal manner. On this basis Jesus, by sharing the bread, identified Judas as His betrayer. He explained, "This is to fulfill the scripture: He who shares my bread has lifted up his heel against me" (John 13:18). Jesus behaved so as literally to fulfill Psalm 41:9 (cf. also John 19:24 and Psa. 22:18).

In a past generation, David L. Cooper gave his concept of the basic principle of prophetic interpretation:

> **When the plain sense of Scripture makes common sense, seek no other sense; therefore, take every word at its primary, ordinary, usual literal meaning unless the facts of the immediate context, studied in the light of related passages and axiomatic and fundamental truths, indicate clearly otherwise.[8]**

A more recent author, Stanley Horton, expresses the same thought in concise summary: "take the prophecies of the Old Testament, as well as those of Jesus and the New Testament, as literally as their contexts allow."[9]

2. Seek the precise meaning of the text

In the effort to understand eschatological texts one should use all of the best tools of scholarship. Evangelicals, committed to the inerrancy and authority of the Scriptures, typically apply

---

8   David L. Cooper, *The World's Greatest Library Graphically Illustrated.* Los Angeles: Biblical Research Society, 1970, p. 11.

9   Stanley M. Horton, *The Ultimate Victory.* Springfield: Gospel Publishing House, 1991, p. 21.

the grammatico-historical (or grammatical-historical) method of biblical interpretation. The Spirit's intended meaning may be clarified by procedures such as: grammatical analysis, the study of the meaning and denotation of the words (lexicography), the study of syntax and word relationships, context, to whom addressed, literary character or genre (is it history? poetry? sermonic?), and the prior history of the text in where, why and how it came to be written (*Sitz im Leben*) and its usage.

3. Interpret nonliteral Scripture according to its genre

Nonliteral Scripture must be interpreted according to its particular literary type or genre. Poetry frequently involves emotional overtones and pictorial representations that embellish literal reality. Jeremiah spoke of God's judgment upon the disobedient people of Judah: "I will completely destroy them and make them . . . an everlasting ruin" (Jer. 25:9). In fact, after seventy years, the people returned and resumed life in the land.

Figurative language must be interpreted according to the implied similarities with reality. "Benjamin is a ravenous wolf" (Gen. 49:27) is obviously a vivid statement about a man's character rather than his physical form. Frequently, Scripture provides the interpretation of symbolic language: "The seven heads are seven hills on which the woman sits" (Rev. 17:9). If the interpretation is not supplied, available information and common sense must combine to derive it.

Similar rules apply to Scriptures interpreted as types. "Just as Moses lifted up the snake in the desert, so the Son of Man must be lifted up" (John 3:14; cf. Heb. 8:5 ". . . make everything according to the pattern [Gk. *tupos* {TU-pos = type}] shown you on the mountain.")

4. Always compare Scripture with Scripture

This principle is spoken of as "interpreting by the analogy of faith," or by "the analogy of antecedent Scripture." The major eschatological doctrines are not just the implication of isolated texts, but consistent themes of Scripture. On occasion, the larger body of biblical text must be allowed to color the interpretation of a particular passage. Though a single verse may appear to favor a divergent view, sound exegesis entails evaluating that view in terms of the consensus of all the other relevant texts. In this pattern "The Bereans . . . examined the Scriptures every day to see if what Paul said was true" (Acts 17:11). One's goal in eschatology should be a system that integrates all Scriptures that concern the future. An obvious defect in method results if the "proof texts" of one system are the "ignored" or "overlooked" texts of an opposing system.

5. Give appropriate place to context

The context of promises and prophecies is basic to interpretation and one must always take it into account. What is
predicted of Israel, or promised to David or to individual
prophets, must be distinguished from a promise to Christian
believers or the church. A common cause of confusion in
eschatology is overlooking the context of the Olivet Discourse
and thus applying to the church that which Jesus assigned to
national Israel. Scripture itself appears to take some liberties in
the rigorous respect of contexts,[10] but the scholar should be
cautious of what is not biblically sanctioned. Two later
discussions—sequential fulfillment and prophetic telescoping
—relate to this matter of context.

6. Base eschatology upon the entire Bible

In eschatology, just as in all doctrinal studies, "all Scripture
is God-breathed and is useful for teaching" (2 Tim. 3:16). The
Testaments are equal as sources of eschatological teaching, and
neither negates nor cancels the other. In his defense before
Agrippa, Paul declared, "I am saying nothing beyond what the
prophets and Moses said would happen" (Acts 26:22).

Eschatological revelation may advance, and by this means
prior insights may be superceded, but the latter views will not
contradict the former. God simply tailors the eschatological
message to the audience. Jesus informed His disciples: "I have
much more to say to you, more than you can now bear" (John
16:12). The Old Testament introduces God's future earthly
Kingdom, but the New adds many facts and details. In contrast,
the Old Testament gives considerable detail about the person of
the Antichrist, while the New is mostly limited simply to reporting the events of his actual rule.

7. Build with affirmation rather than denial

Biblical and theological understanding, perhaps more
rigorously in eschatology than in other areas of theology, is based
upon faith rather than doubt. Essential tools of eschatological
study include an open mind, freedom from prior prejudicial
attitudes, the will to believe, and a commitment to resolve
problems rather than create them. Paul appealed to optimism,
"Everything that was written in the past was written to teach us,
so that through endurance and the encouragement of the
Scriptures we might have hope" (Rom. 15:4). Although one must
maintain careful scholarship and logical rigor, and must not be
naïve, the spirit of critical scepticism will definitely impede the

---

10 e.g., The child Jesus' sojourn in Egypt was said to fulfill the prophecy "Out of
Egypt I called my son" (Matt. 2:15, cf. Hos. 11:1), but in context the prophecy is referring to Israel's deliverance from bondage in Egypt.

development of eschatology. The wise scholar begins with what is clearly understandable in eschatology, and builds, refines and grows in understanding upon that foundation.

8. Recognize one definitive meaning per passage

In seeking, if possible, to interpret Scripture literally, one must ordinarily assign a single meaning to a text, for that is how language is usually used. An interpretation of prophetic texts that speaks of "double fulfillment" (or dual reference, or double sense) should be carefully evaluated. In the seventeenth century, the Puritan John Owen wrote, "If the Scripture has more than one meaning, it has no meaning at all." To see more than one meaning in a text suggests an arbitrary capriciousness by which Scripture means whatever the scholar says it means.

Medieval practices illustrate extremes in multi-interpretations. A single passage of Scripture was seen to have 1) a literal meaning, 2) a moral meaning, 3) an allegorical or typical meaning, and 4) a spiritual or mystical (anagogical) meaning. Clearly, this multi-meaning methodology led to error. To assign a single meaning to a text, however, does not preclude more than one application or illustration of the passage. Also, a literally interpreted Scripture may speak typically, thus enriching its application. The important guideline in these instances is to distinguish the text's basic meaning from its applications.

9. Recognize the possibility of a sequential fulfillment

On occasion, a passage of Scripture speaks of events that are to occur sequentially or cumulatively. Thus, Genesis 3:15 addressed to the serpent, the representative of Satan, spoke of ongoing enmity between him and the woman's offspring, "he [i.e., the human] will crush your head, and you will strike his heel." The crushing of Satan's head began at Calvary and the resurrection, it continues in the church's victories, it will lead to Satan's imprisonment in the Abyss, and finally culminate in his consignment to the lake of burning sulfur (cf. Rev. 20:3, 10).

Most futurists would likely consider that Scriptures illustrating sequential fulfillment would include God's promise to make Abraham the father of nations, or the promises to the Israelites to be given the land of Canaan. That Abraham became the father of sons, and that his descendants attained nationhood, involved an extended sequence of events. The possession of Canaan by the Israelites has thus far seen only temporary fulfillment and the full sequence is yet to be consummated.

10. Recognize the possibility of "prophetic telescoping"

The expression "prophetic telescoping" describes passages that move from one predicted event to another without providing conspicuous clues to extensive chronological gaps between the events that have been predicted. Such Scriptures describe the future in a single view even though the events which are to occur may be widely separated in time. Prophetic perspectives can be visualized as if the prophet on a distant plain is observing successive mountain peaks through a telescope. In such circumstances he is unaware of the width of the valleys that separate one mountain range from the other. This phenomenon is also known as the mountain peak principle or prophetic foreshortening, and some speak of it as a near and far view.

Some examples include 1) the reign of Christ immediately conjoined with His first coming: "Your king comes to you . . . gentle and riding on a donkey. . . . His rule will extend from sea to sea and from the River to the ends of the earth" (Zech. 9:9-10), 2) the events of the day of Pentecost immediately preceding the end time judgment: "I will pour out my Spirit . . . I will show wonders in the heavens and on the earth, blood and fire and billows of smoke" (Joel 2:28, 30), 3) the church, which soon will have thrived on earth for two millennia, not seen in any chronological dimension at all.

In His address in the synagogue at Nazareth Jesus applied Isaiah's prophecy (cf. Isa. 61:1-2) to Himself, but by stopping at a comma, He omitted the final clause (cf. Luke. 4:16-19). Jesus thus separated events which Isaiah had seen in a single vision. If the "year of the Lord's favor" was at that time in history, the "day of vengeance of our God" would not be before at least 2,000+ years. (Jesus' day of judgment will be at Armageddon, cf. Rev. 19:15-20; God's final judgment will be 1,000 years later at the great white throne, cf. Rev. 20:11-14.) By ending the quotation as He did, and recognizing the distinctive "mountain peaks," Jesus both endorsed and clarified Isaiah's prophecy.

Eschatological Identities

asic disagreements in eschatological viewpoints frequently relate to the identity of specific companies of humans. Many nonfuturist views disregard the futurist's distinctions between various groups. The futurist holds, however, that a careful, literal handling of Scripture definitely identifies specific separate bodies of people. Paul's usage in this regard is a frequently cited text: "Do not cause anyone to stumble, whether Jews, Greeks or the church of God" (1 Cor. 10:32). An extended discussion of these issues is important in establishing futurist viewpoints.

The Biblical Term "Church"

Scripture depicts the church as a spiritual body that is described pictorially as the glorious Bride of Christ. "Husbands, love your wives, just as Christ loved the church and gave himself up for her to make her holy, cleansing her by the washing with water through the word, and to present her to himself as a radiant church" (Eph. 5:27). Thus, the church particularly relates to Christ and the Christian era.

The church's distinct origin and identity

The Greek *ekklesia,* (ek-klay-SEE-ah) which in English translates as "church," derives from *ek*, meaning "out," and *klesis*, meaning "a calling." In pre-Christian usage the word had a political connotation, denoting the gathering of citizens summoned by the town crier. When, for the first time in the New Testament, Jesus used the word, He applied a secular word to a new spiritual entity. "On this rock I will build my church, and the gates of Hades will not overcome it" (Matt. 16:18). Notably, at that time He spoke of the church in the future.

Later, Paul provided a brief working definition, "the church, which is his body, the fullness of him who fills everything in every way" (Eph. 1:22-23). Other figures for the church in the New Testament include: temple of God[1] (Eph. 2:21); bride of Christ (Eph. 5:25-27); God's household (Eph. 2:19); and a colony of

---

[1] "Temple" in this usage is *naos* (nah-OS): God's dwelling place; not *hieron* (hee-er-ON): a building.

heaven still living upon earth (Phil. 3:20). Such identifications stress the spiritual nature of the church and dissociate it from an earthly destiny.

While He was present on earth, Jesus spoke of the church as future: "On this rock I will build my church" (Matt. 16:18). Though he had assembled and commissioned His followers (cf. Matt. 28:19), until the Day of Pentecost they lacked the anointing that they needed to fulfill their commission. The completed and perfected church awaited Calvary, Resurrection Sunday, and the Day of Pentecost. On the Day of Pentecost, Peter explained, "this is what was spoken by the prophet Joel" (Acts 2:16), for these happenings partially fulfilled Joel's prophecy (cf. Joel 2:28-29). The larger fulfillment awaits the millennium, preceded by Armageddon (cf. Joel 2:3-32). To say that Joel predicted the bestowment of the Spirit is not to say that he foresaw the church, for the outpoured Spirit is just one element of the church. To predict the fact of the Spirit's outpouring was not to predict God's application of that event.

The church and national Israel

The church and national Israel are fundamentally different bodies, with each existing under its own covenant. When Jesus inaugurated the Lord's Supper, He extended, or mediated, to the church a unique new covenant. "This cup is the new covenant [Gk. *diatheke*] in my blood, which is poured out for you" (Luke 22:20). Paul wrote, "He has made us competent as ministers of a new covenant—not of the letter but of the Spirit" (2 Cor. 3:6). To provide for His eternal priesthood "Jesus has become the guarantee of a better covenant" (Heb. 7:22). The Christian's new covenant offers salvation by faith in Christ's cleansing blood, and His ongoing heavenly intercession. God extends this covenant to all humankind, and for humans in general this covenant is much better than the Abrahamic. Nevertheless, to those Jews not under the new covenant, the old Abrahamic covenant still stands.

The Greek word *diatheke* that Jesus used in Luke 22:20 translates as either covenant or testament. Thus *diatheke* (di-ah-THAY-kay) refers to a will or testament, decree, covenant, compact, contract. In Greek, the familiar designations of Old Testament and New Testament use this word. Since God provided Israel with the Old Testament (or covenant), and the church with the New Testament (or covenant), these actions provide ample precedent to expect that God will supply the people of the millennial kingdom with their own testament-covenant.

Christ does not cause Christian believers to become citizens of Israel, but He abolished the barrier that previously denied non-Jews access to God. Paul wrote that the Gentiles of Ephesus

	NATIONAL ISRAEL	THE CHURCH
ESTAB-LISH-MENT	**IN THE LIFETIME OF ABRAHAM:** "Your name will be Abraham . . . I will establish my covenant as an everlasting covenant between me and you and your descendants after you for generations to come" (Gen. 17:5, 7).	**THROUGH CHRIST'S INCARNATE MINISTRY:** He recruited His first followers (cf. John 1:35-51), but later declared, "I will build my church" (Matt. 16:18). Early in the apostolic era the church was a functioning entity: "Great fear seized the whole church" (Acts 5:11).
CALL-ING	**TO LEAD THE NATIONS AS GOD'S REPRESENTATIVES:** "All peoples on earth will be blessed through you" (Gen. 12:3); "All the peoples on earth will see that you are called by the name of the Lord, and they will fear you. . . . The Lord will make you the head, not the tail" (Deut. 28:10, 13); "The house of Israel will possess the nations as menservants and maidservants in the Lord's land. They will make captives of their captors and rule over their oppressors" (Isa. 14:2).	**TO WITNESS, WIN FOLLOWERS, AND GROW IN CHRIST:** "You did not choose me, but I chose you and appointed you to go and bear fruit—fruit that will last" (John 15:16); "Go and make disciples of all nations, baptizing them . . . and teaching them to obey everything I have commanded you" (Matt. 28:19-20); "You will be my witnesses in Jerusalem, and in all Judea and Samaria, and to the ends of the earth" (Acts 1:8).
RES-PON-SIBIL-ITIES	**OBEY GOD'S LAW OR BE PUNISHED FOR FAILURE:** "Observe therefore all the commands I am giving you today, so that you may have the strength to go in and take over the land. . . . When you have taken it over and are living there, be sure that you obey all the decrees and laws I am setting before you today" (Deut. 11:8, 31-32); "When he does wrong, I will punish him with the rod of men . . . But my love will never be taken away from him" (2 Sam. 7:14-15).	**MAINTAIN FAITH IN CHRIST'S FINISHED WORK:** "Christ . . . forgave us all our sins, having cancelled the written code, with its regulations, that was against us . . . he took it away, nailing it to the cross" (Col. 2:13-14); "Therefore, holy brothers, who share in the heavenly calling, fix your thoughts on Jesus, the apostle and high priest whom we confess" (Heb. 3:1); "Now that faith has come, we are no longer under the supervision of the law" (Gal. 3:25).
RE-SULTS OF GOD'S BLESS-ING	**EARTHLY PROSPERITY, MANY DESCENDANTS, AND A GREAT NAME:** "Then the Lord your God will make you most prosperous in all the work of your hands and in the fruit of your womb, the young of your livestock and the crops of your land" (Deut. 30:9); "God made his promise to Abraham . . . saying, I will surely bless you and give you many descendants" (Heb. 6:13-14); "I have cut off all your enemies from before you. Now I will make your name great, like the names of the greatest men of the earth" (2 Sam.7:9).	**HEAVENLY PROSPERITY, SINS FORGIVEN, MATURING TRIALS:** "Jesus Christ . . . has blessed us in the heavenly realms with every spiritual blessing in Christ" (Eph. 1:3); "Blessed is the man whose sin the Lord will never count against him" (Rom. 4:8); "Blessed is the man who perseveres under trial, because when he has stood the test, he will receive the crown of life" (James 1:12).
IN-HERIT-ANCE	**SECURITY IN THE EARTHLY LAND OF CANAAN:** "The whole land of Canaan . . . I will give as an everlasting possession to you and your descendants after you" (Gen. 17:8); "I will provide a place for my people Israel and will plant them so that they can have a home of their own and no longer be disturbed . . . I will also give you rest from all your enemies" (2 Sam. 7:10-11).	**SECURITY IN THE ETERNAL HEAVENLY REALM:** "He has given us new birth into . . . an inheritance that can never perish, spoil or fade—kept in heaven for you" (1 Pet. 3-4); "The Lord will . . . bring me safely to his heavenly kingdom" (2 Tim. 4:18).

Fig. 2: Israel and the church compared in their basic roots and nature. The differences between the two mark them as separate and distinct entities. Futurism holds that the church was not launched until Christ fulfilled His incarnate ministry.

were "excluded from citizenship in Israel and foreigners to the covenants of the promise, without hope and without God in the world" (Eph. 2:12). He added, "Now in Christ Jesus you who once were far away have been brought near" (v. 13).

To emphasize that those Christian believers who "once . . . were not a people" (1 Pet. 2:10) are now the "people of God," Peter called them a "holy nation." This designation led to his exhortation to see themselves as "aliens and strangers in the world" (1 Pet. 2:11). He clearly was not equating the church with national Israel, which is one of earth's nations. Christians know a Savior and a faith which thus far are unknown to national Israel.

The church's Gentile membership

The church was a new spiritual entity that emerged out of Christ's ministry. Paul spoke of a newly revealed "mystery" [secret, hidden purpose] "that through the gospel the Gentiles are heirs together with Israel, members together of one body, and sharers together in the promise in Christ Jesus" (Eph. 3:6). In these words, he depicts three aspects that have been revealed: 1) non-Jews are heirs together with Israel, 2) non-Jews are members of the body that includes Jews, 3) non-Jews and Jews join in sharing Christ's promises. Thus, the church was a new creation that recruited Jews and non-Jews (i.e., Gentiles) to form a body that uniquely related to Jesus Christ. "His purpose was to create in himself one new man out of the two" (Eph. 2:15).

The concern of the early church was to establish that Gentiles could become Christians and be brought into the church. Since the first Christians were Jewish, they had to learn that the church enjoyed its own distinctive covenant. The issue was debated at the Jerusalem Conference (Acts 15:1-29), and effectively settled by James' quotation from the prophet Amos. "After this I will return and rebuild David's fallen tent . . . that the remnant of men may seek the Lord, and all the Gentiles who bear my name, says the Lord" (Acts 15:16-17; cf. Amos 9:11-12). James saw this prophecy both as a prediction of a Gentile mission in God's program, and also its authorization.

In his citation of Amos, James was seeking to make the point that in the era of the rebuilding of David's fallen tent—which scholars understand as denoting the millennium[2]—Gentiles would be saved, presumably as Gentiles and apart from circumcision. Thus, it is not warranted that they are circumcised now, nor that any other Judaizing elements are required. James did not say that Amos 9:11-12 was being fulfilled in the church, but

---

2 James' expression "after this" is his free citation of Amos' words "in that day." In context, Amos is clearly referring to a future end-time restoration of an earthly Israel—i.e., the millennium.

simply that the idea of the conversion of Gentiles apart from their becoming Jewish proselytes was not contrary to the Old Testament. As incredible as it might be to Jewish traditionalists, God was now providing for the Gentiles through the all-nation commission given to the church. In the millennial kingdom, He would again provide for them.

The Entity Denoted by "Israel"

In Moses' time the Israelites were instructed to pray, "Look down from heaven, your holy dwelling place, and bless your people Israel and the land you have given us as you promised on oath to our forefathers" (Deut. 26:15). The Psalmist rejoiced because "the Lord has chosen Jacob to be his own, Israel to be his treasured possession" (Psa. 135:4). Obviously, to God, Israel is a very special nation of people.

The nation's origin and identity

The nation of Israel emerged out of God's covenant extended to Abraham. "The Lord had said to Abram . . . go to the land I will show you. I will make you into a great nation" (Gen. 12:1-2); "All the land that you see I will give to you and your offspring forever" (Gen. 13:15); "On that day the Lord made a covenant with Abram and said, 'To your descendants I give this land, from the river of Egypt to the great river, the Euphrates'" (Gen. 15:18; cf. also, Gen. 17:8; 22:17). In rejecting Ishmael and providing for Isaac's birth, God demonstrated His vital concern for a particular promised line. He declared, "My covenant I will establish with Isaac whom Sarah will bear to you" (Gen. 17:21).

Israel, then, is a nation of people whose family ancestral roots primarily extend back to Abraham through Isaac and Jacob. Since at the temple's destruction, genealogical records were lost, precise family relationships are known only to God. He is carefully aware of these matters on behalf of His covenant people and He has promised, "I will take the Israelites out of the nations . . . I will gather them from all around . . . I will make them one nation in the land, on the mountains of Israel" (Ezek. 37:21-22).

In spite of God's strict concern for the tribal roots of the Israelites, the Law provided for converts or proselytes to join the nation. "The alien living with you must be treated as one of your native-born. Love him as yourself" (Lev. 19:34; cf. Exod. 12:48). Such Gentile proselytes included Rahab and Ruth in the direct line of Jesus. In Esther's time, "Many people of other nationalities became Jews" (Esther 8:17), and on the Day of Pentecost the audience included "visitors from Rome (both Jews and converts to Judaism)" (Acts 2:10-11). The blood line originating in Abraham was freely enlarged through intermarriage and proselytism, but in God's sight these events caused no confusion nor the loss of identity of the nation's citizens.

The question, "What is a Jew?" continues to generate debate. In biblical usage, however, the name Jew clearly indicates an ethnic, national, and political people, and also, a religion and a culture. The common dictionary definition provides a useful statement: "a member of a nation existing in Palestine from the 6th century B.C. to the 1st century A.D.; a person belonging to a continuation through descent or conversion of the ancient Jewish people." (*Webster's Ninth New Collegiate Dictionary*)

The names that identify the Israelites

In addition to Scripture's use of "Israelites," it also uses "Jews" or "Hebrews." The modern term "Israelis" denotes those Israelites who live in the Republic of Israel.

An "Israelite" is one who relates to Israel [Jacob] the grandson of Abraham. Scripture connects the term to all that associates with an earthly nation, for it speaks of "native-born Israelites" (Lev. 23:42); of a son with "an Israelite mother and an Egyptian father" (Lev. 24:10); and of Israelite "clans and families" (Num. 2:34), "tribal leaders" (Num. 7:2), and "ancestral tribes" (Num. 13:2). The Israelites related to the people of Judah as "fellow countrymen" (2 Chron. 28:11). In His call to Ezekiel, God spoke of the Israelites as a rebellious nation, "Son of man, I am sending you to the Israelites, to a rebellious nation that has rebelled against me" (Ezek. 2:3). In the New Testament, Paul quoted Isaiah, "Though the number of the Israelites be like the sand of the sea, only a remnant will be saved" (Rom. 9:27).

The identification "Jews" began to be used as the remnant returned from captivity (cf. Ezra 4:12). It is a modification of the tribal name "Judah," but it identifies the people of all the tribes, including those who had joined a tribe as proselytes. Though Judah was the fourth son, through the default of his older brothers, his tribe was made the conveyor of the royal Messianic line (cf. 1 Chron. 5:1-2; Gen. 34:25-31; 49:5-7). God acted both in judgment and in sovereignty in choosing the tribe of Judah. When Jesus confirmed that He was "King of the Jews" (cf. Matt. 27:11), He was proclaiming Himself as King of all Israel, since Scripture uses "Jew" and "Israelite" interchangeably. Paul declared, "I am a Jew" (Acts 21:39), but later he wrote, "I am an Israelite" (Rom. 11:1; cf. also Acts 6:1-7).

The name "Hebrew" occurs for the first time in Scripture in identifying Abram, "One . . . came and reported this to Abram the Hebrew" (Gen. 14:13). Joseph and Jonah were each identified as a "Hebrew" (cf. Gen. 39:14; Jonah 1:9), and occasionally God used that designation to apply to any of His covenant people (cf. Exod. 21:2; Deut. 15:12). God chose to identify Himself to Pharaoh as "the God of the Hebrews" (cf. Exod. 3:18; 9:1). As the Philistines confronted the invading Israelites, they regularly referred to them as "the Hebrews" (cf. 1 Sam. 4:9). King Saul's trumpeter sought to rally the people with the call, "Let the Hebrews hear" (1 Sam. 13:3). In New Testament times Paul spoke of himself as "a Hebrew of the Hebrews" (Phil. 3:5). The name "Hebrew" derives from "Eber" in the line of Shem, Abraham's ancestor, favored by Noah's special blessing (cf. Gen. 9:26; 10:21; 11:16-26).

The phrase **"Israel of God"** occurs once in Scripture: "Peace and mercy to all who follow this rule, even ["and" --KJV] to the Israel of God" (Gal. 6:16). The "rule" Paul was advocating was the submission of oneself to the cross of Christ "through which the world has been crucified to me, and I to the world" (Gal. 6:14). In context, he had condemned the Judaizers who were insisting upon the circumcision of Christians. In verse 16 Paul concludes his discussion with a pronouncement of blessing upon all those who trusted the cross. He marks out for a special blessing, however, those Jews who had become Christians, and who, nevertheless, solely trusted the cross rather than the practices of Judaism.

We may conclude that the phrase "Israel of God" simply identifies those among the total family of Christians who in national origin are Jewish— i.e., "Messianic Jews." This view is supported by the newer versions whose scholars render the Greek conjunction *kai* as "even," rather than "and." The simple conjunction "and" would indicate that two groups were being recognized; "even" implies that "Israel of God" is a subgroup within the larger company of Christians.

The perpetuity of the nation of Israel

Scripture distinctively portrays Israel as a perpetually enduring nation of people uniquely favored of God with the promise of a land as an everlasting possession. God declared:

> **"I will raise up your [i.e., David's] offspring to succeed you, one of your own sons, and I will establish his . . . throne forever. . . . I will never take my love away from him. . . . I will set him over my house and my kingdom forever; his throne will be established forever" (1 Chron. 17:11-14; cf. Isa. 60:16-21); "This is what the LORD says, he who appoints the sun . . . who decrees the moon and stars . . . who stirs up the sea so that its waves roar. . . . Only if these decrees vanish from my sight," declares the Lord, "will the descendants of Israel ever cease to be a nation before me. . . . Only if the heavens above can be measured and the foundations of the earth below be searched out will I reject all the descendants of Israel because of all they have done," declares the LORD (Jer. 31:35-37; see Jer. 33:24-36 in** *The Living Bible***).**

Similar passages affirm the perpetuity of Israel's covenant, but
with the added element that failure or disobedience by Israel
would result in punishment.

> **"I will be his father, and he will be my son. When he does wrong, I
> will punish him with the rod of men. . . . But my love will never be
> taken away from him. . . . Your house and your kingdom will en-
> dure forever before me; your throne will be established forever"**
> **(2 Sam. 7:14-16; cf. Psa. 89:30-37).**

The eighty-ninth Psalm clearly declares that though God will
punish Israel for sin, His covenant with the nation will stand as
long as humans can witness the sun and the moon.

A number of biblical references speak of Israel or Judah as
dwelling in the land forever. Thus, "It will be [Israel's] inheritance forever" (Exod. 32:13); "That you [Israel] may . . . pass
[this good land] on as an inheritance to your descendants forever" (Joel 3:20). The word forever is the Hebrew 'olam
(o-LAWM). This word denotes to the vanishing point, to the end of
days, or until time out of mind. In relation to future ages, it indeed signifies eternity, but when applied to the earth, it becomes
a way of saying, as long as the earth stands.

Israel's covenant: extended by God's sovereign act

The chosen descendants of Abraham who comprise national
Israel are the objects of a sovereign God's special favor in His un-
conditionally guaranteed covenanted promises. The effects of
these promises continue into the realm of the everlasting, and
they include a land (cf. Gen. 12:7), a king (Psa. 89:27-37), a restored and regenerated people (Jer. 31:33-34), and even after the
horrors of tribulation, a guaranteed count of survivors of the
flesh and blood offspring of Abraham (Isa. 10:20-23; Zech.
13:8-9). This amazingly generous and remarkable covenant was
granted as a sovereign act of God.

1. **Deity alone enacted the confirming ritual** while Abram
   lay in a deep sleep. Genesis 15:9-21 describes the smoking
   firepot and blazing torch that passed between the divided sacrifices to establish, "the most spectacular blood covenant of
   the Old Testament." The firepot and torch were symbols of
   Persons of the Godhead as God covenanted within Himself to
   make Abram the recipient of the covenant that He was offering. The only condition was God's ability to perform. Hebrews notes, "When God made his promise to Abraham . . . he
   swore by himself" (Heb. 6:13).

2. **The covenant was immutable and its effects everlasting.** The covenant's effectiveness depended solely upon
   God's faithfulness to Israel, not Israel's faithfulness to God.
   God explained this principle to Ezekiel, "This is what the Sovereign Lord says: It is not for your sake, O house of Israel,

that I am going to do these things, but for the sake of my holy name" (Ezek. 36:22). In Genesis 15 God five times declares, "I will," but at no time does He impose commands or requirements upon Abram. All that was asked of Abram was that he place himself in God's custody by journeying from Ur of the Chaldees (cf. Gen. 12). Later God affirmed, "My covenant in your flesh is to be an everlasting covenant" (Gen. 17:13; cf. 17:19; and also 1 Chron. 16:15-17). Hebrews notes, "God wanted to make the unchanging [Gk. *ametathetos*] nature of his purpose very clear to the heirs of what was promised" (Heb. 6:17). The Greek *ametathetos* [am-et-ATH-et-os] signifies unchangeability or immutability. In its outworking, the covenant was to be passed on through the son of promise.

3. **The covenant was repeated to Abram** even when he was guilty of disobedience and unbelief. Abram attempted to fulfill God's promise through Ishmael (Gen. 16), but the covenant's promises remained unchanged. Following this episode, God affirmed, "I will establish my covenant as an everlasting covenant between me and you and your descendants after you" (Gen. 17:7).

4. **Paul affirmed the fact that the covenant** to Israel was still standing centuries later in the Christian era. He spoke of those "of my own race, the people of Israel" who did not know Christ. He saw the tragedy as so much greater because, "theirs is the adoption of sons; theirs is the divine glory, the covenants . . . and the promises" (Rom. 9:4). Israel's covenant status made them a potentially privileged people, and yet Paul found so many living in spiritual poverty.

The terms of Israel's everlasting covenant

Israel's everlasting covenant offers either blessing or curse depending upon the people's response. Much of Israel's history has known the tragedies of the curses, but the promise of blessing still stands. "When [Heb. *kiy*] all these blessings and curses I have set before you come upon you . . . and when you and your children return to the Lord your God and obey him . . . then the Lord your God will restore your fortunes and have compassion on you and gather you again from all the nations where he scattered you" (Deut. 30:1-2). The word *kiy* (kee) is a conjunction indicating causal relation, since, that, for, when, because.[3]

In Moses' declaration, God's promises of the covenant's potential became a firm prophecy of the future (cf. Deut. 30:8-9).

---

3 It is probably unwarranted to attempt to dispute Israel's future on the basis of alternate translations of the Hebrew *kiy*. After seven page-length columns of discussion of the word, Gesenius' *Lexicon* comments, "*kiy* is sometimes of difficult and uncertain interpretation, and in some of the passages quoted [i.e., in his illustrations] a different explanation is tenable."

Previously, God had promised, "They [rebellious Israel] will pay for their sins because they rejected my laws and abhorred my decrees. Yet in spite of this . . . I will not reject them or abhor them so as to destroy them completely, breaking my covenant with them" (Lev. 26:43-44). This Scripture was no doubt partly implemented in the restoration under Ezra and Nehemiah, and it still stands as an abiding and ongoing promise. (See Judg. 2:1; 2 Ki. 13:23; 2 Chron. 21:7; Psa. 89:28; 105:8, 10; Isa. 54:10; 55:3; Ezek. 16:60; 37:26).

The implementation of the covenant

Jesus' advent gave national Israel (some speak of "flesh Israel") an opportunity to appropriate the provisions of the covenant. Their Messiah was present on earth, and He offered Himself as their King. Tragically, they rejected Him. Such events are paralleled by today's sinner who upon hearing a clear presentation of the Gospel chooses to postpone responding to the indefinite future. Where the sinner has no guarantee of life, however, and he may never have another opportunity to respond to the Gospel, national Israel as a nation will yet be saved (cf. Rom. 11:26). God's irrevocable call (cf. Rom. 11:29), and the perpetuity of the covenant, assure that at a future time national Israel will enjoy a further opportunity to accept its Messiah and enter God's kingdom blessings.

In that day when national Israel's survivors accept their Messiah, they will enjoy all the political and earthly advantages of the Abrahamic covenant. The millennial kingdom is not heaven, however, and even millennial Jews will need to accept Christ personally if they are to attain heaven following their life on earth. As one of earth's first citizens, a Jew has a political future either for himself or his descendants, but a vastly greater future awaits those Jews who now receive Jesus Christ as their Messiah-Savior.

Israel's new covenant

In God's own time the unconditional and everlasting covenant to Israel will fulfill all of its promises. But even then, God has special plans for the people of Israel. The writer to the Hebrews quotes Jeremiah 31:31-34:

> "The time is coming, declares the Lord, when I will make a new covenant with the house of Israel and . . . Judah. This is the covenant I will make with the house of Israel after that time, declares the Lord. I will put my laws in their minds and write them on their hearts . . . they will all know me, from the least of them to the greatest. For I will forgive their wickedness and remember their sins no more" (Heb. 8:8, 10-12).

Notably, the new covenant predicted by Jeremiah was Israel's millennial covenant. Jeremiah does not speak of the new covenant that Christ provided for His church (cf. Luke 22:20). The two "new" covenants should not be confused.

The writer to the Hebrews comments, "By calling this covenant 'new,' he has made the first one obsolete; and what is obsolete and aging will soon disappear" (Heb. 8:13). The Abrahamic covenant will stand until it brings the Israelites to their messianic kingdom—i.e., the millennium. At that time, but not before, the new covenant will supercede it. This covenant will provide the spiritual basis for the transformation of flesh and blood Israelites into penitent and devout millennial citizens, and prepare them for eternity in the new Jerusalem.

As noted above, Israel's future new covenant is quite different from the Christian's present new covenant. Christian believers "have come . . . to the church of the firstborn . . . to Jesus the mediator of a new covenant, and to the sprinkled blood" (Heb. 12:22-24). In contrast, at a future time when

> the full number of the Gentiles has come in . . . all Israel will be saved. . . . "The deliverer . . . will turn godlessness away from Jacob. And this is my covenant with them when I take away their sins." As far as the gospel is concerned, they [i.e., the Jews] are enemies on your account; but as far as election is concerned, they are loved on account of the patriarchs, for God's gifts and his call are irrevocable (Rom. 11:25c-29).

The status of the tribes of Israel

Today's people recognized as Jews (or Israelites, Israelis, or Hebrews) include members of all of the original twelve tribes.

The so-called "ten lost tribes" of Israel were not really lost. Though many of the northern kingdom who were taken into captivity (c. 721 B.C.) did not return, some did, and they took their place with Judah in the unified nation. During Nehemiah's restoration, the people with whom he worked are called "Jews" eleven times, and "Israel" twenty-two times. Following the first return, Ezra's dedication of the rebuilt temple recognized represenatatives of all of the twelve tribes. "They offered . . . as a sin offering for all Israel, twelve male goats, one for each of the tribes of Israel" (Ezra 6:17).

In the New Testament the same people are referred to as "Jews" 174 times, and "Israel" 74 times. The prophetess Anna was known to be of the tribe of Asher (Luke 2:36), and Paul knew he was of the tribe of Benjamin (Phil. 3:5). Jesus commissioned His disciples, "Go rather to the lost sheep of Israel" (Matt. 10:6). During the tribulation, the servants whom God will seal will be the "144,000 from all the tribes of Israel" (Rev. 7:4). Scripture names the twelve tribes, and lists the count of 12,000 of each who will be sealed. These are literal flesh and blood Israelites and not allegorical figures whose reality must be interpreted.

Prior to the captivity, members of the ten tribes had joined Judah. When the kingdom was divided after Solomon's death (c. 931 B.C.), "Those from every tribe of Israel who set their hearts on seeking the Lord, the God of Israel, followed the Levites to Jerusalem to offer sacrifices to the Lord. . . . They strengthened the kingdom of Judah and supported Rehoboam" (2 Chron. 11:16-17). Later (c. 900 B.C.) during the spiritual revival under Asa, "he assembled all Judah and Benjamin and the people from Ephraim, Manasseh and Simeon who had settled among them, for large numbers had come over to him from Israel when they saw that the Lord his God was with him" (2 Chron. 11:9). In later history in the southern kingdom, Judah and Benjamin were the prominent members, but all twelve tribes were well represented.

The deportation of the northern tribes apparently was not total. Though the majority of the people were deported, some were left behind (cf. 2 Kings 17). Thus, worshipers at Hezekiah's Feast of Unleavened Bread (c. 715 B.C.), decades after the captivity, included "many people who came from Ephraim, Manasseh, Issachar and Zebulun" (2 Chron. 30:18). When Josiah restored the temple (c. 630 B.C.), funds were "collected from the people of Manasseh, Ephraim and the entire remnant of Israel and from all the people of Judah and Benjamin" (2 Chron. 34:9).

Israel's tribal resurgence is yet future. Jacob's deathbed bestowal of blessings upon his sons prophetically skims the entire history of the Israelites. He instructed, "Gather around so I can tell you what will happen to you in days to come" (Gen. 49:1). Although "last days" is used in some versions, the somewhat general "days to come" more correctly translates the original. What is predicted can validly apply to any time following Jacob's death, and it certainly can await fulfillment until the millennium. The term "last days" will be discussed in the chapter that follows. If what Jacob promised is not evident today, that is not grounds for identifying Israel with the church, or a modern nation or alliance of nations. The last days' identification of tribes and families will be no problem to God.

Today's "Jews" comprise all of the twelve tribes. Upon his deathbed, Jacob conveyed the political and economic strengths of the nation upon Joseph and through him to his sons Ephraim and Manasseh. The ruling line, however, was conveyed through the tribe of Judah (to which Benjamin was attached and largely absorbed). The combination of a ruler, and a nation of people to rule, demanded that all twelve tribes should comprise the chosen descendants of Jacob. What has been called "birthright Israel" (the ten tribes), and Judah (plus Benjamin) is one national body.

Concluding summary

The Jews remain a distinctive nation among the peoples of the earth. They are set apart by family origins, customs, traditions, religion, and to some degree by such matters as shared ideals, language, physical traits, and personal mannerisms. In a multitude of national settings worldwide, the Jewish people, or at least the great majority of them, are distinctly identifiable. God's ancient covenant to Abraham, the father of this people, has never been abrogated. That covenant is unconditional and irrevocable. On the integrity of His own divine character, God has sworn the eternally ongoing perpetuation of the political phenomenon of the nationhood of the Jewish people.

The Church and Israel as Heirs of Abraham

While Scripture clearly distinguishes between the church and Israel as two separate entities, it also reveals that they have much in common.

Abraham the father of us all

The people of Israel (Jews, Hebrews) trace their earthly ancestry to Abraham; the people of the church (Christians) trace their spiritual ancestry to Abraham. Jesus endorsed the Jewish physical heritage in Abraham. "[The Jews] answered him, 'We are Abraham's descendants.' Jesus replied . . . 'I know you are Abraham's descendants'" (John 8:33-34, 37). God revealed to Paul the Christian's descent from Abraham. "If you belong to Christ, then you are Abraham's seed, and heirs according to the promise" (Gal. 3:29; cf. Rom. 4:11). Obviously, there is a fundamental difference between being the chosen biological or earthly descendants of Abraham or being his spiritual descendants.

To distinguish ethnic Jews—Abraham's earthly descendants —and Christians, Scripture depicts Christians as:

1. **Spiritual descendants of Abraham.** They relate to Abraham because of their belief. "Those who believe are children of Abraham" (Gal. 3:7). These born again descendants in the Abrahamic line inherit righteousness that is by faith, rather than a land or a national identity. With Abraham, the spiritual descendant looks for his eternal home in the New Jerusalem. "By faith Abraham . . . was looking forward to the city with foundations, whose architect and builder is God" (Heb. 11:8, 11). Abraham is the patriarch of an earthly nation, and also of all the future citizens of the New Jerusalem.

2. **Gospel believers.** God directly promised Abraham a vast family of biological descendants, but there was also an implicit message that Paul recognized, "The Scriptures . . . announced the gospel in advance to Abraham: 'All nations will

be blessed through you.' So those who have faith are blessed along with Abraham, the man of faith" (Gal. 3:8-9). All gospel believers out of all nations owe to Abraham the legacy of salvation's earthly elements (e.g., Bible, Jesus, first generation of believers). God's choice of Abraham was a notable step in providing the gospel, and believers can look back to him with gratitude.

3. People of faith. "The promise comes by faith, so that it may be by grace . . . to all Abraham's offspring—not only to those who are of the law but also to those who are of the faith of Abraham. He is the father of us all" (Rom. 4:16). Abraham is faith's outstanding pioneer; he is the model, and the universal patriarch of all who walk by faith. "Abraham believed God, and it was credited to him as righteousness" (Rom. 4:3; cf. Gal. 3:6). The convert who enters into the lineage of the faith relationship with God has identified with this very special man: Abraham the friend of God (cf. 2 Chron. 20:7).

The unique inheritance of national Israel

Though the Jews of the New Testament era erred in thinking that they possessed all that God offered (cf. John 8:33), their inheritance did contribute, physically, culturally, and religiously. Paul wrote of "those of my own race, the people of Israel. Theirs is the adoption as sons; theirs the divine glory, the covenants, the receiving of the law, the temple worship and the promises" (Rom. 9:3-4). Previously, Paul had asked, "What advantage, then, is there in being a Jew?" (Rom. 3:1). He answers, "Much in every way! First of all, they have been entrusted with the very words of God" (Rom. 3:2).

In making his point in this passage, Paul implies that the Jew also enjoys God's faithful or immutable covenant (verse 3), God's sanctifying chastening (verse 5), and a redemptive consciousness of sin (verse 20). Though a Jew is without faith, he still has access to much potential spiritual privilege and blessing. "What if some did not have faith? Will their lack of faith nullify God's faithfulness? Not at all!" (Rom. 3:3-4). The unbelieving Jew still retains God's promise of an earthly land for him or his descendants.

Abraham's blessing upon Gentiles

God would have preferred that Abraham's descendants through Isaac (cf. Rom. 9:6-8) qualified both as citizens of an earthly land and citizens of the New Jerusalem. Tragically, their excessive concern with the first deprived most of them of the second. Though they remained Jews nationally, culturally, and in a nominal sense, religiously, they personally lost their special covenant privileges. God's response was to create the church.

Citizenship in Abraham's eternal city of faith was extended to all who would believe. No longer is biological or earthly relationship to Abraham required. "He redeemed us in order that the blessing given to Abraham might come to the Gentiles through Christ Jesus" (Gal. 3:14). The barrier that excluded Gentiles is no more (cf. Eph. 2:15-16).

Redeemed humans, whether Jews or Christians, comprise one body that Peter describes as "a chosen people, a royal priesthood, a holy nation" (1 Pet. 2:9). In Paul's figure, "[Gentiles], though a wild olive shoot, have been grafted in among the others and now share in the nourishing sap from the olive root" (Rom. 11:17). The circle has been enlarged! Paul spoke reverently of "the mystery made known to me by revelation" (Eph. 3:3). He explains, "This mystery is that through the gospel the Gentiles are heirs together with Israel, members together of one body, and sharers together in the promise in Christ Jesus" (Eph. 3:6). Though Israel maintains an exclusive monopoly on a flesh and blood relationship to Abraham, the scarce children of faith among them must share with believing Gentiles who comprise the church. Christians do not become Jews, but they enjoy the spiritual aspects of God's promises to Israel.

In laying down the truth of the doctrine of justification by faith, and humanity's universal spiritual need, Paul addressed his Jewish countrymen with severity.

> If you call yourself a Jew; if you rely on the law and brag about your relationship to God . . . do you not teach yourself? . . . A man is not a Jew if he is only one outwardly, nor is circumcision merely outward and physical. No, a man is a Jew if he is one inwardly; and circumcision is circumcision of the heart, by the Spirit, not by the written code [or "according to the spirit, not the letter of the law" --Knox]. Such a man's praise is not from men, but from God (Rom. 2:17, 21, 28-29).

Paul does not deny that these legalists are Jews, but he is saying that they are depriving themselves of the spiritual and eternal aspects of their covenant. Their Jewishness may have its advantages, but it fails to provide justification. There are two people groups, Jews and Gentiles, but God has a single standard. "There is only one God, who will justify the circumcised by faith and the uncircumcised through that same faith" (Rom. 3:30). A Jew without faith has missed the essential basics of his heritage.

The enduring role of national Israel

In Romans chapter 11 Paul emphasizes that Gentile Christians share but do not displace. Even the sharing is temporary.

> I ask then, Did God reject his people? By no means! . . . God did not reject his people, whom he foreknew. . . . Did they stumble so as to fall beyond recovery? Not at all! . . . But if their transgression means riches for the world, and their loss means riches for the

> Gentiles, how much greater riches will their fullness bring! ... After all, if you were cut out of an olive tree that is wild by nature, and contrary to nature were grafted into a cultivated olive tree, how much more readily will these, the natural branches, be grafted into their own olive tree! (Rom. 11:1-2, 11-12, 24).

National Israel remains a distinct body and the church is not Israel. The earthly nation of Israel has a literal eschatological destiny. God's faithfulness will assure that in the millennium, all surviving earthly descendants of Abraham's line through Isaac will inherit His promise of their Messiah and their land. "And so all Israel will be saved" (Rom. 11:26). Though the salvation of all Israel will be distinguished from the salvation of the Gentiles, the manner of the salvation will be the same. Humans, whether Jews or Gentiles, are saved when they submit to God's proffered grace and they appropriate Christ's victory through Calvary.

The mutual destiny of justified Israelites and Christians

In the new Jerusalem, justified Israelites and redeemed Christians will dwell together. (For a further discussion of this matter see Chapter 14.) The writer to the Hebrews celebrates this remarkable eternal union of Israelites and Christians: "You have come to Mount Zion, to the heavenly Jerusalem, the city of the living God. You have come to thousands upon thousands of angels in joyful assembly, to the church of the firstborn. . . . You have come to God, the judge of all men, to the spirits of righteous men made perfect, to Jesus the mediator of a new covenant" (Heb. 12:22-24).

The new Jerusalem is the city which Abraham anticipated (cf. Heb. 11:10). He will be there among the "righteous men made perfect." Though he foresaw the city, Abraham did not see that the church would be there also, and with the advantage of its faith in Christ's finished work. After recounting the Old Testament heroes, the writer to the Hebrews concludes: "God had planned something better for us so that only together with us would they be made perfect" (Heb. 11:40). The New Testament revelation of the church was the unveiling of a mystery (cf. Col. 1:26-27; Eph. 3:4-6). Though its destiny merges with Israel, the church has its own special history, and it existed neither in fact nor in specific prophecy until the New Testament.

The modern State of Israel

The modern State of Israel emerged in 1948 when the British withdrew from their World War I protectorate. Israel had not been a sovereign state since 63 B.C. when, after 104 years of independence, their native Maccabean rulers were replaced by representatives of Imperial Rome. Today's Jewish citizens of the State of Israel constitute national Israel, although only a portion of world Jewry lives there. The nation is basically secular, and the constitution avoids any direct reference to the name of God. Israel's leaders are morally and legally empowered to speak for the Jews among the world family of nations. It is their right to enter into treaties and covenants on behalf of the nation.

Though the State of Israel confirms Israel's perpetuity, and an Israeli government will facilitate Antichrist's covenant, the modern State is not otherwise seen as the fulfillment of prophecy. The following facts should be noted:

1) The present church age is untimed and unmarked and in this age no dates are identified either for the church or for Israel.

2) The Israelis are united on the basis of Zionism which is primarily political, and on an official basis their belief in God's covenant promises is at best nominal.

3) Biblical designations such as the dry bones that live (Ezek. 37:1-14), the nation born in a day (Isa. 66:8), and the gathering from among all nations (e.g., Deut. 30:3; Neh. 1:9; Jer. 29:14) are events that describe the founding of the millennial kingdom of Israel and they do not relate to the present era.

Israel and the Arabs

The approximately twenty-three modern Arab nations share a common ancestry with the Jews. Since the Arab tribes were launched through Abraham's son Ishmael (Gen. 16:15) and his grandson Esau (Gen. 25:25), with their Egyptian and Hittite wives (cf. Gen. 21:20; 26:34), they join with the Jews in acknowledging Abraham as their patriarch. In Old Testament times, and into the New Testament and early Christian eras, Arabs were Israel's chief neighbors. Most notable among them in biblical references were Edom, Egypt, and Syria.

The rise of Islam, the religion of Mohammed, which emerged following his death in A.D. 632, markedly fueled Arab militarism. Thus, in 638, the Arabs (or Saracens) conquered Jerusalem and took control of the land. They ruled for the next four and one-half centuries, but in 1098 they were defeated and driven out by the European Roman Catholic Crusaders. These latter were barely able to maintain their conquests, and in 1187 the kingdom of Jerusalem was recaptured by the Arabs under the leadership of Saladin. At that time the Crusaders retained only limited outposts in coastal Palestine.

A century and a half later (1244) the Crusaders were permanently replaced by the militant invading Seljuk Turks, who were non-Arab, but converts to Islam. Although Turkey retained political control of Palestine until 1917, the Arabs greatly outstripped them in population growth both in Palestine and throughout the Near East. Thus, when the modern State of

Israel concluded its fourth decade in 1988 its Jewish citizens were outnumbered twenty-seven to one by Arab neighbors of varying degrees of hostility.

The Arab peoples are a major factor on the world scene, but they are not a unified nation with their own prophetic destiny. Nebuchadnezzar's dream image saw a succession of only four world empires: Babylonian, Medo-Persian, Grecian and Roman. In his interpretation, Daniel noted: *"Finally,* there will be a fourth kingdom" (Dan. 2:40). The divisions within the Arab world reflect their forefather, Ishmael, of whom God said, "He will be a wild donkey of a man . . . and he will live in hostility toward all his brothers" (Gen. 16:12). Islam unifies often by identifying common enemies rather than consolidating its followers. Major national groups in the Near East, such as Iran (ancient Persia) and Turkey, are not Arabs although they are predominantly Islamic.

Scripture devotes more predictive prophecy to Edom than to any other Arab peoples. The theme of the prophecy is Edom's doom, however, and that had been fulfilled by the end of the biblical era. Edom fell victim to Assyria's conquests in the same era that the Israelites were conquered.

Though the Bible contains 750 references to Egypt, only 50 are prophetic. A notable text describes millennial relationships: "In that day Israel will be the third, along with Egypt and Assyria, a blessing on the earth" (Isa. 19:24). This threefold coalition will combine Jews with Egyptians who are Arabs, but the Assyrians were probably non-Arabs, though their modern identification is uncertain.

The Bible mentions the Arab nation of Syria scores of times, but it does not give any specific prophecies of the nation's future. In the end time era two ancient Arab tribes will oppose Gog's invasion of Israel: "Sheba and Dedan . . . will say to you, Have you come to plunder?" (Ezek. 38:13). Clearly, hostile relationships between the Jews and the Arabs remain ongoing, but the Arabs are not a major prophetic national body.

The Nature of the Kingdom

In their earlier ministry, both John the Baptist and Jesus shared a similar message: "In those days John the Baptist came, preaching . . . and saying, 'Repent, for the kingdom of heaven is near'" (Matt. 3:1); "From that time on Jesus began to preach, 'Repent, for the kingdom of heaven is near'" (Matt. 4:17). The messages of Jesus and John in these citations from Matthew were identical.

In passages parallel to Matthew in the Gospels the expression is likely to be "kingdom of God." The designation "kingdom of heaven" is unique to Matthew, though he also used "kingdom of God" four times. In at least twenty-seven parallel Scriptures, what is said to be true of the kingdom of heaven, is elsewhere said to be true of the kingdom of God. Thus, most scholars consider the two forms to be interchangeable.

The kingdom in the New Testament era

Jesus used the familiar kingdom language of the prophets, and to His Jewish audiences He proclaimed the kingdom's imminence. He was taken very seriously. "He went on to tell them a parable, because he was near Jerusalem and the people thought that the kingdom of God was going to appear at once" (Luke 19:11). Clearly, they expected a literal kingdom. Jesus called for repentance as a heart preparation, however, and this message the people refused; He called for acceptance of Himself as the Messiah, and this truth the leaders refused. That which Jesus offered was rejected, and He who was Israel's Messiah was nailed to the cross.

Scholars seek an appropriate way to describe events relating to the kingdom. The appeal of John the Baptist, Jesus, and the disciples to prepare for the kingdom was obviously genuine. God's desire for the Jews of that day was that they enthrone the incarnate Christ as their Messiah, but they failed to do so. In response to Jesus' miracles that demonstrated His kingdom powers, the Pharisees declared that He was empowered by the prince of demons. Jesus refuted their claim and He declared, "If I drive out demons by the Spirit of God, then the kingdom of God has come upon you" (Matt. 12:28). Since what Jesus offered was rejected, the fulfillment of God's plan now awaits the kingdom age—the millennium, but this turn of events is no surprise to God. Thus, many scholars feel it is misleading to say that when Christ was on earth God revised His plan and as a consequence He postponed the kingdom.

The offering and rejection of a literal earthly kingdom were simply preludes to God's end time plans. The omniscient God by no means formulates His plans according to the vagaries of human behavior. He allows humans to choose, and He thus makes them responsible for the outcome. The Jews of Jesus' day could have directly entered into the kingdom, just as in Moses' time the people could have entered the promised land a few days after leaving Egypt. In each case, the people chose, and the outcome was then implemented in God's overall plan.

In His later ministry, Jesus responded to the Jews' rejection of the terms of the kingdom. To the chief priests and the

Pharisees He declared, "Therefore I tell you that the kingdom of God will be taken away from you and given to a people who will produce its fruit" (Matt. 21:43). In the parable of the wedding banquet (Matt. 22:1-14) He told of the invited guests who refused to come. The king proceeded with their punishment and destruction, and then he found a new company of guests and the wedding feast proceeded. In His response to Pilate Jesus said, "My kingdom is not of this world. If it were, my servants would fight. . . . But now my kingdom is from another place" (John 18:36).

The resurrected Jesus continued to speak of the kingdom. "He appeared to them over a period of forty days and spoke about the kingdom of God" (Acts 1:3). Just prior to His ascension, Jesus' disciples asked, "Lord, are you at this time going to restore the kingdom to Israel?" (Acts 1:6). In His response, Jesus did not deny that there would be a future kingdom; He simply referred to the indefinite timing. "It is not for you to know the times or dates the Father has set by his own authority" (Acts 1:7). Someday there would indeed be a kingdom. In His closing message to the church, Jesus spoke of Himself as "the Root and the Offspring of David" (Rev. 22:16). By these final words, Jesus made clear that He expects someday to reign upon David's throne, and to take His place as Israel's Messiah.

Present and future kingdom manifestations

The word kingdom in the sense of deity's reign over human subjects occurs 148 times in the New Testament (NIV), with 66 references to the "kingdom of God," 32 to the "kingdom of heaven," and 50 simply to "kingdom." These many Scriptures indicate that ultimately the kingdom will have been manifested in four different forms: 1) today's mystery form, 2) today's visible form, 3) the millennial or Messianic kingdom, 4) the eternal or Father's kingdom.

The kingdom exists today in **mystery form** (i.e., one has to be enlightened to perceive it) in its subjects who are born again and living righteously as they serve their divine King. This kingdom is not a place or area to be shown on a map, but rather, the reigning power and authority of Jesus Christ to which His subjects willingly submit. Jesus launched the kingdom, recruited its first subjects, and laid the foundation for its perpetuation and growth. All humans who have lived since Jesus' day, including those now alive, who have chosen to acknowledge the Lordship of Christ and to submit to His government are in this spiritual or mystery kingdom (cf. Eph. 3:3-11). Believers enjoy a dual citizenship, that of their earthly national homeland, and that provided in Christ. "Our citizenship is in heaven" (Phil. 3:20).

During His years on earth, Jesus proclaimed a non-political kingdom. "My kingdom is not of this world. If it were, my servants would fight to prevent my arrest by the Jews" (John 18:36). When the Pharisees asked "when the kingdom of God would come," Jesus replied, "The kingdom of God is within you" (cf. Luke 17:20-21). These questioners had to be told that the kingdom was there, because they had missed seeing it. By exorcizing demons, Jesus proclaimed both the fact of the kingdom, and also its spiritual rule. He explained, "If I drive out demons by the Spirit of God, then the kingdom of God has come upon you" (Matt. 28).

Jesus taught, "No one can see the kingdom of God unless he is born again" (John 3:3). "No one can enter the kingdom of God unless he is born of water and the Spirit" (John 3:5). "Unless your righteousness surpasses that of the Pharisees and the teachers of the law, you will certainly not enter the kingdom of heaven" (Matt. 5:20). The kingdom depicted in this manner is Jesus' redemptive spiritual kingdom. Today, this mystery kingdom is equivalent to and concurrent with the true church of Jesus Christ on earth comprising all born again believers.

The **visible kingdom** is equivalent to what is often called Christendom, which includes the born again righteous ones who truly belong, and also those who only profess to belong and who are to be separated out in the end time. These facts are taught in Jesus' parables of the wheat and the weeds (Matt. 13:24-30), and the net (dragnet) with its good and bad fish (Matt. 13:47-50). Each parable begins, "The kingdom of heaven is like . . ." The first concludes, "Collect the weeds and tie them in bundles to be burned; then gather the wheat and bring it into my barn" (v.30). Similarly, "They sat down and collected the good fish in baskets, but threw the bad away" (v. 48).

The **millennial kingdom** will be launched when the Jews, in response to their extremity, finally acknowledge their Messiah and Jesus Christ returns as King of the Jews. "I will pour out on the house of David and the inhabitants of Jerusalem a spirit of grace and supplication. They will look on me, the one they had pierced, and they will mourn for him as one mourns for an only child" (Zech. 12:10). Christ will rule on His own terms. "'The days are coming,' declares the Lord, 'when I will raise up to David a righteous Branch, a King who will reign wisely and do what is just and right in the land. In his days Judah will be saved and Israel will live in safety'" (Jer. 23:5-6). In this earthly manifestation of the promised kingdom, Christ will consume and destroy all other kingdoms. "The kingdom of the world has become the kingdom of our Lord and of his Christ" (Rev. 11:15).

Since there is a unity within the trinity, Scripture does not appear rigorous in designating the divine sponsor of the **eternal kingdom.** Peter wrote to those effectually called, "you will receive a rich welcome into the eternal kingdom of our Lord and Savior Jesus Christ." Scripture also states, however, that after the millennium Jesus will surrender the kingdom to the Father. "Then the end will come, when he hands over the kingdom to God the Father after he has destroyed all dominion, authority and power . . . so that God may be all in all" (1 Cor. 15:24, 28).

The kingdom of the Father will be the believer's heaven where he or she is eternally united with the Savior. To the disciples, as He instituted the Lord's Supper in the upper room, Jesus had said, "I will not drink of this fruit of the vine . . . until that day when I drink it anew with you in my Father's kingdom" (Matt. 26:29). Since the Christian knows that "the righteous will shine like the sun in the kingdom of their Father" (Matt. 13:43), it is little wonder that regularly Christians pray, "Thy Kingdom come" (Matt. 6:10 KJV).

THREE

Systems and Methods of Eschatology

In their understanding of eschatological Bible portions, scholars are separated by important differences. Not only must terms and concepts be distinguished, but the basic outlook or perspective determining the method of interpreting Scripture must be decided. If the techniques by which Scripture is approached are different, then it is highly unlikely that the conclusions will agree. The different approaches particularly determine interpretations of the Book of Revelation, but they apply also to interpretations of prophetic Scriptures overall.

Futurist Eschatology

The futurist position generally identifies with premillennialism, and likely with pretribulationism, and with a commitment to the consistent literal interpretation of Scripture.

The nature of the futurist viewpoint

Futurism sees all prophesied specific end time events to be future to the present age. Further, it holds that the church has minimal or no prophecies of its own that can be assigned chronologically. Future events will include the rapture, the tribulation, Antichrist's rule, Armageddon, the second coming, the millennium, and the latter day judgments, but none of these events are yet in place. Today's "signs of the times" cannot be expected to be actual prophesied events, but only the "setting of the stage" for the end time events that are yet to come.

Basic to futurism is the evangelical emphasis upon the consistent literal interpretation of Scripture, and the minimizing of allegorization. Futurism seeks to develop eschatology based on the grammatico-historical approach to biblical interpretation. In futurism's view, eschatological truth that the Holy Spirit intended is assured when one adopts meanings conveyed through vocabulary and grammatical structure, and he or she is guided by a commitment to the historical accuracy of biblical content.

As already noted, futurists acknowledge that their program did not arise as a consistent coherent system until the early nineteenth century. In this present day they consider that the task of developing a comprehensive eschatology is still ongoing. They acknowledge that Christendom may be far from agreement in its doctrines of the end time, but futurists are optimistic that sound biblical scholarship will develop an increasingly expanding circle of established eschatological beliefs.

The futurist view of the last days[1]

Newer Bible versions (e.g., NIV) use the expression "last day" (six times, all in John's Gospel); "last days" (eight times, with three Old Testament and five New Testament occurrences); and "days to come" (fourteen times, all in the Old Testament). Older versions (e.g., KJV) use "latter days" (eight times) rather than "days to come." All but one of John's references identify the "last day" with the resurrection of the believer's body. The final reference is to the sinner at the great white throne judgment.

The expression "last days" denotes the present era four times (Acts 2:17; Heb. 1:2; James 5:3; 2 Pet. 3:3), the tribulation once (2 Tim. 3:1), and the millennium three times (Isa. 2:2; Hos. 3:5; Mic. 4:1). In some references the expression "days to come" refers to the entire span of human history (e.g., Exod. 13:14; Isa. 30:8); in others, it points to the tribulation (Deut. 31:29; Jer. 30:24); or to the millennium (Num. 24:14; Jer. 49:39).

Clearly, the denotation of "last days" and "days to come" (or "latter days") is determined by context. These expressions speak of the future, but they are not technical terms rigidly identifying specific eras. Biblical usage spoke of the "last days" or "days to come" of the Old Testament era (e.g., Gen. 49:1), of human history on earth (e.g., Heb. 1:2), of the Christian era (e.g., 2 Pet. 3:3), and of God's plan for His Son and all people (e.g., Isa. 2:2). These expressions denote a time future to the time of writing, and usually the latter portion of that era, but the context must determine details. It was thus possible for Christians in Paul's time to be living in the last days, just as Christians do today.

The present age and futurist eschatology

Though the futurist typically teaches and preaches predictive biblical truth, valid futurism actually allows very little scope for present applications. Basically, futurism applies prophetic Scripture either to a future day on earth, or to eternity, and it sees today's era on earth only in generalities. If predicted earthly events apply to this age, they do not occur at a point in time, but as continuing characteristics. Even the message of the rapture of the church has been an ongoing promise throughout church history, for God structured the prophetic message to apply to the church of every decade and every century.

---

1 Chapter 10 includes a further discussion of the expression "last days."

Most futurists would endorse Darby's rule of thumb, "All prophecies that apply to earthly events pertain to Israel; all that apply to heaven pertain to the church." The futurist scholar is alert to the "signs of the times," not because they are the fulfillment of prophecy in this age, but because they are the harbingers of what will be. Futurist eschatology sees the church age as uncharted and timeless. In Ironside's classic phrase it is "the great parenthesis" that is an undefined and unmeasured insert between one phase of God's plan for Israel, and the next.

Futurism and premillennialism

As noted previously, futurism commonly identifies with premillennialism. Responding to Scripture on a literal basis leads most people to expect prophetic fulfillment in the future, and to expect Christ to return to earth to launch His millennial rule. Such futurist premillennialism appeared as the dominant view during the apostolic era while the church was developing its theological beliefs.

Unfortunately, the excessive materialism of millennial expectations among its more radical supporters offended many Christians, beginning with the Alexandrian school in the third century. Thus, early in the Christian era, premillennialism fell upon hard times. In recounting these events, the histories of premillennialism, millennialism, and chiliasm come together as a single story. Chapter 13 discusses these matters further.

Preterist Eschatology

The preterist is likely to be a postmillennialist or an amillennialist since the views are often associated, though preterism is not essential to either. The preterist probably will use allegorizing more than the futurist.

The nature and methods of preterism

In this view, the eschatological Scriptures were future at the time that they were written, but they have virtually all been fulfilled in the passing centuries. Thus, the Bible prophecies are now past tense. The term "preterit" (or preterite) is a Latin word meaning "gone by." It is a grammarian's term to designate action in the past without reference to duration or repetition. The Bible scholar who adopts the preterist view of eschatology designates specific historical events and personalities as the fulfillment of scriptural prophecies. Thus, he or she constructs an interpretation that is intended to reconcile history and prophecy.

Typical preterist views have taught that the tribulation consisted of the attack upon Jerusalem by the armies of Rome in A.D. 70, or Emperor Nero's vicious persecution of Christians in the Roman Empire just prior to that time. Preterists identify the expression "last days" as the time between Christ's birth and the destruction of Jerusalem. The millennium has been equated with the outcome of Constantine's conversion, his proclamation of religious liberty in A.D. 313, Christianity's status with imperial patronage, and the subsequent Christianization of the entire Roman Empire.

A popular preterist view that has already been noted involved equating the onset of the tribulation with Emperor Justinian's policies of placing secular authority above that of the church. A non-preterist writer comments, "The Preterist interpretation would resolve [the Book of] Revelation into a handbook of the history of the church under the Caesars." Preterists are likely to assign the fulfillment of all biblical prophecy to events that occurred during the early centuries of the Christian era.

Preterist scholars usually ignore the "mountain peak principle" and typically they see a given Scripture in a single perspective only. They see the Bible prediction of a tribulation to be fulfilled in the events that culminated in Jerusalem's destruction in A.D. 70. Christ came at that time by pouring out His judgment from heaven. Preterist David Chilton reviewed the predicted events of the Olivet Discourse, including the cosmic disturbances and the coming of the Son of Man on the clouds of the sky (cf. Matt. 24:29-31) as follows:

> **It must be stressed that none of these events literally took place.
> . . . Poetically, however, all these things did happen: as far as these
> wicked nations were concerned "the lights went out." . . . In Matthew 24 . . . Jesus was not prophesying that He would literally
> come on the clouds in A.D. 70 (although it was figuratively true).
> . . . In A.D. 70 the tribes of Israel would see the destruction of the
> nation as the result of His having ascended to the throne of
> heaven to receive His kingdom.[2]**

Evangelical preterists seek to equate biblical prophecy with historical events. In *The Beast of Revelation,* Kenneth Gentry argues that the Beast was Nero Caesar (A.D. 37 to 68). This view requires dating the Book of Revelation prior to Nero's anti-Christian rampages. Thus, Gentry dates Revelation prior to A.D. 70. Preterism entails a fundamentally different way of interpreting Scripture, and in Gentry's words, for an evangelical it's a case of "swimming against the tide."

Preterism in the past and present

Luis de Alcazar (1554-1613), a Jesuit friar, is considered a notable representative of the preterist position. In defending the Pope against the Protestant charge that he was the Antichrist, Luis argued that the Antichrist had been an agent of imperial

---

2   David Chilton, *The Great Tribulation.* Fort Worth: Dominion Press, 1987, pp. 20, 25.

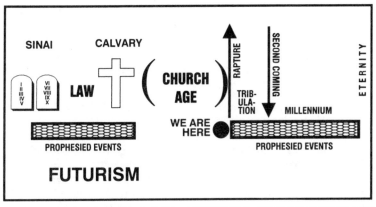

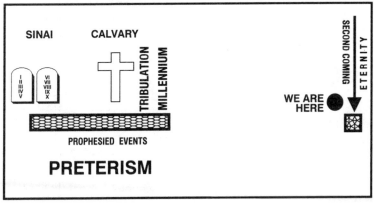

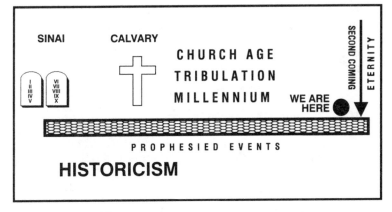

Fig. 3. Three approaches to eschatology. All agree that prophesied events begin early in Israel's history and they continue through Calvary and the resurrection. The views divide sharply, however, in their opinion of the application of end time prophecies.

Rome in the era of the early church. Since Antichrist had died long ago, he could not be the current Pope. A Protestant contemporary, Hugo Grotius (1583-1645), also used the preterist approach. He developed a preterist interpretation to defend his claim that in seventeenth century Europe neither Catholics nor Protestants remained in the millennium.

A notable publication in 1887 contended for the rigorous preteristic position that has been called "full preterism" (or hyper-preterism). The work, by J. Stuart Russell was titled, *The Parousia: A Critical Inquiry into the New Testament Doctrine of Our Lord's Second Coming*. It contended that all end time events, including the second coming and the great white throne judgment, took place during the destruction of Jerusalem in A.D. 70. The usual preterist view still anticipates these end time cosmic events. Russell justified his interpretation by explaining, "Prophecy is poetry, and Oriental poetry also, in which gorgeous symbolical imagery is the vesture of thought."[3] (As the reference to the foregoing citation indicates, Russell's work under a shorter title was republished in 1999.)

Preterism has not been a dominant eschatological system, but among nineteenth and early twentieth century theological liberals it attained a modest following. In the present day it has particularly appealed to some evangelical postmillennialists. They welcome a system disposing of most prophesied events, and freeing them to view living Christians as millennial citizens with the potential for all of the promised blessings and privileges. To a futurist, many preterist interpretations appear arbitrary and subjectively imaginative. Assigning historical people and events to the Bible's descriptions and visions requires both allegory and spiritualization. Some presentations of preterism, however, could probably be compatible with evangelicalism, as well as with liberalism and with versions of a social gospel.

Historicist Eschatology

Historicism is the position held by the majority of Christendom, and though some refer to it as "comprehensivism," historicism is not really a fully developed system of eschatology. In reality, historicism functions chiefly as a method of interpreting Scripture, rather than as a consistent eschatological system.

The overall historicist viewpoint

Historicism in general holds that, apart from the eternal state, all Bible predictions are being fulfilled in this present age. The meaning of what appears to be predictive prophecy will be

---

3   J. Stuart Russell, *The Parousia*. Grand Rapids: Baker Books, 1999, p. 399.

found in what has happened and is happening in the experience of the Christian church on earth. The passage of events—human history—is the sole interpretative standard for predictions. The meaning of concepts, such as Antichrist and tribulation, are found in the Christian's experience of ongoing trials in everyday life on earth. As the third century Alexandrians had taught, much that appears as biblical prophecy is really an allegorical account of the ceaseless struggle between good and evil.

Basic historicism holds that Scripture teaches only two states of existence: this life, and the life to come. The eternal state is the realm which humans enter at death. Many historicists, however, teach that the "end of the world" will occur when Christ returns to earth and officiates at the general judgment of all moral beings. Some see the achievement of an improved life on earth that can be called a millennium, though without a fundamental change of the order of human existence. To the historicist, whatever will occur on earth is now occurring, though perhaps on a much smaller (or larger) scale, and it has been doing so ever since the church age began.

Some specific historicist views

Historicist scholars usually hold that the promises of a restored Israel are to be spiritualized as promises to the church. They see the church as today's true Israel, since it comprises God's people of the new covenant. Some historicists hold that God intends the church to seek to infiltrate secular society so that the two become one. By this means they hope to see the lofty promises of Messiah's kingdom fulfilled. Since this view may lead to postmillennialism, some historicists have adopted this position. The more usual view, however, is amillennialism which holds simply that there is no future millennium, or "as much millennium as we'll ever see is whatever there is here and now."

The doctrine of the return of Christ is acceptable to most historicists, though they differ from futurists in their view of the nature and purpose of His return. The historicist may share the language of immanency, but to him, the second coming is probably only the prelude to the eternal state rather than the inauguration of a new life on earth. A typical historicist wrote, "The Bible teaches that Jesus Christ will return at the end of this gospel age to receive us to Himself and to bring wrath on the unsaved." In some cases, historicists see the second coming as a spiritual or allegorical event, rather than literal.

Historicist methods and applications

The historicist is not interested in the futurist's detailed chronological or dispensational charts. Since he sees all of Scripture speaking either of life today or life in eternity, God cannot relate to humans in programs in which He deals differently in successive eras. Scripture's "thousand years" (Rev. 20:2) is likely symbolic and impressionistic, and meant only to convey impressions or feelings. One errs by counting literal numbers. If a timed prophetic period must be recognized, however, the historicist would likely adopt preterism and assign it in the past. Typically, historicist-preterism suggests that Daniel's seventieth week was the disturbing period in Israel following Christ's crucifixion. Such a preterist interpretation does not clash with the methods of historicism, and its belief poses no conflicts.

In some cases, historicists hold their position more or less by default. They either have not yet pursued studies in eschatology, or out of their studies thus far they have not been able to construct a futurist system acceptable to them. The historicist system is simple and unencumbered, and it at least offers an answer to the meaning of eschatological Scriptures. Since all systems require some allegorizing or spiritualizing of Scripture, the historicist concludes that he is justified in his methodology.

Variants of the historicist system

Historicism's view of eschatology typically spiritualizes Scripture, thus leaving room for a variety of systems. Some of these have a wide following; others are taught by a single author. These systems tend to look upon eschatology as a personal perspective, and they emphasize the "existential impact" of eschatology. To them, eschatology is not God's goal for history, but for each individual human. Eschatology is not so much something to be understood as that which is to be personally experienced.

Cosmic eschatology: This system, associated with Karl Heim, holds that God's eschatological plan is directed toward the scientific redemption of the universe or cosmos. It is a matter of evolutionary upgrading that somehow relates to Scripture and which began with the resurrection of Christ. The final goal is that God will be "all in all." Obviously, such a theory has little in common with an evangelical interpretation of Scripture.

Realized eschatology: This term identifies a more or less conventional historicist position. It sees the themes, symbols, and motifs of eschatology being realized in this age. In His earthly ministry, Jesus fulfilled as much of God's plan as He will ever fulfill on earth, and the kingdom of God is now here. In His teaching, Jesus' eschatology concerned the present and conveyed no idea of futurity—for "the future is now." The sole expectation of the future may be the second coming when the kingdom that is now realized will be "eternally consummated." Spokesmen associated with this view include Charles H. Dodd in his earlier writings, T.F. Glasson, Paul Althaus and Jay E. Adams.

Inaugurated eschatology: This term describes a position similar to Realized, but it denies a distinct second coming that will have specific effect upon the kingdom. Rather, in the present, humans determine Jesus' future in relation to themselves. Thus, not only is the kingdom now realized upon earth, but all that it will ever be in relation to eternity has been inaugurated. Eschatological fulfillment is underway, and for humans, the kingdom comes and comes and comes. Those associated with this system include J.A.T. Robinson, Georg Kummel, the later C.H. Dodd, and with some variation, Anthony Hoekema.

Existential eschatology: According to this system, Jesus had definitely believed in the future kingdom, but His eschatology was mythological because it did not come to pass as He said it would. The meaning of eschatological Scripture is therefore not in its literal affirmations, but in what it can achieve in the believer's present experience. The question is not, "Will it happen this way?" but "Am I experiencing in my own existence the truths of which this Scripture speaks?" Rudolf Bultmann particularly developed and promoted this view.

Consistent or thoroughgoing eschatology: This system holds that a consistent biblical view must see the kingdom as a future, dramatic, eschatological event. Liberalism, which sees the present Christianized society to be the kingdom, is inconsistent. Jesus taught that the kingdom would arrive by a future divine stroke. This non-liberal view is necessary for consistency, but Jesus was wrong[4]. When His expectations failed, He suffered the crucifixion, and He died. His kingdom rule is thus as the crucified One. The believer enters a mystical kingdom by sharing Christ's crucified life and following His example. The end time kingdom is now experienced in the paradox of the suffering and death of Christ. Spokesmen for this view include Albert Schweitzer, Johannes Weiss, and Martin Dibelius.

Theology of Hope eschatology: This view sees all theology to be eschatological; the spirit, outlook, and framework of theology is eschatology. God is not merely within Christians, but He is ahead of them and the future is the mode of God's being. Christ is the future brought into the present. A Christian is one who hopes in the future of God. As mediators of the future of a powerful and loving God, Christians are responsible for doing something about evil in the world. Even if they cannot identify that for which they are hoping, Christians must have hope. This view relates to Jürgen Moltmann whose optimistic hope enabled him to survive a wartime imprisonment.

---

4 Note that though it concludes that Jesus was wrong, consistent eschatology interprets Jesus' beliefs in the standard futurist pattern.

Other historicist terminology: The systems that are the outcome of historicist interpretations are sometimes designated as idealist or synchronous eschatologies. Idealist eschatology results when the prophetic portions of Scripture are spiritualized or idealized as mere symbols or allegories of the conflict of good and evil. Synchronous eschatology is the outcome of ignoring the chronological structure of prophecy, and seeing all events as cyclical or topical. Supposed prophetic Scriptures are simply describing God's final triumph at the end of the world.

Literalism and Allegorism

One's position in eschatology is vitally tied to his or her perspective in regard to the Bible. Paul Lee Tan writes:

> As long as the issue of interpretation remains unsettled, it is futile to debate the schemes and details of Bible prophecy. All questions of prophecy must ultimately be settled within the framework of proper hermeneutics.[5]

What Tan says of Bible prophecy is true of biblical eschatology in general.

The literal approach to eschatological Scripture

As previously stated, literalism asks that, if possible, the words of Scripture be accepted in their normal and literal sense. The words of the Bible should be taken to mean just what the same words would mean in any normal context. Necessarily, unique applications of terms occur (e.g., until Jesus used *ekklesia* to identify His church, the word denoted any called assembly of people), and some Bible descriptions must be understood allegorically. Thus, Jesus explained, "The field is the world, and the good seed stands for the sons of the kingdom. The weeds are the sons of the evil one, and the enemy who sows them is the devil" (Matt. 13:38-39). Common sense should prevail, however, and God through His Holy Spirit should be given credit for being able to communicate intelligibly with humans.

God's manner of fulfilling prophesies in the past supports a literal approach to the interpretation of Scripture. Studies have produced lengthy lists of the detailed, precise, literal fulfillment of prophecies concerning individuals, events, cities, nations, and empires. Examples of these fulfillments include **individuals**—Nebuchadnezzar (Dan. 4), Judas Iscariot (Psa. 41:9 and John 6:64; 13:18-21); **events**—the Noachic flood (Gen. 6), famine (Gen. 41); **cities**—Babylon (Isa. 13:19,20; Jer. 50- 51), Jerusalem (Jer. 25:15-18; 34:1-7; Matt. 24:1-2); **nations**—Ammon (2 Ki.8:8-13; Ezek. 25:1-7), Moab (Isa. 15:1-16; Jer. 48), and of

---

5 Paul Lee Tan, *The Interpretation of Prophecy.* Rockville: Assurance Publishers, 1974, p. 280.

course many prophecies of Israel and Judah; and **empires**—Assyria (Isa. 10:5-34; Nah. 1:1-3:19), Greece (Dan. 8:3-27; 11:2-4).

Scores of explicit prophecies—the usual count is 109—relating to the incarnate life of Jesus Christ were literally fulfilled. Notably, when Matthew concludes the story of the events of Christ's nativity, he notes, "All this took place to fulfill what the Lord had said through the prophet" (Matt. 1:22). In fact, in Matthew alone, the expressions "to fulfill" or "so was fulfilled" or their variants occur at least thirteen times.

Among the early church Fathers, literalism was freely accepted as the common method for the interpretation of prophetic and eschatological Scripture. As schools emerged, the School of Antioch, which identifies with Lucian (martyred in 312), was particularly marked by its commitment to literalism. This school produced such leaders as Chrysostom (354-407) and Theodoret (386-458). Nevertheless, in the matter of hermeneutical approaches to eschatological Scripture, it was not Antioch, but the School of Alexandria under the leadership of Origen (c. 185-254) that chiefly influenced the developing Catholic church. Origen considered literalism only the first level of the meaning of Scripture; the second was spiritual and by it one perceived the "soul" of the Scriptures; the third level was expressed by allegory and it was both anti-intuitive and anti-intellectual.

The Protestant reformers revived literalism as *the* method of interpreting Scripture. John Calvin wrote, "It is the first business of an interpreter to let his author say what he does say, instead of attributing to him what we think he ought to say." Martin Luther declared, "I have grounded my preaching upon the literal Word." Disappointingly, however, these reformers failed to apply literalism to the development of a biblical eschatology. Instead, they maintained, seemingly without critical evaluation, the traditional allegorical amillennialism of Catholicism.

Literalism, as previously noted, was not systematically applied to eschatological Bible passages until the primarily lay movements of the nineteenth century. Some suggest that one of the bases of the nineteenth century futuristic eschatology may have been John A. Ernesti's *Principles of New Testament Interpretation*. This volume promoted literalism, and for fully a century it was a standard text for students of hermeneutics.

A limitation upon literalism: Out of their background, the reformers and their followers, in effect, limited the voice of literal Scripture by their commitment to historic beliefs. This tendency continues to the present, and thus Keith Mathison wrote in his book which defends postmillennialism:

> It is the conviction of this author that the Westminster Confession of Faith is an accurate and faithful summary of the teaching of Scripture. . . . Foundational for this book, providing the vantage point from which we shall proceed, are the Scriptures as the sole source of doctrine, as interpreted by the ecumenical creeds and the Reformed faith.[6]

To require literal Scripture to be interpreted by historic creeds and confessions limits what one will discover in the text. This difference in basic methodology results in eschatologies that differ.

The Allegorical Approach to Eschatological Scripture

To interpret Scripture allegorically is to hold that what is said is to be understood as symbolic, figurative, or metaphorical. The process is also known as spiritualization since it involves giving a spiritual meaning to what is tangible and physical. Commonly, an allegory is described as "an extended metaphor." To the allegorist, the real meaning of Scripture lies beneath the letter of the text.

Some examples of allegorization from a published booklet on the Second Coming[7] include: the drying up of the Euphrates (Rev. 16:12) was the Turkish Empire's passing after World War I; the three evil spirits looking like frogs (Rev. 16:13) are communism, Papal political activity, and Mohammedanism; the British capture of Jerusalem in 1917 marked the end of the time of the Gentiles; and the ten virgins (Matt. 25:1-13) are the ten tribes of Israel, only half of whom are ready to welcome their Lord.

Allegorization, as a method of interpreting written text, derives from the efforts of secular Greek scholars who were seeking to glean added ideas from the Greek philosophers. The method passed from the Greeks to second century (B.C.) Alexandrian Jews who greatly admired Greek culture. In turn, in the second century A.D., the same hermeneutical method passed into the Christian school at Alexandria, and hence into mainstream Christianity. As noted above, Origen, the head of the Alexandrian school, assiduously promoted the system, and in fact some historians refer to him as "Mr. Allegorism."

Augustine (354-430) is thought of as a literalist, but in prophetic and eschatological interpretations he was an allegorist. By the medieval period, and following it, allegorism held sway. Hugo of St. Victor (1096-1141) taught, "First learn what you are to believe, and then go to the Scripture and find it there." He stressed the use of the "eye of the spirit" as a tool to "find" what one seeks

---

6   Keith A. Mathison, *Postmillennialism An Eschatology of Hope*. Phillipsburg: P. & R. Publishing, 1999, p. 8.

7   Wm. Pascoe Goard, "The Second Coming of Our Lord." London: The Covenant Publishing Company, 1945.

in the Bible. Bernard Ramm once noted, "The Bible treated allegorically becomes putty in the hand of the exegete."[8]

Common Eschatological Terms

For the most part, those who use eschatological terms that consist of time designations (e.g., posttribulation, premillennial) are viewing matters from the futurist standpoint. Such distinctions would likely be irrelevant to the historicist and of limited interest to the preterist. They merit, however, a compilation of short working definitions as follows:

Pretribulation: This term usually applies to the time of the rapture and obviously assigns it prior to the tribulation. In common usage, the short form "pretrib" frequently serves as an adjective, and the other forms are similarly abbreviated.

Midtribulation: Since the seven-year tribulation is divided into two periods of three and one-half years, this term denotes the moment of time at the dividing point.

Posttribulation: The prefix "post"means "after, following after, or later," and it classifies time in relation to the tribulation. An event designated as posttribulation would occur following the end of the tribulation period. A posttribulation rapture would subject believers to Antichrist's wrath during the entire seven years. They would then be caught up to meet the Lord in the air as He is on His way from heaven to return to earth.

Premillennial: As a designation of time, premillennial speaks of whatever comes before the millennium. One might find the sentence, "Even the doctrine of a posttribulation rapture allows for the premillennial return of Christ."

Postmillennial: This term denotes that time or era that follows the millennium. A postmillennial coming of the Lord is usually understood to require that humans somehow achieve millennial conditions on earth apart from the personal presence of Jesus Christ. Postmillennialists do not usually require the millennium to be a literal one thousand calendar years.

Amillennial: This term, which means "no millennial [event]," holds that Scripture does not teach a special end time period significantly different from present life on earth. The millennial kingdom is now present on earth in the church. The amillennialist likely does not deny the fact of the millennium, but he or she markedly qualifies what is perceived as the millennium. The only two existences that humans can know are 1) the

---

8 Bernard Ramm, *Protestant Biblical Interpretation* (Third Revised Edition). Grand Rapids: Baker Book House, 1970, p. 30.

present life on earth and 2) eternity. If what is true of the church differs from the Old Testament prophecies, either the church triumphant in heaven is in view, or the interpretation of the Old Testament prophecies must be spiritualized. Among the amillennial "schools" are the Augustinians who hold that all the promises to Israel are now being fulfilled by the church on earth. This position is held by Roman Catholics and some Protestants. Other amillennialists, often those with covenant or presbyterial backgrounds, hold that the promises to Israel are being fulfilled by the church in heaven—the so-called Warfield view.

Application Issues in Eschatology

The position taken in respect to the foregoing views is often more than mere abstract theory. In many cases, eschatological perspectives definitely shape lifestyles and ministry goals.

The **pretribulation** rapture viewpoint tends to see the church's task to be to rescue humankind from the coming destruction. All who have trusted Christ as their personal Savior will be caught up in the rapture. Thus, the major energies of the church must be directed toward evangelism. Also, personal lifestyle in Biblical holiness is important, since believers must live ready to meet Jesus Christ at any moment.

The **posttribulation** rapture perspective holds that the preparation of humans for the tribulation is of vital importance. Evangelism remains a critical necessity, since as many as possible must be spared the deception of the mark of the beast. Believers must study in-depth the strategies of Antichrist and the procedures that will assure survival. Practical preparations may be warranted, including the stockpiling of food.

Those committed to a **postmillennial** return of Christ consider humans responsible to work to achieve what has been predicted for the millennial earth. Evangelical postmillennialists emphasize that they do most to transform humans when they touch their lives with the Christian gospel. In general, however, the postmillennial viewpoint sees evangelism alone as "escapist," and the "rapture mentality" to result in the paralysis of the church. Much is to be done through education, philanthropy, scientific research, political and social action, and whatever other available resources will contribute to the welfare of people and a better world. Whereas the premillennial outlook in regard to human achievements and their potential is usually pessimistic, in these areas postmillennialism is notably optimistic.

Some who hold an **amillennial** commitment to eschatology would share the postmillennial commitment to human progress, but the more typical amillennial position would be resignation to the continuing development of both good and evil. At least on the basis of his or her eschatology, the amillennialist is not preparing for any specifically different earth, but only for eternity. Since in the amillennial view the kingdom is now in effect, national Israel has no predicted future, and Middle East and European political events are of no particular biblical significance.

In **summary**, it is evident that individual believers, churches, and denomination are significantly influenced in their outlook and goals by their eschatological viewpoints. Differences in social concerns, and disagreements in missionary policies and evangelistic thrusts, may link much more closely to divergent eschatologies than to outlooks otherwise.

Premillennial Backgrounds

Most Christians who hold to Christ's premillennial return are probably in some way the heirs of John N. Darby. Many "covenant" theologians are also premillennial, however, and they reject Darbyism. A review of these two backgrounds follows.

Dispensational premillennialism

According to some scholars, the word "dispensational" has been "much maligned." Even though many Christians are heirs of the system, they tend to deny it credit. Apparently, the mistakes and excesses of overzealous students of dispensationalism have resulted in many declaring their rejection of the entire system. As Louis Sperry Chafer once noted, however, "Any person is a dispensationalist who trusts the blood of Christ rather than bringing an animal sacrifice . . . [and] who observes the first day of the week rather than the seventh." What is no longer popular is an excessive emphasis upon dispensationalism (hyperdispensationalism) that made it the key to all biblical understanding, and applied only the epistles to the present church age —the age of grace.

The term "dispensation" defines as "a distinctive management standard used by God in a specified context to work out His purpose." During each dispensation, God imposes a particular rule of life for humans to obey. Biblically justifiable dispensationalism holds that the dispensational rule is merely God's mode of dealing in that era. At all times, either past or future, God's only basis of salvation is by grace through faith in Christ's atoning death. Probably some dispensationalists have hurt their cause because they appeared to lose sight of this truth. Thus, a typical criticism of dispensationalism is that it "does not adequately portray the unity of God's redemptive work."[9]

---

9 Mathison op. cit., p. 19.

Dispensationalists commonly recognize seven earthly dispensations: 1) **Innocence** while Adam and Eve were in the garden and under the rule not to partake of the fruit of the tree of the knowledge of good and evil; 2) **Conscience** during the early ages of life on earth when humans were left to the rule of their own conscience; 3) **Human Government** following the Noachic flood when God delegated authority to human leaders: "Whoever sheds the blood of man, by man shall his blood be shed" (Gen. 9:6); 4) **Promise** or the Patriarchal age during which Abraham and his descendants walked in anticipation of the Lord's promise as He prepared them for nationhood; 5) **Law** began at Mt. Sinai and continued until the church age. God's requirements for humankind were expressed in great detail through the commandments, precepts, and decrees; 6) **Grace** began with the launching of the church and Peter's proclamation of the standard that "everyone who calls on the name of the Lord will be saved" (Acts 2:21); 7) the **Kingdom** or millennial age will begin when Jesus Christ personally returns to earth and assumes the rule of all submissive humans and destroys those who resist.

Dispensationalism applies rigorous analysis to God's ruling standards and those humans with whom He deals. Notably, the nation of Israel, the Gentiles, the church, and millennial citizens are each maintained as distinct entities. Here, then, are methods and conclusions, that through their extensive background contributions and applications, conveniently identify with premillennial and pretribulational literal-futurist eschatology.

Covenant theology premillennialism

A major evangelical school of thought, with seventeenth century Calvinistic roots and contributions from scholars in Switzerland, the Netherlands, and Scotland, is known as federal or covenant theology. It associates particularly with Reformed and Presbyterian churches. The system sees God's dealings with humans to focus on two covenants: the Covenant of Works and the Covenant of Grace. By eating the forbidden fruit, Adam and Eve failed to qualify by the Covenant of Works, and since they were the representatives of the human race, all people became sinners. God thereupon extended to humans the Covenant of Grace (or some prefer the "Covenant of Redemption").

As biblical history proceeded, God expanded the elements of the Covenant of Grace. The additions included the Noachic Covenant, the Abrahamic Covenant, the Mosaic Covenant, and the Davidic Covenant. These all came together and were fulfilled in the New Covenant in Christ. And thus, Keith Mathison explains, "[The] person and covenantal work of Jesus Christ [provide] the central unifying theme of Scripture and the fulfillment of God's redemptive purposes."[10]

A covenant is a pact, agreement, or promise. O.P. Robertson described it as "a sovereignly administered bond-in-blood which relates God and man in a life and death relationship." In covenant theology's view, the Covenant of Grace has been adapted to specific times and peoples, but it has remained substantially the same for all humans. Though Bible history may be divided into specific epochs, the same Covenant of Grace has been consistently mediated by the Lord Jesus Christ. Thus, in Him alone all the offers and promises of the Covenant of Grace find their fulfillment. The salvation of the elect of all ages has been by the grace of God through Christ the Savior.

The covenant theologian's conclusion, which has a major effect upon eschatological beliefs, is that God has only one people: the church. Though this people may have two manifestations, one in the Old Testament and the other in the New, since humans fell, all called out saints comprise the one body in Christ. Israel and the church are not to be distinguished, the 144,000 are the church, the millennial temple is the church, and so is the new Jerusalem. The indicated eschatological outcome of such a view is either postmillennialism or amillennialism.

In fact, however, a company of covenant theologians adopt premillennial eschatology. Though their system freely spiritualizes Scripture, they personally choose to see the 1,000 years of Revelation 20 as a millennium. Since they see only one covenant people, the millennial citizens will be the church, and those preserved through the tribulation also will be the church. Israelites will be included only if they have become Christians. The only return of Christ will be posttribulational. Covenant theologians holding this view are likely to be vitally interested in eschatology. Since many are scholarly writers, their anti- dispensational, posttribulation, but premillennial views have enjoyed widespread dissemination.

An underlying issue

A basic issue that separates futurists from evangelical preterists or historicists is likely to be hermeneutics rather than Biblical exegesis. The futurist interprets literally to a much further degree than those who hold other viewpoints. A nonliteral interpretation views many predictive Scriptures as symbolic, pictorial, or allegorical. Even the literalist must interpret some Scriptures allegorically; thus, for instance, "All the trees of the field will clap their hands" (Isa. 55:12). The nonliteral scholar

---

10 ibid., p. 19.

considers that he or she is simply bringing systematic common sense to biblical interpretation.

Where the literalist-futurist holds that "Israel" means Israel, and "church" means church, the nonliteralist accepts that either term denotes the people of God. To the nonliteralist, God has dealt with His people in two alternate ways, or by two covenants, by requiring works—as He did for Adam or under Moses, or by offering grace—as He does for all sinners. The literalist tends to see a succession of varying conditions imposed by God upon humans during the course of history. Thus, God has extended multiple covenants as He dispensed His rule (or as He imposed dispensations).

Believers, whose centuries-long tradition teaches only a distinction between works and grace, are understandably reluctant to adopt the apparently complex distinctions of futurism. Also, it means abandoning many allegorical interpretations in favor of the literal. The issue is not merely what is taught in particular passages, but the basic methodology to be applied in interpretation. Further, what is accepted for one passage must be reconciled with all other relevant passages. Such a far-ranging turnaround can, understandably, provoke firm, and even heated resistance.

FOUR

The Rapture

Futurist eschatology sees the rapture of believers, by being caught up to meet Jesus in the air, as the culmination of the church age and the next step in God's program. Popularly, the rapture is seen as "the great escape of the church," and the beginning of the final countdown. This chapter will discuss the issues involved in the doctrine of the rapture.

The background of the rapture doctrine

In the early church the expectation of the return of Jesus Christ appears to have popularly complemented the reality of a personal spiritual experience. Writings such as *The Didache* (c. 100-125), the *Epistle of Barnabas* (early 2nd century), and the *Shepherd of Hermas* (c. 140) speak of Christ's return, though they are ambiguous in its timing. Irenaeus (c. 130-c. 200) taught the return of Christ, but he appears to have been a posttribulationist. Thus, though these writers supported the fact of the return of Christ for His people, they probably did not understand the rapture the way modern futurists do. And whatever the earlier views, by the fourth century they were largely abandoned.

As previously noted, though the systematic structured rapture doctrine did not really arise until the first quarter of the nineteenth century, the doctrine of the rapture was occasionally heard in prior centuries. Thus, the volume *Millennium, Last Days Novelties,* published in 1788 by Pastor Morgan Edwards of Philadelphia, included an enlightened discussion of the doctrine of the pretribulation return of Christ.

In the development of the doctrine of the rapture of the church, J.N. Darby (1800-1882) used his unique two-phase return view to harmonize Christ's imminent return with His conquering return at tribulation's end. Darby saw both a private rescue to deliver the church from the coming tribulation, and a spectacular military action at tribulation's close to deliver penitent Israel from Antichrist. The private rescue was the rapture, and the military action, the second coming.

Others who developed and popularized Darby's views included Presbyterian George Duffield in *Dissertations on the*

Prophecies Relative to the Second Coming of Jesus Christ (1842), and William Trotter in *Plain Papers on Prophetic and Other Subjects* (1860's). The volume *Jesus Is Coming* by Methodist William E. Blackstone was published in 1878. By 1925 this work had been translated into 36 languages, and 770,000 copies had been sold. An admirer described it as "the most forceful presentation of premillennialism ever written." Other works in this period included Charles Henry Mackintosh, *Papers on the Lord's Coming* (1878), and James H. Brookes' *Maranatha* (1870's).

In addition to his book, Brookes, who was a Presbyterian, sponsored the summer Niagara Bible Conferences, and until his death in 1897, edited the prophetic magazine, *Truth*. Brookes' large following included Cyrus I. Scofield (1843-1921). This Congregationalist, perhaps aided by his legal training, prepared a Bible edition with extensive notes that supported, among other doctrines, the pretribulation rapture. *The Scofield Reference Bible*, which was first published in 1909, had sold at least three million copies in North America by mid-century. In revised formats it still continues to be marketed.

As the twentieth century progressed, systematic teaching on the subject of the rapture shifted from the prophetic conference to the Bible college classroom. Many evangelical denominations, particularly those whose statement of faith was shaped during the century, adopted positions similar to that of Darby. Their training institutions naturally reflected the views of their sponsors. Much popular preaching, and many twentieth century hymns have enthusiastically supported a rapture doctrine.

The nature of the rapture

Scripture describes the rapture and its subjects in a notable and well-known text:

> **We who are still alive, who are left [Gk. *perileipomai*] till the coming [Gk. *parousia*] of the Lord, will certainly not precede those who have fallen asleep. For the Lord himself will come down from heaven, with a loud command, with the voice of the archangel and with the trumpet call of God, and the dead in Christ will rise first. After that, we who are still alive and are left [Gk. *perileipomai*] will be caught up [Gk. *harpadzo*] together with them in the clouds to meet the Lord in the air. And so we will be with the Lord forever[1] (1 Thess. 4:15-17).**

This Scripture clearly affirms that a day is coming when Jesus Christ will descend to catch up to Himself both dead and living

---

[1] *perileiponai* (per-ree-LIFE-o-my): remain, be left behind, to leave over, to survive; *parousia* (par-oo-SEE-ah) see next page; *harpadzo* (har-PADS-oh): to carry off, to snatch up, to take away (the passive of this verb in verse 17 denotes an action that is performed "in such a way that no resistance is offered").

believers. In context, the subjects are the "dead in Christ" and believers who are living.

The word "rapture," though not strictly biblical, derives from the older Latin version of the above passage. The Latin for "caught up" in verse 17 is *rapturo*, and its root is *rapere* which means "to grasp, seize, or catch away." This Latin word is an appropriate translation of the Greek *harpadzo*, for at the rapture believers will be seized and caught away upward. As they are brought into the presence of Christ (cf. 1 Thess. 4:14), their mortal bodies will instantly be transformed to become glorified and incorruptible.

The meeting in the air launches the raptured believers on their heavenly journey. Although the rapture is a coming of Jesus Christ, He stops short of an actual return to earth. The Bible's wording was previously cited: "We . . . will be caught up . . . in the clouds to meet the Lord in the air." Jesus promised "In my Father's house are many rooms. . . . I am going there to prepare a place for you. And if I go and prepare a place for you, I will come back and take you to be with me that you also may be where I am" (John 14:2-3). This verse clearly depicts the rapture as a catching away of believers into Jesus' heavenly dwelling place and to the prepared rooms in the Father's house.

Although a *parousia* in secular usage could involve the welcoming of the arrival of a visiting dignitary, it does not have this meaning in biblical accounts of Jesus' return in the rapture. The believers who are caught up are not a welcoming party who return with Him to earth, but resurrected or transformed humans whom He has come to take to His home. Jesus awakens and assembles both dead and living believers so that "God will bring with Jesus" (1 Thess. 4:14) those manifesting faith in Christ's resurrection promises. As soon as they are assembled, He will transport the entire company to their prepared home in heaven, "And so we will be with the Lord forever" (1 Thess. 4:17).

A passage parallel to 1 Thessalonians 4:15-17 describes the rapture as a dramatic occasion.

> Listen, I tell you a mystery [Gk. *mysterion*][2]: We will not all sleep, but we will all be changed—in a flash, in the twinkling of an eye, at the last trumpet. For the trumpet will sound, the dead will be raised imperishable, and we will be changed (1 Cor. 15:51-52).

For "mystery" some versions use "secret" or "God's hidden purpose." The word indicates a truth that is eternal in God's mind but which is made known only to those selected by God in His chosen time. The rapture is an event that God has planned

---

2 *mysterion* [moos-TAY-ree-on]: secret, secret rite, secret teaching, mystery.

uniquely for believers. It is His special way of achieving the resurrection and/or translation of believers in Jesus Christ.

Both of the above passages refer to a trumpet. In Bible times, trumpets (mentioned 119 times in the NIV) were used to summon assemblies (Num. 10:7; Matt. 24:31), emphasize announcements (1 Sam. 13:3), proclaim a coronation (1 Kings 1:34), or signal an army's movements (2 Sam. 2:28). Clearly, the expression "last trumpet" was a common idiom and not an out-of-context reference to the seventh trumpet of Revelation 11:15. The use of trumpets in Bible times includes the following:

1) In Jerusalem in the New Testament era, a temple trumpet was sounded to mark the Sabbath. Jerome wrote, "It was the custom for one of the priests to stand and give notice, by the sound of a trumpet, in the afternoon of the approach, and on the following evening of the close of every Sabbath day." The people commonly scheduled their lives by trumpet signals, just as many in a later generation marked time by bells or factory whistles.

2) In Roman practice, preliminary trumpets would signal the stages of the breaking up of an army camp. At the last trumpet the army would start to march.

3) Conventional dating systems place the writing of Corinthians at about A.D. 54 and Revelation at about A.D. 95. If Paul wrote to the Corinthians four decades earlier than John's angel trumpets in Revelation, Paul's readers could only understand "last trumpet" in terms of the common idiom.

The fact that the rapture is a mystery or "secret" tends to complicate its description. The rapture is an inner-circle event involving only born again believers—probably only a minority portion of earth's population; it will leave the vast majority of humans untouched. For those involved, however, the rapture will be far from secret.

The rapture will involve Jesus' commanding shout, the archangel's voice, and God's trumpet. For the believer, the rapture will be the most ecstatically exciting event he or she has ever known. Perhaps for other humans, it will parallel God's confirmation of Jesus' ministry. "The crowd that was there and heard it said it had thundered; others said an angel had spoken to him" (John 12:29). For all its dramatic awesomeness, the rapture will be explained away by those who deny spiritual realities.

Biblical language and the rapture

Various Greek terms are used in Scripture to speak of the rapture, (and also of the conquering second coming). Three are particularly notable as follows:

Parousia (par-oo-SEE-ah) denotes a coming into the presence of, arrival, or advent. This term occurs twenty-four times in the New Testament, and it clearly applies to the rapture: "Now, dear children, continue in him, so that when he appears we may be confident and unashamed before him at his coming [Gk. *parousia*]" (1 John 2:28). The term also, however, applies to the second coming: "[The lawless one] whom the Lord Jesus will . . . destroy by the splendor of his coming [Gk. *parousia*]" (2 Thess. 2:8).

Epiphaneia (ep-if-AN-i-ah) describes an appearing, manifestation of what has been hidden, becoming visible, or bringing to light. The word occurs six times in the New Testament, and it refers to the rapture, "I charge you to keep this command without spot or blame until the appearing [Gk. *epiphaneia*] of our Lord Jesus Christ" (1 Tim. 6:14), and also to what seems to be the second coming, "Christ Jesus . . . will judge the living and the dead, and in view of his appearing [Gk. *epiphaneia*] and his kingdom, I give you this charge" (2 Tim. 4:1). The word also occurs in 2 Thessalonians 2:8 which is cited above, "[The lawless one] whom the Lord Jesus will . . . destroy by the splendor [Gk. *epiphaneia*] of his coming." This context illustrates its connotation as "a bringing to light."

Apokalypsis (ap-ok-AL-oop-sis) speaks of a revelation, disclosure, exposing to view, bringing to light, or unveiling. Among the eighteen occurrences of this word in the New Testament, some identify the rapture. "You do not lack any spiritual gift as you eagerly wait for our Lord Jesus Christ to be revealed [Gk. *apokalypsis*]" [lit. "eagerly awaiting the revelation of our Lord Jesus Christ"] (1 Cor. 1:7). Others identify the conquering second coming: "God is just: He will pay back trouble to those who trouble you. . . . This will happen when the Lord Jesus is revealed [Gk. *apokalypsis*] [or "in the revelation of the Lord Jesus] from heaven in blazing fire with his powerful angels" (2 Thess. 1:6-7). The word *apokalypsis* emphasizes the revealing of the Christ who is now hidden.

In addition to using the above three terms, on four occasions the New Testament designates Christ's return by the verb *phaneroo* (fan-er-OH-oh) which is translated as show or reveal oneself, be revealed, appear to someone. "When he appears, we shall be like him" (1 John 3:2; cf. Col. 3:4; 1 Pet. 5:4; 1 John 2:28). The common verb "to come" (Gk. *erchomai* [ER-khom-my] is also used. It translates as to come, come back, return, appear). "So you also must be ready, because the Son of Man will come [Gk. *erchomai*] at an hour when you do not expect him" (Matt. 24:44). An even more common usage is the participial form in a structure that parallels English usage. "At that time men will see the Son of Man coming [Gk. *erchomenos*] in clouds with great power and glory" (Mark 13:26). *Erchomenos* (erch-O-men-os) simply means coming. In a single instance the common verb ***horao*** (used in the passive voice) is applied to Christ's return. "Christ . . . will appear [*horao*] a second time, not to bear sin, but to bring salvation" (Heb. 9:28). *Horao* (hor-AH-oh) denotes see, notice, (in passive) to be seen, to become visible, to appear.

The stage of Christ's return depicted in Titus 2:13 is debated, "We wait for the blessed hope—the glorious appearing [Gk. ***epiphaneia***] of our great God and Savior, Jesus Christ." The import and application of this verse are more evident in a strictly literal translation, "Looking for the blessed hope and the appearing of the glory of the great God and our Savior, Christ Jesus" (NASB, margin). This rendering, and the context that places the verse in the "present age" (v. 12), appear to identify Titus 2:13 as a statement about the rapture.

The purpose of the rapture

Jesus Christ will use the rapture to bring His people to Himself. Paul wrote of "the coming of our Lord Jesus Christ and our being gathered to him" (2 Thess. 2:1). As previously cited, Jesus promised the rapture in His last message to His disciples: "If I go and prepare a place for you, I will come back and take you to be with me that you also may be where I am" (John 14:2-3). The rapture message is a great comfort and encouragement: "And so we will be with the Lord forever. Therefore encourage each other with these words" (1 Thess. 4:17-18). God has scheduled the rapture to precede the tribulation when He wages war against rebel humankind. By means of the rapture, God delivers His people from the arena of His outpoured tribulation judgments upon earth's inhabitants. The rapture is His way of calling home His ambassadors before war begins.

The rapture opens the door to other events in God's program. The believer's status in the life to come and his or her relationship to Christ must be determined. Thus, God has scheduled the bema judgment: "We must all appear before the judgment seat [Gk. *bema*] of Christ, that each one may receive what is due him for the things done while in the body, whether good or bad" (2 Cor. 5:10). A *bema* (BAY-ma) is a rostrum, a tribunal, or judgment-seat. Also scheduled are celebrations and festivities involved in the long-awaited union of Christ and His church.

Oriental weddings involved betrothal, presentation, and the celebration with a marriage supper. Christ relates to His church under these images. Paul wrote, "I promised you to one husband, to Christ, so that I might present you as a pure virgin to him" (2 Cor. 11:2); and "Christ loved the church and gave himself up for her to make her holy . . . and to present her to himself as a radiant church, without stain or wrinkle or any other blemish" (Eph. 5:25-27). John describes the end time fulfilment, "The wedding of the Lamb has come, and his bride has made herself ready. . . . Blessed are those who are invited to the wedding supper of the Lamb!" (Rev. 19:7, 9). An appropriate gap between the rapture and the marshaling of participants for the second coming allows for these important events.

In the earlier decades of the twentieth century, the rapture was popularly presented under the figure, "Behold, the bridegroom cometh!" Preferred exegesis in most circles no longer applies the parable of the ten virgins (Matt. 25:1-13) to the rapture, but so-called "nuptial theology" is otherwise well developed in the New Testament.

The subjects of the rapture

All who constitute the true church of Christ, whether living or dead, will be included in the rapture. "We will not all sleep, but we will all be changed" (1 Cor. 15:51); "We believe that God will bring with Jesus those who have fallen asleep in him" (1 Thess. 4:14). The one qualification is faith in Jesus Christ. Those who faithfully partake of the Lord's Supper confirm His coming for them. "Whenever you eat this bread and drink this cup, you proclaim the Lord's death until he comes" (1 Cor. 11:26). Believers who have availed themselves of Christ's redemption can now joyfully anticipate His coming. Paul wrote, "We will glory in the presence of our Lord Jesus when he comes" (1 Thess. 2:19).

Though most evangelicals reject the partial rapture theory[3] that teaches that only those of superior spirituality will be raptured, Scripture clearly relates the rapture to those with prepared hearts and lives. The expectation of His coming should motivate to Christian piety. "To those who eagerly wait [Gk. *apodechomai*] for Him He will appear a second time, apart from sin, for salvation" (Heb. 9:28 NKJV). The verb *apodechomai* (a-po-DECK -oh-my) is translated eagerly wait for, welcome, receive favorably.

An evidence of eagerly awaiting Christ's appearance is **regular church attendance.** "Let us not give up meeting together . . . but let us encourage one another—and all the more as you see the Day approaching" (Heb. 10:25). The response to distractions should be **patient perseverance.** "Be patient and stand firm, because the Lord's coming is near" (James 5:8). An ongoing relationship of **abiding in Christ** is the ideal preparation. "Continue [or abide] in him, so that when he appears we may be

---

3 For a discussion of the partial rapture theory see page 79.

confident and unashamed before him at his coming" (1 John 2:28). Candidates for the rapture direct their vision and perspective toward Jesus Christ, they are more aware of heavenly treasures than earthly, and their lifestyle and values give first place to Christ's imminent return. These challenging standards are not really different from those expected of every believer.

The Christian hope will be gloriously fulfilled the moment that the believer sees Jesus and is forever united with Him.

> Now we are children of God, and what we will be has not yet been made known. But we know that when he appears, we shall be like him, for we shall see him as he is. Everyone who has this hope in him purifies himself, just as he is pure (1 John 3:2-3); Jesus said: "I shall lose none of all that he has given me, but raise them up at the last day. For my Father's will is that everyone who looks to the Son and believes in him shall have eternal life, and I will raise him up at the last day" (John 6:39-40).

The rapture is the first event that the living believer will experience that involves life in a realm beyond the earth. The believer qualifies only because of the merits of Jesus Christ.

The imminency of The rapture

Belief in the imminency of the rapture is considered the central feature of pretribulationism. To say that the rapture is imminent is to say that Scripture predicts no event that must precede it. Thus, the futurist holds that no specific scriptural signs or predicted milestones alert to the nearness of the rapture. Since Jesus could come at any moment, believers are always to be ready for His coming, and they are to watch expectantly. Biblical inferences and statements that indicate the rapture's imminency include the following:

> In the final chapter of Revelation, Jesus three times declared: "I am coming soon!" (Rev. 22:7, 12, 20). John responded, "Amen. Come, Lord Jesus" (v. 20).
>
> New Testament Christians were taught the Aramaic greeting, *Maranatha*: "Come, O Lord" (cf. 1 Cor. 16:22, KJV).
>
> "The Lord is near" (Phil. 4:5).
>
> Jesus concluded the parable of the master returning from the wedding banquet with the admonition, "You also must be ready, because the Son of Man will come at an hour when you do not expect him" (Luke 12:40).
>
> "Therefore you do not lack any spiritual gift as you eagerly wait for our Lord Jesus Christ to be revealed" (1 Cor. 1:7).
>
> "The Lord's coming is near" (James 5:8).
>
> "You need to persevere so that when you have done the will of God, you will receive what he has promised. For in just a very little while, 'He who is coming will come and will not delay'" (Heb. 10:36-37).
>
> "You turned to God from idols to serve the living and true God, and to wait for his Son from heaven" (1 Thess. 1:9-10).

Christians in every era who are eagerly anticipating Christ's return are safeguarded from accommodating themselves to the values, priorities and spirit of the world. Belief in the imminency of Christ's return safeguards the believer's spiritual health.

To deny that there are signs definitively identifying the time of the rapture is not to deny the possibility of clues. Scripture's descriptions of conditions marking the last days of the church are obviously also descriptions of conditions at the time of the rapture. The emergence of trends and events (e.g., technologies, political developments, human lifestyles) that set the stage for Antichrist, Armageddon and the second coming underscore the rapture's imminency. David Allen Lewis comments,

> There are no primary signs of the Rapture. . . . However, every sign of the Second Coming is a sign of the Rapture. For if the Second Coming is close at hand, then the Rapture is even closer.[4]

Scripture passages that scholars commonly consider to describe conditions on earth today and that declare that they are speaking of the last days include the following:

> There will be terrible times in the last days. People will be lovers of themselves, lovers of money, boastful, proud, abusive, disobedient to their parents, ungrateful, unholy, without love, unforgiving, slanderous, without self-control, brutal, not lovers of the good, treacherous, rash, conceited, lovers of pleasure rather than lovers of God—having a form of godliness but denying its power (2 Tim. 3:1-5).

In today's world one can easily find multiple illustrations of each of these eighteen characteristics marking the end of the present church age.

> Listen, you rich people, weep and wail because of the misery that is coming upon you. . . . Your gold and silver are corroded. Their corrosion will testify against you and eat your flesh like fire. You have hoarded wealth in the last days. Look! The wages you failed to pay the workmen . . . are crying out against you (James 5:1, 3-4).

Collapsing financial investments and the exploitation of workers are signs of the last days. Even though the general trend of investments may be upward, one can hear numerous stories of disastrous collapses of investment funds.

> In the last days scoffers will come, scoffing. . . . They will say, "Where is this coming he promised? Ever since our fathers died, everything goes on as it has since the beginning of creation" (2 Pet. 3:3-4).

The rejection and ridicule of the doctrine of the return of Christ proves that it will occur soon.

> The Spirit clearly says that in later times some will abandon the faith and follow deceiving spirits and things taught by demons. . . . They forbid people to marry and order them to abstain from certain foods, which God created to be received with

---

4 David Allen Lewis, *Signs of His Coming*. Green Forest: New Leaf Press, 1997, pp. 30-31.

thanksgiving by those who believe and who know the truth"
(1 Tim. 4:1, 3).

Most scholars understand the expression "later [or latter] times"
as approximately equivalent to "last days." Glaring perversions
of the Christian gospel, including the pursuit of the occult, are all
too common.

Another approach in establishing both the imminency and
the immediacy of the rapture is to review current events. Since
the Bible depicts the tribulation and second coming to require
certain political, economic, social, and religious conditions, if
these are evident, the rapture must be near. Today's Christians
ought to learn from Jesus' criticism of the Pharisees and Sadducees: "You know how to interpret the appearance of the sky, but
you cannot interpret the signs of the times" (Matt. 16:3).

Developments of special interest to prophetic scholars include the following:

**the Ecumenical Movement (as the foundation of a world reli-
gious system) (1910, 1948),**

the State of Israel (1948),

the European Union (1993 [its predecessors began in 1957]),

Israel's conquest of Jerusalem (1967),

the rise of the Arab League (1964),

the emergence of Middle East oil wealth (late 20th century),

a world-shaping spirit of nationalism,

the human rights movements,

globalization

A particular current development may not prove the immediacy
of the rapture, but certain events may make more plausible the
predicted onset of the tribulation that follows the rapture.

The time of the rapture

To say that the rapture is imminent is neither to date it nor
to agree to the possibility of legitimately doing so. Jesus' words
about the second coming apply also to the rapture. "No one
knows about that day or hour, not even the angels in heaven, nor
the Son, but only the Father. . . . Therefore keep watch, because
you do not know on what day your Lord will come. . . . So you also
must be ready, because the Son of Man will come at an hour
when you do not expect him" (Matt. 24:36, 42, 44).

To the disciples' question concerning the time of the establishment of the kingdom (i.e., the millennium), Jesus answered,
"It is not for you to know the times or dates the Father has set by
his own authority" (Acts 1:7). A Bible believer who knew the date
of the launching of the millennium would know that the rapture
would be not more than seven years previous to that date. God

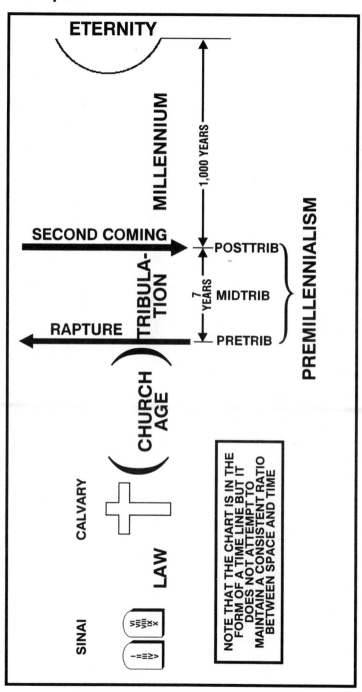

Fig. 4: The sequence of scriptural events and various theories of the rapture's timing.

chooses to withhold from humans the information that would allow date setting. Anyone who sets dates for the rapture is in contradiction of the explicit message of Scripture.

The Pretribulation Rapture

Most futurists believe that pretribulationism, on the basis of consistent literal interpretation, best integrates and harmonizes prophetic Scripture. It satisfactorily recognizes basic distinctions such as those between Israel and the church, and it coordinates all relevant Old and New Testament Scriptures and leaves none without application and meaning.

1. Notable background facts

Though "pretribulation rapture" is not a biblical expression, it correctly denotes what the Bible teaches.

1) **Five New Testament verses speak of a future tribulation (or distress).** The first four verses are from Jesus' Olivet Discourse. "Then there will be great distress [Gk. *thlipsis megale*[5]]" (Matt. 24:21); "Immediately after the distress [Gk. *thlipsis*] of those days" (Matt. 24:29); "Those will be days of distress [Gk. *thlipsis*]" (Mark 13:19); "In those days, following that distress [Gk. *thlipsis*]" (Mark 13:24). The fifth verse identifies the martyred tribulation saints who are in heaven prior to the end of the tribulation. "These are they who have come out of the great tribulation [Gk. *thlipsis megale*]" (Rev. 7:14).

2) **The tribulation is Daniel's seventieth 'seven' (or 'week').** Jesus clearly made this connection. "When you see the abomination of desolation which was spoken of through Daniel the prophet . . . then there will be great tribulation" (Matt. 24:15, 21 NASB). Daniel had written, "[The ruler who will come] will confirm a covenant with many for one 'seven.' In the middle of the 'seven' he will put an end to sacrifice and offering. And . . . he will set up an abomination that causes desolation" (Dan. 9:27). The seventieth week fulfils God's prophecy through Moses: "When you [i.e., Israel] are in distress [tribulation KJV] and all these things have happened to you, then in later days you will return to the Lord your God and obey him" (Deut. 4:30).

3) **The tribulation is the time of God's outpoured wrath.** As God acts to fulfil His six goals in Daniel 9:24, He has reserved the seven years of Daniel's seventieth week for a revised strategy. What the gospel of grace has not done in nearly

---

5 *thlipsis* (THLIP-sis): affliction, anguish, distress, pressure, oppression, tribulation. Among common versions only the NIV renders it "distress," the others retain "tribulation"; *megale* (meg-AL-ay): big, large, mighty, exceedingly great.

2,000 years, He will undertake to achieve by the outpouring of wrath and judgment. At that time, He will repeat the strategy that He used against Babylon: "The Lord has opened his arsenal and brought out the weapons of his wrath, for the Sovereign Lord Almighty has work to do" (Jer. 50:25). The seven-year seventieth week is a discrete time-entity involving God's commitment to act out of wrath, but at the outset His wrath is chiefly manifested by His choice to abandon humans to their destructive pathway. David wrote, "God is a righteous judge, a God who expresses his wrath every day" (Psa. 7:11). In the tribulation, rebellious humans become aware of divine wrath only through the calamities resulting from the sixth seal. "Hide us from the face of him who sits on the throne and from the wrath of the Lamb!" (Rev. 6:16).

4) **Events change dramatically at midweek.** The seven-year week of years begins with Antichrist's confirmed covenant providing Israel with a sense of security. Thus, life goes on more or less normally for the first half of the week. Disaster breaks loose, however, at midweek. Jesus described a sudden and radical change: "Let no one on the roof of his house go down to take anything out of his house. Let no one in the field go back to get his cloak" (Matt. 24:17-18). He then spoke of outpoured judgmental catastrophe so severe that, "If those days had not been cut short, no one would survive" (Matt. 24:22). The seven-year period begins with hopeful optimism but ends in chaos.

2. Evidences for a pre-seventieth week rapture

The seventieth week, as previously noted, is an individually distinct block of time in which God is committed to resorting to the strategy of wrath. At the outset of the seven years, God's wrath is passive. While naive and rebellious humans align with Antichrist, God manifests "great patience" but sees them as "the objects of his wrath prepared for destruction" (Rom. 9:22). Since the entire seven years is characterized by divine wrath, a promise of escape from wrath is a pretribulation promise.

1) **This timing fits the prophetic calendar.** Out of various contexts, Scripture speaks of future events: the building of Christ's church (Matt. 16:18), the rapture, an end-time period of false peace based on a covenant, and God's outpoured wrath. Repeatedly, the Bible mentions a time span of three and one-half years. Daniel reveals the relationship and sequence of these time periods. After an indefinite interruption following Calvary (cf. Dan. 9:26), the final seven year period will occur. Jesus, as previously noted, in applying Daniel's prophecy to the end time, spoke of two dramatically different three and one-half year periods. Neither He nor Daniel, however, indicated that the church would have any part in that

final week. The promise was, "Seventy 'sevens' are decreed for *your* people [i.e., Israel]" (Dan. 9:24). Daniel's calendar provides for the growth and complete removal of the church prior to the events of his final seven years.

2) **Paul taught a rapture prior to the revelation of Antichrist.** His letters to the Thessalonians responded to the teaching that the rapture had already occurred. Paul wrote,

> **"Concerning the coming of our Lord Jesus Christ and our being gathered to him, we ask you, brothers, not to become easily unsettled or alarmed by some prophecy . . . saying that the day of the Lord has already come. . . . That day will not come until the rebellion [Gk. *apostasia*] occurs and the man of lawlessness is revealed" (2 Thess. 2:1-3).**

Apostasia denotes defection from truth, falling away, forsaking, rebelling, abandonment.[6] Note the sequence of events in 2 Thessalonians 2:1-8— 1) the rapture: "our being gathered to him" (v. 1); 2) the day of the Lord—tribulation: "the rebellion occurs and the man of lawlessness is revealed" (v. 3); 3) the second coming: "the Lord Jesus will overthrow . . . and destroy by the splendor of his coming" (v. 8). Paul thus explained that they could not have missed the rapture and be in the tribulation because essential events (the apostate religion and the revelation of Antichrist) would confirm that the tribulation was underway. Though the Antichrist will first be revealed by his negotiation of a covenant with Israel, he will be more dramatically manifested three and one-half years later when he proclaims himself deity.

3) **Someone now restraining immorality must be removed** from the earth before Antichrist is revealed. In order to assure the Thessalonians that the tribulation had not begun, Paul provided a further fact about God's plan: "the secret power of lawlessness is already at work; but the one who now holds it back will continue to do so till he is taken out of the way. And then the lawless one will be revealed" (2 Thess. 2:7-8). First someone will be taken away from an involvement on earth—one who now restrains the secret power of lawlessness. A departure from an active role on earth of a force that is so influential on behalf of morality must in some way identify with the rapture of the church. This passage clearly dates the rapture prior to the tribulation.

4) **The rapture's role in physical redemption** implies a pre-seventieth week occurrence. Throughout the Christian

---

6 Kenneth S. Wuest's New Testament translation reads: "the aforementioned departure (of the church to heaven) comes first . . ." Unfortunately, although the roots would allow *apostasia* to be so rendered, current popular lexicons and versions do not support it. Writers such as E. Schuyler English and Gordon Lewis, however, endorsed Wuest's view.

era the rapture has been an eagerly awaited joyous event. "We . . . groan inwardly as we wait eagerly for . . . the redemption of our bodies" (Rom. 8:23). The believer anticipates translation as the Christian era ends, and the Israelites again take their place as God's chosen people on earth.

5) **The angelic promise implies a pre-seventieth week rapture.** At the ascension site, the men in white promised, "This same Jesus, who has been taken from you into heaven, will come back in the same way you have seen him go into heaven" (Acts 1:11). He left with only the awareness of His disciples, and in peace and blessing. The second coming with its judgments and conquest would not be a return under similar conditions. The rapture of believers must be prior to the resumption of the program of the seventy weeks.

6) **The rapture marks the end of the church age.** In the great commission Jesus established His relationship to the soul-winning disciples according to a time limit. "Surely I am with you always, to the very end of the age" (Matt. 28:20). Paul saw the rapture as the termination of this present age. "The grace of God . . . teaches us . . . to live self-controlled, upright and godly lives in this present age, while we wait for the blessed hope—the glorious appearing of our great God and Savior, Jesus Christ" (Titus 2:11-13). The present church age ends with the rapture when Christ's bride is complete, and God moves to fulfil His covenant promises to Israel.

A pre-seventieth week rapture separates Israel and the church. The seventy weeks pertain to Israel. "Seventy 'sevens' are decreed for your people and your holy city" (Dan. 9:24). Israel's day ended for the time being with the temple curtain's tearing as Jesus died. Israel will again assume center stage when the church is translated and Antichrist extends to the nation his gratuitous but deceitful covenant.

7) **For the rapture to be imminent it must be the next prophesied event.** From Bible times believers have been charged to "eagerly wait for . . . [the] Lord Jesus Christ to be revealed" (1 Cor. 1:7; cf. Phil. 3:20). The New Testament uses the theme of the imminency of the pretribulation rapture as an incentive to practice godliness. Though signs mark the course of the tribulation, and specific milestones launch later events, there are no conditions to be fulfilled nor specific indicators that mark the countdown to the rapture. Though the rapture is signless, it will be the spectacular dramatic sign that announces the beginning of the tribulation.

8) **God's people are not destined to suffer His wrath.** As Jesus opens the seals at the beginning of the tribulation, earth's inhabitants begin to suffer warfare, famine and

plague. Though He is God's Lamb, He thus launches the "great day of [his wrath]" (Rev. 6:17). Yet Paul speaks of the Thessalonian converts who now "wait for his Son from heaven . . . —Jesus, who rescues us from the coming wrath" (1 Thess. 1:10). The seven outpoured bowls which follow are "filled with the wrath of God" (Rev. 15:7). But Paul wrote, "God did not appoint us to suffer wrath but to receive salvation through our Lord Jesus Christ" (1 Thess. 5:9); "How much more shall we be saved from God's wrath through [Christ]" (Rom. 5:9); "God's wrath comes on those who are disobedient" (Eph. 5:6). These Scriptures assure believers that they are exempt from God's wrath, and the obvious way to achieve this exemption is by a pretribulation rapture.

Because Scripture so unequivocally declares that believers will be spared God's wrath, scholars who disagree on other matters are likely agree on this truth. Thus, posttribulationists such as J. Barton Payne, George E. Ladd, or Robert H. Gundry suggest that the Lord will in some way spare His true church from His outpoured wrath.

9) **The response of society to tribulation's wrath excludes believers.** At the time that the seven seals have been broken and the sixth of the seven trumpets sounded, Scripture notes that all of tribulation's citizens are either: (A) dead, (B) unrepentant. "The rest of mankind that were not killed by these plagues still did not repent of the work of their hands; they did not stop worshiping demons and idols" (Rev. 9:20). Christians do not belong in such a society.

10) **The rapture's role in encouragement implies pretribulationism.** Scripture presents the rapture message as one of encouragement. Paul concluded his description of the Rapture, "Therefore encourage each other with these words" (1 Thess. 4:18). An end time program that begins with the deliverance of God's people can rightly be the basis of encouragement; if it were to begin with tribulation, it would be a depressing threat. Elsewhere, as already noted, Paul called the rapture "the blessed hope" (Tit. 2:13).

11) **The fulfilment of God's promise to Philadelphia extends to the entire church.** "I will keep you from (Gk. *ek*: from, out of, of, outside of) the hour [Gk. *hora*] of trial that is going to come upon the whole world to test those who live [Gk. *katoikeo*] on the earth" (Rev. 3:10). Though this little Asian church no longer exists, the trial upon the whole world is yet future. One is kept from a time of trial by a deliverance that assures one's absence. Thus, in the next verse Jesus promises, "I am coming soon" (Rev. 3:11), and these words imply that He is coming as deliverer. The designation "hour" (*hora* [HO-rah]) implies the time of day, a space of time, a

structured period of time, a season, the time when something takes place. The word *katoikeo* (kat-oy-KEH-o), describing the status of those who are to suffer the hour of trial, denotes settled dwellers or permanent residents, and it thus indicates that the victims of the tribulation are those firmly identified with all that is human and earthly.

12) The tribulation is always linked to groups apart from the church. In the four references to the tribulation (or "distress") in the Olivet Discourse, Jesus was speaking to the disciples as representatives of the Jewish nation (cf. Matt. 24:21, 29; Mark 13:19, 24; Luke 21:23). The Jewish nation is addressed in references to the end time tribulation in Deuteronomy 4:30; Daniel 12:1; and Jeremiah 14:8. In Jeremiah 30:7 the tribulation is called "a time of trouble for Jacob," and it thus singles out the Jewish nation. The "hour of trial" of Revelation 3:10 is "to test those who live on the earth."

13) In the major account of earth's tribulation, the church is not mentioned. Though "church" or "churches" occurs nineteen times in the first three chapters of Revelation (NIV), the church is not identified again until chapter 19, and not named until 22:16. Chapters 6 through 19 describe God's twenty-one tribulation judgmental acts upon rebellious humans. In this period, His servants on earth are not the church, but rather the 144,000 Jews who are marked with a protecting seal (cf. Rev. 7:1-8).

During this time the twenty-four elders, who are in the heavenlies, represent the church (plus also Israel's justified saints) since 1) they are clothed in white (therefore manifesting Christ's righteousness) and 2) they wear crowns (therefore judged and rewarded) (cf. Rev. 4:4; 5:8; 7:11; 11:16; 14:3; 19:4). The twenty-four elders are first introduced as heaven's citizens in Revelation chapter 4, just prior to the onset of the tribulation. Most futurists see twenty-four as the sum of twelve tribes of Israel and twelve apostles, and they also link the number to the twenty-four divisions of the priesthood of Israel (cf. 1 Chron. 24:1-19).

14) The rapture will occur prior to any changes in the world order. The discussion of the rapture's imminency noted that one of the arguments of scoffers in the last days will be that nothing has changed. "Ever since our father's died, everything goes on as it has since the beginning of creation" (2 Pet. 3:4). A world class peacemaker, at last implementing peace, will mark a momentous change. Those who scoff at the message of Christ's return will be silenced by Antichrist's amazing covenant that apparently, but deceptively, dramatically changes life involvements and expectations for humans on earth.

As a later discussion will point out (see p. 186), the dual outcome of the rapture is the translation of living believers and the
resurrection of those who have died. Scholars typically see four
phases of the first resurrection, and the rapture is the second of
these phases. First resurrection events began with "Christ as
firstfruits," and the fourth phase will not occur until weeks after
the millennium begins. Thus first resurrection events occur over
an extensive time span—so far nearly 2,000 years is the indicated
minimum. The fact that the rapture is also a resurrection event
contributes no definitive information to determine the time that
the rapture will occur. It is on the grounds of evidences such as
the thirteen cited above that pretribulationists see the rap-
ture/resurrection occurring prior to the tribulation.

The Midtribulation Rapture Theory

Midtribulationism[7] holds that the rapture will occur three
and one-half years after the tribulation begins, and three and
one-half years before Christ's Armageddon victory. In this view,
by remaining on earth during the first half of the tribulation, the
church will undergo persecution that will enable it to fulfill its
destiny. Paul wrote, "In fact, everyone who wants to live a godly
life in Christ Jesus will be persecuted" (2 Tim. 3:12). Other arguments supporting this position include the following:

1. The rapture occurs at the "last trumpet" (or trump) (1 Cor.
   15:51-52), and the earliest that the seventh and last trumpet
   could sound is at midtribulation (cf. Rev. 11:15). In this view
   the issue is fixing the time of the seventh trumpet.

The pretribulationist agrees that the seventh trumpet is
likely no earlier than midtribulation, but he or she denies that
the last trumpet of Corinthians is the seventh trumpet. Paul's
last trumpet and John's seventh trumpet are different events.
The last trumpet of the gospel age is quite a different event from
the last trumpet sounded during the tribulation. In Corinthians,
the trumpet sounds first and the resurrection and translation
follow; in Revelation, resurrection and translation occur first
and then the trumpet sounds. In 1 Thessalonians 4:15-17, the
trumpet that is mentioned is identified as "the trumpet call of
God" (v. 16). In contrast, "The seventh angel sounded his trumpet" (Rev. 11:15). The seventh trumpet will proclaim the inauguration of the millennium, not the rapture. Paul's last trumpet
proclaims the end of the gospel age as Christians know it. Since,

---

7 The term owes its origin to its opponents. Two of its earlier spokesmen, Norman B. Harrison (*The End: Re-Thinking the Revelation* [1941]), and
   James O. Buswell (*A Systematic Theology of the Christian Religion* [1963])
   considered themselves pretribulationist, and posttribulationist, respectively. Gleason Archer also taught midtribulationism, and he considered
   himself a pretribulationist.

as previously noted, Revelation was written three decades after Corinthians, Paul could not have been referring to John's vision involving the sounding of the seven trumpets.

2. Since the Bible clearly identifies the "great tribulation" (Rev. 7:14) to be only three and one-half years in duration (cf. Rev. 12:6; 13:5), a rapture three and one-half years before Christ's victory would effectively deliver believers from the wrath of God. One should distinguish between the seven year tribulation and the three and one-half year wrath of God.

The evidences that indicate a pre-seventieth week rapture answer this argument. As noted there, the chronology of the end time is built around Daniel's seventieth week, and only a seven-year interval between the rapture and the second coming adequately accommodates all events.

3. Some midtribulationists note that the judgmental seals (Rev. 6:1- 8:5) are comparatively mild, and believers need to be removed only when the seal events are completed at midtribulation. If the seals are not in the picture, fewer judgments will need to be scheduled in the second three and one-half years.

The pretribulationist agrees that though the seals begin mildly, by the sixth seal a total cosmic upheaval has taken place. Further, he or she again raises the point of the total seven-year chronology. The judgmental events of the seals, trumpets, and bowls are God's arsenal of strategies and not timed campaigns. They are not the basis for calculating the time of the rapture.

4. The resurrection of the two witnesses (Rev. 11:3-13) embodies, or at least symbolizes, the rapture of the church. The symbol of olive trees is applied to the witnesses (Rev. 11:4) and also to the church (Rom. 11:17). Scripture reports concerning the witnesses, "They heard a loud voice from heaven saying to them, 'Come up here.' And they went up to heaven in a cloud" (Rev. 11:12). This upward call is commonly taken to occur at midtribulation.

The pretribulationist rejects the identification of the two witnesses with the church. The witnesses had power to destroy enemies, shut heaven, and turn water to blood, and such a ministry is not that of Christian servants. Paul's illustration of the ingrafted olive branch was not meant to identify the church, but to reveal its relationship and status. The association of the two witnesses with olive trees spoke of their unlimited anointing (cf. Zech. 4:1-14). The olive tree was simply a convenient illustration. If Revelation does provide a symbol of the rapture, it is the invitation to John at the beginning of the tribulation, "Come up here" (Rev. 4:1). Also, one should note that though the midtribulation translation of the two witnesses appears valid to many, the timing of their translation is debated, and it can scarcely serve as a solution of another problem.

5. The phrase, which many consider is speaking of the removal of the Holy Spirit since He indwells the church, "till he is taken out of the way" (2 Thess. 2:7) is literally "until he be taken out of the midst [Gk. *mesos*]." These words are clearly a reference to Daniel's phrase "in the middle [or midst] of the sevens [or week]" (Dan. 9:27). Thus, the removal of the church and the Holy Spirit is dated at midtribulation.

The pretribulationist answers that the connection of the language between Thessalonians and Daniel is coincidental. The Greek *mesos* (MEH-sos) indeed means "midst" or "middle," but it also means "in communion with" or "in close personal relationship with." The use of the word relating to the Holy Spirit does not signify a time, but it is His way of relating to the church.

6. The elect of Matthew 24:22 and Mark 13:20 are not Jews but Christians.

Appropriate sections in this book discuss this very fundamental difference in interpretation.

The Prewrath Rapture

This view combines elements of both the midtrib and the posttrib positions. Its spokesmen include Marvin Rosenthal in *The Pre-Wrath Rapture of the Church* (1990), and Robert Van Kampen in *The Sign* (1992). Van Kampen wrote, "The essence of the prewrath position is that Christ will rapture His church immediately after He cuts short the great tribulation by Antichrist and immediately before He unleashes His day-of-the-Lord judgment on the ungodly world."[8] As presented by these collaborating colleagues, the prewrath rapture view differs not merely on the timing of the rapture but on numerous details of virtually the entire end time scenario.

Some of the more notable divergencies of interpretation from conventional futurist eschatology include the following: 1) the timing of the rapture is determined by the onset of the Day of the Lord, which lasts only a few months and is the outpoured wrath period of the tribulation, and this makes it a "three-fourths-trib" rapture, 2) there is no clear distinction between the church and Israel, 3) the rapture is included in the second coming, 4) the rapture will only become imminent when Antichrist launches the great tribulation, and therefore the church should be looking for the rise of the Antichrist, 5) Antichrist's coalition

---

8   Robert Van Kampen, *The Sign*. Wheaton: Crossway Books, 1992, p. 278.

of ten nations is not the Roman Empire revived but the resurgence of previous world empires plus Gog's allies (cf. Ezek. 38), **6)** the seals, trumpets and bowls occur successively in a strict timed sequence, **7)** the seventh trumpet and the seven seals occur in the thirty-day period after the seventieth week has ended, **8)** the Jews become the victims of Antichrist's persecution in the great tribulation because the archangel Michael's protection is withdrawn, **9)** though Antichrist continues to rule after the rapture he is "paralyzed" and unable to continue active persecution, and **10)** Armageddon occurs at the end of the thirty-day period that follows the seventieth week.

The answers to these views are found in the presentation of the orthodox futurist doctrines that are the content of this book.

The Partial Rapture Theory

This view holds that the rapture is a unique reward granted to qualifying members within the church. Typically, the rapture is restricted to those believers who are watching and waiting, or for those of superior spirituality or holiness. Some versions reserve the rapture for the "overcomers" or the 144,000, or the "bondslaves." Some teach that the prepared (as the wise virgins of Matthew 25:1-13) will be admitted to the wedding supper, and therefore caught up in the rapture, while the unprepared will be excluded and presumably left to endure the tribulation on earth. The rapture is thus seen as a reward to a special group, so that it contrasts with salvation which is by grace to all who believe.

Variants of the view see multiple rapture events during the years of the tribulation as specific groups qualify for rapture. Some scholars suggest that the rigors of the tribulation will awaken and purge the lukewarm and bring them to respond to the Lord's upward call. Thus, the great uncountable multitude (Rev. 7:9-17), the male child snatched up to God's throne (Rev. 12:5), and the Lord's coming like a thief to the one "who stays awake and keeps his clothes with him" (Rev. 16:15).

Texts that partial rapture theorists feel support their views include the following:

Be always on the watch, and pray that you may be able to escape all that is about to happen, and that you may be able to stand before the Son of Man (Luke 21:36); Two men will be in the field; one will be taken and the other left (Matt. 24:40); I want to know Christ . . . and so, somehow, to attain to the resurrection from the dead (Phil. 3:10-11); The Lord, the righteous Judge, will award [a crown] to me on that day—and . . . also to all who have longed for his appearing (2 Tim. 4:8); Christ . . . will appear a second time . . . to bring salvation to those who are waiting for him (Heb. 9:29); Since you have kept my command to endure patiently, I will also keep you from the hour of trial that is going to come upon the whole world (Rev. 3:10).

Those committed to the total rapture of the entire church respond that to teach a partial rapture based on believers' qualifications is to impugn the efficacy of Christ's provision of justification and positional sanctification. Although believers may be at various stages of spiritual growth, every genuine believer is justified and sanctified. Scripture declares,

> **Since we have now been justified by his blood, how much more shall we be saved from God's wrath through him (Rom. 5:9); Therefore, since we have been justified through faith, we have peace with God through our Lord Jesus Christ (Rom. 5:1); You were washed, you were sanctified, you were justified in the name of the Lord Jesus Christ and by the Spirit of our God (1 Cor. 6:11); We have been made holy through the sacrifice of the body of Jesus Christ once for all (Heb. 10:10).**

The texts from Luke 21:36 and Matthew 24:40 cited above (in the first quotation section) as supporting the partial rapture view concern the second coming rather than the rapture. The other cited texts relate to the challenge to develop progressive sanctification to the level of positional sanctification. God sees Christians sanctified in Christ, and they count on His provision to qualify them in His sight. Christians are responsible for progressing in their lifestyle, but even at their best they cannot offer their virtues to negotiate God's favors. For all that they are before Him, they depend upon His provision of grace and mercy.

The pretribulationist sees the rapture as a divine response to the believer's status in view of God's intention to launch the tribulation. Scripture teaches the future judgment and reward of Christians, but under the figures of crowns and administrative posts. The rapture transforms believers from the scene of forthcoming divine wrath into the realm of their actual heavenly citizenship. All believers who comprise the church will be raptured, for Christ has only one church and not two or more. That one church is a complete entity and not due to be dismembered. The promise to the Corinthians declared simply, "We will *all* be changed" (1 Cor. 15:51).

The Posttribulation Rapture Theory

Posttribulationism holds that the rapture will not take place until the close of the tribulation which the church will have endured. This position sees the church's triumph through tribulation, and it often dwells on the "cleansing effect of suffering and persecution." The two-phase return of Christ is likely to be denied, so that the rapture and the second coming are one event. Many posttribulationists are also amillennialists so that Christ's one time return is "the end of the world." This view identifies many of the futurist's end time events either as history or as present events to be spiritualized.

Statements supporting postribulationism span the centuries of church history. Most agree that posttribulationism was taught or implied in the writings of the Fathers in the *Epistle of Barnabas* (an anti-Jewish 2nd century anonymous letter), by Justin Martyr (c. 100-165), by Tertullian (c. 155-220), and Lactantius (c. 250-320). Irenaeus (c. 130-c. 200) described events that identify with Scripture's description of the tribulation, and he noted that rulers of that era will "put the church to flight." These tribulation events will end with the glorious coming of the Lord. This aspect of his teaching appears to imply a commitment to a posttribulation rapture.

Later supporters of posttribulationism have included Charles Wesley, Edward Bickersteth, Henry Alford, J.A. Seiss, Edward J. Carnell, George E. Ladd, J. Barton Payne, and Robert H. Gundry.[9]

Not all posttribulationists agree in their doctrinal beliefs and emphases, but among the views that are likely to be found are the following:

1. The rapture is simultaneously a resurrection and the glorious unveiling of Christ. A single event includes resurrection, transformation, translation, and all of the victories at Armageddon. Thus, for instance, the same event is being described in Matthew 24:30 "All nations . . . will see the Son of Man coming on the clouds of the sky, with power and great glory," and 1 Thessalonians 4:16-17 "The Lord himself will come down from heaven . . . and the dead in Christ will rise first. . . . And so we will be with the Lord forever."

2. Israel and the church are two views of the same body and not to be distinguished. The terms "elect" and "saints" in the end time identify the church rather than Jewish believers.

3. If, as is the case for many evangelicals, the posttribulationist believes in a specific tribulation period, and also the imminency of Christ's return (or at least impending), he or she may define imminency broadly enough to allow for a tribulation period between the present day and the return. Posttribulationists are not rigorously bound to a seven-year tribulation, and they may see it as of greater or lesser length.

4. The "last trumpet" of Corinthians and the seventh trumpet of Revelation are merged into one.

---

9 Paul Feinberg's discussion of the views of J. Barton Payne, George E. Ladd, and Robert H. Gundry deals helpfully with some of the technical grammatical aspects of their arguments. See Paul D. Feinberg "The Case for the Pretribulation Rapture Position" in *Three Views on the Rapture*. Stanley N. Gundry, Editor, pp. 50-86. Grand Rapids: Zondervan Publishing House, 1996.

5. The tribulation is primarily the outpouring of the wrath of Satan, and the wrath of God should be either minimized or denied entirely. For God's people to be forced to endure the tribulation, is not inconsistent with His ways, particularly since God will intervene to preserve and mature His people.

6. The Book of Revelation cannot be interpreted in literal futurism. It is not the case that the Gentiles will be evangelized by 144,000 Jewish evangelists during the tribulation, nor that Revelation chapters 4 through 18 portray the church in heaven. Any evangelization during the tribulation will be by the church which is still functioning on earth.

The pretribulationist's overall answer to posttribulationism is that it does not do justice to literal Scripture, and it overlooks vital biblical distinctions (e.g., "Do not cause anyone to stumble, whether Jews, Greeks of the church of God" [1 Cor. 10:32]). The pretribulationist likely holds that posttribulationism takes as figurative or spiritual what is meant to be literal, and the system tends to generalize what is given as a specific.

Some posttribulationist statements about the necessary suffering of Christians are seen by their opponents to be based on out-of-context individual Scriptures rather than the overall teaching of the Bible. Church fathers cited as posttribulationists (e.g., Justin Martyr, Tertullian) appear to have supported their view on this basis. In at least some cases, in responding to posttribulationism, what must first be settled are the rules of biblical scholarship and hermeneutical approach. The divisive issue is more likely to be the method of interpretation rather than the understanding of biblical chapter and verse.

The Second Coming of Christ

S cripture clearly teaches that the return of Jesus Christ to earth is the decisive crucial event which separates this age from the next. It will be an awesome dramatic event with far-reaching effects, not only on earth, but throughout the entire universe. "In those days, following that distress [Gk. *thlipsis*][1], the sun will be darkened, and the moon will not give its light; the stars will fall from the sky, and the heavenly bodies will be shaken. At that time men will see the Son of Man coming in clouds with great power and glory" (Mark 13:24-26).

The Overall Second Coming Concept

The expression "second coming" denotes that at some time, in some way, Jesus Christ who came as Bethlehem's Babe will once again invade human events on earth. Those who speak of the second coming likely have a particular event in mind, though the expression specifies neither the mode, the occasion, nor the precise objective of the return. Christ's second coming is usually seen, however, as the occasion when as judge and conqueror He confronts and overthrows human rebels and inaugurates His promised Kingdom.

The combination of words "second coming" is not strictly Biblical, but there are many references to the "coming of Christ" that concern His coming for the second time. The words "second" and "coming" were first combined by Justin Martyr (A.D. c. 100-165) who wrote of "two comings . . . the second when, according to prophecy, He shall come from heaven with glory." The use of the phrase "second coming" naturally followed. The alternate form "second advent" is a language variant with the identical meaning. An "advent" is an arrival or a coming.

The Old Testament depicts the second coming as a literal event involving the personal and visible earthly presence of Jesus Christ. Scriptures describing the event are as follows:

---

1 The word *thlipsis* (THLIP-sis) was discussed on page 70 and it is mentioned further on page 127.

> I know that my Redeemer lives, and that in the end [latter day, at last] he will stand upon the earth (Job 19:25); Before me was one like a son of man, coming with the clouds of heaven. . . . He was given authority, glory and sovereign power; all peoples, nations and men of every language worshiped him (Dan. 7:13-14); Sud - denly the Lord you are seeking will come to his temple; the mes - senger of the covenant, whom you desire, will come (Mal. 3:1); On that day his feet will stand on the Mount of Olives, east of Jerusa - lem, and the Mount of Olives will be split in two from east to west. . . . Then the LORD my God will come, and all the holy ones with him (Zech. 14:4-5).

The second coming and its conquests end Jesus' heavenly resi-dence. "The Lord says to my Lord: 'Sit at my right hand until I make your enemies a footstool for your feet'" (Psa. 110:1).

The New Testament continues the prophecies of Jesus' sec-ond coming.

> When Christ, who is your life, appears, then you also will appear with him in glory (Col. 3:4); The Lord is coming with thousands upon thousands of his holy ones to judge everyone, and to convict all the ungodly (Jude 14-15); "For as lightning that comes from the east is visible even in the west, so will be the coming of the Son of Man" (Matt. 24:27); "'The sun will be darkened, and the moon will not give its light; the stars will fall from the sky.' . . . At that time men will see the Son of Man coming in clouds with great power and glory. And he will send his angels and gather his elect" (Mark 13:24-27); Look, he is coming with the clouds, and every eye will see him, even those who pierced him; and all the peoples of the earth will mourn because of him (Rev. 1:7).

These Scriptures establish that Jesus will return personally in His second coming. It will be a literal, visible, dramatic event.

Paul wrote to the Thessalonians, "May he strengthen your hearts so that you will be blameless and holy in the presence of our God and Father when our Lord Jesus comes with all his holy ones" (1 Thess. 3:13). Since the second coming will follow the Bema judgment[2] of raptured believers, Paul desired that on this occasion these people should fully qualify in God's sight. Paul thought of the Thessalonians, along with all who would comprise the church, as the company of those who would serve as Jesus' honor guard when He returned to earth in conquering majesty.

The second coming, with its judgments and blessings, relates to those who dwell upon earth. As will be explained, His coming results in the destruction of Antichrist's armies and those who identify with them. Further, His coming is the occasion of the conversion and preservation of the Jewish nation. As an outcome of His presence on earth He launches His millennial kingdom, and assumes the earthly rule of all surviving humans. The end time great white throne judgment, which determines the eternal

---

2 See Chapter Eleven.

destinies of moral intelligences, does not occur until after the millennium.

Scriptural Descriptions of Jesus in His Second Coming

A composite of the various passages provides an impressive glimpse of Jesus' person and His achievements at His second coming. Scripture depicts Him as:

The rider on a white horse (Rev. 19:11)

Coming in a cloud with power and great glory (Luke 21:27)

The Ancient of Days (Dan. 7:9)

Faithful and true (Rev. 19:11)

Justly judges and makes war (Rev. 19:11)

Eyes like blazing fire (Rev. 19:12)

The hair of His head white like wool (Dan. 7:9)

His clothing as white as snow (Dan. 7:9)

A notable gold crown on His head (Rev. 14:14)

Many other crowns on His head (Rev. 19:12)

A sharp sickle in His hand (Rev. 14:14)

Only He knows His true name (Rev. 19:12)

His robe has been dipped in blood (Rev. 19:13)

He is known as the Word of God (Rev. 19:13)

His throne is flaming with fire (Dan. 7:9)

He is accompanied by all his holy ones (1 Thess. 3:13)

He is followed by heaven's armies (Rev. 19:14)

His feet stand on the Mount of Olives (Zech. 14:4)

A sharp sword comes out of His mouth (Rev. 19:15)

He comes to rule the nations with an iron scepter (Rev. 19:15)

He comes to administer the wrath of God (Rev. 19:15)

He displays the name: KING OF KINGS AND LORD OF LORDS (Rev. 19:16)

He comes as the great prince and protector of Israel (Dan. 12:1)

He captures and imprisons the beast and false prophet (Rev. 19:20)

With His sword He destroys Antichrist's armies (Rev. 19:21)

The Purposes of The Second Coming

Scripture describes the important outcomes that will be achieved by Jesus' second coming. At this time He comes to:

Rescue and restore Israel

By means of the second coming Jesus will deliver the Jews from Gentile domination. "Jerusalem will be trampled on by the Gentiles until the times of the Gentiles are fulfilled. . . . At that time they will see the Son of Man coming in a cloud with power and great glory" (Luke 21:24, 27). Jesus' immediate purpose will be to rescue the penitent Jews from destruction at the hand of Antichrist and his armies.

> On that day I will set out to destroy all the nations that attack Je -
> rusalem. And I will pour out on the house of David and the inhab -
> itants of Jerusalem a spirit of grace and supplication. They will
> look on me, the one they have pierced, and they will mourn for
> him as one mourns for an only child (Zech. 12:9-10); I will gather
> all the nations to Jerusalem to fight against it. . . . Then the Lord
> will go out and fight against those nations, as he fights in the day
> of battle (Zech. 14:2-3).

The outcome of Jesus' victory and His assumption of the rule of the earth will be the fulfillment of the many promises to the nation of Israel.

> " 'I will bring back my exiled people Israel; they will rebuild the
> ruined cities and live in them. . . . I will plant Israel in their own
> land I have given them,' says the L ORD your God" (Amos 9:14-15).

Judge the nations

Though there will still be a future eternal judgment, in the second coming Jesus will judge earthlings. "This will happen when the Lord Jesus is revealed from heaven in blazing fire with his powerful angels. He will punish those who do not know God and do not obey the gospel of our Lord Jesus." (2 Thess. 1:7-9; cf. also Jude 14-15 quoted above). In his sermon on the Areopagus, Paul declared, "[God] has set a day when he will judge the world with justice by the man he has appointed." (Acts 17:31); to Timothy Paul wrote, "Christ Jesus . . . will judge the living and the dead, and in view of his appearing and kingdom" (2 Tim. 4:1). Jesus described these events,

> "When the Son of Man comes in his glory, and all the angels with
> him, he will sit on his throne in heavenly glory. All the nations
> will be gathered before him, and he will separate the people . . . as
> a shepherd separates the sheep from the goats" (Matt. 25:31-32).

Resurrect the righteous dead

Christian believers will have been resurrected at the rapture and thus this resurrection will provide for other groups. The martyrs of the tribulation will be resurrected at this time. "Those who had been beheaded because of their testimony for Jesus and . . . had not worshiped the beast or his image and had not received his mark . . . came to life and reigned with Christ a thousand years" (Rev. 20:4-5). It is widely held that this will be the occasion of the resurrection of Old Testament saints. "At that time your [i.e., Daniel's] people . . . will be delivered. Multitudes who sleep in the dust of the earth will awake; some to everlasting life, others to shame and everlasting contempt" (Dan. 12:1-2).

Conquer Satan

Following His triumphal return to earth as King of kings and Lord of lords (Rev. 19:16), Jesus will dispatch an angel to deal with Satan. "I saw an angel coming down out of heaven . . . holding in his hand a great chain. He seized . . . Satan, and bound him for a thousand years! He threw him into the Abyss, and locked and sealed it over him, to keep him from deceiving the nations anymore until the thousand years were ended" (Rev. 20:1-3).

Assume kingship of the earth

Christ's descent in the second coming has been described as "the most dramatic and shattering event in the entire history of the universe." Malachi wrote, "Who can endure the day of his coming? Who can stand when he appears?" (Mal. 3:2). John describes this event:

> I saw heaven standing open and there before me was a white horse, whose rider is called Faithful and True. With justice he judges and makes war . . . his name is the Word of God. The armies of heaven were following him. . . . Out of his mouth comes a sharp sword with which to strike down the nations. "He will rule them with an iron scepter." . . . he has this name written: KING OF KINGS AND LORD OF LORDS (Rev. 19:11, 13-16).

The above passage links the second coming with Jesus' becoming the world's absolute ruler. As He assumes His rule of the nations "The Lord will be king over the whole earth. On that day there will be one Lord, and his name the only name" (Zech. 14:9). Isaiah prophesied, "See, darkness covers the earth . . . but the Lord rises upon you and his glory appears over you. Nations will come to your light, and kings to the brightness of your dawn" (Isa. 60:2-3). Zechariah wrote, "Then the survivors from all the nations that have attacked Jerusalem will go up year after year to worship the King, the Lord Almighty, and to celebrate the Feast of Tabernacles" (Zech. 14:16). The millennium is the direct outcome of the second coming.

Backgrounds of the Second Coming Concept

As previously mentioned, the medieval church lost sight of a literal second coming of Christ. The Reformation accorded the doctrine only a limited comeback. Protestantism tended to see the latter day milestones as interchangeable events, including the second coming, the end of the world, and the end time general judgment. Declarations included the *Belgic Confession* (1561), "Our Lord Jesus Christ will come again from heaven, corporal and visible, as he ascended with great glory and majesty," and the Church of England's *Thirty-Nine Articles* (1571), "He ascended into Heaven, and there sitteth until he return [sic]."

Until modern times, date-setting predictions of the second coming expected His end time conquering judgment and the end of the world rather than the rapture of Christians. Among some

RAPTURE	SECOND COMING
In the air	**To earth**
"We . . . will . . . meet the Lord in the air" (1Thess. 4:17).	"His feet will stand on the Mount of Olives" (Zech. 14:4).
To believers	**To all humans**
"He will appear a second time . . . to bring salvation to those . . . waiting for him" (Heb. 9:28).	"All nations . . . will see the Son of Man coming on the clouds of the sky, with power" (Matt. 24:30).
At any moment	**At Armageddon's close**
"[We] eagerly wait for . . . [the] Lord Jesus Christ to be revealed" (1 Cor. 1:7).	"This horn was waging war against the saints . . . until the Ancient of Days came" (Dan. 7:21-22).
Voices accompany Christ	**Heaven's armies accompany**
"With a loud command, with the voice of the archangel and with the trumpet call of God" (1 Thess. 4:16).	"The armies of heaven were following him" (Rev. 19:14; cf. Jude 14).
Christ claims His Bride	**Christ assumes earth's rule**
"The wedding of the Lamb has come, and his bride has made herself ready" (Rev. 19:7).	"Out of his mouth comes a sharp sword with which to strike down the nations. 'He will rule them with an iron scepter'" (Rev. 19:15).
Tribulation begins	**Millennium begins**
"I will . . . keep you from the hour of trial that is going to come upon the whole world" (Rev. 3:10).	"[Those who had] not worshiped the beast or his image . . . came to life and reigned with Christ a thousand years" (Rev. 20:4).
Faithful dead resurrected	**Human rebels destroyed**
"The dead in Christ will rise first" (1 Thess. 4:16).	"[The armies of the kings of earth] were killed with the sword . . . of the rider on the horse" (Rev. 19:21).

Fig. 5: The rapture and second coming compared and contrasted. They are clearly two separate events.

notable "prophets" Joachim of Floris (or Fiore) (1132-1202) predicted Christ's return in 1260; John Napier, the inventor of loga-
rithms, presumably used his new mathematical tool to calculate
Christ's return sometime between 1688 and 1700; "five or six
honest enthusiasts" among the early Methodists "foretold the
world was to end on the 28th of February" (1762); and John
Albrecht Bengel (1687-1751), otherwise a conscientious and productive Lutheran scholar, predicted Christ's coming in 1838.

In nineteenth-century North America, a major stir was created by the predictions of William Miller (1782-1849). Miller won
a large following with his teaching that the second coming would
occur October 22, 1844. Miller's views were based on a historicist
interpretation of Daniel's 2300 days as 2300 years beginning in
457 B.C. When Christ did not return in 1844, Miller revised his
doctrine to teach that He had come in the heavenlies and from
there He was proceeding with His "investigative judgment." He
thus will determine who qualifies to enter His eternal kingdom,
and to divide the saved from the lost. The doctrine of an investigative judgment is still held by today's Seventh Day Adventists.
It will be discussed in Chapter Eleven under the topic of the judgment of the believer's sins.

Orthodox scholars hold that virtually all date-setting attempts result because of defective hermeneutics. Scholars in
some way add to the literal sense of Scripture, and though their
intentions are good, the outcome is error. Paul Lee Tan writes:

> **Once date-setting starts, interpreters must spiritualize and
> allegorize prophecy in order that the rest of the prophetic Scrip -
> tures might fit into the date schemes thus evolved. Interpreters
> who set dates work under a hodge-podge of spiritualized prophe -
> cies enmeshed in a literalistic framework** [3]

Nineteenth century literalist eschatology, by its message of a
two-stage return involving first a private rescue and then a great
military victory, clarified both the nature and the timing of the
second coming. In the twentieth century date-setters still appeared, but most who set dates focused on the rapture rather
than the second coming. With the resurgence of posttribulationism in the century's final decades, however, some
date-setters spoke of an event when they expected Christ to come
as Ruler and Judge of all mankind.

The Importance of The Second Coming

The expectation of Christ's conquering return to earth will
direct the focus of Christian work and witness, and provide its

---

[3] Paul Lee Tan. *The Interpretation of Prophecy*. Rockville: Assurance Publishers, 1974, p. 209.

own unique orientation to Christian service. It is difficult to attach too much importance to this doctrine.

1) **It is prominent in Scripture.** Though many Old Testament Scriptures speak of the second coming, the main emphasis is in the New Testament. Scholars have counted a total of 318 New Testament references to Christ's return, most of them referring to the second coming. This total is equivalent to one reference to each twenty-five verses. More references are concerned with the second coming than with any other doctrine, including either saving faith, or the atoning blood of Christ. The only New Testament books that lack an explicit reference to Christ's second coming are Galatians, 2 John, 3 John, and Philemon.

2) **It is a foundational scriptural doctrine.** Jesus Christ must return to earth to fulfill the covenant promises to Israel, to assume rulership of the world, and to judge and reward humans. Christ's appropriation of His victory over Satan awaits the second coming. He will thus be launched upon His rule as the Jews' Messiah and the King of all mankind. For the unbeliever, the second coming will involve judgment; for the believer it will be an opportunity for worship. "Those who do not obey the gospel of our Lord Jesus . . . will be . . . shut out from the presence of the Lord and from the majesty of his power on the day he comes to be glorified in his holy people" (2 Thess. 1:8-10).

3) **It has impressive practical consequences.** Knowledge of Christ's promised return, whether it is the rapture or the second coming, powerfully motivates God's people to holiness, spiritual maturity, dedication, and evangelism. The bankruptcy of human leadership becomes evident, and the pains and pleasures of life find their right perspective. Notably, almost all passages in the New Testament that speak of Christ's second coming are associated with virtuous living. Paul wrote, "May he strengthen your hearts so that you will be blameless and holy in the presence of our God and Father when our Lord Jesus comes with all his holy ones" (1 Thess. 3:13). John saw the purifying aspect of the anticipation: "We know that when he appears, we shall be like him. . . . Everyone who has this hope in him purifies himself, just as he is pure" (1 John 3:2-3). Dwight L. Moody once commented, "I have felt like working three times as hard ever since I understood that my Lord was coming back again."

Variant Concepts of the Second Coming

Some scholars consider the biblical promise of the personal return of Jesus Christ to be only a spiritual or allegorical event. They hold that the expression "second coming" is not to be taken literally, and they suggest various nonliteral meanings. In each case, the literal view responds with an appropriate defense.

1) The second coming was fulfilled on the day of Pentecost when He returned to earth in the person of the Holy Spirit.

The literal view responds that the Third Person is not the Second, and that years after Pentecost the disciples were still declaring the promise of Jesus' coming. Jesus taught that the Holy Spirit was His replacement on earth. "The Father . . . will give you another Counselor" (John 14:16).

2) The second coming occurs on each occasion when one experiences conversion and Jesus Christ comes into his or her life.

The literal view accepts the spiritual reality of conversion, but insists on a physical reality at the second coming. "This same Jesus . . . will come back in the same way you have seen him go into heaven" (Acts 1:11).

3) The second coming should be considered an aspect of the destruction of Jerusalem in A.D. 70 since the Olivet Discourse (Matt. 24:3-25:46) combines these events.

Literalism responds that Jerusalem's destruction under Titus with the scattering of the Jews and God's judgment stroke was indeed the nearer fulfillment of Christ's prophecy, but the larger fulfillment and Christ's coming awaits the end time. Some three decades after the destruction of Jerusalem John prayed, "Amen, Come, Lord Jesus" (Rev. 22:20).

4) The second coming occurs whenever a believer dies.

Literal theology sees the soul at death proceeding to Christ, not vice versa. At death the believer is placed in the grave and the body begins corruption; at Christ's coming the believer abandons the grave and the body puts on incorruption.

5) The second coming will be achieved by the conversion of the world since Jesus said, "This gospel of the kingdom will be preached in the whole world as a testimony to all nations, and then the end will come" (Matt. 24:14).

The literalist answers that worldwide proclamation is not worldwide conversion, and evangelism will never totally succeed. The end time will see worldwide proclamation because of energetic evangelism and communications technology, but even these efforts will not guarantee conversions. Jesus indicated that He will return to an apostate world scene when He asked: "When the Son of Man comes, will he find faith on the earth?" (Luke 18:8). The world will offer homage to Christ in response to His conquest, not to achieve His return.

The Time of the Second Coming

Christ's second coming is in the closing moments of Armageddon when the armies of earth will be poised totally to annihilate Israel. Thus, the second coming is very specifically linked to events on earth. In contrast, the rapture's timing can be plotted only generally by observing human events that could be the basis for the predicted world scene during the tribulation. The rapture will occur at the time of God's sovereign choice, but from that moment forward, the final countdown begins. Humans cannot say when the count will begin, but they do know that the second coming will occur after the seven-year tribulation.

Scripture indicates that the second coming will be a surprise to the people of earth. "So you also must be ready, because the Son of Man will come at an hour when you do not expect him" (Matt. 24:44); "At that time men will see the Son of Man coming in clouds with great power and glory. . . . Be on guard! Be alert! You do not know when that time will come" (Mark 13:26, 33); "Be always on the watch, and pray that you may be able to escape all that is about to happen, and that you may be able to stand be fore the Son of Man" (Luke 21:36); "Behold, I come like a thief! Blessed is he who stays awake and keeps his clothes with him" (Rev. 16:15). Other Scriptures that speak of Christ's coming as a thief include, Matt. 24:43; Luke 12:39; 1 Thess. 5:2; 2 Pet. 3:10, and Rev. 3:3. In context, all of the foregoing Scriptures speak of the second coming, rather than the rapture.

The second coming will surprise earthlings because almost all of those it affects will have been totally indifferent to Bible prophecy. These subjects will be chiefly Gentile rebels and newly converted Jews, and neither group will be informed about New Testament teachings. Humans who deny and reject such well attested events as the birth, death, and resurrection of Jesus will readily explain away predictions of the second coming. The same attitudes that enabled the scholars to identify for Herod the place of Christ's birth, and then personally do nothing about it, will assure that mankind in general is not informed (cf. Luke 2:3-6). The repeated biblical exhortations to watchfulness will be obeyed only by the handful of gospel converts who somehow escape martyrdom during the tribulation.

Even for humans who are aware of Daniel's prophecies and who are on earth during the tribulation, the exact date of the second coming may be uncertain. Once it has occurred, the rapture's date will be precisely known, but the tribulation, which begins with Antichrist's covenant, may be vaguely dated due to an earlier signing and a later implementation. Also, Jesus indicated that tribulation time would in some way be modified. "If those days had not been cut short, no one would survive, but for the sake of the elect those days will be shortened" (Matt. 24:22). This statement's meaning is debated, but if God's purposes are

achieved within less than seven years, it is within His preroga-
tives to terminate the tribulation ahead of schedule. Thus, at all
times the valid human response is one of watchfulness.

The Olivet Discourse and the Second Coming

The Olivet Discourse (Matt. 24:1-25:46; Mark 13:1-36; Luke
21:5-36) is Jesus' major statement concerning His second coming. The disciples asked Him two questions, with the second in
two parts:

1) *When will the temple be destroyed?* ("When will this happen?"—Matt. 24:3)

2) *What will be the sign of your [second] coming, and what will
   be the sign of the end of the [present] age?*

In interpreting Jesus' response to these two questions, futurist
scholars have proposed two apparently conflicting viewpoints:

Viewpoint 1: Jesus inserted a message to the disciples in their
newly achieved status as Christians before He answered their
questions. This view has been widely and popularly held, and
it is frequently the basis of sermons on "The Signs of the
Times." Typically the enumerated events[4] in Matthew
24:4-14 are compared with present day statistics. The fulfillment of these events, or their prevalence, is seen as evidence
that the end of this age is near—and thus Christ's return is
imminent. On the other hand, the disciples, and all Christians who succeed them, are informed that they can expect
troubles and disasters on this earth during the gospel age.
Peace, prosperity, and tranquility await the age to come.

Viewpoint 2: Jesus proceeded directly to answer their questions
and He spoke to the disciples as Jews. This view assumes that
Jesus did not answer what He was not asked. It holds that Jesus was speaking of His coming as Israel's Messiah, not as a
Bridegroom claiming His bride, the church, in the rapture.
Though the disciples were Christ's followers, their approach
and mind set at this time was Jewish and their questions concerned the Jewish temple, the return of the Jewish Messiah,
and the end of the times of the Gentiles. Jesus replied to them
as representatives of the Jewish nation. Thus, the pronouns
"you," beginning with verse 4, address not merely His immediate hearers, but also future generations of Jews. (e.g., "You
will be handed over to be persecuted and put to death, and
you will be hated by all nations because of me"—Matt. 24:9. A
common excuse for anti-Semitism is the nation's alleged role
in crucifying Jesus.)

---

4   A suggested list: false Christs, wars, famines, earthquakes, persecution of be-
      lievers, false prophets, increasing wickedness, spiritual coldness, the
      worldwide dissemination of the gospel.

Perhaps these two viewpoints can be reconciled by applying Jesus' words in this section primarily to the temple and Jewish nation, and secondarily to the church and the Christian expectation of the rapture. Life on earth is tenuous, and humans in every age can expect to undergo birth pains (cf. v. 8). Such events, intensifying as the age advances, mark the church age, and they will similarly mark the tribulation period. This earthly life, even at its best, falls drastically short of the joys and blessings of Christ's millennial reign.

Jesus' reply to the disciples' questions

In answering question one, Jesus did not tell when the temple would be destroyed, but He gave advice for the behavior of those who would suffer these calamities. At the first hint of trouble they were to escape with utmost urgency. Further, He gave a clue to identify the imminency of these events: "When you see Jerusalem being surrounded by armies, you will know that its desolation is near" (Luke 21:20). As Rome prepared to destroy Jerusalem in A.D. 70, Titus' armies first laid siege to the city, but after a time they withdrew. Those Jews who followed Jesus' warning and left the city during the interval were spared. When the armies returned they were totally ruthless in their siege and destruction of the city.

In answering question two, Jesus gave a number of signs of His coming: the proclamation of the gospel of the kingdom to all nations, a period of severe distress (or great tribulation—cf. Matt. 24:21; Rev. 7:14), cosmic upheavals, His sign in the sky, and human fearfulness (cf. Matt. 24:14-30; Mark 13:24-26; Luke 21:25-26). The kingdom proclamation and His coming are closely linked, for the earthly kingdom will be launched by Jesus' coming at the end of the tribulation. The kingdom depends upon His presence on earth.

The disciples may not have realized it, but the fulfillment of the two events concerning which they inquired was to be widely separated in time. The destruction of the temple was completed in A.D. 70. The second coming of Christ is yet to occur nearly twenty centuries later. The two events were to have much in common, and Jesus intertwined their descriptions. The culmination of events in A.D. 70, however, brought tragedy, destruction, and the total dismantling of the temple. The culmination of events at the second coming will be the glorious visible return of Jesus and worldwide penitence, but there will have been prior destruction and desolation paralleling A.D. 70. The preterit view (see p. 43) sees only the similarities, and in the opinion of the futurist, it therefore confuses the two events.

A key to recognizing the imminency of the temple's destruction, the second coming, and kingdom's inauguration is the unique expression, "the abomination [Gk. *bdelugma*] that causes desolation [Gk. *eremosis*]" (Matt. 24:15; Mark 13:14). The word *bdelugma* (beh-DEL-oog-mah) means that which arouses God's wrath, a thing detestable in God's sight, an abomination—particularly one connected with idolatry; *eremosis* (er-EM-mo-sis) means a devastation, destruction, or desolation. The phrase is made more understandable in various versions. Thus: "the abomination of desolation"—KJV; "the desolating sacrilege"—RSV; "the destructive desecration"—Williams New Testament; "the Foul Desecration"—20th Century New Testament; or "the appalling Horror"—Moffat. The language identifies spiritual desecration rather than physical destruction. Its victims are left neglected, sorrowful, wretched, and disconsolate.

Jesus' answer to question one applied to the destruction of the existing temple—the second or Herod's temple. His answer to question two necessarily applied to a reconstructed third temple. In relation to the destruction of Herod's temple, the threat of desecration of the scared site was a sign of imminent danger. In relation to Christ's coming and the end of the age, the emergence of the desolating abomination in the reconstructed temple will be a critical sign. Jesus' reference to Daniel's "abomination that causes desolation" (Dan. 9:27) identifies end-time events with Daniel's seventieth "seven" (or "week"). Thus, Jesus' second coming will follow a seven-year tribulation period, the midpoint of which is marked by the desolating abomination. A further discussion of this topic follows in Chapter 8.

The gospel of the kingdom

The significance of Jesus words "this gospel of the kingdom will be preached to the whole world" (Matt. 24:14) is debated. Once again there are two viewpoints:

Viewpoint 1) holds that there is only one gospel and it is the gospel that Jesus, the disciples, and Paul preached in the New Testament era. Scriptures supporting this view are Acts 20:25 "I [i.e., Paul] have gone about preaching the kingdom"; Acts 28:23 "[Paul] declared to them the kingdom of God and tried to convince them about Jesus"; and Acts 23:31 "[Paul] preached the kingdom of God and taught about the Lord Jesus Christ." This gospel, the eternal gospel, will continue to be proclaimed during the tribulation. "I saw another angel flying in midair, and he had the eternal gospel to proclaim to those who live on the earth—to every nation, tribe, language and people" (Rev. 14:6).

Ed Hindson supports this position and based upon it he makes the following application:

> Since Matthew has already shown in his parables that the pres -
> ent form of the kingdom is the church, it seems proper to inter -
> pret the events in this discourse as relating to the entire Church
> Age and culminating during the tribulation period. Thus, the
> "signs" . . . of the end are general characteristics of the present
> age, which shall be intensified as this age moves toward its con -
> clusion.[5]

The biblical text does not definitively settle whether the gospel is
to be merely announced in all nations, or believed in all nations.

Viewpoint 2) holds the gospel of the kingdom is the message of repentance preached by John the Baptist and by Jesus as
His ministry began. "John the Baptist came, preaching . . . and
saying, 'Repent, for the kingdom of heaven is near'" (Matt.
3:1-2); "Jesus began to preach, Repent, for the kingdom of
heaven is near" (Matt. 4:17; cf. Matt. 3:1; 4:23; 10:7). This message declares the way to God (i.e., by repentance) and it was relevant in the pre-Church era and it will again be relevant during
the tribulation. On the other hand, the Church's "gospel of
Christ[6]" is the "gospel of God's grace" (Acts 20:24) which "is the
power of God for the salvation of everyone who believes" (Rom.
1:16). Paul wrote, "Our gospel came to you not simply with
words, but also with power, with the Holy Spirit and with deep
conviction" (1 Thess. 1:5). The gospel of Christ provides the miracle of the new birth whereas the repentance call of the gospel of
the kingdom asks for human works and in the tribulation will
frequently lead to martyrdom.

Supporters of Viewpoint 2) point out:

1) The gospel of the kingdom's concern is repentance, and it differs from the Christian gospel preached by Paul. "I preached
   . . . that Christ died for our sins . . . that he was buried and he
   was raised on the third day . . . and that he appeared to Peter,
   and then to the Twelve" (1 Cor. 15:2-5).

2) When Christ sent the apostles to preach the kingdom message,
   He instructed, "Do not go among the Gentiles or enter any
   town of the Samaritans. Go rather to the lost sheep of Israel"
   (Matt. 10:5-6). Following Calvary and His resurrection, He
   sent forth the apostles with the Christian gospel and He instructed them, "Therefore go and make disciples of all nations" (Matt. 28:19).

One's choice from the above viewpoints affects his or her
view of salvation during the tribulation. If the gospel is

---

5   Ed Hindson, *Earth's Final Hour.* Eugene: Harvest House Publishers, 1999,
        p. 64.

6   The phrase "gospel of Christ" occurs eight times in the New Testament
        (NIV): Rom. 15:19; 1 Cor. 9:12; 2 Cor. 2:12; 2 Cor. 9:13; 2 Cor. 10:14; Gal.
        1:7; Phil. 1:27; and 1 Thess. 3:2.

unchanging, then humans would come to God during the tribulation in response to the same message that draws sinners to Christ today. Since futurists hold that the church is a distinct entity, however, tribulation saints are not considered to be added to the church. Almost all will suffer martyrdom. Thus there is ground to hold that tribulation humans will need to hear a gospel message that is unique to them and that will prepare them for the kingdom. Since Christ's literal earthly kingdom is to be launched at the close of the tribulation, a gospel message of repentance appears to be the appropriate preparation.

Though what is to be understood by the gospel of the kingdom may be debated, it is clear that it will be a gospel (i.e., good news). It may be necessary to adapt God's gospel to the specific needs of the hearers, but the message will always tell what must be done to be reconciled to God. A Christian evangelist proclaiming the gospel of Christ may stress repentance when dealing with a profligate rebel, but to a tender sensitive seeker he might speak of love and mercy. The gospel of the Bible is adaptable and multifaceted, and its message is comprehensive enough to embrace the needs of all humans.

The "elect" of the Olivet Discourse

At His second coming, Jesus' angels "will gather his elect from the four winds" (Matt. 21:31). In Scripture, "elect" [or "chosen ones"] is a generic term, and those identified are determined by context. On occasion, Paul used the term to refer to Christians, "I endure everything for the sake of the elect [Gk. *eklektos*], that they too may obtain . . . salvation" (2 Tim. 2:10). The Greek *eklektos* (ek-lek-TOS) means chosen, select, elect, those (or one) chosen by God. Peter wrote "to God's elect" (1 Pet. 1:1). It is said, however, that out of sixteen occurrences of the word "elect" in the New Testament, only seven are an obvious and undisputed reference to those who comprise the church.

In the Old Testament, Isaiah used the equivalent Hebrew term to refer to the nation of Israel. "I will bring forth descendants from Jacob, and from Judah those who will possess my mountains; my *chosen people* [*bachiyr*, KJV—elect] will inherit them" (Isa. 65:9). The Hebrew *bachiyr* (baw-KHEER) is translated chosen one(s) or elect. Other Old Testament references to "elect" or "chosen ones" include, 1 Chron. 16:13; Psa. 105:6, 43; and Psa. 106:15. In addressing Israel, Moses used the verbal form, "The Lord your God has chosen you [elected you] out of all the peoples on the face of the earth to be his people, his treasured possession" (Deut. 7:6). More than forty Old Testament references apply some form of the term "elect" (often the verb form "elected") to individuals or groups to whom God so related. The usual translation is "chose" or "chosen." At least eleven times in the Old Testament, individuals or groups are designated by God as "elect" or "chosen ones." It is understandable that Jesus would have used the word "elect" in the usual fashion to which His hearers were accustomed to hear it.

The context requires that the elect of the Olivet Discourse should be Jews since they are the people to whom "the abomination that causes desolation" will be a threat. For their sake the days of the tribulation will be shortened (Matt. 24:22; Mark 13:20); they will be subject to the deceptive wiles of a false messiah and false prophets (Matt. 24:24; Mark 13:22), and at Christ's second coming He will dispatch His angels to gather them from the "four winds" (Matt. 24:31; Mark 13:27).

Though the Jewish elect are assembled by angels, Christ will have personally gathered His bride, the church, by means of the rapture prior to the tribulation. Christ's coming at this time (Matt. 24:30-31; Mark 13:26-27) is His glorious second coming which occurs some seven years after the rapture. Whereas the rapture achieves the translation of dead and living Christians, this return unleashes conquering power and awesome glory; it relates to all humans and, because of its destructive stroke upon rebels, in many it evokes mourning and desolation. The elect, the penitent Jews, are gathered to begin life anew as citizens of Messiah's Israel during the millennium.

Olivet applications and parables

Much of the material that follows in the Olivet Discourse concerns preparedness for the future. The illustrations comparing human fate in the tribulation to that of people during the days of Noah (Matt. 24:37-41) are the reverse of the rapture. In this passage those who are "taken" suffer judgment, and those who are "left" survive to enter the millennium. The occasion is the selection of millennial citizens, and thus it differs from the rapture's selection of the celestial Bride of Christ.

The theme of the parable of the faithful and wise servant and also of the parable of the ten virgins is watchfulness. Some are ready and some are not. The second coming involves the immediate judgment of the sheep and the goats, and anyone who is unprepared for His return will be classified with the latter. "He will cut him in pieces and assign him a place with the hypocrites" (Matt. 24:51). The parable of the talents teaches the need for careful stewardship. The parable of the sheep and goats teaches concerning future judgment. Jesus did not so much assign His coming to a specific time in the future, but rather He taught that all of life should be lived in anticipation of His promised coming. The important issue is the quality of present life.

OLIVET DISCOURSE (Matt. 24, 25; Mark 13; Luke 21:5-36)

1. WHEN WILL THE TEMPLE BE DESTROYED?
2. WHAT WILL BE THE SIGN OF YOUR COMING?

GENERAL INCONCLUSIVE SIGNS

"THESE THINGS MUST HAPPEN FIRST, BUT THE END WILL NOT COME RIGHT AWAY"
(Luke 21:9)

FALSE CHRISTS (Matt. 24:5)
WARS AND RUMORS (Matt. 24:6)
FAMINES (Matt. 24:7)
EARTHQUAKES (Matt. 24:7)
PESTILENCES (Luke 21:11)
CHRISTIAN JEWS PERSECUTED (Mark 13:9; Luke 21:12)

POSITIVE SIGNS RELATING TO THE TWO QUESTIONS

1. THE DESTRUCTION OF THE TEMPLE

CHRISTIAN JEWS PERSECUTED (Mark 13:9; Luke 21:12)
CITY SURROUNDED (Luke 21:22)
ABOMINATION CAUSING DESOLATION
(Matt. 24:15; Mark 13:4)
JERUSALEM TRAMPLED ON (Luke 21:24)
TEMPLE DESTROYED

TIME ⬇

───────────────────────────── **A.D. 70**

ISRAEL DISPERSED (Luke 21:24)

2. THE SIGNS OF CHRIST'S COMING

COSMIC UPHEAVALS (Matt. 24:29; Luke 21:25-27)
ENDURING REMNANT (Matt. 24:13)
GOSPEL OF KINGDOM PREACHED WORLDWIDE (Matt. 24:14)
ETHNIC JEWS PERSECUTED (Matt. 24:9)
APOSTASY (Matt. 24:10)
ABOMINATION CAUSING DESOLATION
(Matt. 24:15; Mark 13:14)
FALSE MIRACLES (Matt. 24:24)
"EATING AND DRINKING, MARRYING AND GIVING
IN MARRIAGE (Matt. 25:38)

From
A.D. 70
to the
rapture
plus the
7 years
of the
tribu-
lation

⬇

───────────────────────────── **SECOND COMING**

JUDGMENT OF SHEEP AND GOATS (Matt. 25:31-46

Fig. 6: In the Olivet Discourse Jesus described two very different events—1) a near event (the temple's destruction in A.D. 70), and 2) a distant event (His second coming at the end of the age).

The sprouting fig tree

Jesus said, "Now learn this lesson from the fig tree: As soon as its twigs get tender and its leaves come out, you know that summer is near" (Matt. 24:32). The symbolism in this statement is debated, and two viewpoints compete:

Viewpoint 1): The fig tree is a symbol of national Israel. This view is supported by various instances when a fig tree has been used to symbolize Israel, and it is compared to the use of an eagle as a symbol of the United States. Advocates of this view feel that they have scriptural support in Hosea 9:10. In that text the LORD is quoted as saying, "When I found Israel . . . it was like seeing the early fruit on the fig tree."

Viewpoint 2): There is really no clear cut biblical identification of Israel with a fig tree as a standing national symbol. Hosea 9:10 is an incidental comparison only. In speaking of the fig tree, Jesus was teaching about the inevitability of the cycle of nature rather than identifying Israel. In Luke's version, Jesus actually said, "Look at the fig tree and all the trees. When they sprout leaves, you can see for yourselves that summer is near" (Luke 21:29-30).

Though Viewpoint 2) is probably not the most popular at the present time, it appears to many futurists to have a better logical and biblical basis.

The generation that will not pass away

Jesus said, "When you see all these things [i.e., the signs of the end of the age], you know that it is near, right at the door. I tell you the truth, this generation [Gk. *genea*]⁷ will certainly not pass away until all these things have happened" (Matt. 24:33-34; cf. Luke 21:32). These words follow His discussion of the fig tree and the emergence of its leaves as a sign. Many of those who link the fig tree to Israel hold that the proclamation of the State of Israel in 1948 was the leafing of the tree, and this date is therefore pivotal. Date setters have fixed on this date as a basis for predicting the date of the Lord's return.

The futurist suggests possible interpretations of Jesus' words concerning the generation that would survive. **1)** Jesus was teaching the relative brevity of the tribulation by declaring that the same generation that witnesses the end-time devastation will also witness the second coming. This group will be the final generation or race of the church age. Or **2)** He may have been making the reassuring point that in spite of Antichrist's efforts the Jewish nation (Gk. *genea*) will not be annihilated by its enemies, but it will survive as a nation to experience the coming of

---

7 *genea* (gen-eh-AH): generation, race, kind, nation (cf. Luke 16:8, 21:32; Mark 13:30).

the Messiah. Or 3) By "this generation" Jesus meant those alive at the time He was speaking. He was thus referring only to His prediction of the temple's forthcoming destruction. In fact the temple was destroyed less than four decades from the time that He was speaking, and at least some of His hearers could be expected to be still alive.

Preterists tend to focus on this latter interpretation and to identify "this generation" with Jesus' Jewish contemporaries. They thus consider that the horrors of Jerusalem's destruction in A.D. 70 were the fulfillment of Jesus' prophecies of the tribulation end-time destruction. They hold that Jesus' specification that the present generation would still be alive, establishes that all that was predicted was fulfilled during the lifetime of at least some of Jesus' listeners. The futurist insists that what happened in A.D. 70 by no means fulfilled literal Scripture that describes great cosmic upheavals and Christ's glorious second coming (cf. Matt. 24:29-30; Mark 13:24-26; Luke 21:25-28).

Near and far views

The Olivet Discourse describes two destructions of Jerusalem, and thus it entails both a near and a far application. Matthew and Mark stress the end time or latter day destruction, while Luke stresses that of the first century. The nearer fulfillment was the destruction under Titus in A.D. 70; the far fulfillment will involve the terrors of the great tribulation when the False Prophet will set up an image in honor of the Antichrist and demand that everyone worship it (cf. Rev. 13:14-17). The discourse clearly charted the course of these coming events. Just as Christians in A.D. 70 found the worth of these insights, and they escaped when Rome attacked Jerusalem, so those who will pay heed to this guidebook will be better able to cope with the events that lead to Christ's second coming.

The Luke 17:20-37 Discourse

Jesus' sermon in Luke 17 closely parallels the Olivet Discourse though it was given a few weeks previously. In Luke's account, Jesus had been asked by the Pharisees when the kingdom of God would come. Jesus' answer to the question, and His further remarks to the disciples, made the point that the kingdom would be launched catastrophically by His second coming "like the lightning, which flashes and lights up the sky from one end to the other" (Luke 17:24).

In these words, just as in the Olivet Discourse, Jesus is not speaking of the rapture, but of the second coming. Humans during the tribulation will attempt to maintain normal lifestyles, and they will be caught by surprise when Jesus is revealed as the conquering King. In His conquest, all who resist Him will suffer judgment and they will perish. Only those who penitently accept Him will be spared to begin millennial life (cf. Luke 17:33).

Language usage in the clause "one will be taken [Gk. *paralambano*] and the other left [Gk. *aphiemi*]" (vv. 34,35) supports the understanding of the first group being taken in judgment and the second left free to enter the millennium. (*paralambano* [para-lam-BAN-oh]: to take, to take over, receive; *aphiemi* [af-EE-ay-me]: to forsake, leave, forgive). Some suggest that "taken" (*paralambano*) is to be understood as in John 14:3 "I will . . . take [*paralambano*] you to be with me." This same verb is used, however, to describe the taking of one for a negative purpose. Thus, "The devil took him [Jesus] to the holy city" (Matt. 4:5), and "The governor's soldiers took Jesus into the Praetorium" (Matt. 27:27). Though the verb "left" occurs in a negative sense in Revelation 2:4 "You have forsaken [*aphiemi*] your first love," it also clearly denotes positive outcomes: "The servant's master . . . canceled [*aphiemi*] the debt" (Matt. 18:27); "Forgive [*aphiemi*] us our debts" (Matt. 6:12). Forgiven humans who are spiritually debt free are spared to enter the millennium.

The Intermediate State

The expression "intermediate state," though not biblical, is commonly used to refer to what awaits humans immediately following death. Biblical references to this topic are incidental and incomplete, and thus in our theology, in the words of Truett Bobo, "we can but stammer weakly." Nevertheless, at least some insights can be found in Scripture, and these merit attention.

The Bible's Portrayal of the Experience of Death

Scripture uses various figures and inferences to depict death:

undergoing the destruction of our tent: "Now we know that if the earthly tent we live in is destroyed [*kataluo*], we have a building from God, an eternal house in heaven, not built by human hands" (2 Cor. 5:1), (*kataluo* [kat-a-LOO-oh]: to destroy, demolish, dismantle, tear down).

losing one's clothing: Paul adds that we eagerly look forward to being "clothed" in that eternal body "because when we are clothed, we will not be found naked [*gumnos*] (v. 3). (*gumnos* [goom-NOS]: naked, stripped bare, without an outer garment, poorly dressed, uncovered). The context indicates that Paul saw death as the total loss of one's clothing, and not merely becoming lightly clothed—all elements of the earthly body are left behind. Thus, he continues, "For while we are in this tent, we groan and are burdened, because we do not wish to be unclothed [*ekduo*], but to be clothed with our heavenly dwelling, so that what is mortal may be swallowed up by life" (2 Cor. 5:4), (*ekduo* [ek-DO-oh]: to strip, plunder, undress).

being away from the body: "We are confident, I say, and would prefer to be away from [*ekdemeo*] the body and at home with [*endemeo*] the Lord" (2 Cor. 5:8), (*ekdemeo* [ek-day-MEH-oh]: to leave, get away from, take a long journey; *endemeo* [en-day-MEH-oh]: to be at home).

a departure *(exodos*[1]): "I think it is right to refresh your memory as long as I live in the tent of this body, because I know

---

1   Note that Latin influence changed the spelling of the name of the second book of the Bible.

that I will soon put it aside, as our Lord Jesus Christ has made clear to me. And I will make every effort to see that after my departure [*exodos*] you will always be able to remember these things" (2 Pet. 1:13-15), (*exodos* [EX-od-os]: departure, death, decease).

a departure (*analuo*): "For I am already being poured out like a drink offering, and the time has come for my departure [*analuo*]" (2 Tim. 4:6), (*analuo* [an-a-LOO-oh]: to unloose, to untie, to cast off, to depart, to die).

Changes Occurring at Death

Scripture speaks of at least three changes that occur when the human dies:

1. The spirit departs

At death the spirit of bodily life, departs. On the cross, as He was about to die, Jesus prayed, "Father, into your hands I commit my spirit" (Lk. 23:46). Similarly, "While they were stoning him, Stephen prayed, 'Lord Jesus, receive my spirit'" (Acts 7:59). James wrote, "the body without the spirit is dead" (James 2:26). Solomon described death: "the dust returns to the ground it came from, and the spirit returns to God who gave it" (Eccl. 12:7). In the case of Jairus' daughter: "Her spirit returned, and at once she stood up" (Luke 8:55).

2. The body "sleeps"

The body at death is ordinarily laid in the ground and, at least in the case of believers, it is described as "sleeping." "Brothers, we do not want you to be ignorant about those who fall asleep [*koimao*], or to grieve like the rest of men, who have no hope" (1 Thess. 4:13). (*koimao* [koi-MA-oh]: to sleep, fig. to sleep the sleep of death; "cemetery" which means "sleeping place" derives from this root.) By depicting the believer's death as sleep, Scripture conveys the concepts of: rest, assurance, and renewal.

Though to Jesus, death's conqueror, death is only a sleep, He was misunderstood when He spoke of death in this fashion. "Our friend Lazarus has fallen asleep; but I am going there to wake him up. . . . Jesus had been speaking of his death, but his disciples thought he meant natural sleep" (John 11:11, 13). In the case of Jairus' daughter, Scripture reports, "'Stop wailing,' Jesus said. 'She is not dead but asleep.' They laughed at him, knowing that she was dead" (Luke 8:52-53).

The body that is asleep in death usually is allowed to decay in the ground. Eventually, it returns to its constituent elements. "For dust you are and to dust you will return" (Gen. 3:19). This process deprives the human of an instrument that his spirit can animate in order to express itself in the material world.

3. The person enters the intermediate state

Traditionally, a human is depicted as existing in the intermediate state as a "soul" (Heb. *nephesh* [NEH-fesh], Gk. *psyche* [psooch-HAY]). In the original, this word is more or less equivalent to "person, personality, or human being," and it identifies that of which a human basically consists. Thus, it is legitimate to speak of a "person" in the intermediate state, though with the understanding that a distinctive connotation of the word is implied. We should note that the biblical usages of *psyche* and its derivatives are very different from popular or scientific usage.

Older Bible versions (e.g., KJV) of Genesis 2:7 use the traditional word "soul." "The Lord God formed man of the dust of the ground [body], and breathed into his nostrils the breath of life [spirit]; and man became a living soul [*nephesh*]." Newer versions replace "soul" in this context with "being."[2] This basic human being, or what some call the "disembodied soul," survives death and passes into the intermediate state. Peter described God's provision in Old Testament terms: "You will not abandon my soul [Gk. *psyche*] to Hades" (Acts 2:27, lit. trans.). The Psalmist wrote, "God will redeem my soul [*nephesh*] from the hand of Sheol" (Psa. 49:15, lit. trans.).

Biblical Views of the Intermediate State

1) **At death, the believer proceeds into Christ's presence;** he or she is, of course, awaiting resurrection and temporarily without a body. (See 2 Cor. 5:8 previously quoted.) Jesus promised the thief on the cross, "I tell you the truth, today you will be with me in paradise" (Luke 23:43). Paul spoke of his desire: "I am torn between the two: I desire to depart and be with Christ, which is better by far; but it is more necessary for you that I remain in the body" (Phil. 1:21).

2) **At death the unbeliever is sent to a realm of judicially imposed suffering.** He or she also, is without a physical body, though events are described in terms of a body. "The rich man also died and was buried. In hell [*Hades*], where he was in torment, he looked up and saw Abraham far away, with Lazarus by his side. So he called to him, Father Abraham, have pity on me and send Lazarus to dip the tip of his finger in water to cool my tongue, because I am in agony in this fire" (Luke 16:22-24).

---

2   Newer Bible translations still use "soul" as the rendering of *nephesh* and *psyche* but not at all consistently. In many cases, they translate the original with personal pronouns "I, me, you, or him." In some instances, they use words such as "heart, mind, or thing." Sometimes, they omit any reference to an entity (e.g., The literal "unto the saving of the soul" in Hebrews 10:39 is rendered simply "are saved").

3) **The believer's intermediate realm is called "paradise."** In Luke 16:23 the popular Hebrew name "Abraham's side" (or bosom) is used. The "paradise," to which Jesus promised to transport the penitent thief (cf. Luke 23:43), means "an enclosed park." In recounting his experience, Paul indicates that paradise is now in the third heaven (cf. 2 Cor. 12:2, 4). Because paradise is in heaven, believers who enter the afterlife are popularly said to be in heaven.

4) **The human continues conscious existence in the intermediate state** even without a body. The thief would have needed to be conscious to enjoy Christ's promise of fellowship in paradise. For the rich man to suffer in Hades or for Lazarus to be comforted required consciousness for each. John wrote, "Blessed are the dead who die in the Lord" (Rev. 14:13). The word "blessed" means "happy," and only those who are conscious can be happy. The consciousness of humans in the after life means there is memory of the previous life on earth. The rich man remembered his five brothers. Presumably, at least for believers, what is known and remembered in some way screens out the painful and ugly.

5) **The intermediate state is one of incompleteness.** The portrayal of the mode of existence in the after life becomes more explicit as one proceeds through the Scriptures.

In several **Old Testament** passages (e.g., Job 26:5, Psa. 88:10, Prov. 9:18, Isa. 14:9) the word rendered "dead" is the Hebrew *raphaim* [raw-faw-EEM] which is the plural of *rapha* (raw-FAW). This word is defined: "dead, deceased, that which is sunken or powerless, evening shadows or shades of night, or fig. a ghost." The revised *Gesenius Hebrew and English Lexicon* identifies *raphaim* as: "[the] name of [the] dead in Sheol." This language suggests a somewhat vague shadowy or even ghostly existence.

In the **New Testament,** Paul wrote, somewhat enigmatically, of God's provision for the after life.

Now we know that if the earthly tent we live in is destroyed, we have a building from God, an eternal house in heaven, not built by human hands. . . . For while we are in this tent, we groan and are burdened, because we do not wish to be unclothed but to be clothed with our heavenly dwelling, so that which is mortal may be swallowed up by life (2 Cor. 5:1, 4).

Scholars debate how to understand these words, and two viewpoints are suggested:

Viewpoint 1) holds that Paul was simply writing about the believer's anticipated resurrection body. Futurists hold that the rapture will involve the resurrection and the reunion of the believer with his or her glorified body.

Viewpoint 2) holds that God will provide a temporary body in the afterlife. This body will be especially created by God to provide a vehicle through which the believer will be able to function and relate in the intermediate state. At the rapture, this intermediate body will be replaced by the believer's own resurrected and glorified body.

Since the text in 2 Corinthians 5 is not definitive, and there is no other agreed upon information about an intermediate body, the expectation of a temporary body in the after life appears to be a minority view not widely held.

The Intermediate State vs. the Eternal State

Most scholars struggle to define the precise distinctions between the intermediate and eternal states. Scripture portrays the believer as immediately in the presence of Jesus after departing from this life, and yet there is the future expectation of the rapture when the dead in Christ will rise. As an outcome of that event "we will be with the Lord forever" (1 Thess. 4:17). Similarly, the dead sinner finds himself immediately in a place of torment, although his formal sentencing and incarceration await the great white throne judgment.

The disembodiment of humans is fundamental to the intermediate state. A comparable existence during the tribulation is that of the souls under the altar (cf. Rev. 6:9-11). Their strange location under the altar, and their cry, "How long, Sovereign Lord?" clearly imply a temporary status. Though they are in heaven and can talk to the Lord, their fellowship is limited and restrained. They are given a white robe, but "they were told to wait a little longer" (v. 11). Those presently in the intermediate state are similarly with Christ in a place of great blessing. Nevertheless, only the eternal state will see the fulfilment of all their promises and expectations.

As explained elsewhere, many Bible scholars hold that the location of the departed changes in the eternal state.[3] In addition, Scripture is interpreted as teaching that the departed undergo a change of status. Not only is the person once again embodied, but also he or she is officially and legally confirmed in that status. The intermediate state might compare with the circumstances of a newly arrived immigrant who remains in a holding center in the new land until an application for residence can be approved. Similarly, it might compare with the circumstances of an apprehended lawbreaker who is in custody until he can be brought to trial. Prior to the completion of the legal process, the immigrant

---

3   The believer is transferred from paradise to the new Jerusalem. The sinner is transferred from Hades to the lake of fire.

is present in the country, and the lawbreaker is in prison, but the full destiny of each is yet future.

The Old Testament Sheol[4]

The Hebrew word for the place of those whose bodies are left behind on earth is *Sheol* (sheh-OLE). *Sheol* means "that which is hollow," or "that which continually asks," and it denotes a place that is never full and is insatiable in its demands. Older versions usually translate *Sheol* as "hell" or "grave"; newer versions render it as "grave, death, realm of death," or in some cases leave it untranslated. Scholars suggest it would have been less confusing to have left *Sheol* in the text, although "realm of death" or "domain of death" are probably appropriate replacements.

The Old Testament usage of the word Sheol supports the following conclusions:

1. Sheol was the usual expected future destiny of humans

Jacob said, "In mourning I will go down to the grave [*Sheol*] to my son" (Gen. 37:35); David said of Joab, "Do not let his gray head go down to the grave [*Sheol*] in peace (1 Kings 2:6); the Psalmist wrote, "My life draws near the grave [*Sheol*]" (Psa. 88:3), and he asked rhetorically, "What man can live and not see death, or save himself from the power of the grave [*Sheol*]?" (Psa. 89:48); Hezekiah pleaded, "In the prime of life must I go through the gates of death [*Sheol*]?" (Isa. 38:10).

Two notable Old Testament exceptions to this pattern were Enoch and Elijah. They were granted the privilege of skipping this step, just as Christians will escape death in the rapture.

2. The term Sheol commonly denoted the grave

Hannah declared, "The Lord brings death . . . he brings down to the grave [*Sheol*]" (1 Sam. 2:6); Job said of the wicked, "They spend their years in prosperity and go down to the grave [*Sheol*] in peace" (Job 21:13); the Psalmist wrote of those trusting in themselves, "Like sheep they are destined for the grave [*Sheol*], and death will feed on them . . . their forms will decay in the grave" (Psa. 49:14); Isaiah described Babylon's dead king: "All your pomp has been brought down to the grave [*Sheol*] . . . maggots are spread out beneath you" (Isa. 14:11).

3. Sheol also denoted a realm of conscious beings beyond the grave

Isaiah wrote, "The grave [*Sheol*] below is all astir to meet you at your coming; it rouses the spirits of the departed to greet

---

4   Since the word Sheol has been adopted into the English language, when discussing it we will print it as an ordinary word. When we wish to show usage in the Hebrew text, however, we will print it in italics. This same system will apply to the Greek term Hades.

you . . . They will all respond, they will say to you, 'You also have become weak, as we are'" (Isa. 14:9-10). Those within Sheol observe and comment on events: "From within the grave [*Sheol*] the mighty leaders will say of Egypt and her allies, 'They have come down and they lie with the uncircumcised'" (Ezek. 32:21). Fugitives from God cannot escape Him even in Sheol: "If I go up

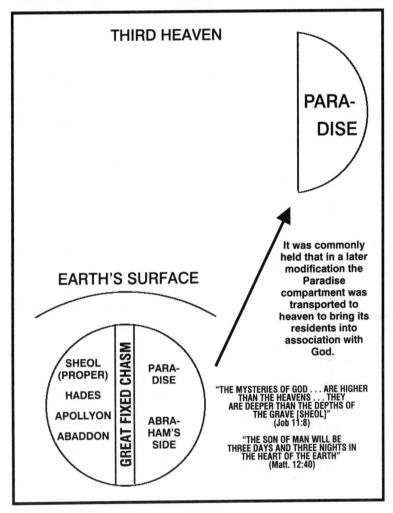

Fig. 7: A view of Sheol based upon the teaching of the Apocrypha. This view reflects belief in Old Testament times, though a two-compartment Sheol is not specifically taught there. Many Christian scholars formerly diagramed life after death in this way, but today's trend is the simplified view of Figure 8 (p. 113).

to the heavens, you are there; if I make my bed in the depths [*Sheol*], you are there" (Psa. 139:8). The Psalmist saw Sheol as an enclave of evil, "Let [my enemies] go down alive to the grave [Sheol], for evil finds lodging among them" (Psa. 55:15).

Because Sheol is the realm of the afterlife, there is no communication with those still living on earth. Thus David wrote, "No one remembers you when he is dead. Who praises you from the grave?" (Psa. 6:5). In relation to living humans on earth and in sharing the worship of the LORD, the dead are silent and without a voice. "It is not the dead who praise the LORD, those who go down to silence; it is we who extol the LORD" (Psa. 115:17-18); "The grave [*Sheol*] cannot praise you . . . the living—they praise you" (Isa. 38:18-19).

4. Sheol associates with the wicked and their punishment

In dealing with Korah's rebels, Moses prayed, "But if the Lord brings about something totally new . . . and they go down alive into the grave [*Sheol*], then you will know that these men have treated the Lord with contempt" (Num. 16:30); Moses depicted God as declaring, "For a fire has been kindled by my wrath, one that burns to the realm of death [*Sheol*] below" (Deut. 32:22); Job said, "The grave [*Sheol*] snatches away those who have sinned" (Job 24:19); David saw Sheol as the destiny of the wicked at the hand of a God of justice, "The wicked return to the grave [*Sheol*]" (Psa. 9:17, cf. v. 16); an anonymous Psalmist spoke of "the anguish of the grave [*Sheol*]" (Psa. 116:3); and Solomon describes those who consort with the woman called Folly and he concludes, "Her guests are in the depths of the grave [*Sheol*]" (Prov. 9:18).

5. The righteous, sooner or later, escape Sheol

Old Testament Scriptures include various spokespersons who speak of the destiny of the righteous. "You will not abandon me to the grave [*Sheol*]" (Psa. 16:10—David); "I will dwell in the house of the Lord forever" (Psa. 23:6—David); "God will redeem my life [soul, NIV footnote] from the grave [*Sheol*]; he will surely take me to himself" (Psa. 49:15—anon.); "You guide me with your counsel, and afterward you will take me into glory" (Psa. 73:24—Asaph); "For great is your love toward me; you have delivered me from the depths of the grave [*Sheol*]" (Psa. 86:13—David); "The path of life leads upward for the wise to keep him from going down to the grave [*Sheol*]" (Prov. 15:24—Solomon); "Punish him [one's child] with the rod and save his soul from death [*Sheol*]" (Prov. 23:14—Solomon); "Shall I ransom them [rebellious Israel] from the power of Sheol? Shall I redeem them from Death?" (Hos. 13:14 [NRSV]—God).

It is evident, that at least ultimately, the righteous escape Sheol. They do not belong there because it is a place where the wicked are punished. Most scholars hold that the manner in which God has provided for the righteous in regard to Sheol is not given in Scripture. Thus any theory in this regard is interpretive, and as later discussions will indicate, the subject is a matter of debate.

6. Only passing hints describe Sheol's nature

Job taught that humans in Sheol do not return to earth: "He who goes down to the grave [*Sheol*] does not return" (Job 7:9). Though in the passage that follows Job did not name Sheol, he described the afterlife (which to him was Sheol) as a realm of gloom and shadow: "I go to the place of no return, to the land of gloom and deep shadow . . . where even the light is like darkness" (Job 10:21-22). Job's friend, Zophar, depicted the location of Sheol in the lowest depths, for he spoke of God's mysteries as "deeper than the depths of the grave [*Sheol*]" (Job 11:8).

In Old Testament usage the term *Abaddon* (ab-ad-DONE) appears to parallel and perhaps overlap *Sheol*. Thus: "Death [*Sheol*] and Destruction [*Abaddon*] are never satisfied" (Prov. 27:20; cf. Job 26:6, 28:22, 31:12; Psa. 88:11; Prov. 15:11). The Gesenius *Lexicon* defines Abaddon: "Place of ruin in Sheol for lost or ruined dead."

In summary, the Old Testament teaches: 1) All humans anticipate the grave (*Sheol*), 2) For the wicked, the realm of the afterlife (*Sheol*) is a place of punishment, 3) For the righteous, though their bodies are in the grave (*Sheol*), their afterlife realm is Abraham's side (Paradise) in God's presence. (Note that Sheol denotes both the grave and the realm of the afterlife.)

The Traditional Jewish View of Sheol

The Jewish understanding of Sheol derived more from the post canonical Apocrypha, Pseudepigrapha, and Talmud than the Old Testament. In this extra-biblical literature, the Jews taught that all humans proceeded to Sheol at death, but that Sheol included two divisions, regions, or compartments: 1) the abode of the wicked and condemned (Sheol [proper]), and 2) the abode of the righteous and justified (Abraham's side, Paradise). A later modification saw the Paradise compartment transported to God's heavenly realm. The two-compartment underworld has appealed to some evangelical scholars, but the majority now reject it, for it seems to exceed what is taught in the Old Testament.

The New Testament Hades

In His account of the rich man and Lazarus (cf. Luke 16:19-31), Jesus neither endorsed nor amended the traditional

Jewish view. As Jesus described events, both men arrived at the grave and in their afterlife one was assigned to punishment and the other to blessing. The realm of punishment is called *Hades* ([HA-days] hell-NIV, KJV) which is widely accepted as the Greek equivalent of *Sheol*. The realm of blessing is spoken of as "Abraham's side (bosom, arms)." Between the two realms there was "a great chasm (gulf)," that prevented any crossing over.

Hades remains the dwelling place of the wicked dead until the great white throne judgment (cf. Rev. 20:11; 21:1). At that time, "The sea gave up the dead that were in it, and death and Hades gave up the dead that were in them, and each person was judged according to what he had done" (Rev. 20:13). Since there is no death in eternity, and there will be no prisoners remaining in Hades, God will obliterate each of these realms. "Then death and Hades were thrown into the lake of fire" (Rev. 20:14).

As we have seen, in identifying the region of the righteous in the life to come, Jesus used not only "Abraham's side," but also "paradise" (cf. Luke 23:43 "Today you will be with me in paradise"). This term was also used by Paul to identify a heavenly realm. Paul spoke of being "caught up to the third heaven" (2 Cor. 12:2), and then in the restatement of the event, being "caught up to paradise" (v. 4). These two descriptions of the same event indicate that in Paul's day paradise was thought to be in the third heaven.

The expression "paradise of God" occurs in Revelation. "To him who overcomes, I will give the right to eat from the tree of life, which is in the paradise of God" (Rev. 2:7). The expression in this context seems to proceed beyond the intermediate state, and thus it may be taken as a general nontechnical designation of the state of future blessing. The tree of life identifies with the new Jerusalem in eternity (cf. Rev. 22:2), and it there relates to the believer's eternal abode.

Hades and Christ's Victories

At His death, Jesus fulfilled His prophecy: "the Son of Man will be three days and three nights in the heart of the earth" (Matt. 12:40). The expression "heart of the earth" seems very clearly to denote more than the tomb into which Jesus' body was placed. Other Scriptures that suggest that during His days in the grave, Jesus entered the realm of the dead in Hades include "[He] ascended on high [but] . . . [He] also descended to the lower earthly places" (Eph. 4:8-9); and "For Christ . . . was put to death in the body but made alive by the Spirit, through whom also he went and preached to the spirits in prison" (1 Pet. 3:18-19). Apparently the early church endorsed the reality of Jesus' activity in the realm of death, for the Apostles' Creed, which arose by the end of the fourth century, states that Jesus was "crucified, dead and buried," and it adds, "He descended into hell [*Hades*]."

Though what Jesus did in the realm of the dead while His body was in the grave may be debated, Scripture clearly declares His resurrection. In his address on the Day of Pentecost Peter stated, "Christ . . . was not abandoned to the grave [*Hades*], nor did his body see decay" (Acts 2:31). Jesus' emergence from the dead is seen as a victory, not only over the grave but over the realm of afterlife. Thus Jesus could declare to John, "I was dead,

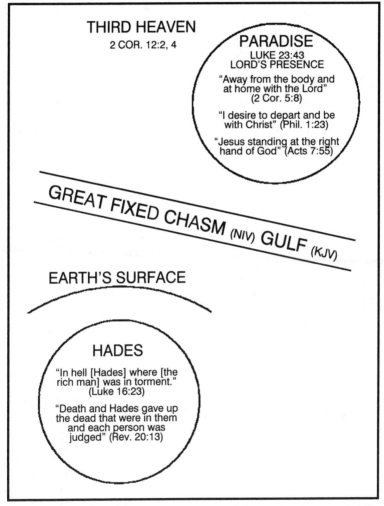

THIRD HEAVEN
2 COR. 12:2, 4

PARADISE
LUKE 23:43
LORD'S PRESENCE

"Away from the body and at home with the Lord" (2 Cor. 5:8)

"I desire to depart and be with Christ" (Phil. 1:23)

"Jesus standing at the right hand of God" (Acts 7:55)

GREAT FIXED CHASM (NIV) GULF (KJV)

EARTH'S SURFACE

HADES

"In hell [Hades] where [the rich man] was in torment." (Luke 16:23)

"Death and Hades gave up the dead that were in them and each person was judged" (Rev. 20:13)

Fig. 8: A proposed schema of the New Testament portrayal of the realms of Hades and Paradise as they now exist.

and behold I am alive for ever and ever! And I hold the keys of death and Hades" (Rev. 1:18). He now has the authority to call the dead from their grave (which He will do by the rapture), and the authority to call the wicked from Hades (which He will do in the end time judgment).

Paul applied Psalm 68:18 to Christ's ascension, "When he ascended on high, he led captives in his train and gave gifts to men" (Eph. 4:8). Until the late twentieth century, many scholars held that this verse described an important transitional event when Christ emptied Sheol-Hades of righteous dead and transported them to Paradise in heaven. This interpretation supported the view that until Christ's resurrection and ascension Sheol-Hades consisted of two compartments with the wicked dead in one (sometimes called Hades Proper) and the righteous dead in the other (Abraham's side or Paradise). The more likely interpretation today applies Ephesians 4:8-9 to the overall general theme of Christ's resurrection victory and its beneficial gifts to so many. Christ's resurrection assures that death, which as it were held captives in its clutches, is no longer the victor.

The reality of a heavenly paradise is not denied by Peter's words: "David did not ascend to heaven, and yet he said, 'The Lord [Jehovah] said to my Lord [Messiah—the future king]:' "Sit at my right hand"'" (Acts 2:34). On this occasion, Peter was providing proof that Jesus is the Messiah. Thus, he contrasted the earthly king David with his greater Son who, prophetically, David could see being invited to the heavenlies to sit at the Lord's right hand. Peter stated that "David did not ascend to heaven" to make clear that David is not speaking of himself in a heavenly setting, and thus the statement does not concern the location of Sheol or Paradise.

The interpretation of Peter's statement in his epistle is a matter of debate: "[Jesus] was put to death in the body but made alive by the Spirit, through whom also he went and preached [kerusso] to the spirits in prison" (1 Pet. 3:18b-19). (kerusso [keh-ROOS-oh]: announce, proclaim aloud, preach, speak publicly). Some apply these words to Jesus' announcement in Hades of His victory over death since even the wicked dead needed to know that they were awaiting resurrection to face a future judgment. Commentators are more likely, however, to see it as a proclamation confirming the condemnation of the evil spirits being held captive in the Abyss, or a similar prison. These spirits relate particularly to the time of Noah, and they thus are distinguished from later humans who have died and entered the realm of the afterlife. Another possible interpretation of the passage is to consider that it is saying that in the pre-flood era the preincarnate

Jesus used Noah as His channel to convey His message. Most evangelicals would firmly deny that this preaching involved a post-earthly-life opportunity for conversion.

The Two-Compartment Sheol/Hades View

Many older evangelical works support this view and they argue in its favor. Those who disagree respond as follows:

1) The Old Testament nowhere states that Sheol consisted of two compartments,

2) Though the righteous spoke of going down to Sheol, these references can be understood to say only that the righteous anticipated the physical grave,

3) Jesus' experiences in the realm of the afterlife can be explained in terms of His relationships to the wicked dead,

4) As previously noted, Ephesians 4:8-9 can be interpreted as a general comment on the fruits of Christ's victory and it does not necessarily speak of a cosmic event that in one stroke modified the realm of the afterlife,

	Intermediate State	Eternity
Entrance	**Death:** "The rich man . . . died and was buried. In hell [Hades] . . . he looked up" (Luke 16:22-23)	**Judgment:** "Death and Hades gave up the dead that were in them, and each person was judged" (Rev. 20:13).
Location	**In the depths of the earth:** "The Son of Man will be three days and three nights in the heart of the earth" (Matt. 12:40)	**At God's great white throne:** "I saw a great white throne. . . . And I saw the dead, great and small, standing before the throne" (Rev. 20:11-12)
Destiny	**Second Resurrection:** "I saw the dead, great and small, standing before the throne" (Rev. 20:12).	**Condemnation:** "If anyone's name was not found written in the book of life, he was thrown into the lake of fire" (Rev. 20:15).

Fig. 9: The destiny of the unconverted in their afterlife in the intermediate state and in eternity.

5) Though in the account of the rich man and Lazarus (cf. Luke 16:19-31) the rich man could see Lazarus and Abraham, and he could converse with Abraham, these circumstances would not demand that Hades (proper) and Abraham's side were adjacent. In the spirit world distances are irrelevant,

6) Paul's words are thought to teach an immediate heavenly destiny for the righteous dead.

Hades, the Abyss, Abaddon, Apollyon, Tartarus

Scripture's "Abyss" (Gk. *abussos* [AH-boos-os]) is the place of detention of demons (Luke 8:31), and of Satan during the millennium (cf. Rev. 20:1-3), and the place of confinement of spirits of evil and darkness who are God's special enemies. Antichrist is twice said to come up out of the Abyss (cf. Rev. 11:7; 17:8), and this place is the source of the demonic spirit motivating and empowering him. The tormenting "demon locusts" (cf. Rev. 9:3-5), emerge from the opened Abyss. Scripture twice notes that the Abyss is a locked enclosure with the key in heaven's custody (cf. Rev. 9:1; 20:1). The demons possessing the man of Gadera anticipated it as the place of their torment (cf. Matt. 8:29). Thus, they "begged [Jesus] repeatedly not to order them to go into the Abyss" (Luke 8:31).

In addition to translating *abussos* as "Abyss" our Bibles also render the word as: deep, depths below, or bottomless pit. In Revelation 9:1-2 the Greek word *phrear* (a well, pit, or shaft) combines with *abussos*. The resulting expression may be rendered "shaft of the Abyss." In Greek tradition, *phrear* (FREH-are) was the "pit or shaft leading down into the depths of Hades." In the New Testament era, popular concepts of the realm of the afterlife tended to derive from Greek mythology. Thus, it was widely held that the wicked dead, Satan, and his demonic angels are all confined in the same underworld. In this view, Abyss would be an alternate name for Hades proper. A more rigorous approach to Scripture requires the separation of these two realms, and limits Hades to the wicked dead humans, whereas the Abyss is the dwelling place of all other evil spirits.

Paul's reference to Christ in the Abyss in Romans 10 is thought to be a rhetorical device rather than a specific doctrinal statement In arguing for the non-repeatability of the finished work of Christ, Paul personified righteousness, and he depicted it as asking, "Who will ascend into heaven? (that is, to bring Christ down) or Who will descend into the deep [Gk. *abussos*]? (that is, to bring Christ up from the dead)" (Rom. 10:6-7). We suggest that in using Abyss as the opposite of heaven Paul was simply sketching the two extreme possible destinies, and not intending to make a definitive theological statement.

The name Apollyon, which is the Greek equivalent of the Hebrew Abaddon, apparently identifies the Abyss, and thus depicts it as the realm of the spirits of evil and darkness. In the sole New Testament reference, the terms are personified. "[The demon-locusts] had as king over them the angel of the Abyss, whose name in Hebrew is Abaddon, and in Greek, Apollyon" (Rev. 9:11). The name of the king was also the name of his realm.

The single biblical reference to Tartarus does not define it. "God did not spare angels when they sinned, but sent them to hell [*tartaroo*] putting them into gloomy dungeons [or chains of darkness --KJV]" (2 Pet. 2:4). (*tartaroo* [tar-tar-O-oh]: to thrust down to Tartarus, to hold captive in Tartarus. Peter uses the word as a participle, and it might be rendered "tartarizing them.") This passage seems to describe Tartarus under terms appropriate for the Abyss—the place of confinement of spirit beings of evil and darkness being "held for judgment" and thus awaiting their day in God's court.

The word Tartarus in pagan Greek eschatology, from which it is borrowed, denoted the equivalent of Hades proper. The Greek version of the intermediate state, just as the Jewish, taught two underworld regions: Elysium, the abode of the righteous, and Tartarus, the abode of the wicked. In using the verbal form of a secular word equivalent to our word "hell," Peter may not have intended a theological label. The *Lexicon* defines Tartarus, "thought of by the Greeks as a subterranean place lower than Hades where divine punishment was meted out."

The New Testament View of the Righteous Dead

The New Testament does not associate the righteous dead with Hades. Rather, it depicts them in the presence of the Lord. Thus, as we have noted, Paul wrote, "We are confident, I say, and would prefer to be away from the body and at home with the Lord. So we make it our goal to please him, whether we are at home in the body or away from it" (2 Cor. 5:8-9). In his final moments "[Stephen] looked up to heaven and saw the glory of God, and Jesus standing at the right hand of God"(Acts 7:55). Then, "while they were stoning him, Stephen prayed, 'Lord Jesus, receive my spirit'" (Acts 7:59). As he entered the afterlife, Stephen clearly expected to join Jesus in heaven.

As we have noted, the status of existence of the righteous dead is unclear in Scripture. The believer's relationship in being "at home with the Lord" appears to be preliminary. The formal union with Christ awaits the rapture when "the dead in Christ will rise first . . . to meet the Lord in the air" (1 Thess. 4:16-17). The granting of rewards awaits the Bema judgment. It would seem, that in whatever sense the believer enters the Lord's presence, the relationship at the outset is restricted and limited—the word "intermediate" remains appropriate.

Whether the righteous dead are aware of events on earth, has no definitive Biblical answer, but there are two possible hints. The souls under the altar (tribulation martyrs) knew that God's judgment upon earth was delayed (cf. Rev. 6:9-10). Abraham knew that the rich man had received "good things" in his lifetime, and that the rich man's five brothers on earth had "Moses and the Prophets" to warn them of their future destiny (cf. Luke 16:25-29). Thus, there may be some awareness of events on earth, at least to the degree that God judges that it is desirable for the departed to know what is occurring.

	Intermediate State	**Eternity**
Entrance	**Death:** "The beggar died and the angels carried him to Abraham's side" (Luke 16:22).	**Rapture:** "The dead in Christ will rise first. After that, we who are alive . . . will be caught up together" (1 Thess. 4:17).
Location	**With Christ in Paradise:** "I desire to depart and be with Christ"; "A man . . . was caught up in the third heaven. . . . [He] was caught up to paradise" (Phil. 1:23; 2 Cor. 12:2, 4).	**New Jerusalem:** "We are looking for the city that is to come"; "I saw the Holy City, the new Jerusalem" (Heb. 13:14; Rev. 21:2).
Destiny	**Bodily resurrection:** "The trumpet will sound, the dead will be raised imperishable. . . . For the perishable must clothe itself with . . . immortality" (1 Cor. 15:52-53).	**United with the Lord:** "Now the dwelling of God is with men, and he will live with them"; "The throne of God and of the Lamb will be in the city" (Rev. 21:3; 22:3).

Fig. 10: The destiny of the redeemed in their afterlife in the intermediate state and in eternity.

As an overall principle, it would seem warranted for the departed to be spared insights into events on earth. Such knowledge would mostly bring them anxious concerns, yet they would be helpless to intervene. In matters such as these, we can at least cite God's basic operating axiom: "Will not the Judge of all the earth do right?" (Gen. 18:25).

The Doctrine of the Intermediate State in History

Mention of the state of the human following death is found in the writings of Justin Martyr, Irenaeus, Tertullian, Origen, Ambrose, and Augustine. In the era of these Fathers, however, little was done to develop the doctrine of the intermediate state. Usually, the life that followed the death of the physical body was portrayed as a dreamy semiconscious existence that continued until the soul was reunited with the resurrection body.

Nevertheless, three traditional statements on this subject teach a responsive intermediate state. Thus: "During the time which intervenes between a man's death and the resurrection at the last, men's souls are reserved in secret storehouses at rest or in tribulation according to each soul's deserts" *Enchiridion,* Augustine (354-430); "Among the secret abodes of which Augustine speaks, we must also reckon heaven and hell. . . . The reason why a distinction is drawn between the time before and time after the resurrection is because before the resurrection they are there without the body whereas afterwards they are with the body" *Summa Theologica,* Thomas Aquinas (1224-1274); "The souls of the righteous, after their warfare is ended, obtain blessed rest where in joy they wait for the fruition of promised glory, and thus the final result is suspended till Christ the Redeemer appear" *The Institutes,* John Calvin (1509-1564).

Similarly, the *Westminster Confession of Faith* (1646) clearly gave place to a waiting period following death and prior to the believer's redemption or the sinner's judgment.

> The souls of the righteous, being made perfect in holiness, are received into the highest heavens, where they behold the face of God in light and glory, waiting for the full redemption of their bodies: and the souls of the wicked are cast into hell, where they remain in torments and utter darkness, reserved to the judgment of the great day. Beside these two places for souls separated from their bodies, the Scripture acknowledgeth none.

As we have noted, modern scholars remain cautious in their pronouncements regarding the intermediate state. A typical statement illustrates exemplary restraint:

> The period between death and the resurrection may be described as an existence better than our present one in that it is a "being with Christ." Yet it is not the Christian hope, and the reason is clear: it is an existence which still lies under the curse of sin. It is

man being with God, but lacking an element integral to his nature and without which he is incomplete, namely a body.[5]

Some Rejected Theories of the Intermediate State

Orthodox Protestantism lacks a complete and dogmatic doctrine of the intermediate state, but it does conclude that some teachings in this area are false.

The Doctrine of Purgatory

Most Protestants consider that the Roman Catholic doctrine of purgatory expands the intermediate state beyond scriptural warrant. The doctrine holds that at death all "ordinary Christians" are assigned to the fire of purgatory (as a state or condition more than as a place) to be purged from their sins. The "fire of purgatory does not differ from the fire of hell, except in point of duration." (Bellarmine). "Mortal" sin (sin against the law of God or the Church—of which almost all humans sooner or later are guilty) can be remitted in its eternal aspects by baptism, or an act of perfect contrition and confession. The remission of "venial" sin (minor sins committed without full intention or consent) is by temporary affliction of the soul. For these sins, good works such as almsgiving, penance, masses, and indulgences will reduce punishment in purgatory.

In the Catholic view, for those assured of ultimately reaching heaven, purgatory exists to make up for shortcomings of good works. As Gilmore comments, "The modern man does not believe he is wicked enough to deserve hell, but that he is sufficiently bad to require purgatory."[6] Some modern Catholics deny that purgatory is a place or condition of torment and horror, and they relate it to joy. They add, however, that to the degree that purification is needed, suffering is the tool that is used.

The doctrine of purgatory is a comparatively recent addition to Roman Catholic beliefs. Although both Ambrose (339-397) and Augustine (354-430) suggested preliminary versions, the doctrine was actually not fully defined until the Councils of Lyons (1274) and Florence (1439). The belief in purgatory was reaffirmed, and guidelines for its application were formulated, by the Council of Trent (1545-63).

Catholics hold that one remains in purgatory until purified, however long that may take. Purgatory is compared to an incubator that warms one up rather than an incinerator that burns one up. Catholic practice usually limits masses said on behalf of

---

5 Truett E. Bobo, *An Evangelical Theology of the Intermediate State*. Pasadena: Fuller Theological Seminary, 1978. Unpublished Doctor of Philosophy Dissertation, p. 335.

6 John Gilmore, *Probing Heaven*. Grand Rapids: Baker Book House, 1989, p. 139.

the deceased to a few years, although they may continue for decades. The soul in purgatory cannot help itself, but friends on earth, by prayers and the saying of masses, can shorten the duration of a soul's punishment. Tradition assigns to the Pope special jurisdiction over purgatory through the power of the keys, and thus he can offer indulgences to hasten the soul's release.

Bible-believing Protestants reject the doctrine of purgatory since its primary support is in 2 Maccabees 12:39-46, a book which most Protestants exclude from the biblical canon. Scriptures that are cited are considered not relevant (e.g., Isa. 4:4; Mic. 7:8; Zech. 9:11; Mal. 3:2-3; Matt. 3:11; 5:22, 25-26; 12:32; 1 Cor. 3:12-15; 1 Pet. 3:18-20; Jude 22-23; Rev. 21:27). Protestants point out that the doctrine of purgatory in its traditional form, makes death a threat, for even the devout Catholic must detour through purgatory on the way to Christ's presence.

The Protestant sees no need of purgatory, for he cites Scriptures such as: "By one sacrifice he has made perfect forever those who are being made holy" (Heb. 10:14); "Death has been swallowed up in victory" (1 Cor. 15:54); and "The blood of Jesus, his Son, purifies us from all sin" (1 John 1:7). It has been rightly said, "On the ground that the saving work of Christ is really finished, purgatory must be denied." The purgatory (i.e., cleansing, purging) of Calvary is the only one that counts.

The Doctrine of Soul Sleep

This doctrine holds that at death souls fall asleep and they do not awaken until the eternal state. Thus, the whole doctrine of the intermediate state is bypassed, but the second coming and the future judgments are not denied. At first glance those Scriptures that speak of death as a sleep seem to support this view—this topic was previously discussed. Notably, the heavenly messenger had declared to Daniel "Multitudes who sleep in the dust of the earth will awake: some to everlasting life, others to shame and everlasting contempt" (Dan. 12:2).

The logical simplicity of the soul sleep doctrine (which is given the technical name psychopannychy) has strong appeal, but it is not taught in the Bible as a whole. Scripture indicates that a human remains active and conscious in the afterlife. Soul sleep confuses the appearance of the body with the state of the soul. As Tertullian pointed out, "Souls do not sleep even when men are alive. It is the province of bodies to sleep." Sleep is a suitable image of death since death resembles sleep, but similarity of appearance is the only connection between death and sleep. Jesus rightly spoke of death as sleep because He was death's conqueror, and to Him death was no more permanent than a period of restful sleep.

Salvation in the Intermediate State

The claim that in the intermediate state those who died in their sins may yet be reconciled to God periodically has appeared. Origen in the third century and Schleiermacher in the nineteenth each hinted at this doctrine, and Universalists and Restorationists favor it. Often, it is spoken of as "second chance," or "second probation." The second chance doctrine denies that death ends the opportunity for decision. It should not be confused with the possibility of salvation during the tribulation.

Two verses in Peter are used to defend the second chance doctrine: "For this is the reason the gospel was preached even to those who are now dead" (1 Pet. 4:6); and "[Christ] went and preached to the spirits in prison" (1 Pet. 3:19). In context, however, the first text declares that preaching the gospel to humans who reject it and die in their sins is not in vain, for it validates God's judgment. The second text has already been discussed. Christ simply proclaimed His conquest of death. He did not offer freedom to imprisoned spirits, but He confirmed His power and victory and thus implied the inevitability of judgment.

Second chance supporters argue that an opportunity to accept the Lord after death would be the unevangelized's first chance, but Scripture teaches otherwise. "Man is destined to die once, and after that to face judgment" (Heb. 9:27); "now is the day of salvation" (2 Cor. 6:2). Paul points out that all humans have access to truths concerning God, for creation, conscience, and history each reveal Him. "For since the creation of the world God's invisible qualities—his eternal power and divine nature—have been clearly seen, being understood from what has been made, so that men are without excuse" (Rom. 1:20; cf. 1:18-2:16). Evangelistic efforts may fall short, but all humans have access to knowing God.

Communication With Those Who Have Died

Some cultures teach that the dead, particularly deceased ancestors, can communicate with living humans. These views usually associate with animistic beliefs. Ancestor spirits are the "living dead" who, as they are remembered by those still alive, remain a vital part of society. They are the "spiritual doubles" released through the decomposition of the body that follows death. Ancestor spirits are seen as embodying wisdom, and knowledge of both the past and the future. The loss of the body is a "good," and a transition to essential existence with new and greater powers. It is to be both expected and desired that these ancestor spirits will communicate with those alive on earth. They may speak directly through dreams, and indirectly through revelations and impressions to the medium or the shaman.

Scripture accepts the possibility of humans communicating with the dead, but it firmly prohibits the practice. Mediums and spiritists (or spiritualists) are under the judgment of God (cf. Lev. 20:6, 27; Deut. 18:11-12). The medium of Endor was able to "bring up" Samuel, but the event involved a rebel whom God had rejected (cf. 1 Sam. 28:6-25). Since Samuel's appearance in spirit form terrified the medium, clearly God had intervened.

On the other hand, communications claiming to be from the departed may be either human trickery or demonic impersonation. God's law instructed, "Do not turn to mediums or seek out spiritists, for you will be defiled by them" (Lev. 19:31). Isaiah taught that God's people should consult Him, not ancestral spirits. "When men tell you to consult mediums and spiritists, who whisper and mutter, should not a people inquire of their God? Why consult the dead on behalf of the living?" (Isa. 8:19).

God intends that death normally ends all relationships between the deceased and those alive on earth. Solomon wrote (though perhaps as a skeptic rather than a spokesman for divine truth), "The dead know nothing; they have no further reward, and even the memory of them is forgotten. Their love, their hate and their jealousy have long since vanished; never again will they have a part in anything that happens under the sun. . . . In the grave, where you are going, there is neither working nor planning nor knowledge nor wisdom" (Eccl. 9:6, 10). In the account in Luke 16:19-31 the rich man sought to send a message to those on earth only through the miracle of a resurrected Lazarus, and he had no suggestion of a spirit communication. The Psalmist described the dead as "those who go down to silence" (Psa. 115:17). Job predicted his anticipated death, "Only a few years will pass before I go on the journey of no return" (Job 16:22).

Scripture teaches that death totally removes a human from relating actively to the living, but it does not discourage wholesome memories. "The memory of the righteous will be a blessing, but the name of the wicked will rot" (Prov. 10:7). Remembering the life and teaching of a departed saint may significantly influence the living. "By faith Abel offered God a better sacrifice than Cain did. . . . And by faith he still speaks, even though he is dead" (Heb. 11:4). Abel, and the other heroes of faith of Hebrews, are models whose history—but not their surviving spirit—sends a vital message. "Therefore, since we are surrounded by such a great cloud of witnesses (or "with all these witnesses to faith around us like a cloud"—NEB) . . . Let us fix our eyes on Jesus, the author and perfecter of our faith" (Heb. 12:1-2). The Lord Jesus Christ, not dreams or spirit communications, is the believer's proper focus in his or her search for wisdom and truth.

Limbo and Prayers for the Dead

The doctrine of limbo is not biblical, and it is rejected by evangelicals, but it has been widely taught in traditional Catholicism. Most modern Catholics, however, usually ignore or outright reject this doctrine. The name "limbo" means "edge, fringe, or border." In Catholic tradition, limbo is the realm of those who do not deserve hell, but who fail to qualify for heaven. Typically, infants who die without baptism are assigned to limbo. There they are denied the happiness of saints, but spared the privations of sinners in hell. God thus avoids the injustice of either the unqualified in heaven or the undeserving in hell. Protestant evangelicals are likely to see limbo as a man-made theory, and they typically respond to the issues by referring them to God's sovereign goodness (cf. Gen. 18:25).

Prayers to be said for the dead are found in Jewish and Roman Catholic prayer books, and in some liturgical Protestant worship materials. Such prayers are not found in the Bible, however, for there the dead are seen to be in God's hands and beyond human intercession. The universal church includes the church triumphant (i.e., believers now in paradise), but believers alive on earth cannot become involved in the present lives of those now living in the life to come. Our privilege is limited to remembering the earthly life of those choice children of God who are now departed, and joyfully anticipating the future day when once more we will be united with them in His presence.

Reincarnation

This view associates particularly with eastern religions. It holds that humans are given a new identity at death, and that they are reborn as a new creature that may be another human, or even a god, but it could be an animal. Through successive rebirths, which may extend to hundreds of thousands, the human is gradually purified and thus "saved."

Obviously, Scripture teaches that there is no program for humans to save themselves, and that there is no chance for salvation beyond this life. Humans retain their identity in the after life, and they do not become other people or other creatures.

SEVEN

The Tribulation Period: Part 1

The tribulation (or "distress" NIV) is the next major event that God has scheduled for this earth. Scripture has much to say about this coming catastrophe, so that more biblical prophecies pertain to the tribulation than to any other period. The futurist holds that except for the rapture, all unfulfilled prophecies await the tribulation period or thereafter.

Biblical Names for the Tribulation

The expression "tribulation period" is not in the Bible, and in the NIV the word "tribulation" is used only once to designate the end time chaos (cf. Rev. 7:14). Jesus in the KJV four times spoke of tribulation, but as we have noted (p. 70), His word *thlipsis* is rendered "distress." The tribulation identifies with Daniel's seventieth 'seven' (or "week" —KJV) (cf. Matt. 24:15, 21; Dan. 9:27). Daniel's reference provides a time frame for God's prophecy through Moses, "When you are in distress [tribulation, —KJV; Heb. *tsar*] and all these things have happened to you, then in later days you will return to the LORD your God and obey him" (Deut. 4:30). (*tsar* [TSAR]: a tight place, anguish, affliction, distress, tribulation). This end time season warrants the usage of the expression "tribulation period."[1]

The English word "tribulation" is from the Latin *tribulum*, the threshing-sledge which was repeatedly drawn over heaps of gathered sheaves to press the grain out of the heads. In a second step, winnowing separated the grain from the chaff.

Scripture refers to the tribulation period by a variety of expressions including the following:

His wrath (indignation, fury). This term, or its synonyms, is the most common biblical name for the tribulation. The word "wrath" translates at least four words in Hebrew. "The earth will shake from its place at the wrath [Heb. *'ebrah*] of the LORD Almighty" (Isa. 13:13, cf. Zeph. 1:15:18); "The LORD is

---

1 Some suggest that the expression "seventieth week" would be more scriptural than "tribulation period." In fact, Daniel identifies the seventieth 'seven' (week) only as the 'seven' that comes after seven plus sixty-two 'sevens,' and he avoids naming it.

angry with all nations; his wrath [Heb. *chemah*] is upon all their armies" (Isa. 34:2, cf. 63:3); "I am going to tell you what will happen later in the time of wrath [Heb. *za'am*] ... the appointed time of the end" (Dan. 8:19, cf. Isa. 26:20; Jer. 10:10); "He will crush kings on the day of his wrath [Heb. *'aph*]" (Psa. 110:5). Translations are: *'ebrah* [eb-AW]: anger, rage, wrath, passionate outburst; *chemah* [khay-MAH]: heat, anger, hot displeasure, fury, rage, wrath; *za'am* [ZAH-am]: state of being angry, wrath, rage, indignation; *'aph* [AF]: the nose, a snort in passionate anger, anger, fierceness of anger.

The Greek New Testament uses two words: "Jesus . . . rescues us from the coming wrath [Gk. *orgee*]" (1 Thess. 1:10, cf. 1 Thess. 5:9, Rev. 6:16, etc.); "I saw in heaven . . . seven angels with the seven last plagues—last, because with them God's wrath [Gk. *thumos*] is completed" (Rev. 15:1, cf. Rev. 14:10, 14:19, 15:7, 16:1). These words may be combined: "He treads the winepress of the fury [Gk. *thumos*] of the wrath [Gk. *orgee*] of God Almighty" (Rev. 19:15, cf. 16:19). Lexicons render these words: *orgee* (or-GAY): violent emotion, ire, anger, abhorrence, indignation, wrath; *thumos* [thoo-MOS]: anger at white heat, boiling anger, fierceness, indignation, wrath.

time of trouble for Jacob. "How awful that day will be! None will be like it. It will be a time of trouble for Jacob, but he will be saved out of it" (Jer. 30:7). These words describe the Babylonian captivity as the near disaster, but the greater fulfilment is the tribulation. Israel will be saved by Christ's Armageddon victory and His millennial rule. In that day it will be said of the Israelites, "No longer will foreigners enslave them. Instead, they will serve the LORD their God and David their king . . . 'All who devour you will be devoured; all your enemies will go into exile'" (Jer. 30:8-9, 16).

a time of distress (or trouble). "There will be a time of distress [Heb. *tsarah*] such as had not happened from the beginning of nations" (Dan. 12:1, (*tsarah* [tsaw-RAW]: adversity, affliction, anguish, distress, tribulation. This word is the feminine of *tsar* which is used in Deuteronomy 4:30.) Zephaniah wrote of the "great day of the LORD" and described it as "a day of distress [*mutsaq*]" (Zech. 1:15). (*mutsaq* [muts-ACK]: to be under pressure or constraint, to be distressed).

The use of "distress" to replace "tribulation" in Jesus' Olivet Discourse has been discussed (see preceding page).

the Lord's day of vengeance. "For the LORD has a day of vengeance, a year of retribution, to uphold Zion's cause" (Isa. 34:8). During the tribulation, while Satan pours out his wrath upon God's people—the Jews; God simultaneously pours out His judgmental wrath upon Satan's citizens—rebellious sinners.

the great day of God's wrath. "Hide us from the face of him who sits on the throne and from the wrath of the Lamb! For the great day of their wrath [Gk. *orgee*] has come, and who can stand?" (Rev. 6:16-17). Father and Son share in the outpouring of divine wrath. When tribulation's victims declare "the great day of their wrath has come" they acknowledge that they are feeling the outcome of God's wrath against humans. Ten times in Revelation, God is depicted as acting in wrath: 6:16, 17; 11:18; 14:10, 19; 15:1, 7; 16:1, 19; 19:15. God's wrath may require time to gain momentum. The rain began the day that Noah entered the ark, but it was days or weeks before floods drowned all of earth's creatures.

the day of the LORD: This phrase will be discussed later.

Other terms used to denote the tribulation include: **dreadful** (Mal. 4:5); **anguish, trouble, ruin, darkness, gloom, clouds, blackness** (these seven terms are all in Zechariah 1:15); **calamity** (Matt. 24:22), and **horror** (Mark 13:19).

The Nature of the Tribulation

As we have noted, Jesus' word for the tribulation in four passages in His Olivet Discourse was *thlipsis* (THLIP-sis) meaning: pressure, or figuratively oppression, affliction, distress or tribulation. In the NIV this word is translated as "distress," and only in Revelation 7:14 is it given as "tribulation." In forty other New Testament references, *thlipsis* is used as a general term to speak of the pains of war, onerous circumstances, birth pains, the sufferings of the persecuted, and the sufferings of Jesus (cf. Col. 1:24). These usages confirm that God's plan to deal with human rebels is to send a period of oppressive distress upon them.

Many Scriptures that do not use the word tribulation speak of this latter day calamitous time:

> The earth will shake from its place at the wrath of the LORD Almighty, in the day of his burning anger (Isa. 13:13); The great day of the LORD is near . . . that day will be a day of wrath, a day of distress and anguish, a day of trouble and ruin, a day of darkness and gloom . . . he will make a sudden end of all who live in the earth (Zeph. 1:14-15, 18); If anyone worships the beast . . . he, too, will drink of the wine of God's fury, which has been poured full strength into the cup of his wrath (Rev. 14:9-10).

The seven-year tribulation is God's ultimate strategy to achieve the salvation of as many humans as possible. In this final harvest time, God causes mankind's earthly home to become hostile; while simultaneously He allows Satan to launch Antichrist's harsh demands and fierce persecutions. In place of loving forbearance, God responds to human rebels in outpoured wrath. For multitudes, violence and terror succeed where mercy and grace have not, and they become a vast company of tribulation saints. Others, even under these drastic events, continue to defy God and thus suffer destruction. The tribulation concludes, with heaven's citizens greatly increased in number, and all surviving humans on earth ready to enter the millennium as believers.

The tribulation is a seven-year period

The Book of Revelation describes the tribulation in detail but it does not specify a seven-year period. We have noted (p. 70), however, that the tribulation extends for seven years as Daniel's seventieth 'seven.' Many Scriptures speak of the tribulation, but only Daniel reveals its seven-year duration (cf. Dan. 9:27). Daniel wrote, "in the middle of the 'seven' [the ruler who will come] . . . will set up an abomination that causes desolation" (v. 27). Jesus used this phrase to say, "When you see standing in the holy place the abomination that causes desolation . . . then there will be great distress [tribulation --KJV]" (Matt. 24:15, 21). The "abomination" marks the beginning of the second half of a seven-year period, and though the first half is unnamed, the second three and one-half year period is a time of "great tribulation."

The time period stressed in Revelation is three and one-half years—depicted by three different formulas in five Biblical references (see p. 134). At least four of the references (Gentiles trample Jerusalem, Antichrist wars with saints, Jews preserved in desert [two verses]) are usually thought to concern the second half of the seven-year period. The fifth reference concerns the duration of the ministry of the two witnesses (Rev. 11:3), and if the 1,260 days are prior to the abomination, the full seven-years of the tribulation are specifically programmed.

Scripture is very clear, however, that the seven-year period begins when the ruler "will confirm a covenant with many for one 'seven'" (Dan. 9:27). Events proceed, outwardly at least, smoothly and favorably for the first three and one-half years. The watchword for this period is "Peace and safety" (1 Thess. 5:3). This auspicious beginning largely explains the mass acclaim and submission to Antichrist of the second three and one-half years. There is as much time before the abomination as after it, and the two periods total seven years.

The Day of The LORD[2] and the Tribulation

We have noted that Zechariah 1:14-18 sees the end-time tribulation as the "great day of the LORD." In 1 Thessalonians 5:2

---

2 In the eighteen occurrences in the Old Testament the form is "Day of the LORD" since the expression translates "Day of Jehovah [or Yahweh]." (cf. *adonai* [ad-own-I] = Lord) The New Testament form in the six occurrence is "Day of the Lord" since there are no other Greek words for Lord to be distinguished. (Gk. *kurios* [KUR-i-os] = Lord).

"day of the Lord" similarly refers to the tribulation: "The day of the Lord will come like a thief in the night." In context, 1 Thessalonians 4:13- 5:11 is discussing the rapture as the means of deliverance from the scheduled tribulation (cf. 4:17). Paul affirms: "For God did not appoint us to suffer wrath" (5:9).

The expression "day of the LORD" was used anciently to speak of a sovereign's day of conquest. It portrayed a mighty warrior-king who would complete a major conquest in a single day by achieving a swift and decisive victory over his enemies. "The day of the LORD" occurs twenty-four times in Scripture (NIV), and near variants (day of God, day of Christ, His day, the day), bring the total to thirty-one references. The occasions that these identify may be discussed in chronological order:

1. **Past military judgments.** Nations who suffered a day of the LORD by a military stroke include: *ISRAEL* (conquered by Assyrians in eighth century) "Why do you long for the day of the LORD? That day will be darkness, not light. . . . I will send you into exile beyond Damascus" (Amos 5:18, 27); *JUDAH* (conquered by Babylon in sixth century) "The day of the LORD is near. . . . At that time I will search Jerusalem . . . and punish those who are complacent" (Zeph. 1:7, 12); *BABYLON* (fell to Medo-Persia in the sixth century) "Wail, for the day of the LORD is near; it will come like destruction from the Almighty. Because of this, all hands will go limp, every man's heart will melt" (Isa. 13:6-7); (cf. also, *EGYPT* [Ezek. 30:3]; *EDOM* [Oba. 15]).

2. **The end time tribulation.** We have already noted and commented on 1 Thessalonians 5:2-3. In addition, Paul wrote, "[Do not become] alarmed by some prophecy, report or letter . . . saying that the day of the Lord has already come" (2 Thess. 2:2). The "day of the LORD" prophecies against Judah and Edom in their larger application extend to all nations, and in this secondary sense depict the end time tribulation (cf. Zeph. 1:14, 18; Oba. 8, 10, 15).

3. **The second coming at Armageddon.** "The day of the LORD is coming. . . . a large and mighty army comes. . . . Before them the earth shakes, the sky trembles, the sun and moon are darkened, and the stars no longer shine" (Joel 2:1-2, 10); "Multitudes, multitudes in the valley of decision! For the day of the LORD is near in the valley of decision" (Joel 3:14); "A day of the LORD is coming when . . . I will gather all the nations to Jerusalem to fight against it; the city will be taken . . . Then the LORD will go out and fight against those nations" (Zech. 14:1-3; cf. also Mal. 4:5; Rev. 16:13-14).

4. **The judgments of God's court.** "Hand this man over to Satan, so that the sinful nature may be destroyed and his spirit

saved on the day of the Lord" (1 Cor. 5:5); "You will come to understand fully that you can boast of us just as we will boast of you in the day of the Lord Jesus" (2 Cor. 1:14; cf. also Phil. 2:16); "He who began a good work in you will carry it on to completion until the day of Christ Jesus" (Phil. 1:6);

5. **The millennium or kingdom age.** "The day of the LORD is near for all nations . . . and the house of Jacob will possess its inheritance. . . . Deliverers will go up on Mount Zion . . . [and] the kingdom will be the LORD's" (Oba. 15, 17, 21).

6. **The renovation of the earth by fire.** "The day of the Lord will come like a thief. The heavens will disappear with a roar; the elements will be destroyed by fire, and the earth and everything in it will be laid bare" (2 Pet. 3:10).

As prior comments establish, "day of the Lord" indeed denotes the seven-year tribulation, but it also identifies other occasions. In these uses, the expression does not merely identify a specific chronological event or time interval, but rather it speaks of God's methodology. It describes God at work intervening in human lives, whether pouring out His wrath upon Satan's citizens, or renewing heaven and earth to establish the eternal age. Thus, "day of the Lord" depicts God's unleashing of a cataclysmic stroke to fulfil "His day" in earthly events. As He implements His day, God achieves a further stage in the outworking of His divine plan for mankind.

God's Purposes in the Tribulation

The tribulation is God's final program to rescue sinners from Satan's clutches. His tribulation purposes include:

1. **To glean Gentile converts.** Thus, "Before me was a great multitude that no one could count, from every nation, tribe, people and language, standing before the throne and in front of the lamb. They were wearing white robes and were holding palm branches. . . . These are they who have come out of the great tribulation; they have washed their robes and made them white in the blood of the Lamb" (Rev. 7:9, 14).

2. **To bring Israel to Himself.** Ezekiel wrote, "As I judged your fathers in the desert of the land of Egypt, so I will judge you, declares the Sovereign LORD. I will take note of you as you pass under my rod, and I will bring you into the bond of the covenant. I will purge you of those who revolt and rebel against me" (Ezek. 20:36-38). God revealed His intentions to Jeremiah, "Though I completely destroy all the nations . . . I will not completely destroy you. I will discipline you but only with justice" (Jer. 30:11). Zechariah wrote of disasters that would fall upon the Jewish people and result in the death of two-thirds of the nation. He continued, "One-third will be

left. . . . This third I will bring into the fire; I will refine them like silver and test them like gold. They will call on my name and I will answer them" (Zech. 13:8-9). Previously, Zechariah had prophesied the outpouring of God's grace so that the Jews would penitently look upon "the one they have pierced"—their crucified Messiah (cf. Zech. 12:9-11).

3. **To deal with rebellious humanity.** God declared, "I will punish the world for its evil, the wicked for their sins" (Isa. 13:11). God's wrath is directed toward "kings of the earth, the princes, the generals, the rich, the mighty, every slave, and every free man" (cf. Rev. 6:15-17). Jesus described His role, "When the Son of Man comes in his glory . . . he will sit on his throne. . . . All the nations will be gathered before him. . . . He will put the sheep on his right and the goats on his left. Then the King will say . . . to those on his left, Depart from me, you who are cursed" (Matt. 25:31-34, 41).

4. **To select millennial citizens.** To those on His right Christ says, "Come, you who are blessed by my Father; take your inheritance, the kingdom prepared for you" (Matt. 25:34). Jesus interpreted the parable of the wheat and the weeds, "At the end of the age [the] Son of Man will send out his angels, and they will weed out of his kingdom everything that causes sin. . . . Then the righteous will shine like the sun in the kingdom of their Father" (Matt. 13:40-41, 43). At Armageddon "the kings of the earth and their armies" will be "killed with the sword that came out of the mouth of the rider on the horse [i.e., Jesus Christ]" (Rev. 19:21). Humans not identifying with Antichrist become millennial citizens. Micah prophesied, "In the last days the mountain of the LORD's temple will be established . . . and peoples will stream to it. Many nations will come and say, 'Come, let us go up to the mountain of the LORD'" (Mic. 4:1-2).

5. **To deal with Satan.** At mid-tribulation, Satan will be cast down to earth. "The great dragon was hurled down—that ancient serpent called the devil or Satan, who leads the whole world astray. He was hurled to the earth, and his angels with him" (Rev. 12:9). Following Armageddon, he will be bound and thrown into the abyss, which will be "locked and sealed . . . over him, to keep him from deceiving the nations anymore until the thousand years [are] ended" (Rev. 20:3).

The Tribulation and Daniel's Seventieth Week

In Chapter 9 of Daniel, which has been called "the backbone of Bible chronology," God revealed that He had scheduled a timed series of successive events upon His people. In the final seven years of this period, which were to be detached from those preceding, there would be a treacherous ruling prince and the blasphemous "abomination that causes desolation." The events of this seventieth week are described in detail in the Olivet Discourse (Matthew chapters 24 and 25), and in the Book of Revelation (chapters 4 through 19).

We have noted that Daniel's "weeks" or "sevens" are literally "heptads" (Heb. *shabua* [shaw-BOO-ah]) which are seven year intervals, just as a decade is a ten-year interval. All but the final seven years of the 490 years that they identify relate to the time of the Jews' restoration from captivity following Daniel's lifetime. The "seventy sevens" specifically relate to Israel (your people) and to Jerusalem (your holy city), and not to a timed sequence for the church.

The first sixty-nine weeks

God's plan and the goals that He intended become evident in an annotated and expanded version of Daniel 9:24:

> Seventy 'sevens' [or "heptads" totaling 490 years] are decreed for your people [the Jews] and your holy city [Jerusalem] [1] to finish transgression [end Israel's willful rejection of their Messiah], [2] to put an end to sin [permanently end Israel's secular humanistic life patterns], [3] to atone for wickedness [Israel in penitence to be reconciled to the One "whom they have pierced"], [4] to bring in everlasting righteousness [establish Christ's millennial reign. Christian believers enjoy Christ's imputed righteousness (Rom. 3:21) but everlasting righteousness does not yet rule the moral universe], [5] to seal up vision and prophecy [fulfill all prophecies concerning national Israel and make future prophecies unnecessary] and [6] to anoint the most holy [establish Jesus as their anointed Messiah and consecrate the temple for worship that it may be filled with the divine shekinah].

As the chronology proceeds, there is a break after 49 years. Scripture does not explain the reason for the division of the weeks into 7 + 62, though 49 years may have seen notable achievements in the temple and city's restoration. Also, after 49 years there may have been a memorable year of Jubilee. The first 49 restorative years are described in Daniel 9:25

> Know and understand this: From the issuing of the decree to restore and rebuild Jerusalem [identified as the edict of Artaxerxes Longimanus in 445 B.C., cf. Ezra 7:17-25] until the Anointed One [Christ], the ruler, comes, there will be seven 'sevens' [49 years], and sixty-two 'sevens' [434 years, total 49 + 434 =483 years]. It [Jerusalem] will be rebuilt with streets and a trench [lit. "that which has been dug" but some versions translate "wall"—a protecting escarpment (a low cliff) is implied], but in times of trouble [cf. Samaritan opposition].

The next break in the chronology is after 69 "sevens" when Jesus Christ is crucified (cut off)—commonly dated in A.D. 32. According to Sir Robert Anderson's classic chronology, the day of Christ's triumphal entry was the last day of the 69th week. He dated the edict of Artaxerxes Longimanus to restore temple worship and establish government in the land (cf. Ezra 7:17-19, 25) as March 14, 445 B.C. He dated the triumphal entry as April 6, A.D. 32. In this dating, the intervening period was 476 years and 24 days. Thus, the elapsed time in days was {[476 x 365] = [173,740 days] + {24 days} + leap years {116 days} = 173,880 days. In turn, the 69 "sevens" of the prophetic period, with 360 day years, would total {69 x 7 x 360} = 173,880 days.

In A.D. 70, fewer than four decades after Christ's crucifixion, Jerusalem fell to the invading Roman army. These events are described in Daniel 9:26

> After the sixty-two 'sevens' [plus the first 7 sevens for a total of 69 'sevens' or 483 years] the Anointed One will be cut off [suffer the death penalty] and will have nothing [perhaps because He was forsaken by the Father and His disciples, or perhaps these words should be rendered, "but not for himself"]. The people of the ruler who will come will destroy the city [since the Romans were the people who destroyed the city, the future ruler {Antichrist} will relate to the Roman Empire] and the sanctuary. The end will come like a flood: War will continue until the end, and desolations have been decreed [these words suggest both what the Romans did to Jerusalem, and what Antichrist will yet do].

The seventieth 'week'

Daniel's account pauses after the seventh "seven," and after the next sixty-two—that is, after the sixty-ninth. By then Messiah is crucified, Jerusalem destroyed, and the nation desolate. The seventieth "seven" begins with a ruler making a seven-year covenant with "many"—evidently Jewish leaders. After the sixty-ninth "seven" the sanctuary is destroyed, but by the seventieth it is rebuilt and again in use. Between the sixty-ninth and seventieth "seven" are the centuries of Jewish dispersion, their return, and the reestablishment of their institutions. Also, during this era is the extended period of the church age. The rapture of the church and Antichrist's covenant with Israel, clears the way for God to proceed with the final seven years.

In spite of the long gap of time between the sixty-ninth and seventieth "seven," the seventy weeks are a connected whole. What prevailed at the end of sixty-nine "sevens" will again prevail as the seventieth "seven" begins. Not only will there be a State of Israel, but also a major political power parallel to ancient Imperial Rome. This major political power may well be recognized as the Revived Roman Empire.

The seventieth week is described in Daniel 9:27—

> He [the subject is now the future ruler—Antichrist] will confirm a covenant with many[3] [representatives of the Jews] for one 'seven' [seven years]. In the middle of the 'seven' [after three and

---

3 Note that the acceptance of the covenant is not unanimous. It is said to be the only Bible covenant that is not received by the whole nation.

one half years] he will put an end to sacrifice and offering [the Jewish worship system honoring the LORD [Jehovah or Yahweh]. And on a wing [or possibly, the summit] of the temple he will set up an abomination that causes desolation [such as an idolatrous image] until the end that is decreed is poured out on him [Armageddon]. One version reads, "Upon the wing [of the temple] there will be idols of the desolator."

In chapter 9, Daniel depicts a seven-year tribulation, but he had previously noted that Antichrist would persecute the Jews for only half of this time. "The saints [these are Jews] will be handed over to him for a time [1 year], times [2 years] and half a time [6 months]" (Dan. 7:25). The three and one-half year interval occurs six times in Revelation. It is given as 42 months for the time that the Gentiles would trample the holy city (11:2), or the time that Antichrist would utter blasphemies and make war with the saints (13:5-8); it is given as 1,260 days (prophetic months have exactly 30 days) for the time that the two witnesses minister (11:3), or the duration of the wilderness refuge that God provides the woman (the Jews) (12:6), and this latter event is also given as "time, times and half a time" (12:14).

The seven-year tribulation will consist of two three and one-half year periods, one very different from the other. Paul depicts the beginning and middle of the seven years: "While people are saying, 'Peace and safety,' destruction will come on them suddenly, as labor pains on a pregnant woman" (1 Thess. 5:3). Antichrist's seven-year covenant provides for "Peace and safety" only until "the middle of the 'seven'." At that time he treacherously unleashes vicious persecution upon the Jews who have renewed their Old Testament worship practices (cf. Dan. 9:27).

Antichrist's destruction of the Jews ends with Jesus' second coming. Jesus spoke of a shortening of the tribulation. "If those days had not been cut short, no one would survive, but for the sake of the elect those days will be shortened" (Matt. 24:22, cf. Mark 13:20). Since the duration of the tribulation is given in Scripture six times, however, the reduction of the number of days seems unlikely. Other possibilities include, 1) the shortening will be nominal (cf. The disciples were spoken of as the "eleven" [Mark 16:14], although only ten were present.), 2) the individual days are shortened in duration with fewer than normal hours—such an outcome associates with the fourth trumpet, 3) Jesus was affirming that only the latter half of Daniel's seventieth week would involve active destructive tribulation.

The Onset of the Tribulation

The seven-year tribulation period begins with Antichrist's covenant, but there are also specific acts by God. As Satan gears up for his attacks, God likewise implements His strategies.

Antichrist's covenant with the Jews

The tribulation is launched by Antichrist's covenant with Israel. "[Antichrist] will confirm a covenant with many for one 'seven'" (Dan. 9:27). Evidently Israel's borders are guaranteed, Israel is assigned total control of the land, and the resumption of temple worship is approved. Isaiah describes this covenant, perhaps in secondary fulfilment, in chilling terms:

> Hear the word of the Lord, you scoffers who rule this people in Jerusalem. You boast, We have entered into a covenant with death, with the grave we have made an agreement. When an overwhelming scourge sweeps by, it cannot touch us, for we have made a lie our refuge and falsehood our hiding place.... Your covenant with death will be annulled. . . . When the overwhelming scourge sweeps by, you will be beaten down by it (Isa. 28:14-15, 18).

The covenant that Israel's leaders so proudly exhibit is soon cruelly violated.

The imagery of the little horn of Daniel 7 suggests that at the outset Antichrist will be a minor figure who represents a confederacy of nations with links to the ancient Roman Empire. Nevertheless, he has sufficient status that, on behalf of the confederacy, he can negotiate a supposedly binding treaty with Israel. Scripture gives no terms for the treaty, but we can assume that, in addition to favoring Israel, it will purport to foster global peace through a settlement of Middle East hostilities. Israel would surely honor as her protector and benefactor the one bringing her such a treaty.

Israel's tribulation temple

Since Antichrist's covenant will favor the revival of Israel's sacrificial system of worship, the tribulation will see a structure or center where traditional Old Testament sacrifices are offered. Though Scripture gives no account of the source of such a temple, if it is to be functioning during the tribulation period, its planning and construction will likely be prior to that time. Students of prophecy monitor with great interest proposals and discussions for the rebuilding of Israel's temple.

In the decades since Israel captured the Temple Mount in 1967, Israeli organizations have become involved in activities related to the rebuilding the temple. Their projects have included schools for training priests in Old Testament rituals, tracing family lines to find those who qualify for the priesthood, researching the correct temple site, reconstructing the ritual implements that are required in sacrificial worship, preparing vestments for priests, and attempting to breed a strain of cattle to provide a sacrificial red heifer. A virtually "perfect" animal, with every hair the appropriate color, is required for the ashes that produce the water of cleansing (cf. Num. 19:1-10).

Since there is no known account of the destruction of the ark of the covenant, some believe it still exists on earth, and they continue to promote efforts to search for it. Traditions speak of hiding places in Ethiopia or in tunnels in the Temple Mount, and some suggest that both the original and a replica survive. Though a new ark could be built, the finding of the original ark would provide great incentive to rebuild the temple, for it was the transferred ark that assured continuity between the first and second temples. Some Christian observers hold that God raptured the ark at the temple's destruction in A.D. 70, and it was this ark that John saw in heaven (cf. Rev. 11:19).

God's acts of judgment

Daniel enjoyed a vision of God, the divine Judge, during the tribulation period.

> **The Ancient of Days took his seat. His clothing was as white as snow.... His throne was flaming with fire.... Thousands upon thousands attended him.... The court was seated, and the books were opened (Dan. 7:9-10).**

Immediately following this vision of the heavenly Judge, Daniel's view returned to events on earth, including the end of the tribulation and Antichrist's destruction. He thus links the Judge and the tribulation. The books that were opened (v. 10) involved the people of that generation, just as the open books at the great white throne judgment (Rev. 20:12) will involve those who at that time are summoned before God's judgment throne.

The Book of Revelation describes God's judgmental acts during the tribulation under the figures of 7 seals, 7 trumpets, and 7 bowls (vials). These events depict the result of God's plan being outworked, and as the seals are broken, the trumpets sounded, and the bowls poured out, He adds whatever was symbolized to His arsenal of weapons against Satan's subjects. Since the fifth and seventh seals, and the seventh trumpet and seventh bowl are proclamations, the symbols actually depict only seventeen judgments. When these judgments are concluded, man's environment is in shambles and earth's population is decimated.

There is a logical order to the seals, trumpets, and bowls, and each one is assigned a sequence number. The explicit purpose of the seventh seal was to prepare the way for the seven angels with the seven trumpets (cf. Rev. 8:1-2). The finality of the seven bowls is stressed, "I saw . . . seven angels with the seven last plagues—last, because with them God's wrath is completed" (Rev. 15:1). Thus, the tribulation provides for a beginning and an ending of a series of twenty-one divine enactments. Scripture reports them in sequence, but God would be free to use two or more concurrently, and if He chose, to use them randomly. It can be expected that the disciplinary judgments will require a span of time just as it did for the ten plagues upon Egypt.

The seven seals (Rev. 6:1-17; 8:1) portray God's preliminary strokes of tribulation judgments. They are modes by which God works, and their effects are felt shortly after the seven-year period begins. The seals were personally opened by Jesus, the divine Lamb who had been slain. They included,

1) **The white horse**—Antichrist, as a counterfeit Christ, begins his seven-year rule by deceptive diplomacy and progressive conquest. He thus apparently succeeeds in achieving a false peace. In contrast, Christ will conquer by a single stroke. Daniel's prediction of a future ruler (commonly seen as Antiochus Epiphanes who ruled 175-164 B.C.) applies as a type of Antichrist: "He will cause deceit to prosper, and . . . when they feel secure, he will destroy many" (Dan. 8:25).

2) **The red horse**—By his "power to take peace from the earth" (Rev. 6:4) he unleashes anarchy, warfare, and bloodshed. These outcomes reflect the policies of the rider on the white horse. Jesus had predicted, "wars and rumors of wars" (Matt. 24:6). Since God was sovereignly in control, these riders were "given" objects (a crown, a large sword).

3) **The black horse**—Famine, deprivation, and suffering resulting from the warfare. Rationing, with up to 1,000% inflation is indicated, but some luxuries are left untouched.

4) **The pale** (Gk. *chloros*) **horse**—The unleashing of Death and Hades to claim the body and soul of one-fourth of mankind. (*chloros* [khlo-ROS]: pale, greenish, ashen, dun-colored)

5) **Souls under the altar**—Antichrist's martyrs—tribulation citizens who had paid the price for denying him, are now seen at the place of sacrifice. Jesus had said, "You will be handed over to be persecuted and put to death" (Matt. 24:9).

6) **Cosmic upheavals**—Six prior catastrophic events will lead up to the seventh bowl judgment (cf. Rev. 16:17-21) and the preparation for the millennium. Peter quoted Joel's prophecy concerning these events (cf. Acts 2:17-20).

7) **Silence**—An ominous period of foreboding and "the silence of solemn worship"[4] prior to the sounding of the seven trumpets. The silence gives opportunity for the prayers of the saints to be featured (cf. Rev. 8:3-4).

---

4   Ed Hinson, *Earth's Final Hour.* Eugene: Harvest House Publishers, 1999, p. 129. Hinson compares the events at this time to those of temple ritual after the offering of a sacrificial lamb. At that time, priests would fuel an incense censer from the golden altar and offer incense and also distribute coals in a golden bowl. During these solemn ceremonies, deep silence would prevail.

The seven seals proclaim that Jesus Christ has His program of outpoured judgments, but not apart from a loving sensitivity to those who react to their misery by responding to Him.

The Two Witnesses and the 144,000

The two witnesses, as their name implies, are to be a voice for God during the era of the Antichrist and the False Prophet. The 144,000 are identified as "servants," and "they [who] follow the Lamb wherever he goes" (Rev. 14:4). That the description of the "great multitude . . . who have come out of the great tribulation" directly follows the account of the appointment of the 144,000 strongly suggests that these servants were soul-winning evangelists (cf. Rev. 7:9-17). Also, they are called "firstfruits" (Rev. 14:4), implying that they themselves were converts at the beginning of the tribulation. During both the years of deceptive "peace and safety," and the years of "great tribulation," God will maintain His agents on earth. They will be there to lead to Him those who penitently respond to God's judgmental acts.

Scripture does not specify the time when these ministries begin. The fact that the two witnesses prophesy 1,260 days (Rev. 11:3) strongly suggests that they identify with either the first or last half of the tribulation. Since the time span of 1,260 days immediately follows the designation of 42 months (Rev. 11:2), many feel that the same three and one-half year period is indicated. This view would depict the two witnesses, and probably the 144,000, surviving and ministering during the final three and one-half years of tribulation. These ministries would be in spite of Antichrist's fierce persecutions and God's outpoured wrath.

A brief comment by Stanley Horton favors the above view. Horton speaks of the seven years and he assigns the forty-two months—1,260 days—to "probably the latter half."[5] In a more extended discussion, Mark Hitchcock cites Revelation 11:1-3, and he comments,

> **The two witnesses will minister during the same forty-two month or three-and-a-half-year period that the temple is being trampled by the nations. This period of time is clearly the last half of the tribulation.[6]**

The alternate view places the two witnesses and the 144,000 in the first three and one-half years. It holds that it is the death of the witnesses that triggers the tribulation's outpouring of wrath. This view is supported by Tim LaHaye who wrote, "These two witnesses are . . . here to preach and witness during the entire

5 Stanley M. Horton, *Ultimate Victory*. Springfield: Gospel Publishing House, 1991, p. 156
6 Mark Hitchcock, *The Complete Book of Bible Prophecy*. Wheaton: Tyndale House Publishers, 1999, p. 123.

first half of the tribulation."[7] Charles Ryrie wrote, "Two powerful witnesses will be active during the first part of the tribulation
. . . Antichrist finally kills them at the midpoint of the tribulation."[8] It would appear that there is greater logical support to assign the witnesses to the first three-and-one-half years, but the
conclusion must be based on Scripture rather than logic. Thus,
Mark Hitchcock's linking of the witnesses with Revelation
11:1-3 deserves careful attention.

Gog and the Armies of Magog War Against Israel

Chapters 38 and 39 of Ezekiel describe this major end time
war involving Israel. These chapters provide the sixth and final
prophecy of Israel's future that God gave Ezekiel on the eve of
the arrival of news of Babylon's conquest of Jerusalem. Most of
the account consists of a prophetic denunciation of "Gog, of the
land of Magog" and the celebration of Israel's deliverance from
his attack. The prophecy depicts Gog's war as a Gentile effort to
conquer Israel in the end time, though the war is not dated.

Evidence that Gog's war is a tribulation event

Suggestions for the time of Gog's war include: prior to the
tribulation, during the tribulation, in an interval between the
tribulation and the millennium, or during the millennium. Evidences that Gog's war is during the tribulation are:

1) The time reference that is given points to the tribulation. "After many days . . . in future [Heb. *achariyth*] years you will invade a land" (Ezek. 38:8). (*achariyth* [akh-ar-EETH]: last,
end, hence the future). The last opportunity for the nations
to relate to one another as they do now will be during the
tribulation.

2) Israel is depicted as living in her land in peaceful and secure
affluence. Antichrist's tribulation covenant will temporarily
create such circumstances.

3) This event is prior to the Israelites' national penitence and acceptance of their Messiah which occurs at Armageddon
which is at tribulation's end. At this time they recognize God
only to the degree that His holy name is no longer profaned
(cf. 39:7). Thus, the victory of Gog's war leaves the nation
with an upgraded, but still nominal, acknowledgment of
their God. The war finds a nation representing Israel in the
land, but they are there basically on a secular basis and not
as end time penitents (cf. Deut. 30:4-8).

7 Tim LaHaye, *Rapture Under Attack*. Sisters: Multnomah Publishers Inc.,
   1998, p. 61.
8 Charles Ryrie, *Countdown to Armageddon*. Eugene: Harvest House Publishers, 1999, pp. 177-178.

4) Gog's war could not be either in an interval after the tribulation or during the millennium because at Armageddon Christ comes as conqueror to "strike down the nations" and "rule them with an iron scepter" (Rev. 19:15). All human rebels are destroyed at Armageddon and there are no more predator type humans until Satan's release.

5) Gog's war is distinct from Gog and Magog's threat to Jerusalem at the close of the millennium (Rev. 20:7-10). To describe that event, "Gog and Magog," is the generic name for the nations "in the four corners of the earth" who march "across the breadth of the earth" and surround "the camp of God's people." This entire vast army is consumed by fire from heaven (cf. 20:9). In Ezekiel, Gog is the leader from the land of Magog who with his northern allies (38:6) comes to plunder Israel (38:16), but God uses him as an example to the nations (cf. 38:16). Gog's followers destroy one another (38:21), and their bodies are eaten by scavengers. Gog's war is part of Israel's national history. Gog and Magog's threat is Satan's last abortive thrust against God's rule of the universe.

Gog's War is not Armageddon

Gog's war is sometimes thought of as an earlier skirmish that years later culminated in Armageddon. It seems warranted, however, to distinguish Gog's war from Armageddon proper. Some of the differences that are suggested are as follows: **1)** Gog comes with only an eight-nation power base (cf. Ezek. 38:2, 5-6) and there are uninvolved observer nations (Ezek. 38:13; 39:7), but Armageddon will involve all nations (Rev. 16:14; 19:19); **2)** Gog is motivated by greed (Ezek. 38:12), but demonic spirits motivate Antichrist's followers (Rev. 16:13-16); **3)** Gog attacks Israel (Ezek. 38:16), but at Armageddon Antichrist and his armies are "gathered together to make war against the rider on the horse and his army" (Rev. 19:19); **4)** Prince Gog falls in battle "on the mountains of Israel" (39:4) and he is given "a burial place in Israel" (39:11); the captive Antichrist and the False Prophet are "thrown alive into the fiery lake of burning sulfur" (Rev. 19:20); **5)** The scene of battle under Gog is primarily "the mountains of Israel" (39:2); Armageddon, on the other hand, is named for its battleground in the Valley of Megeddo.

Since both wars involve God's total destruction of the enemy, they each result in scavengers' suppers (cf. Ezek. 39:17-20; Rev. 19:17-18), but this does not establish that they are the same war. When David confronted Goliath, they each threatened to give the other's flesh to "the birds of the air and the beasts of the field" for that was the usual destiny of one defeated in battle (cf. 1 Sam. 17:44, 46). The Bible typically depicts the total defeat of an enemy as the occasion of a scavengers' supper.

The war's timing in relation to the tribulation

Scripture reports that the house of Israel will require seven months to bury the dead of Gog's armies (cf. Ezek. 39:12). Further, "those who live in the towns of Israel will go out and use the weapons for fuel and burn them up. . . . For seven years they will use them for fuel" (39:9). For Israel to enjoy this seven-year fuel supply, this war must occur shortly after the beginning of the seven-year tribulation. Perhaps the Jews, apparently protected by Antichrist's covenant, will cancel their burdensome military budget in favor of disarmament. The nation's vulnerability will provoke Gog's evil scheme, "I will invade a land of unwalled villages" (38:11). Ezekiel's references to ancient armaments (v. 9) use vocabulary and concepts that would have communicated with readers prior to the twentieth century. The technology of that day will know how to use salvaged war materials for fuel.

Identifications and outcomes of the war

Scripture twice notes that Gog of the land of Magog comes from "the far north" (38:15; 39:2), and also, his ally Beth Togarmah is "from the far north" (38:6). Over the centuries, Magog has been variously identified as an Arab nation (Jewish Midrash view), one of the original Russian tribes (Pliny and Josephus), or the Goths —Germanic tribes (held by various Jewish writers). The allies are tentatively identified as: Ethiopia (Cush), Libya (Put), Iran (Persia), possibly Germany (Gomer), and Turkey (Togarmah). National identities derived from biblical names are tenuous at best, and today's research tends to discredit prior claims. Agreed upon impressions suggest that Magog and his allies are nations that adjoin the territory of the Roman Empire but are not part of it. Thus, they come against Israel from all directions. The defeat of these neighbor states may become a factor in Antichrist's surprising rise to power.

Ezekiel makes no mention of Israel's efforts to defend her- self, nor of any active allies. Sheba and Dedan (38:13), which are taken to be Arab tribes (cf. Gen. 10:7), simply engage in verbal protests. Israel's spectacular victory will be the result of direct divine action. The account of Gog's destruction extends for more than thirteen verses (38:18 through 39:6) and this led one writer to comment, "The prophet's vision carries with it many of the characteristics of a nuclear war."

The Tribulation World Empire

The rise and fall of world empires was twice depicted in Daniel's visions. In each case, Christ's kingdom replaces the last human empire. In Daniel 2:44-45 He is the smiting rock who sets up a kingdom that will never be destroyed, in Daniel 7:13-14 He is the Son of man who receives an everlasting dominion. The human empire that He overthrows in each vision is a league of ten nations which emerges from the fourth great world empire.

The Ten Nation Confederacy (The Revived Roman Empire)

Nebuchadnezzar's dream (Daniel chapter 2) of the "enormous, dazzling statue" saw a succession of four world empires. Daniel interpreted the vision: the golden head—Nebuchadnezzar and the Babylonian Empire; the silver chest and arms —the Medo-Persian Empire; the belly and thighs of bronze—the Greek Empire; and the legs and feet of iron and clay —the future great and powerful Roman Empire. "As iron breaks things to pieces, so it will crush and break all the others" (Dan. 2:40). The statue featured ten "toes . . . partly iron and partly clay . . . so the people will be a mixture and will not remain united, any more than iron mixes with clay. In the time of those kings, the God of heaven will set up a kingdom" (Dan. 2:42, 44).

In his parallel dream vision (Daniel chapter 7), Daniel saw a sequence of four animals depicting a similar succession of empires. The lion represented Babylon, the bear represented Medo-Persia, the leopard represented Greece, and the fourth, so-called nondescript beast, represented Rome. "It had large iron teeth; it crushed and devoured its victims and trampled underfoot whatever was left . . . and it had ten horns" (Dan. 7:7). The heavenly onlooker explained to Daniel, "The ten horns are ten kings who will come from this kingdom" (Dan. 7:24).

Centuries later, the apostle John also was given a vision of a similar nondescript beast. John's beast, which was scarlet in color, "was covered with blasphemous names and had seven heads and ten horns" (Rev. 17:3). The angel interpreted, "The ten horns you saw are ten kings . . . who for one hour will receive authority as kings along with the beast [Antichrist] . . . They will make war against the Lamb, but the Lamb will overcome them" (Rev. 17:12, 14). The seven heads appear to represent the succession of world powers. (See next section).

Though the ten toes of Nebuchadnezzar's dream image, and the ten horns of the beasts of Daniel's and John's vision indicate a coalition of ten kingdoms, this ten-kingdom division did not occur historically. The Roman Empire did not end with a catastrophic stroke by the divine Smiting Stone. In fact, the ancient Roman Empire crumbled from within into inconclusive powerlessness. The political kingdom was replaced by ecclesiastical Rome, so that, as Scripture portrays Rome, its history is not yet finished. The fulfilment of the prophecies of Daniel and John require a future resurgence of the Roman Empire. In this resurgent or revived form it must be based in a federation of ten constituent states. This distinctive political entity will constitute the power nucleus of the tribulation world empire, and it will be the basis of Antichrist's world empire.

The resuscitated revived head

Scripture seeks to identify the origins of Antichrist. The angel noted, "The beast, which you saw, once was, now is not, and will come up out of the Abyss" (Rev. 17:8). He explained, "The seven heads . . . are . . . seven kings. Five have fallen, one is, the other has not yet come; but when he does come, he must remain for a little while. The beast who once was, and now is not, is an eighth king. He belongs to the seven and is going to his destruction" (Rev. 17:10-11). In context, the seven kings are specifically linked to Rome and its common literary identification as the city built on seven hills. This sequence of seven kings, with Antichrist the eighth in succession, is variously understood—

It is a succession of world powers. Daniel saw four world powers because he began with his own day. Actually, six impinged upon Israel: Egypt, Assyria, Babylonia, Medo-Persia, Greece, and Rome. The revived Roman Empire, the seventh power, was the composite of the previous world powers with all their rapaciousness and humanistic-satanic roots. Antichrist's empire is the eighth, proceeding from the seventh. In endorsing this view, Horton speaks of the beast who is the eighth and he comments, "he belongs to and culminates the same Babylonian world system that preceded him."[9]

It is a succession of governmental systems. Ancient Rome experimented with a series of six systems of government: kings, consuls, dictators, decemvirs (a body of 10 magistrates), military tribunes, and emperors—rulers of an empire consisting of various nations in an enforced federation. It became an empire when its armies conquered other nations. This view sees a revival of the Roman Empire or the seventh system and then its apparent demise. Out of the seventh, however, the eighth or Antichrist's empire emerges.

It is a succession of Roman rulers. Though there were many more than six Roman rulers by John's time, most of them were of limited influence and some were considered to be usurpers. It is thus possible to compile a selective list of six, beginning with Julius Caesar and ending with the incumbent, Domitian, who was cruel, lustful, and blasphemous. This view holds that Antichrist revives and embodies Domitian's traits to become the seventh ruler. Following his apparent death and resuscitation, he proceeds in his own right as the eighth ruler.

9   Horton, op. cit., p. 248.

The scenario of a fatal wounding and a spectacular recovery associates with Antichrist. "One of the heads of the beast [the tribulation empire] seemed to have a fatal wound, but the fatal wound had been healed. The whole world was astonished and followed the beast [Antichrist]" (Rev. 13:3). There are two further references to this incident: "[The False Prophet] made the earth and its inhabitants worship the first beast, whose fatal wound had been healed" (Rev. 13:12); "He [the False Prophet] ordered them [inhabitants of the earth] to set up an image in honor of the beast who was wounded by the sword and yet lived" (Rev. 13:14).

These Scriptures, taken literally, appear to describe the miraculous recovery of a fatally injured human. They suggest the scenario of Antichrist's suffering a death wound early in his career, but then experiencing, by satanic power, a sensational and widely publicized healing. Alternately, the language is taken by some to suggest that an ambitious leader, who first suffers ignominious failure and political defeat, later achieves a remarkable comeback both militarily and politically.

Perhaps this miracle recovery will see a double fulfilment, just as the seven heads of the beast represent both Rome and a succession of kings (cf. Rev. 17:9-10). It may be that there will not only be the physical recovery of a fatally wounded Antichrist, but also of the revived Roman Empire. The emergence of the eighth out of the seventh seems to speak almost in resurrection terms. Thus, the seventh kingdom may conveniently be spoken of as the Revived Roman Empire, and the eighth kingdom and its ruler may be spoken of as the *Resuscitated Revived Roman Empire*.

EIGHT

The Tribulation Period: Part 2

In general, during the first three and one-half years of the tribulation, life on earth will proceed more or less normally. Although Christians will have been translated, and with them they will have taken their preserving influence as the "salt of the earth" (Matt. 5:13), worldly humans under the leadership of Antichrist will attempt to encourage the best of humanistic values. Peace and prosperity will be proclaimed, and to some degree achieved. God's judgmental acts in the seals and trumpets will be seen as upheavals of nature, and mankind will use his utmost ingenuity to cope with them. During this time, the majority of people in Israel and the nations will know only the good aspects of Antichrist's rule. Probably he will maintain a fairly low profile as he gathers momentum for his future intentions. Ironically, Antichrist's emergence, and the beginnings of his rise to power, will be largely through his success in negotiating a peace treaty with and on behalf of Israel.

The Midpoint of the Tribulation

At the midpoint of the tribulation, Antichrist reveals his true nature and he ruthlessly embarks upon his intended goals. Satan joins him on earth, and satanic and demonic forces greatly increase their activity. For His part, God escalates the severity and frequency of His outpoured judgments. These developments result in great loss of human life, and the reduction of the earth to an ecological disaster.

The abomination that causes desolation

Antichrist's action to break his covenant with Israel is first of all a religious action. "In the middle of the 'seven' he will put an end to sacrifice and offering. And on a wing of the temple he will set up an abomination that causes desolation" (Dan. 9:27). He thus rescinds the Jewish freedom to worship through animal sacrifices and grain offerings, and he proceeds to desecrate the temple. This desecration appears to be explained in Paul's description of the "man of lawlessness." "He will oppose and will exalt himself over everything that is called God or is worshiped, so that he sets himself up in God's temple, proclaiming himself to be God" (2 Thess. 2:4). It may be that what is set up in the temple is actually his image which later will be animated by the skills of the False Prophet (cf. Rev. 13:15).

The desecration of the temple by Antichrist will be similar to previous events of this kind. In 167 B.C., the Greco-Syrian ruler of Israel, Antiochus Epiphanes, set up what is thought to have been an image of Zeus within the temple precincts, he rededicated the Jewish temple to the worship of Olympian Zeus, and he proceeded to offer a sow upon the temple altar. This event is alluded to in Daniel 8:9-14 and called "the rebellion [or transgression] that causes desolation" (8:13). In A.D. 70, while the temple was aflame and Jerusalem was being sacked, the Roman soldiers brought the official standards of their legions and set them up outside the eastern gate. There they offered sacrifice and proclaimed Titus the Victorious Commander.

It was to this latter event that Jesus primarily referred in the Olivet Discourse. At that time He warned His Jewish hearers to plan to take flight when they saw "standing in the holy place 'the abomination that causes desolation,' spoken of through the prophet Daniel—let the reader understand" (Matt. 24:15). It is thought that in Greek the expression "abomination that causes desolation" may be taken as a parody or insulting pun of the name "Jupiter Olympus." (The Roman Jupiter and the Greek Zeus were considered to be the same supreme god seen from different national perspectives.)

Antichrist's assumption of despotic power

Antichrist's appropriation of despotic power is depicted symbolically by Daniel. He tells of his vision of a nondescript beast (which we know portrays both the original and revived Roman Empire) with ten horns. He proceeds, "There before me was another horn, a little one, which came up among them; and three of the first horns were uprooted before it" (Dan. 7:8). In response to Daniel's question about the little horn, the heavenly messenger explained, "he will subdue three kings. He will speak against the Most High and oppress his saints and try to change the set times and the laws. The saints will be handed over to him for a time, times and half a time" (7:24-25).

In Scripture, a horn is a symbol of governmental power and, as a "little horn," Antichrist prior to midtribulation, is apparently a subordinate ruler. He will serve under a "king" who is one of ten independent rulers who possess more or less equal powers. By overthrowing three of these rulers, Antichrist suddenly becomes a "super ruler," for he now has their combined strength. Aided by his notable personal skills, and with Satan's support, he promptly parleys this status into absolute domination of the entire ten nation federation.

The Book of Revelation provides a different vision of the rise of Antichrist. John "saw a beast coming out of the sea. He had ten horns and seven heads" (Rev. 13:1). As John's vision continued, this beast, representing world dominion, merged with the ruler of the world—the beast that we call Antichrist. In the transposition there is the account of the resuscitated head. "One of the heads of the beast seemed to have had a fatal wound, but the fatal wound had been healed. The whole world was astonished and followed the beast" (Rev. 13:3).

Though the mechanics of the resuscitation are debated, it seems clear that Antichrist's cause receives a powerful boost by an apparent miracle of satanic origin. We have noted that scholars debate whether the miracle is a physical recovery, a political comeback, or the revival of the Roman Empire.

Satan cast down to the earth

In the eternal councils of God, Satan was a defeated foe in past eternity. Jesus said, "I saw Satan fall like lightning from heaven" (Luke 10:18). The death of Christ on Calvary legally verified Satan's defeat, but it will not be until midtribulation that God moves to appropriate the victory that Christ achieved. A vision of the event was given to John. "There was war in heaven. Michael and his angels fought against the dragon, and the dragon and his angels fought back. . . . The great dragon was hurled down—that ancient serpent called the devil or Satan . . . was hurled to the earth. . . . When the dragon saw that he had been hurled to the earth, he pursued the woman who . . . was given the two wings of a great eagle, so that she might fly to the place . . . where she would be taken care of for a time, times and half a time, out of the serpent's reach" (Rev. 12:7, 9, 13-14).

The casting down of Satan occurs at midtribulation. The event allows him to launch an attack upon the Jews, but because of God's protecting care, they escape and take refuge for the remaining three and one-half years. For this final period, Satan as a dragon is present personally to oversee the programs he seeks to impose upon humans on earth: "The dragon stood on the shore of the sea" (Rev. 13:1). He proceeds to empower Antichrist, "The dragon gave the beast his power and his throne and great authority" (Rev. 13:2).

The satanic dragon is one of the sources of the demonic spirits that lure human leaders into becoming involved in Armageddon. "I saw three evil spirits that looked like frogs; they came out of the mouth of the dragon, out of the mouth of the beast and out of the mouth of the false prophet. They are spirits of demons" (Rev. 16:13-14). Satan remains active on earth until the conclusion of Armageddon. "I saw an angel coming down out of heaven.

... He seized the dragon, that ancient serpent, who is the devil, or Satan, and bound him for a thousand years. He threw him into the Abyss" (Rev. 20:1-3).

Israel suffers violent persecution

Scriptures describing Satan's persecution of Israel during the tribulation have been cited above. Israel is represented by the woman clothed with the sun, with the crown of twelve stars, and the mother of the male child who is to rule all the nations with an iron scepter (cf. Rev. 12:1-5). We have noted that as Satan's persecution is unleashed, this woman is able to take flight to a desert refuge for the final three and one-half years of the tribulation (cf. 12:13-14, cf. v. 6). The text proceeds, "Then from his mouth the serpent spewed water like a river . . . to sweep her away with the torrent. But the earth helped the woman by opening its mouth and swallowing the river that the dragon had spewed out of his mouth" (Rev. 12:15-16). Most scholars consider this flood to be symbolic, but there is no consensus of what is implied. It is clear, however, that Satan's efforts against Israel will have limited effectiveness.

Daniel spoke of Israel's future distress. "There will be a time of distress such as has not happened from the beginning of nations until then" (Dan. 12:1). Prior to these words Daniel had written, "At that time Michael, the great prince who protects your people, will arise [Heb. 'amad]" (12:1). The import of this clause is debated. Although 'amad (aw-MAD) means: to stand up, to dwell, to arise, to come on the scene, it can also mean, to stand aside, be inactive, or desist. Some hold that it is Michael's withdrawal that permits Antichrist's fierce destruction of Jewry. A more appealing view is to consider that he arises, or places himself on the alert, so that he can proceed with his role in fulfilling the third clause of the verse, "everyone whose name is found written in the book—will be delivered" (12:1).

Zechariah's prophecy of the destruction of the Jews just prior to their acknowledgment of the divine lordship may be applied to the tribulation period. Zechariah predicted better than a 66 percent casualty rate. "In the whole land . . . two-thirds will be struck down and perish; yet one-third will be left in it. This third . . . I will refine . . . like silver. . . . They will call on my name and I will answer them; I will say, 'They are my people,' and they will say, 'The Lord is our God'" (Zech. 13:8-9). This passage affirms God's use of the tribulation's horrors to produce penitence within His ancient chosen people.

In the Olivet Discourse, which is addressed to Israel, Jesus had said, "Then you will be handed over to be persecuted and put to death, and you will be hated by all nations because of me. At that time many will turn away from the faith and will betray and hate each other, and many false prophets will appear and deceive many people" (Matt. 24:9-10). These words indicate tragic times for Israel during tribulation's terrors.

Antichrist destroys ecumenical religion

This event may not take place immediately at the mid-tribulation, but it must occur shortly afterward. When Antichrist is proclaimed the object of mankind's worship, religious competition will no longer be tolerated. His target will be the ecumenical religious organization that will have emerged after the rapture of the true church. Because this organization is associated with the city of Babylon (cf. Rev. 17:5), this event is often spoken of as "the destruction of ecclesiastical Babylon."

In Revelation 17 ecumenical religion is depicted under the figure of the great prostitute. John tells of his vision of the events that were to lead to her destruction:

> **I saw a woman sitting on a scarlet beast that was covered with blasphemous names and had seven heads and ten horns. The woman was dressed in purple and scarlet, and was glittering with gold, precious stones and pearls. She held a golden cup in her hand.... This title was written on her forehead: Mystery Babylon the great the mother of prostitutes ... the woman was drunk with ... the blood of those who bore testimony to Jesus" (Rev. 17:3, 4-6).**

The woman is seen to depict traditional liturgical religion, and particularly, traditional Christendom. Her vestments of purple and scarlet, the gold, jewels, and the cup reinforce the image, and so does her role as the one shedding the blood of true believers in Jesus. The identification with Babylon links with the legend of the goddess Semiramis who was said to have conceived supernaturally and given birth to a son, Tammuz. Babylon's mother-child cult was thus launched as a center of human rebellion against God. The city of Babylon is Satan's city. This city is named 260 times in Scripture and, among cities, only Jerusalem is named more frequently.

In John's time, the Babylonian cult had moved its center to Asia Minor, and its headquarters were in Pergamos. Thus, in addressing the church there, John spoke of "your city—where Satan lives" (Rev. 2:13). Not only is Babylon the mother of "idolatrous religionism," but also the channel of demonism and Satanism. Tragically, this immoral, idolatrous, anti-God, satanic cult proceeded to infiltrate Christianity. It succeeded so well that by A.D. 378 much of this ancient mystery religion had been transferred bodily into the Christian church. Even the former title of the high priest of Babylonianism, *"pontifex maximus,"* now was applied to the Pope.

The angel responsible for John's vision provided clues to identify both the woman and the beast upon which she rode. "The woman you saw is the great city that rules over the kings of the earth" (Rev. 17:18). For 1,000 years the city of Rome, first as a military power, and then as the spiritual headquarters of the Holy Roman Empire, indeed ruled the earth. The beast is linked with seven heads and ten horns (cf. 17:9-13), and although the symbolism is debated, it definitely can be seen as identifying the political structure and system that will prevail in the tribulation period. Thus, the beast is Antichrist's kingdom. The fact that, at the outset, the woman rides the beast (v. 3) is taken to imply that ecumenical religion uses Antichrist to enhance its cause. He appears deceptively submissive and compliant, and the religionists falsely conclude that they are in control.

The turnaround comes when Antichrist and the confederacy he rules conclude that they must be rid of all outside religious domination. "The beast and the ten horns . . . will hate the prostitute. They will bring her to ruin and leave her naked; they will eat her flesh and burn her with fire. For God has put it into their hearts to accomplish his purpose by agreeing to give the beast their power to rule" (Rev. 17:16-17). Perhaps Antichrist will enact laws that allow no other religion except his own and that close all religious institutions and confiscate their property. The destruction of what had been a powerful and entrenched religious system will free Antichrist to proceed with his radical religious program for the final half of the tribulation.

Tribulation saints

In his description of the little horn (i.e., Antichrist) that had uprooted three others, Daniel writes, "This horn was waging war against the saints and defeating them. . . . The saints will be handed over to him for a time, times and half a time" (Dan. 7:21, 25). Daniel proceeds, however, to describe the results of the destruction of the little horn, "Then the sovereignty, power and greatness of the kingdoms under the whole heaven will be handed over to the saints, the people of the Most High" (Dan. 7:27). Thus, the saints are to be the objects of Antichrist's fierce persecution during the tribulation, but they become earth's ruling citizens in the era that follows Antichrist's destruction.

Fig. 11: A graphic representation of the seven-year tribulation period—Daniel's seventieth week. The seven years are divided into two periods of 3½ years (42 months or 1,260 days) each. The chart is in the form of a time line, and the sequence of events seems valid, but most scholars do not consider their timing, except for the events at midpoint, to be definitively given in Scripture.

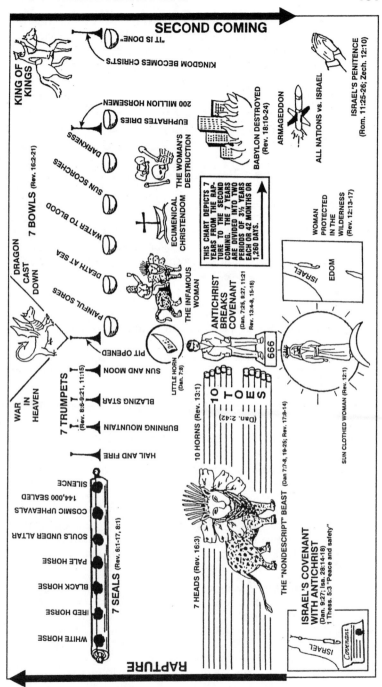

Daniel's sole concept of saints was that they were Jewish believers, and this view persists in all seven of his references to saints. In seventeen other references to saints elsewhere in the Old Testament, they are similarly portrayed. In the Old Testament, saints are God's people in the land (Psa. 16:3), who joined the priests in worship (Psa. 132:9), so that the assembly of saints was the assembly of the people of Israel (Psa. 149:1-2).

In the New Testament, the word saints occurs forty-five times in the pattern of Old Testament usage to identify assemblies of believers (cf. Rom. 1:7; Eph. 1:1; 2 Cor. 1:1). Twelve of these occurrences are in Revelation, with five being references to saints on earth. The experience of these latter parallels just what Daniel had prophesied. "He [i.e., Antichrist, the beast from the sea] was given power to make war against the saints and to conquer them" (Rev. 13:7). In the era of the Acts and the Epistles, church saints were on earth. In Revelation, church saints are in heaven, but saints which are spoken of on earth are clearly Jewish. Tribulation saints are Jewish believers who have accepted their Messiah.

The Man Called Antichrist

For humans on earth the central figure in the tribulation is the Antichrist. As Satan's special emissary, he serves to unite both sinful mankind and evil spiritual forces in a final desperate rebellion against God. Antichrist is a flesh and blood human, but Satan will empower him supernaturally.

Biblical titles for this end time ruler

The Antichrist first appears in Scripture in Daniel, and then he reappears in the New Testament in both Paul's and John's writings. His Biblical titles include:

1) **The Beast.** "I saw a beast coming out of the sea. He had ten horns and seven heads, with ten crowns on his horns, and on each head a blasphemous name" (Rev. 13:1). The ten crowns imply multiple ruling authority. In the Book of Revelation, the title "Beast" is used thirty-six times to speak of the Antichrist. Since his origin is specified in the above verse, in order to distinguish him from the False Prophet, he is sometimes referred to as "the beast from the sea."

2) **The Antichrist.** Though this name is the most common in popular usage, in Scripture it occurs only in two of John's epistles. John applies the name to other enemies of Christ who actively promote evil, as well as to the end time tyrant. John wrote, "Children, it is the last hour, and even as you have heard that Antichrist is coming, even now many antichrists have come" (1 John 2:18, lit. trans.). In addition to this twofold use of the word (the second time in the plural),

John uses it three other times (cf. 1 John 2:22, 4:3; 2 John 1:7). In newer Greek texts it is only in the reference cited that the singular "antichrist" is used without an article. In Greek, the use of the article with proper nouns is optional, just as it is in English as the above literal translation illustrates. In 2:18 the one Antichrist who is future is clearly distinguished from "many antichrists" of the past and present. Repeatedly there have been, and now are, humans who embody the spirit and behavior patterns that will find their ultimate culmination and manifestation in an evil world superman.

3) **The Man of Lawlessness (or Sin —KJV).** "That day will not come until the rebellion occurs and the man of lawlessness (Gk. *anomia*) is revealed, the man doomed to destruction [the son of perdition KJV] . . . he sets himself up in God's temple proclaiming himself to be God" (2 Thess. 2:3-4). (*anomia* [an-om-EE-ah]: state of being without law, the frame of mind whereby one despises God's law). Antichrist will rebel against all of God's laws. In many Greek manuscripts, but not those that scholars today consider most authoritative, the key word in this verse is not *anomia*, but *hamartia* [ham-ar-TEE-ah] which is another of the common Greek words for "sin." This difference in the Greek text is the usual reason for the difference between the English versions.

4) **The Lawless One (the Wicked —KJV).** "Then the lawless one [Gk. *anomos*) will be revealed, whom the Lord Jesus will overthrow with the breath of his mouth" (2 Thess. 2:8). (*anomos* [AN-om-os] one whose lifestyle is destitute of [God's] law so that he lives in total violation of it). Note that the two preceding titles, which are both Pauline, are similar and come from the same root word. There are subtle differences, nevertheless, including the fact that *anomia* is feminine and *anomos* is masculine. As the definitions have sought to indicate, *anomia* refers to a hostile attitude toward God's law; *anomos* describes one's lifestyle when judged by that law.

5) **The King.** This title, together with the three that follow, is provided by Daniel. "A stern-faced king [a king of fierce countenance —KJV], a master of intrigue, will arise" (Dan. 8:23), "The king will do as he pleases [according to his will —KJV]. He will exalt and magnify himself above every god and will say unheard of things against the God of gods. He will be successful until the time of wrath is completed" (Dan. 11:36). In these accounts, Daniel transcends his description of Antiochus Epiphanes and events near at hand, and he moves to a description of Antichrist in the end time. As a king, Antichrist is the political ruler, but he has a passion to be involved in religion.

6) The Ruler (or Prince —KJV) who will come. This text has previously been discussed: "The ruler [Heb. *nagid*] who will come will confirm a covenant with many for one 'seven'" (Dan. 9:26-27). (*nagid* [naw-GHEED]: commander, governor, leader, noble, prince, chief ruler).

7) The Little Horn. "There before me was a fourth beast—terrifying and frightening and very powerful. . . . It was different from all the former beasts, and it had ten horns. . . . [T]here before me was another horn, a little one, which came up among them; and three of the first horns were uprooted before it. This horn had eyes like the eyes of a man and a mouth that spoke boastfully" (Dan. 7:7-8). As we have previously noted, a "horn" denotes governmental authority. The apparent significance of Antichrist's designation as a "horn, a little one" is that in his roots and legitimate status he is a lesser ruler or official, below someone else.

8) The Worthless (or idol —KJV) Shepherd. He will be a false leader and a deceiver who will betray Israel and all humans who put their trust in him. "I am going to raise up a shepherd over the land who will not care for the lost, or seek the young, or heal the injured, or feed the healthy, but will eat the meat of the choice sheep, tearing off their hoofs. Woe to the worthless [Heb. *'elil*] shepherd" (Zech. 11:16-17). (*'elil* [el-EEL]: that which is good for nothing, an idol).

Characteristics and attributes of Antichrist

The name "Antichrist" means "instead of" or "opposed to" Christ. This man will be a counterfeit who superficially and deceptively attempts to fulfill Christ's role on earth. Scripture provides numerous insights into his actions and character:

1) He will be a human but with supernatural satanic powers. "The dragon [i.e., Satan] gave the beast [i.e., Antichrist] his power and his throne and great authority" (Rev. 13:2). In effect, Antichrist will become an incarnation of Satan.

2) He will deny Jesus' role as Messiah. "The man who denies that Jesus is the Christ . . . is the antichrist—he denies the Father and the Son" (1 John 2:22).

3) He will be a clever propagandist ("a master of intrigue"), powerful ("very strong"), a deceiver ("cause deceit to prosper"), and a destroyer ("he will destroy many") (Dan. 8:23-25). Although chapter 8 is primarily describing Antiochus Epiphanes, beginning with verse 23, the description transcends earlier history. At least in secondary fulfillment, it is considered to relate to Antichrist in the end time.

4) A miracle recovery will launch his career. "One of the heads of the beast seemed to have had a fatal wound, but the fatal wound had been healed. The whole world was astonished and followed the beast" (Rev. 13:3). This miracle recovery was discussed at the close of the previous chapter.

5) Satanically empowered miracles will appear to validate his rule. "The coming of the lawless one will be in accordance with the work of Satan displayed in all kinds of counterfeit miracles, signs and wonders" (2 Thess. 2:9).

6) He will claim to be deity. "He will oppose and will exalt himself over everything that is called God or is worshiped, so that he sets himself up in God's temple, proclaiming himself to be God" (2 Thess. 2:4); "All inhabitants of the earth will worship the beast" (Rev. 13:8); "He will show no regard for the gods of his fathers" (Dan. 11:38). In his program to establish his own deity and secure worship for himself, Antichrist will eventually demonstrate hatred for all other organized religions. Scholars speculate whether Antichrist, in proclaiming himself to be God, will also claim that he is the Christ.

7) He will arrogantly blaspheme God and persecute God's people. "The king . . . will exalt and magnify himself above every god and will say unheard-of things against the God of gods" (Dan. 11:36); "He will speak against the Most High and oppress his saints. . . . The saints will be handed over to him for a time, times and half a time" (Dan. 7:25). The saints who are oppressed for three and one-half years are the Jews who will be the special objects of Antichrist's hatred.

The identification of antichrist

In the well-known text, John provides a hint concerning Antichrist's identity. "This calls for wisdom. If anyone has insight, let him calculate the number of the beast, for it is a man's number. His number is 666" (Rev. 13:18). God thus chose to provide humans with an important clue by which to identify Antichrist. It no doubt will be specifically significant when the time comes, but thus far in human history, no identification has proved to be valid. The most notable reason, of course, why 666 has not identified the Antichrist is that he has not yet come.

Since Hebrew, Greek, and Latin use letters of the alphabet as numbers, each lends itself to the transposition of a name into a number. This replacement of a name by a concept with the same numerical value (i.e., a number) is called *gematria* (also written *gimatriya*) from Hebrew roots, or *hisopsephia* (also written *isopsephia*) from Greek roots. In 1889, Nathaniel West reviewed the numerous "solutions" to the identity of 666 in his day:

The Protestants found it in "Vicar of the Son of God," written Latinly, Vicarius Fillii Dei, on the Pope's tiara. The Catholics found it in the word Luther, and both Catholics and Protestants found it in the name Mahomet [i.e., Muhammad], while pagans see it in the word Messias [i.e., Messiah]. Modern critics found it in the words Nero Caesar written Hebrewly, although it is known that John wrote in Greek. Some Germans see it in Gallos Kaiser, the Gallic Caesar [i.e., Napoleon], while some Frenchmen see it in Bismarck, the German aristocrat.

In the third century Origen held that the Antichrist was false doctrine. Joachim of Floris (c. 1145-1202) taught that Antichrist was a composite of state hostility, church corruption, and heresy. In the twentieth century some declared that Antichrist was communism. Scripture, however, teaches that Antichrist is a man (cf. "that day will not come until . . . the man of lawlessness is revealed, the man doomed to destruction" 2 Thess. 2:3).

The nationality of Antichrist is often discussed, but Scripture does not provide any sure clues. It cannot be shown that the Jews would accept a covenant only with a Jewish leader, for the State of Israel today can display many treaties with Gentiles. That Antichrist "will show no regard for the gods of his fathers" (Dan. 11:37) indicates simply that he will reject his religious roots. It does not specifically establish a Jewish background.

Particularly in the era that led to the Reformation, various voices opposed to Catholicism declared that the Pope was the Antichrist. Notable leaders including John Wycliffe (1329-1384), Martin Luther (1483-1546) (at least in his earlier years) and John Foxe (1515-1587) (author of *Foxe's Book of Martyrs*) each held this view. More tolerant modern Protestants have recognized that since the Pope regularly confesses, "I believe in God, the Father almighty, maker of heaven and earth, and in Jesus Christ, His only Son our Lord," he cannot be the Antichrist. Scripture notes that "the antichrist . . . denies the Father and the Son" (1 John 2:22).

Most scholars hold that Antichrist could not be a resurrected (or resuscitated) historical person such as Judas, Nero, or Hitler, for the concept exceeds Scripture. "Man is destined to die once, and after that to face judgment" (Heb. 9:27). Antichrist's healing evokes wonder, but it is not presented as a miracle resurrection.

Those who nominate Judas as a candidate attempt a Biblical defense: Jesus called Judas a "devil" (John 6:70-71), Judas never called Jesus "Lord" but only "master," and both Judas and Antichrist are spoken of as "doomed to destruction" (or "son of perdition" —KJV) (cf. John 17:12; 2 Thess. 2:3). Most scholars, however, prefer to hold that Judas, and other nominees, simply exemplified the traits and attitudes of the future Antichrist. Though they will not be personally resurrected, the treacherous spirit of past tyrants will be perpetuated. The situation compares with John the Baptist's ministry that fulfilled the expectation of Elijah's return as Messiah's forerunner.

A summary of Antichrist's exploits

Scripture provides information about a number of Antichrist's activities, and these may be enumerated as follows:

1) a treaty granting peace and protection to Israel,

2) various consolidating victories that by mid-tribulation result in popular approval that enables him to assume world rulership. These appear to include:

   a) assisting in or profiting by the defeat of Gog's armies,

   b) recovering from near destruction (political or personal),

   c) being indwelt by Satan who is cast down to earth,

   d) destroying ecumenical religion and replacing it with his own,

   e) placing his image in the temple and demanding that people worship it,

   f) launching systematic persecution upon Christ's converts.

3) his destruction by Jesus at the second coming.

Antiochus Epiphanes as a forerunner of Antichrist

The most notable forerunner of Antichrist was Antiochus IV Epiphanes (c. 215-164 B.C.) ("Epiphanes" means "God made manifest"). This ruler was in the line of succession of General Seleucus who had established the Syrian Division of the former empire of Alexander the Great. Since Palestine was on the frontier of his empire, he attempted to use drastic methods to maintain control of the Jews and force them to conform to his Greek religion and culture. Daniel had predicted the fourfold division of Alexander's Empire following the conqueror's sudden demise after his career symbolized by a flying shaggy goat with a prominent horn (cf. Dan. 8:5, 21). He also saw the later emergence of a distinctive ruler under the figure of "another horn, which started small." Daniel described the events of his vision:

> At the height of his power his large horn was broken off, and in its place four prominent horns grew up toward the four winds of heaven. Out of one of them came another horn, which started small but grew in power ... toward the Beautiful Land. ... It set itself up to be as great as the Prince of the host; it took away the daily sacrifice from him, and the place of his sanctuary was brought low. ... Then I heard a holy one speaking, and another holy one said to him, "How long will it take for the vision to be fulfilled—the vision concerning the daily sacrifice, the rebellion that causes desolation?" (Dan. 8:8-9, 11, 13).

Just as Antichrist will desecrate the temple with his "abomination that causes desolation" (Matt. 24:15), Antiochus similarly desecrated the temple. As we have noted, in 167 B.C., Antiochus acted to defy Israel's Lord and mock Jewish temple worship by

offering a sow on the altar and setting up an image of Jupiter
within the temple precincts. Daniel predicted that the sanctuary
would be "trampled underfoot . . . 2,300 evenings and mornings"
(Dan. 8:13-14). Though there is some difficulty in deciding upon
the beginning of this time period, most scholars agree that it
ended when the Jewish leaders, known as the Maccabees, threw
off the Syrian yoke in 165 B.C. The interval from 168 to 165 is
sometimes called the "Maccabean tribulation."

In Daniel's account, Gabriel was instructed to tell the meaning of the vision (cf. 8:16). He proceeded to give clear interpretations in terms of national identities for the symbolic animals. For
four verses beginning with verse twenty-three, however, Gabriel's words became a poem which most scholars agree consists
of predictions that transcend Antiochus, and become a description of the future Antichrist.

Traits that particularly apply to the Antichrist of the "distant future" (cf. v. 26) are: stern-faced (or fierce featured), master of intrigue (specialist in sinister schemes) (v. 23), empowered
from beyond himself, to cause astounding devastation (ruthless
destroyer) (v. 24), deceit to prosper (dishonesty and deception
reign), to consider himself superior (proud and opinionated), to
destroy those who feel secure, stand against the Prince of princes
(against Christ), to be destroyed other than by human power (by
Christ's judgment stroke) (v. 25).

It is important to note that the "small" (Heb. *mitstsehiyrah*
[mits-tseh-ee-RAW]) horn of Daniel 8:9 is quite distinct from the
"little" (Heb. *ze'eyr* [zeh-AYR]) horn of Daniel 7:8. Older translations rendered both Hebrew words by "little," but newer versions apply "little" only to the horn of chapter 7. The chapter 7
horn came up among ten horns and uprooted three; the horn of
chapter 8 came out of one of four horns. The little horn of chapter
7 depicts Antichrist who emerges out of ten members states of a
revived Roman Empire; the small horn of chapter 8 depicts
Antiochus IV who emerged out of the Seleucid Division of Alexander's Empire.

The Satanic Triad

One of Satan's most common tactics is to copy God's patterns and strategies, but always for ulterior purposes. It is no
surprise to find that the holy trinity is imitated in the "counterfeit trinity" comprised of Satan, Antichrist, and the False
Prophet. The designation "Satanic triad," avoids associating Satan with the sacred term "trinity." The three persons of this triad
are seen in a single verse, "The devil, who deceived them, was
thrown into the lake of burning sulphur, where the beast and the
false prophet had been thrown" (Rev. 20:10).

Satan, the fountainhead of evil

Much of the evil that is evident on earth during the tribulation results directly from the personal presence of Satan following his casting down from heaven. John quoted the heavenly voice, "Woe to the earth and the sea, because the devil has gone down to you! He is filled with fury, because he knows that his time is short" (Rev. 12:12). Not only does Satan, as a dragon, persecute the Jews, but John reports, "Then the dragon . . . went off to make war against . . . those who obey God's commandments and hold to the testimony of Jesus" (Rev. 12:17).

We have noted that Satan empowers Antichrist (cf. Rev. 13:2). Apparently, this empowering is so thinly disguised that humans see beyond it to Satan himself. "Men worshiped the dragon [Satan] because he had given authority to the beast [Antichrist]" (Rev. 13:4). Scripture does not credit the False Prophet's miracle power to Satan, but that would be the obvious source. It is said concerning the False Prophet, "He was given power to give breath to the image of the first beast" (Rev. 13:15).

Satan's destiny following the close of the tribulation was included in John's vision. "I saw an angel coming down out of heaven. . . . He seized the dragon, that ancient serpent, who is the devil, or Satan, and bound him for a thousand years. He threw him into the Abyss, and locked and sealed it over him, to keep him from deceiving the nations anymore" (Rev. 20:1-3). As long as he is allowed to continue his associations on earth, Satan will strive to deceive as many humans as he can.

The Antichrist, evil incarnate

The identity, nature, and exploits of the Antichrist have already been discussed. Concerning him John wrote, "All inhabitants of the earth will worship the beast—all whose names have not been written in the book of life belonging to the Lamb that was slain from the creation of the world" (Rev. 13:8). In many ways, worship of Antichrist is worship of Satan.

The False Prophet, the one who implements evil

Although introduced as the "beast coming out of the earth" (Rev. 13:11), he is later referred to as the "False Prophet" (cf. Rev. 16:13; 19:20; 20:10). Scripture provides no significant clues concerning his origin or associations, though his role as a prophet suggests the possibility that he might be an apostate Jew. It is generally understood that the False Prophet will be, as it were, Antichrist's Minister for Religious Affairs. He will support the cause of Antichrist, even to the extent of working miracles, and erecting an image of Antichrist to which he gives the powers of breathing and speaking. He will require worship of Antichrist or his image, and he will impose the death penalty upon those who refuse. "He was given power to . . . cause all who refused to worship the image [of Antichrist] to be killed" (Rev. 13:15). No doubt, the False Prophet will be responsible for a great company of tribulation saints who are promoted to glory as martyrs for their faith.

A notable project of the False Prophet will be to enforce participation in the "mark of the beast." "He also forced everyone, small and great, rich and poor, free and slave, to receive a mark [Gk. *charagma*] on his right hand or on his forehead, so that no one could buy or sell unless he had the mark" (Rev. 13:16). (*charagma* [KHAR-ag-mah]: an engraved mark, an impression made by a stamp, a brand on an animal, an engraved figure or statue). In the original, the beast's mark is mentioned seven times in Revelation (but eight times in the KJV), and for all who receive it, the decision is tragic and irrevocable. To receive the mark one must, in effect, worship Antichrist. "If anyone worships the beast and . . . receives his mark on the forehead or on the hand, he, too, will drink of the wine of God's fury" (Rev. 14:9-10). Since the Greek *charagma* is the root of the English word "character" it is suggested that the "mark of the beast" will entail, not merely submission to an "imprinting," but a major volitional and moral choice comprising a deliberate degeneration of character.

NINE

The Tribulation Period: Part 3

For the final three and one-half years of the tribulation, Satan and his followers feverishly increase their activity. God responds by implementing the full horrors of His judgments, including the final seven bowls. Satan, working through Antichrist and the False Prophet, uses subtle and powerful deceptions to win multitudes of human followers. But even in these dark hours, God reaps a great company of converts, many of them by martyrdom. The contest ends with Armageddon and the glorious triumph of Jesus Christ.

The Conclusion of God's Judgments

Since the tribulation is characterized by God's outpoured judgments, they must begin at or near the beginning of the seven years. By the end of the tribulation, God has launched twenty-one divine enactments—seventeen strokes of judgment and four proclamations. Significantly, modern ecologists, from a purely secular understanding, have begun to predict some of the same dire events that the Bible portrays as God's tribulation judgments. Defiant humans will probably see only natural causes, and deny the hand of God in earth's catastrophes.

The seven trumpets proceed out of the seventh seal (cf. Rev. 8:1-2). The trumpets, each sounded by an appointed angel, are described in Revelation 8:7 to 9:16, and 11:15. They involve:

1) **Hail and fire with blood**— one-third of trees and green grass (which doesn't usually burn) burned up, and "a third of the earth was burned up" (Rev. 8:7). These latter words suggest raging fires upon earth.

2) **Meteoric mass**— a mountain-like burning mass falling into the sea leaves it seriously polluted, destroying one-third of the marine life (perhaps accounting for the blood) and one-third of the ships. Huge waves caused by the impact of the falling mass may cause the sinking of the ships.

3) **Star Wormwood**—as [bitter] volcanic ash or radioactivity, it contaminates and pollutes one-third of the fresh water sources, causing the deaths of many humans. They die as a result of drinking the polluted water.

4) **Sun, moon, stars darkened**—output reduced by one-third, or perhaps rotation patterns altered and the daily cycle reduced to sixteen hours (cf. Matt. 24:22). These changes would seriously affect the earth's temperature and weather.

5) **Abyss (bottomless pit) opened**—an angel from heaven unlocks the pit permitting the exodus of demon locusts that cause humans excruciating suffering for five months. Even the release provided by death will be denied the sufferers.

6) **200 million horsemen dispatched**—either a vast army of Asiatics, or a demon army of death angels responsible for destroying one-third of mankind. This vast destruction of humans is attributed to the horses rather than their riders.

7) **Christ's Kingdom proclaimed**—the proclamation at this point is by way of anticipation.

Following the sixth trumpet judgment, John gives us a candid report of attitudes on earth:

> **The rest of mankind that were not killed by these plagues still did not repent of the work of their hands; they did not stop worshiping demons, and idols of gold, silver, bronze, stone and wood [a commentary on tribulation religion] . . . Nor did they repent of their murders [a lifestyle that allowed such], their magic arts [Gk. *pharmakeia*], their sexual immorality [Gk. *porneia*], or their thefts.[1] (Rev. 9:20-21).**

The final seven judgments are described as "the seven bowls (vials —KJV) (Gk. *phiale)* of God's wrath," and again, each in turn, is poured out by an appointed angel. (*phiale* [fee-AL-ay]: a bowl, a broad shallow cup). The seven bowls are described in Revelation 16:2-17, and their effects include:

1) **Ugly painful sores**—an infirmity falling upon Antichrist's worshipers. These sores compare with the boils that the Egyptians suffered during the ten plagues (cf. Exod. 9:9).

2) **Seas turn to blood**—all remaining life in the sea is destroyed. The sea becomes "blood like that of a dead man." The expression indicates a liquid that is decaying and rotting.

3) **Fresh water turns to blood**—this plague is in retaliation for Antichrist's shedding of the blood of believers. Though water will be loathsome, it apparently will not be toxic.

4) **Sun scorches**—as they are seared by the heat, humans curse the name of God. Earth's citizens will recognize that God has sent this intense heat wave, but they refuse to repent.

5) **Darkness**—especially upon Antichrist's subjects. Its intensity highlighted the severe pains that humans were suffering.

---

1 The original words in this verse are defined: *pharmakeia* [far-mak-EYE-ah]: sorcery, witchcraft, use of drugs, cf. pharmacy; *porneia* [por-NIGH-ah]: prostitution, all types of unchaste sexual acts, cf. pornography.

6) **Euphrates dries**—this event prepares for the westward march of the armies, presumably of Asiatic kings. They will thus be prepared to fulfill their destiny in the soon-to-occur battle of Armageddon.

7) **Earthquake**—an occurrence of vast proportions causing a total revision of the earth's topography, great loss of life, and the destruction of much of man's handiwork on earth. It can be seen as God's final stroke as He obliterates whatever would mar the millennial earth.

God's judgments associated with the sixth trumpet result in the destruction of one-third of mankind. Other judgments must destroy additional multitudes, and the drastic ecological upheavals must result in a vast death toll. The rapture and the martyrdom of believers would reduce earth's population by hundreds of millions, and at the least, the tribulation judgments will destroy half the world's population. Nevertheless, whatever the statistics, there will be enough surviving humans that they willingly will undertake to make war against the omnipotent Lord Jesus Christ (cf. Rev, 19:19).

The People of God During the Tribulation

In spite of prevailing wickedness during the tribulation, multitudes of converts will turn to God. He will provide an effective evangelistic witness, and under the Spirit's conviction and the drastic circumstances, many will respond in penitence. The rapture will undoubtedly shock lukewarm religionists into active faith. Stocks of Bibles, and written and recorded materials will continue to witness, even though the church has gone. Thus, Scripture speaks of several groups of tribulation converts.

1) The 144,000 Jewish servants

We have suggested that this group may be seen as a company of soul-winning evangelists. In listing their tribal origins, Scripture emphasizes their Jewishness. In this list, the tribes of Ephraim and Dan are omitted, but the total of twelve is maintained by naming both Joseph and Manasseh as individual tribes, and including the tribe of Levi. A reason for Dan's omission may have been that it was the first tribe to practice idolatry. In the eighteen enumerations of the tribes in Scripture, one tribe is always omitted, so that the total always stands at twelve as it does in this enumeration.

In John's vision of the Lamb with the 144,000 on Mount Zion (Rev. 14:1-5), facts concerning them are revealed: 1) they "had been redeemed from the earth," Their redemption must have occurred in the early days of the tribulation, for those previously redeemed were taken in the rapture. 2) they were "those who did not defile themselves with women." Since marriage is not a defilement (cf. "the marriage bed kept pure" Heb. 13:4), this reference is either to sexual purity, or to spiritual abstinence from the seductions of false religions (some of which involved immoral sexual practices), 3) absolute devotion to Christ had been the basis of their lives, 4) they were "purchased from among men," 5) they were "offered as firstfruits to God and the Lamb," and 6) they had been scrupulously truthful and blameless.

Scholars do not agree on the status of this company at this time. One view sees them as Jews who had accepted Christ following the rapture. For three and a half years they had been His witnesses on earth. They had then suffered martyrdom and at this time in their after life they were in the presence of Christ in the heavenly Zion prior to His second coming. Another view is that they are the godly nucleus of Israel and because they were sealed they have survived the tribulation and are now with Christ as He prepares to launch His millennial reign from the earthly Mt. Zion. The first view seems to accommodate the overall picture more adequately.

Whether the 144,000 are martyred Jewish believers or the firstfruits of millennial citizens, they are indisputably among God's tribulation people whom He very especially prizes and protects. Their lives on earth during the tribulation testify that sanctified godliness and unswerving faithfulness are freely possible even in the most difficult and ungodly surroundings.

2) The souls under the altar

When the fifth seal was opened, John saw the souls under the altar. He reported in some detail what he had seen.

> I saw under the altar the souls of those who had been slain because of the word of God and the testimony they had maintained. They called out in a loud voice, "How long, Sovereign Lord, holy and true, until you judge the inhabitants of the earth and avenge our blood?" Then each of them was given a white robe, and they were told to wait a little longer, until the number of their fellow servants and brothers who were to be killed as they had been was completed (Rev. 6:9-11).

A number of insights derive from John's vision: 1) they had all arrived in glory through martyrdom, 2) they had believed and practiced God's Word and all who did so could expect a similar fate, 3) they ask for vengeance upon their murderers who still live on earth and thus they do not conform to present standards that instruct "pray for those who mistreat you" (Luke 6:28), 4) they are so concerned about the injustice that they cry in a loud voice, but they address God as "Sovereign Lord" rather than by a typical Christian address, 5) their cry is heard but the answer is delayed, 6) their white robes confirm their status as justified in Christ, 7) the persecution and martyrdom of such believers will continue to the end of the tribulation. Items 3) and 4) above distinguish this group from church saints.

Apparently the souls of tribulation saints remain "under the altar" awaiting Christ's resurrection call. Their state compares with Christian saints now waiting in Paradise for the rapture and the provision of their resurrection bodies. In Old Testament rituals, drink offerings and the blood of sacrifices collected under the altar. As he awaited martyrdom, Paul saw himself to be a drink offering. "For I am already being poured out like a drink offering, and the time has come for my departure" (2 Tim. 4:6).

3) The great uncountable multitude

Following John's vision of the sealing of the 144,000, he was granted the vision of the great multitude. Though Scripture does not expressly identify the multitude as the fruit of the ministry of the 144,000, as we have noted, the fact that the description of the multitude immediately follows that of the 144,000 suggests a cause and effect relationship. The heavenly elder proceeded to explain the identity of the multitude.

> **There before me was a great multitude that no one could count, from every nation, tribe, people and language, standing before the throne and in front of the Lamb. They were wearing white robes and were holding palm branches. . . . These are they who have come out of the great tribulation; they have washed their robes and made them white in the blood of the Lamb. Therefore, they are before the throne of God and serve him day and night in the temple. . . . Never again will they hunger; never again will they thirst. The sun will not beat upon them. . . . And God will wipe away every tear from their eyes (Rev. 7:9, 14-17).**

Notable facts concerning this company include the following: 1) the group is very large and totally multinational, 2) white robes spoke of justification through Christ and palm branches of their participation in worshiping Him, 3) they have suffered death on earth during the time of the great tribulation, 4) they had undergone drastic exposure and deprivation, 5) they died with faith in Christ's shed blood, 6) they died under brutal, painful, sorrowful circumstances, 7) in heaven they serve God in His temple and thus have a different destiny from that of the church which in heaven is Christ's bride.

Scripture does not designate the great multitude as martyrs, but obviously they were victims of destructive persecution. Perhaps they suffered deprivation and starvation that led to their death because they refused to accept the mark of the beast so that they could buy and sell. They are thus a distinctive group of saints, and neither Jewish evangelists nor martyr-converts.

The great multitude are tribulation casualties, but they are distinguished from the tribulation martyrs of Revelation 6:9-11 (souls under the altar) or 20:4-5 (company of the beheaded).

While the multitude stands before God, wears white robes, and holds palm branches, it is not certain that they possess resurrection bodies. The souls under the altar also were given white robes, and yet apparently they were left in their disembodied state and told to wait a little longer. By the time the millennium is under way, however, all tribulation saints will have been given their resurrection bodies as a phase of the first resurrection (see Rev. 20:4-5).

4) The company before the sea of glass

Prior to the dispatch of the seven angels with the bowls of God's wrath, John saw a special company of people in heaven.

> And I saw what looked like a sea of glass mixed with fire and, standing before the sea, those who had been victorious over the beast and his image and over the number of his name. They held harps given them by God and sang the song of Moses the servant of God and the song of the Lamb (Rev. 15:2-3).

The King James Version expands their identification: "them that had gotten the victory over the beast, and over his image, and over his mark, and over the number of his name." The Greek word for "mark" (*charagma*), however, is not actually in the text.

We are not told how these saints were victorious, but in some way they had completely rejected the beast's system. Their rejection had caused them to lose their lives, but they had found them again. Since they were in glory during the seven-year tribulation, apparently they had died prematurely. Scripture does not call them martyrs, though perhaps they were. Their deaths may have resulted from artificial famines resulting from Antichrist's restrictions upon trade. They would thus have been martyrs only indirectly.

5) The company of the beheaded

In his vision of the beginning of the millennium, John identified the company of the beheaded in conjunction with those "who had been given authority to judge." He reported his vision:

> I saw the souls of those who had been beheaded because of their testimony for Jesus and because of the word of God. They had not worshiped the beast or his image and had not received his mark on their foreheads or their hands. They came to life and reigned with Christ a thousand years (Rev. 20:4).

The fact that they "came to life" implies that they received resurrection bodies. Since this group had been beheaded, it is obvious that they were martyrs who were set apart by their mode of execution. They were martyred because they defied Antichrist.

6) The Jews as nationals and as converts

As we have seen, the tribulation directly concerns the Jewish people, and one of its major goals is to bring them to accept their Messiah. When Armageddon ends, all surviving Jews will be

Jesus' loyal subjects, poised to receive His millennial blessings. Scriptures depicting the outworking of God's goals include:

> When you are in distress and all these things have happened to you, then in later days you will return to the LORD your God and obey him. For the LORD your God . . . will not abandon or destroy you or forget the covenant with your forefathers (Deut. 4:30-31).

> "On that day the LORD will shield those who live in Jerusalem, so that the feeblest among them will be like David. . . . On that day I will set out to destroy all the nations that attack Jerusalem. And I will pour out on the house of David and the inhabitants of Jerusalem a spirit of grace and supplication. They will look on me, the one they have pierced, and they will mourn for him as one mourns for an only child, and grieve bitterly for him" (Zech. 12:8-10).

> All Israel will be saved, as it is written: "The deliverer will come from Zion; he will turn godlessness away from Jacob. And this is my covenant with them when I take away their sins" (Rom. 11:26-27).

> He [i.e., the Antichrist] will speak against the Most High and . . . the saints will be handed over to him for a time, times and half a time. But the court will sit, and his power will be taken away and completely destroyed forever. Then the sovereignty, power and greatness of the kingdoms under the whole heaven will be handed over to the saints, the people of the Most High (Dan. 7:25-27).

The attack upon the Jews and the providential protection of a select group was described by Daniel:

> At that time Michael, the great prince who protects your people, will arise. There will be a time of distress [for Daniel's people] such as has not happened from the beginning of nations until then. But at that time your people—everyone whose name is found written in the book—will be delivered (Dan. 12:1).

The "man clothed in linen" explained that the duration of this "time of distress" would be "for a time, times and half a time," and that "When the power of the holy people has been finally broken, all these things will be completed" (Dan. 12:7). Israel will be ready to acknowledge their Messiah when their own strength and traditional religious assumptions have been totally shattered by Antichrist and the onset of Armageddon.

With the world's armies against them, and in the face of the threat of total annihilation, the Jews undergo a national conversion. Presumably, those Jews who continue the traditional rejection of Christ become victims of Armageddon's destruction. The survivors respond to their prior rejection of the Messiah with sincere life-changing penitent grief. The entire living nation of Israel is prepared for its vital millennial role. The tribulation has effectively achieved that which God had planned thousands of years previously (cf. Deut. 4:30-31; Jer. 39- 41).

The tribulation saints in summary

Six groups have been described, but the descriptions may involve two views of the same group. It is clear, that both the souls under the altar, and the company of those beheaded, were martyrs. The fact that the uncountable multitude and the company before the sea of glass were in glory while the tribulation was still in process would indicate that they died under unnatural circumstances resulting from Antichrist's cruelties. Likely, also, such events would explain the presence of the 144,000 on Mount Zion. Thus, two of the five groups appear as formal martyrs, and three appear as haphazard victims of Antichrist's policies. The living Jewish saints are in a separate category, and their immediate reward is physical survival into the millennium.

Conversion During the Tribulation

The tribulation is the seventieth "week" of the time period determined for Israel (cf. Dan. 9:24). It is future, but it is a continuation of Old Testament times. The church age, with all its unique privileges, has run its earthly course, and Christ has chosen His Bride and called her from this earth by means of the rapture. The calling out of a people of God is now appropriate to the times and conditions that prevail.

1) **The primary call will be to repentance.** The pre-church gospel called to repentance, and this was the message of Old Testament prophets, John the Baptist, and Jesus. "Repent! Turn from your idols and renounce all your detestable practices!" (Ezek. 14:6; cf. Jer. 8:6; Amos 5:14, 15; Jonah 3:7-9; Zech. 1:4); "John the Baptist came, preaching . . . and saying, Repent, for the kingdom of heaven is near" (Matt. 3:1-2); "From that time on [as Jesus began His preaching ministry] Jesus began to preach, 'Repent, for the kingdom of heaven is near'" (Matt. 4:17).

2) **The ministry model will be that of the pre-church era.** The church appeal is that of a loving Savior seeking a bride; the tribulation appeal is that of a King seeking penitent citizens for His soon-to-be-launched kingdom. In Old Testament fashion, John the Baptist addressed his hearers, "You brood of vipers! Who warned you to flee from the coming wrath?" (Matt. 3:7) Scripture describes the ministry of the two witnesses during the tribulation, "They will prophesy for 1,260 days, clothed in sackcloth. . . . If anyone tries to harm them, fire comes from their mouths and devours their enemies . . . These men have power to shut up the sky so that it will not rain during the time they are prophesying; and they have power to turn the waters into blood and to strike the earth with every kind of plague as often as they want" (Rev. 11:3,

5-6). Destructive miracles are not usually God's provision to confirm the Christian gospel.

3) **The Holy Spirit will confirm ministry efforts.** The outpoured Spirit will not be withdrawn. What began on the day of Pentecost remains an ongoing process that will continue until the second coming. "I will pour out my Spirit in those days . . . I will show wonders in the heaven above and signs on the earth below, blood and fire and billows of smoke. The sun will be turned to darkness and the moon to blood. . . . And everyone who calls on the name of the Lord will be saved" (Acts 2:18-21; cf. Matt. 24:29-31). The Holy Spirit will convict, impress, and confirm the message to those who hear. He will be especially active during the cosmic disturbances of the tribulation period.

Paul wrote, "The secret power of lawlessness is already at work; but the one who now holds it back will continue to do so until he is taken out of the way" (2 Thess. 2:7). The one who holds back the power of lawlessness—often spoken of as the restrainer—is frequently seen as the Holy Spirit. Some suggest that, during the tribulation, He will cease His present work on earth and return to His pre-church relationship. Though He was present, His indwelling was limited to chosen people (e.g., prophets). (cf. "He lives with you and will be in you" [John 14:17]).

Notwithstanding the foregoing, it is evident that the Spirit in this age primarily expresses Himself through the church. Thus it appears preferable to see the Spirit-indwelt church to be the restrainer as it exercises its anti-corruptive influence as the salt of the earth (cf. Matt. 5:13). Though the word for church (*ekklesia* [ek-clay-SEE-ah]) is feminine in Greek, the masculine article ("the one who holds") implies the personification of the church as the living body of Christ. The rapture will remove the church from earth and end its present social and cultural influence, but the Holy Spirit will still be able to continue His work in humans during the tribulation.

4) **Justification will depend upon Christ's sacrifice.** The justified status granted to tribulation humans who repent will depend on Christ's finished work on Calvary, just as it does for today's converts. Paul commented on the ministry of John the Baptist: "John's baptism was a baptism of repentance. He told the people to believe in the one coming after him, that is, in Jesus" (Acts 19:4). Notably, the heavenly elder explained to John concerning the great multitude in white robes: "These are they who have come out of the great tribulation; they have washed their robes and made them white in the blood of the Lamb" (Rev. 7:14).

5) The tribulation saints are a distinct body. In Old Testament times God had Israelite [or Jewish] saints, "He has raised up for his people a horn [a king], the praise of all his saints, of Israel, the people close to his heart" (Psa. 148:14). Today, God has His church saints, for Paul wrote to, "all the saints in Christ Jesus at Philippi" (Phil. 1:1). When the church saints have been raptured or "harvested," God will proceed with a new company. Thus, the 144,000 are the firstfruits among the tribulation saints, "They were purchased from among men and offered as firstfruits to God and the Lamb" (Rev. 14:4).

Scripture confirms the fact of God's tribulation saints. "The saints will be handed over to him [Antichrist] for a time, times, and half a time" (Dan. 7:25); "[Antichrist] was given power to make war against the saints and to conquer them" (Rev. 13:7). The eternal destiny of all saints is the new Jerusalem. Church saints are resurrected and united with Christ at the rapture; Jewish or Old Testament saints, and tribulation saints are resurrected after the second coming.

The Surviving Sheep Nations

Those Gentiles who survive the tribulation and are not destroyed in Armageddon are a people of God, who along with the Jews, enter the millennium in their natural human bodies. Only those who align with Christ and His people will escape His destructive judgment associated with Armageddon.

> When the Son of Man comes in his glory, and all the angels with him . . . [a]ll the nations will be gathered before him, and he will separate the people one from another as a shepherd separates the sheep from the goats. He will put the sheep on his right. . . . Then the King will say . . . "Come, you who are blessed by my Father; take your inheritance, the kingdom prepared for you since the creation of the world" (Matt. 25:31-34).

In this passage Jesus explains that people's kindness to His people is accepted as a personal kindness to Him. He declares the principle, "Whatever you did for one of the least of these brothers of mine, you did for me" (Matt. 25:40).

Other Scriptures similarly make the point that though multitudes of rebels are destroyed by Christ, there are those humans who meet His terms and enjoy a glorious future.

> This will happen when the Lord Jesus is revealed from heaven in blazing fire with his powerful angels. He will punish those who do not know God and do not obey the gospel of our Lord Jesus. . . . [O]n that day he comes to be glorified in his holy people and to be marveled at among all those who have believed (2 Thess. 1:7-8, 10); "At the end of the age. The Son of Man will send out his angels, and they will weed out of his kingdom everything that causes sin and all who do evil. . . . Then the righteous will shine like the sun in the kingdom of their Father (Matt. 13:40-41, 43).

Not only the Jews, but the Gentiles also, are selected and approved to continue their life in the millennium by their response to the pressures of the tribulation, including events at Armageddon. These "saved" Gentile converts are not church saints, for these latter were raptured seven years previously. The reward to the Gentile converts is to be welcomed as the initial citizens of the millennial kingdom.

Preludes to Armageddon

The Scriptural description of end-time conflicts seems to require two wars that precede Armageddon. These events are not essential to the overall understanding of the tribulation, however, and they may be thought of as tentative proposals. They depend, at least in part, upon what one takes as primary or secondary in Scriptural interpretation.

Possible preliminary wars

The prophet Daniel, beginning at 11:21, describes the exploits of Antiochus Epiphanes. As we have noted, however, from verse 36 onward, the language transcends the scope of Antiochus' blasphemous deeds. Scripture proceeds to describe an even more heinous end-time King who demands worship for himself—we know him as Antichrist. Daniel says, "He will be successful until the time of wrath [Heb. *za'am*] is completed" (11:36). (*za'am* [ZAH-am]: state of being angry, wrath, rage, indignation, tribulation—see p. 126).

Concerning this King who exalts himself, (i.e., Antichrist), Daniel writes: "At the time of the end the king of the South will engage him in battle, and the king of the North will storm out against him with chariots and cavalry and a great fleet of ships" (Dan. 11:40). The outcome of this attack by the North and South upon Antichrist will be a major victory for the latter, and an excuse for him to pillage the land of Israel (cf. v. 41). Antichrist's victory at this time apparently will precipitate his ambitious dreams of world conquest, and the achieving of total control of all of earth's citizens.

The second conflict of the latter half of the tribulation involves either a threat or a declaration of war upon Antichrist. "Reports from the east and the north will alarm him, and he will set out in a great rage to destroy and annihilate many. He will pitch his royal tents between the seas at the beautiful holy mountain. Yet he will come to his end, and no one will help him" (Dan. 11:44-45). These events appear to set the stage for Armageddon. At the news that a vast army from the east, and a revived (?) northern bloc, is marching against him, Antichrist takes refuge in the land of Israel. This gathering of nations, and others who also join, results in Armageddon. Antichrist is destroyed, of course, not by the kings of the East and the king of the North, but by the conquering Lord Jesus Christ.

The destruction of commercial Babylon

Chapter eighteen of Revelation reports the destruction of the Babylon that represents the world's system of trade and commerce. The opening phrase "After this" (or After these things) separates these events from what went before. Antichrist and his federation of nations are responsible for the destruction of ecclesiastical Babylon (cf. 17:16-17), but the destruction of commercial Babylon appears to be a direct act of God. "Her sins are piled up to heaven, and God has remembered her crimes. . . . She will be consumed by fire, for mighty is the Lord God who judges her" (18:5, 8); "Rejoice, saints and apostles and prophets! God has judged her for the way she treated you" (18:20).

Detailed descriptions in this chapter indicate that a literal city's destruction is being reported. The destruction is almost instantaneous, for the kings who observe her will cry, "Woe! Woe, O great city, O Babylon, city of power! In one hour your doom has come! (18:10). Twice there is reference to "the smoke of her burning," and the voice from heaven declared, "her plagues will overtake her: death, mourning and famine" (v. 8). The list of items traded in Babylon totals thirty (cf. vv. 11-13), and ends with "bodies and souls of men," implying trade in slaves and prostitutes. There is special mention of losses to sea captains and those with trading fleets—perhaps fleets of cargo aircraft.

This Babylon represents unprincipled rapacious commercialism. The kings of earth are said to have committed adultery with her, probably in the sense that they participated in illicit and dishonest business agreements. The money control exercised by Babylon caused leaders to forsake good judgment. Babylon's commercialism was an ongoing behind-the-scenes force leading to the persecution of believers. "In her was found the blood of prophets and of the saints" (v. 24).

Scholars do not agree in identifying the commercial Babylon that is to be destroyed. Suggestions include 1) various actual cities such as Rome, London, New York, or a revived literal Babylon in modern Iraq, 2) the overall world economic system with its currencies, stock markets, and its standards of monetary value. The latter appears to have the wider following, though the apparent destruction of a literal city cannot be overlooked.

The Battle of Armageddon

The composite expression "Battle of Armageddon" does not occur in Scripture, but each of its terms does. "They go out to the kings . . . to gather them for the battle [Gk. *polemos*]" (Rev.

16:14); (*polemos* [POL-em-os]: armed conflict, war, battle, fight); "They gathered the kings together to the place that in Hebrew is called Armageddon" (Rev. 16:16). The outcome of that gathering is described in Scripture as the vast destruction of human life that accompanies the conquering return of Jesus Christ. The term "battle" is supported by popular lexicons, although it is noted that the original could denote an entire war. Since Armageddon is a total world conflict, its logistics may require more than a few days, but Scripture leaves these matters unspecified.

Biblical expressions that identify Armageddon and its outcomes include: "the great and dreadful (terrible KJV) day of the LORD" (Joel 2:31; Mal. 4:5), "the harvest" (Joel 3:13), "a day of vengeance (the day of the LORD's vengeance —KJV)" (Isa. 34:8), "the day that is coming (the day cometh —KJV)" (Mal. 4:1), the great winepress of God's wrath (Rev. 14:19), and "the great day of God Almighty" (Rev. 16:14).

The place and the combatants

The name "Armageddon" comes from roots (Har-Megiddo) which are thought to mean "the mount (or hill) of slaughter." The Megiddo region of Palestine constitutes the triangular Esdraelon Valley with an area of 52,000 square kilometers (20,000 sq. mi.) between two ridges that radiate south and east from Mount Carmel. It is the site of the intersection of Africa, Europe, and Asia, and is rightly described as the "crossroads of the world." History, beginning about 1500 B.C., records at least ten major battles that were fought in the Valley of Megiddo.

In addition to Megiddo as the battle site, prophetic Scripture also names the Valley of Jehoshaphat. "Let the nations be roused; let them advance into the Valley of Jehoshaphat, for there I will sit to judge all the nations on every side" (Joel 3:12). Traditionally, the Valley of Jehoshaphat has been considered an alternate name for the Kidron Valley between Jerusalem and the Mount of Olives. This view is challenged, however, and some hold that it is simply another name for Esdraelon. One view is that the Valley of Jehoshaphat is not yet in existence, but it will be the name of the "great valley" (Zech. 14:4) that will result when the Mount of Olives divides at Christ's coming.

All of the nations of earth participate in this last great conflict. God declared,

"Therefore wait for me," declares the LORD ... "I have decided to assemble the nations, to gather the kingdoms and to pour out my wrath on them" (Zeph. 3:8); I will gather all the nations to Jerusalem to fight against it. ... Then the LORD will go out and fight against those nations (Zech. 14:2-3); I saw three evil spirits that looked like frogs ... they go out to the kings of the whole world, to gather them for the battle on the great day of God Almighty"

(Rev. 16:13-14); I saw the beast and the kings of the earth and their armies gathered together to make war against the rider on the horse [i.e., Jesus] and his army (Rev. 19:19).

The earth's nations come together to fight one another, but at the last minute they direct their hostility against the Jews and their Messiah. As one commentator remarked, "It's not clear who fights with whom about what. Getting there is half the war."

The course of the battle

Armageddon's beginnings are reported: "The sixth angel poured out his bowl on the great river Euphrates, and its water was dried up to prepare the way for the kings from the East" (Rev. 16:12). Antichrist considers the possible invasion of an army from the East to be a threat to Europe (cf. Dan. 11:44), and it may be that the king of the North sees potential supporting allies in his contest with Antichrist (cf. Dan. 11:45). Apparently the three frog-like evil spirits exploit these or similar human jealousies and ambitions so that before long there is the major assembly of nations at Armageddon (cf. Rev. 16:16). Though God has ordained the gathering, He uses the evil spirits to accomplish His purpose. The prophet Joel had written,

> "I will gather all nations and bring them down to the Valley of Jehoshaphat.... for there I will sit to judge all the nations on every side. Swing the sickle, for the harvest is ripe. Come, trample the grapes, for the winepress is full." ... The LORD will roar from Zion and thunder from Jerusalem.... But the Lord will be a refuge for his people, a stronghold for the people of Israel (Joel 3:2, 12-13, 16; cf. Zech. 3:8, 14:2).

The armies of the nations of earth gather to fight one another, but they suddenly change their purpose and attack the Israelites. Scripture does not tell of the scheming negotiations that lead up to this outcome. As the one-sided battle proceeds, the Jews retreat from Megiddo and attempt a last stand in Jerusalem. The entire land, from Megiddo to Edom becomes a battlefield, from north to south 320 kilometers (200 miles) and west to east 160 kilometers (100 miles).

Zechariah revealed God's plan: "I will gather all the nations to Jerusalem to fight against it; the city will be captured, the houses ransacked, and the women raped" (Zech. 14:2). The prophet indicates a two-thirds casualty rate. "In the whole land, declares the Lord, two-thirds will be struck down and perish; yet one-third will be left in it" (Zech. 13:8). Jeremiah had written, "How awful that day will be! None will be like it. It will be a time of trouble for Jacob, but he will be saved out of it" (Jer. 30:7).

At this point the Jews repent and acknowledge Jesus as their Messiah. This remarkable turnaround by Israel has already been discussed. Jesus Christ suddenly becomes their Champion and Defender. "On that day the L ORD will shield those who live in

Jerusalem. . . . On that day I will set out to destroy all the nations that attack Jerusalem" (Zech. 12:8-9). Isaiah depicts Jesus the conqueror coming from the direction of Edom. "Who is this coming from Edom, from Bozrah [a location south of the Dead Sea], with his garments stained crimson . . . robed in splendor, striding forward in the greatness of his strength?" (Isa. 63:1).

As Christ appears, Antichrist and the nations find themselves with a new enemy, and once again they change the purpose of the war. "I saw the beast and the kings of the earth and their armies gathered together to make war against the rider on the horse and his army" (Rev. 19:19). Daniel had told of his vision of the little horn—Antichrist. "This horn was waging war against the saints and defeating them, until the Ancient of Days [i.e., Christ] came and pronounced judgment in favor of the saints of the Most High" (Dan. 7:21-22). For human armies to attack Jesus Christ and the armies of heaven has been called, "mankind's most effective attempt at suicide." Antichrist's armies will be instantly destroyed.

The glorious second coming of Christ

The final phase of Armageddon is heaven's invasion of earth. Jesus, the rider on the white horse, comes as the Deliverer of His people, and heaven's conqueror against earth's rebels.

> **The armies of heaven were following him, riding on white horses and dressed in fine linen, white and clean. Out of his mouth comes a sharp sword with which to strike down the nations. . . . He treads the winepress of the fury of the wrath of God Almighty (Rev. 19:14-15). This will happen when the Lord Jesus is revealed from heaven in blazing fire with his powerful angels. He will punish those who do not know God and do not obey the gospel of our Lord Jesus. They will be punished with everlasting destruction and shut out from the presence of the Lord (2 Thess. 1:7-9). The ten horns . . . will make war against the Lamb, but the Lamb will overcome them because he is Lord of lords and King of kings (Rev. 17:12-14).**

A smiting plague will destroy Antichrist's armies. "This is the plague with which the LORD will strike all the nations that fought against Jerusalem. Their flesh will rot while they are still standing on their feet, their eyes will rot in their sockets, and their tongues will rot in their mouths" (Zech. 14:12).

The destruction of Antichrist's rebels at Christ's second coming will create a river of blood across the entire 320-kilometer length of the land of Israel. "They were trampled in the winepress outside the city, and blood flowed out of the press, rising as high as the horses' bridles for a distance of 1,600 stadia[2]" (Rev.

---

2 The distance of 1,600 stadia is equivalent to about 300 kilometers or 180 miles.

14:20). Flocks of carrion birds will gather to "eat the flesh of kings, generals, and mighty men, of horses and their riders, and the flesh of all people, free and slave, small and great" (Rev. 19:18). In the Olivet Discourse, Jesus had said, "Wherever there ia a carcass, there the vultures will gather" (Matt. 24:28). John describes the event as "the great supper of God" (Rev. 19:17).

Christ's Armageddon victory constitutes the total overthrow of human governments, and it clears the way to launch His millennial reign. The satanic triad is summarily removed from the earthly scene:

> **The beast was captured, and with him the false prophet. . . . The two of them were thrown alive into the fiery lake of burning sulphur (Rev. 19:20); The lawless one will be revealed, whom the Lord Jesus will overthrow [Gk. *aneireo*] with the breath of his mouth and destroy [Gk. *katargeo*] by the splendor of his coming (2 Thess. 2:8)[3] I saw an angel . . . [who] seized the dragon . . . or Satan, and bound him for a thousand years. He threw him into the Abyss, and locked and sealed it over him (Rev. 20:1-3).**

Haggai describes Christ's conquering second coming and the dramatic transformations that will result. "'In a little while I will once more shake the heavens and the earth, the sea and the dry land. I will shake all nations, and the desired of all nations will come, and I will fill this house with glory,' says the LORD Almighty" (Hag. 2:6-7).

David had described the Father's words to the Son, "Sit at my right hand until I make your enemies a footstool for your feet" (Psa. 110:1). Jesus has remained at the Father's right hand since the ascension, but the relationship will change when He comes to earth to appropriate Armageddon's victory, and launch His glorious millennial rule.

---

3 *aneireo* (an-ire-EH-oh): slay, kill, put to death; *katargeo* (cat-are-GEH-oh): abolish, bring to an end, wipe out, destroy.

TEN

The Resurrection of the Dead

The English word "resurrection" is from the Latin *resurrectio* [res-er-RECK-tee-oh] which translates the Greek *anastasis* [an-AS-ta-sis]. It means "to stand up or to rise again." In addition to the noun *anastasis*, the Greek Testament uses two verb forms, *egeiro* [eg-EYE-ro] and *anistemi* [an-IS-tay-me], which in this context are usually translated "rise." "Martha answered, 'I know he will rise again [Gk. *anistemi*] in the resurrection [Gk. *anastasis*] at the last day'" (John 11:24); "The dead in Christ will rise [Gk. *anistemi*] first" (1 Thess. 4:16); "For if the dead are not raised [Gk. *egeiro*], then Christ has not been raised [Gk. *egeiro*] either" (1 Cor. 15:16).

Resurrection is defined as: "the raising up of the body so that it is released from the powers of death and made to live." By resurrection, God transforms those who have lived on earth into beings suitable for a permanent future existence. The resurrection of believers has been called "the grand finale of redemptive history." Though achieving resurrection transcends human powers, it is not a problem to God for "if God can bring a body from the womb, He certainly can bring one from the tomb."

Though the expression "resurrection of the body" is not biblical, the futurist applies the term resurrection only to the physical body. This viewpoint holds that the life to come is not primarily the life of an immortal soul, but the life of a resurrected body. The resurrection of the soul is not a Biblical concept, and to speak of a "spiritual resurrection" is to use allegorical language to describe an event of another kind—regeneration.

The doctrine of resurrection is unique to Christianity. Jesus returned from death in a new mode of life that would never die. He promised believers, "I am the resurrection and the life. He who believes in me will live, even though he dies; and whoever lives and believes in me will never die" (John 11:25-26)

Someone has noted that "The most startling characteristic of the first Christian preaching is its emphasis on the resurrection." On at least five occasions reported in the Book of Acts, speakers proclaimed the doctrine of the resurrection as a fundamental truth (cf. Acts 2:31; 4:2, 33; 17:18, 32; 23:6, 8). Christians reported not merely the story of a dead man being restored to life, but the emergence of resurrection life as God's provision for all who believe.

Resurrection Teaching in the Old Testament

Many Old Testament Scriptures portray the resurrection of the physical body:

> You will not abandon me to the grave, nor will you let your Holy One see decay (Psa. 16:10);
>
> In righteousness I will see your face; when I awake, I will be satisfied with seeing your likeness (Psa. 17:15);
>
> You guide me with your counsel, and afterward you will take me into glory (Psa. 73:24);
>
> [The LORD] will swallow up death forever. The Sovereign LORD will wipe away the tears from all faces (Isa. 25:8);
>
> Multitudes who sleep in the dust of the earth will awake: some to everlasting life, others to shame and everlasting contempt (Dan. 12:2);
>
> I will ransom them from the power of the grave; I will redeem them from death (Hos. 13:14; cf. also, Hos. 6:2);
>
> Your dead will live; their bodies will rise. You who dwell in the dust, wake up and shout for joy . . . the earth will give birth to her dead (Isa. 26:19).

The final verse cited above is especially forthright, and it has been called "the Bible's first clear statement of a resurrection."

Job expected a literal resurrection: "After my skin has been destroyed, yet in my flesh I will see God; I myself will see him with my own eyes—I, and not another" (Job 19:26-27). Abraham had faith in a future resurrection, although we learn of it primarily through a New Testament Scripture. "By faith Abraham, when God tested him, offered Isaac as a sacrifice. . . . Abraham reasoned that God could raise the dead" (Heb. 11:17, 19).

The resuscitation of three persons in the Old Testament speaks of a wider resurrection. The widow's son (1 Kings 17:21-22), the Shunammite's son (2 Kings 4:32-36), and the man who touched Elisha's bones (2 Kings 13:20-21) each lived after death, though they died again and they are yet to experience ultimate resurrection. Resuscitation is a return of life to the body; resurrection not only renews the life, but it also transforms the body to equip it for its celestial destiny. Some see a resurrection promise in Old Testament types: Joseph's restoration to his family after having been sold into Egypt, Jonah emerging from the whale, and Daniel emerging from the lion's den.

On occasion, the Old Testament links individual human resurrection with the national resurrection of the Israelites. Ezekiel was given the vision of the valley filled with very dry bones that came to life. In the application of that vision God declared, "O my people, I am going to open your graves and bring you up from them. . . . I will put my Spirit in you and you will live, and I will settle you in your own land" (Ezek. 37:12, 14).

The Old Testament teachings concerning a bodily resurrection convinced most Jews, but not the Sadducees. In describing Paul's defense before the Sanhedrin, Luke added parenthetically, "The Sadducees say that there is no resurrection, and that there are neither angels nor spirits" (Acts 23:8). To mock belief in the resurrection, the Sadducees came to Jesus with their timeworn story of the woman who had had five husbands. Jesus replied by quoting Exodus 3:6 "I am . . . the God of Abraham, the God of Isaac and the God of Jacob." He thus made the point that though the patriarchs had died, they were still alive and claiming the LORD as their God. Death was not the cessation of existence for humans, but entrance into a new mode of life.

Greek philosophy generally accepted the immortality of the soul, but denied the resurrection of the body. Thus, when on Mars Hill Paul spoke of bodily resurrection, he met sharp resistance. "When they heard about the resurrection of the dead, some of them sneered, but others said, 'We want to hear you again on this subject'" (Acts 17:32). Paul even confronted skeptical Christians: "How can some of you say that there is no resurrection of the dead?" (1 Cor. 15:12)

Resurrection Teaching in the New Testament

A total of one hundred and twenty-six NewTestament texts are considered to refer in some way to the idea of resurrection. In forty of these texts the Greek term *anastasis*, which as previously noted, is the usual word for "resurrection," occurs forty-two times. In virtually all instances *anastasis* denotes not only a rising up out of death, but also a transformation from the condition of physical death. Paul summarized the New Testament attitude toward resurrection when he wrote, "If only for this life we have hope in Christ, we are to be pitied more than all men" (1 Cor. 15:19).

Resurrection teaching by Jesus and Paul

Jesus taught a future bodily resurrection. "A time is coming when all who are in their graves will hear [the Son of man's] voice and come out—those who have done good will rise to live, and those who have done evil will rise to be condemned" (John 5:28-29); "My Father's will is that everyone who looks to the Son . . . shall have eternal life, and I will raise him up at the last day" (John 6:40). Jesus described Himself to Martha in remarkable terms: "I am the resurrection and the life. He who believes in me will live, even though he dies" (John 11:25).

Paul repeatedly affirmed this doctrine, and he regularly included it in his spoken messages. When he spoke at Antioch, he referred to Jesus' resurrection four times (cf. Acts 13:30, 33-34, 37), and at Athens, "Paul was preaching the good news about Jesus and the resurrection" (Acts 17:18). In his defense before Governor Felix he spoke of the prophets and added, "I have the same hope in God as these men, that there will be a resurrection of both the righteous and the wicked" (Acts 24:15). He asked of King Agrippa and his Jewish accusers, "Why should any of you consider it incredible that God raises the dead?" (Acts 26:8)

In his writings also, Paul saw bodily resurrection to be a basic concept. Typical examples would be: "By his power God raised the Lord from the dead, and he will raise us also" (1 Cor. 6:14), and, "[The Lord Jesus] will transform our lowly bodies so that they will be like his glorious body" (Phil. 3:21).

New Testament resurrections

The resurrection of Jesus Christ is a pivotal event in the New Testament. He had predicted His resurrection under the figure of the rebuilt temple (John 2:19, 21), and the sign of the prophet Jonah (cf. Matt. 12:39-40; 16:4; Luke 11:29). He portrayed His resurrection as the one miraculous sign of His Messiahship. The Gospels report the empty tomb (cf. Matt. 28:6; Mark 16:6; Luke 24:3; John 20:2, 6, 8, 12), and the message of the angel, "Why do you look for the living among the dead?" (Luke 24:5) In 1 Corinthians 15, Paul develops the spiritual and theological significance of Christ's resurrection:

> But Christ has indeed been raised from the dead, the firstfruits of those who have fallen asleep. For since death came through a man, the resurrection of the dead comes also through a man (1 Cor. 15:20-21); But someone may ask, How are the dead raised? With what kind of body will they come? . . . So will it be with the resurrection of the dead. The body that is sown is perishable, it is raised imperishable; it is sown in dishonor, it is raised in glory; it is sown in weakness, it is raised in power; it is sown a natural body, it is raised a spiritual body (1 Cor. 15:35, 42-44).

Jesus Christ's resurrection victory uniquely characterizes the message and character of Christianity.

The New Testament tells of five individuals, apart from Jesus, who were restored to earthly life after having died. These included Jairus' daughter (Matt. 9:18-26); the son of the widow of Nain (Luke 7:11-15); Lazarus (John 11:1-46); Dorcas (Tabitha) (Acts 9:36-42), and Eutychus (Acts 20:9-12). These people, just as their Old Testament counterparts, were raised to die again since their bodies were revived by not transformed (they were resuscitated rather than resurrected), but their experience substantiates the expectation of resurrection.

The special resurrection at the time of Christ's crucifixion was a confirming sign of Christ's victory over death. "When Jesus had cried out again in a loud voice, he gave up his spirit. At that moment . . . the tombs broke open and the bodies of many holy people who had died were raised to life. They came out of the tombs, and after Jesus' resurrection they went into the holy city and appeared to many people" (Matt. 27:50-52).

This return to life is usually thought to have been a true resurrection consisting of chosen firstfruits of Old Testament saints. The destiny of these resurrected ones is often linked with Paul's quotation of Psalm 68:18 "When he ascended on high, he led captives in his train" (Eph. 4:8). Apart from this special demonstration, for all others the resurrection remains future. Years later, Paul warned of certain heretics, "They say that the resurrection has already taken place, and they destroy the faith of some" (2 Tim. 2:18).

The Doctrine of Resurrection in History

The early church accepted the Pauline thesis that the resurrection was an essential truth of Christianity. "If you confess with your mouth, Jesus is Lord, and believe in your heart that God raised him from the dead, you will be saved" (Rom. 10:9).

Resurrection teachings by the fathers

In the writings of the church fathers, the resurrection of Christ was one of the topics of major concern. Extant references to resurrection include those of: Clement of Rome (c. 30-100) "[God] made the Lord Jesus Christ to be the firstfruits when He raised Him from the dead"—(*Epistle to the Corinthians*); Ignatius (c. 35-107) "[The church] rejoices in the passion of our Lord and in His resurrection without wavering"; Irenaeus (c. 130-202) wrote that the "[church throughout the world confessed belief in] the resurrection of the flesh."

Athenagoras, a professor in Athens and a Christian convert, produced a complete treatise on the subject of the resurrection of the dead. He wrote prior to A.D. 180, and he described resurrection as necessary if man is to fulfill his true human potential. Many see this viewpoint as excessively earthly or material. Also, Athenagoras is criticized for making no mention of Christ's resurrection as the ground for Christian expectation. Fragments of a work of the same era, often attributed to Justin Martyr (c. 100-165), present the resurrection on a more distinctly biblical basis, though still with an excessive materialistic bias.

The materialistic view of resurrection

Tertullian (c. 160-220) wrote: "Flesh shall rise again, wholly in every man, in its own identity, in its absolute integrity." (*On the Resurrection of the Flesh*). Because of this emphasis on the flesh, Tertullian was judged by many to be too materialistic in his concept of resurrection, though perhaps he merged resurrection and millennial bodies.

Origen (c. 185-254), reacted against a materialistic resurrection: "As from the grain of corn an ear rises up, so in the body there lies a certain principle which is not corrupted and from which the body is raised in incorruption" (*Against Celsus*). For Origen, resurrection was essentially spiritual. The believer's resurrection body would not relate to the natural in substance, organs, or form, but only in underlying spirit. He wrote, "Here we see with eyes, act with hands, walk with feet. But in that spiritual body we shall be all sight, all hearing, all activity."

In his later writings, Jerome (c. 347-420) sided with Tertullian against Origen. Augustine (354-430), in his earlier writings, inconsistently endorsed both positions, but eventually he took a stand in favor of a Tertullian-like materialistic resurrection. Pope Gregory I (c. 540-604) promoted materialistic resurrection as a dogmatic article of faith in the Catholic church. Out of this background, Thomas Aquinas (1224-1274) taught that Christ's resurrection body, which was the pattern for all believers, consisted of flesh, bones, and even blood integrally present without diminution. Thus, in his view, a perfect resurrection was necessarily materialistic.

Creedal statements of resurrection

As early as the second century, and not later than the fourth, the developing creeds of the church took note of bodily resurrection. The *Athanasian Creed* affirmed: "All men shall rise again with their bodies"; and the *Nicene Creed* declared, "I look for the resurrection of the dead." The *Apostles' Creed* in the Latin version speaks of belief in the "resurrection of the flesh." This non-Biblical expression was likely introduced to counteract Origen's spiritual resurrection. The English version of the Creed declares simply, "I believe in . . . the resurrection of the body." The intention of these creeds, and other classic Christian statements, has been to express a firm commitment to a literal bodily resurrection.

The same avowed literalism is evident in the *Catechism* that emerged from the Council of Trent (1545-1563). "The identical body, which belongs to each of us during life, shall, though corrupt, and dissolved into original dust, be raised up again to life. . . . Man is, therefore, to rise again in the same body with which he served God, or was a slave to the devil." Most Protestants prefer a less speculative and more biblical statement of these matters. Thus, the Church of England's *Thirty-Nine Articles* (1563,

1571) sees Christ's accomplishments as the pattern of resurrection. "Christ did truly arise again from death, and took again His body, with flesh, bones, and all things appertaining to the perfection of man's nature, wherewith He ascended into Heaven."

Scriptural Teachings Concerning Resurrection

The Bible does not answer all our questions, but it specifically tells us that through resurrection Jesus Christ "will transform our lowly bodies so that they will be like his glorious body" (Phil. 3:21). The resurrection body will possess some present properties, such as life; it will also have new and glorious powers to equip the resurrected one for eternal existence. Resurrection on biblical terms, involving infusing life in that which was dead, is a totally supernatural event.[1]

The believer's resurrection body

The nature of the believer's resurrection body will be determined by the present body, but that body will be changed so as to participate in the nature of Christ's resurrection body. Resurrection is God's provision to transform bodies of dead humans into a state of incorruptibility and immortality. Some qualities and characteristics of the resurrection body of the believer are given in Scripture as follows:

1) **Its model is Jesus Christ.** "Just as we have borne the likeness of the earthly man, so shall we bear the likeness of the man from heaven" (1 Cor. 15:49); "We know that when he appears, we shall be like him, for we shall see him as he is" (1 John 3:2).

2) **It is imperishable.** "The body that is sown is perishable, it is raised imperishable [free from decay]" (1 Cor. 15:42); "They can no longer die" (Luke 20:36).

3) **It is glorious.** "It is sown in dishonor [humiliation], it is raised in glory [splendor]" (1 Cor. 15:43); "The power that enables him to bring everything under his control ... will transform our lowly bodies so that they will be like his glorious body" (Phil. 3:21)

4) **It is powerful.** "It is sown in weakness [feebleness], it is raised in power [full of strength]" (1 Cor. 15:43).

5) **Its realm is spiritual.** "It is sown a natural body, it is raised a spiritual body" (1 Cor. 15:44). It is not that the resurrection body consists of spirit, but that its nature is adapted to functioning in the spiritual realm of the life to come.

---

1 Scholars point out that the supernatural nature of resurrection, strictly applied, invalidates comparisons with natural events. An apparently dead seed or bulb may germinate and grow, but only because it contains a living germ. Human death involves the departure of the spirit of life.

6) Sex distinctions will not longer determine specific roles. "Those who are considered worthy of taking part . . . in the resurrection from the dead will neither marry nor be given in marriage" (Luke 20:35).

Christ's resurrection body provides a preview of what the resurrected believer can expect. To call Christ the "firstfruits" is to declare that the "crop" has come to fruition, and the harvest will be successful. His experience establishes that there will be more of the same. The resurrection body of Jesus could be seen and touched, and He could sit down with His disciples and eat food (cf. Luke 24:39-43; John 20:20, 27; 21:12-15). Nevertheless, His body was not subject to time, space, or material limitations (cf. Mark 16:12, 14; Luke 24:31, 36; John 20:19, 26). On two occasions He passed through walls to enter the room where His disciples were meeting (cf. John 20:19, 26).

Jesus spoke of Himself as "flesh and bones" (Luke 24:39), rather than flesh and blood. The resurrected Christ was recognized by those who knew Him in His prior life, though with some confusion—perhaps because they believed He was dead. His body appears to have represented both a continuity with His previous body, and also a discontinuity. On the one hand, the resurrected Christ functioned entirely independently of the laws of nature and the limitations of matter. On the other hand, on occasion, He freely chose to act in conformity to the requirements imposed upon physical bodies.

Christ's resurrection guarantees the resurrection of believers. Paul argues this thesis in 1 Corinthians 15 which has already been cited. Peter saw Jesus as "the author of life" (Acts 3:15), and the source of victory over death. Jesus revealed Himself to the aged John exiled on Patmos. "I am the Living One; I was dead, and behold I am alive for ever and ever! And I hold the keys of death and Hades" (Rev. 1:18). Sixty or more years previously, just prior to the cross, Jesus had said to John and the disciples, "Because I live, you also will live" (John 14:19). Paul expressed his personal expectations, "I want to know Christ and the power of his resurrection and the fellowship of sharing in his sufferings, becoming like him in death, and so, somehow to attain to the resurrection from the dead" (Phil. 3:10-11). Similarly, he reassured the Romans, "He who raised Christ from the dead will also give life to your mortal bodies through his Spirit, who lives in you" (Rom. 8:11).

The future body and the present one

There is continuity between the body laid in the grave and the resurrection body, but not exact duplication. "When you sow, you do not plant the body that will be, but just a seed, perhaps of wheat or of something else. But God gives it a body as he has determined, and to each kind of seed he gives its own body" (1 Cor. 15:37-38). The analogy is to a plant that emerges from a sown seed. What is placed into the ground determines what comes out, but the seed, and the plant that grows, are not the same objects. The seed provides information directing the assembly of the material elements that will comprise the living plant. The qualities of the believer's resurrection body will be determined by his or her prior earthly body, but the resurrection body will derive its nature and essence from its own realm.

Whatever changes the resurrection accomplishes, the personality and identity of the individual will not be lost. Resurrected humans will be recognizable and identifiable. "Now we see but a poor reflection as in a mirror; then we shall see face to face. Now I know in part; then I shall know fully, even as I am fully known" (1 Cor. 13:12). Stephen instantly knew the resurrected Jesus, "Stephen . . . looked up to heaven and saw the glory of God, and Jesus standing at the right hand of God" (Acts 7:55). The disciples on the Mount of Transfiguration identified those they saw in the after life. "Just then there appeared before them Moses and Elijah, talking with Jesus" (Matt. 17:3).

In the foregoing pattern, the dead rich man in Hades identified others in the after life. "The rich man . . . looked up and saw Abraham far away, with Lazarus by his side" (Luke 16:23). Although Moses, Elijah, Abraham and Lazarus in the after life would not yet have had resurrection bodies, they were readily recognizable. Job's words of resurrection recognition are a classic: "I know that my Redeemer lives, and that in the end he will stand upon the earth. And after my skin has been destroyed, yet in my flesh I will see God; I myself will see him with my own eyes—I, and not another" (Job 19:25-27).

Other issues regarding resurrection

Various attempts to explain the resurrection body have been rejected by Christendom. Origen depicted resurrection as the soul's experience in putting on a better garment than its former body which is now decaying in the grave. Critics spoke of his view as the "topcoat theory." In the nineteenth century, W.N. Clarke taught that at death the body is abandoned to be known no more. Both views fail to account for Christ's role as firstfruits, and they provide no adequate link between the two bodies.

Scripture hints that resurrected believers not only experience a transformed body, but also an inner moral change. "We know that when he appears, we shall be like him, for we shall see him as he is" (1 John 3:2); "You have come to God, the judge of all men, to the spirits of righteous men made perfect" (Heb. 12:23).

God's method of achieving this Christlikeness is not really explained, but it is evident that He does not excuse believers from exercising maximum efforts while they live on earth to seek to grow in grace and achieve the image of Christ.

Scripture says very little about the resurrection body of the sinner. Daniel wrote, however, "Multitudes who sleep in the dust of the earth will awake: some to everlasting life, others to shame and everlasting contempt" (Dan. 12:2). This verse implies that the resurrection of the sinner will parallel that of the believer. The sinner's resurrection body will fit him for a lost eternity.

The Time of The Resurrections

Since Scripture speaks of the "first resurrection" (cf. Rev. 20:5b) it implies that there is a second resurrection. Paul spoke of an orderly sequence of resurrections . "In Christ all will be made alive. But each in his own turn: Christ, the firstfruits; then, when he comes, those who belong to him" (1 Cor. 15:22-23).

The first resurrection

John wrote: "I saw the souls of those who had been beheaded because of their testimony for Jesus. . . . They came to life and reigned with Christ a thousand years. . . . This is the **first resurrection**" (Rev. 20:4-5). It is evident, however, that he is speaking of tribulation saints, and these are only one group among those included in the first resurrection. Thus, this resurrection is best understood when it is seen to include four phases.

The first phase of the first resurrection primarily focused on the resurrection of "Christ, the firstfruits" (see 1 Cor. 15:23 above). It may also have included as firstfruits the "many holy people who . . . [at the moment of Jesus' death] came out of the tombs and after Jesus' resurrection they went into the holy city and appeared to many people" (Matt. 27:52-53). This select circle of holy people are thought by many to have modeled an actual resurrection rather than only a resuscitation.

Only this phase of the first resurrection is completed; all other phases await the future work of Christ. Jesus taught, "My Father's will is that everyone who looks to the Son and believes in him shall have eternal life, and I will raise him up at the last day" (John 6:40). The "last day" can be understood as the last day of this church age, and the last day(s) of the tribulation—the final or seventieth "week" of the Old Testament era.

The second phase of the first resurrection is the rapture of the church. Paul wrote that "the dead in Christ will rise first" (1 Thess. 4:16); "Christ, the firstfruits; then . . . those who belong to him" (1 Cor. 15:23). The original of Philippians 3:11 suggests a

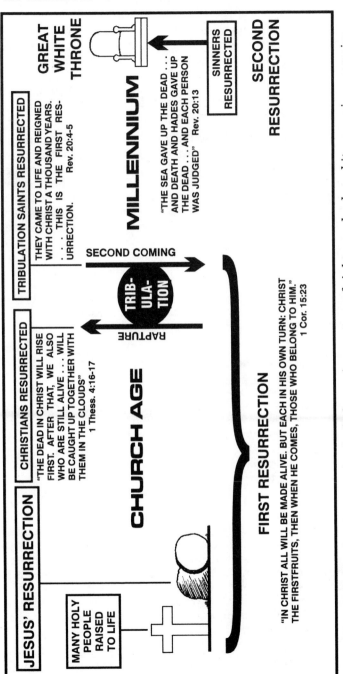

Fig. 12: The first resurrection includes various groups of righteous dead, and it occurs in successive stages. The second resurrection is a one-occasion event.

prior phase of the first resurrection. "I long to know Christ and the power shown by his resurrection . . . so that I may perhaps attain as he did, the resurrection [Gk. *eksanastasis*] from the dead" (Phil. 3:10-11, Phillips). (*eksanastasis*: [ex-an-AS-ta-sis] (lit.) out-resurrection, an uprising from, "earlier resurrection"—Rotherham, "resurrection that lifts me out from among"—Williams). Among resurrections, the church, at the rapture, enjoys one that exclusively is its own.

The third phase of the first resurrection is the raising up and translation to heaven of the tribulation saints. Scripture provides no details of the timing of these activities, but they must be completed by the beginning of the millennium following the conclusion of the tribulation. The martyrs who are specifically said to be in the first resurrection come to life in time to reign with Christ a thousand years (cf. Rev. 20:4-6). The great uncountable multitude were in heaven when John saw them (Rev. 7:9-17), apparently while the tribulation was in progress on earth. We previously noted (p. 165) that whether they were already resurrected is a matter of speculation. Possibilities include: 1) they were in heaven but were still awaiting bodily resurrection, or 2) they had already had their own special resurrection event, or 3) John saw them as they would be at the close of the tribulation.

The fourth phase of the first resurrection is for Old Testament believers—some refer to this group as "precross saints." Daniel was instructed, "From the time that the daily sacrifice is abolished . . . there will be 1,290 days. Blessed is the one who waits for and reaches the end of the 1,335 days. As for you . . . at the end of the days you will rise to receive your allotted inheritance" (Dan. 12:11-13). Thus, Daniel and all Old Testament believers, were promised their own future resurrection. Two times are given: one is thirty days, and the other seventy-five days, after Armageddon. The latter appears to be God's choice for the actual resurrection.

The significance of the thirtieth day in the above formula is not given, but possibilities are: 1) it marks the resurrection of the last group of tribulation saints, or 2) it provides an appropriate period for the cleansing of the temple. In Israel, thirty days has precedence as the duration of a period of mourning or cleansing (cf. Deut. 34:8; Num. 20:29). When King Hezekiah found that there was a shortage of priests, he postponed the Passover celebration for thirty days (cf. 2 Chron. 30:1-4).

Seventy-five days after Armageddon will be a desirable time for the resurrection of Old Testament saints. At that time the debris and confusion of the tribulation will have been dealt with, and Christ will be proceeding to launch the millennium. Also, this two and a half month period following Armageddon may be necessary for living Jews who survived the tribulation to be regathered to Palestine.

In the Jewish calendar, the period from the Day of Atonement (*Yom Kippur*) to Hanukkah is always set at seventy-five days. Hanukkah celebrates the defeat of Antiochus (who, as we have seen, prefigured Antichrist), and the cleansing and rededication of the temple in the time of the Maccabees. The same interval of seventy-five days would speak to the Jews with appropriate relevance.

Other Biblical designations of the first resurrection are "the resurrection of the righteous [or just]" (Luke 14:14); "the resurrection from the dead" (Luke 20:34); "a resurrection of life" (John 5:29 NASB), and "a better resurrection" (Heb. 11:35). John wrote, "Blessed and holy are those who have part in the first resurrection . . . they will be priests of God and of Christ and will reign with him for a thousand years" (Rev. 20:6).

The second resurrection

Those humans out of the entire span of history, who died as unbelievers and apart from God's saving grace, will have missed the first resurrection, and therefore they must await the second. Scripture describes the second resurrection, "I saw the dead, great and small, standing before the throne. . . . The sea gave up the dead that were in it, and death and Hades gave up the dead that were in them, and each person was judged according to what he had done" (Rev. 20:12-13).

Obviously, the second resurrection involves an immediate judgment which will be discussed later. It occurs following the millennium, and therefore it is separated from the last phase of the first resurrection by one thousand years. "The rest of the dead did not come to life until the thousand years were ended" (Rev. 20:5). In the NASB this event is rendered: "a resurrection of judgment" (John 5:29), but in the KJV the phrase is, "the resurrection of damnation." Paul identified it as "a resurrection of . . . the wicked [unjust —KJV]" (Acts 24:15).

Scripture indicates that in the raising of the dead the same kind of event will occur in both the first and second resurrections. We note John's use of language as he describes the faithful martyrs at the close of the tribulation. "They came to life (*zao*)[2] and reigned with Christ a thousand years. (The rest of the dead did not come to life (*zao*) until the thousand years were ended.)

2 *zao* (ZA-oh): to be physically alive, to become alive again, to live on—the identical Greek word is used in both occurrences.

This is the first resurrection" (Rev. 20:4-5). In each case a bodily resurrection is indicated, and we know that the first resurrection will provide a body that equips the believer to reign with Christ a thousand years.

The last day

Scripture (NIV) includes five occurrences of the expression "last day" which refer to the first resurrection. Four of these references are from Jesus' bread of life discourse where Jesus affirmed the resurrection of those who were His. Thus, "No one can come to me unless the Father who sent me draws him, and I will raise him up at the last day" (John 6:44, cf. 6:39-40, 54). Martha apparently understood the fact of this (first) resurrection, for speaking of Lazarus "Martha answered, I know he will rise again in the resurrection at the last day" (John 11:24). In the one other New Testament use of the expression "last day," however, Jesus is definitely speaking of the second resurrection. "For the one who rejects me . . . that very word which I spoke will condemn him at the last day" (John 12:48). We must conclude that the New Testament usage of "last day" is not precise, and the expression denotes points of time that are up to 1,000 years apart.

ELEVEN

The Divine Work of Judgment

The administration of judgment is an important aspect of God's work in relating to His moral creatures. In many contexts the word "judgment" associates with an evaluative sorting or separation leading to condemnation and punishment. Judgment may also result, however, in a reward for the one evaluated. Thus, God assumes His role as judge for the sake of the righteous as well as for the sinners. If there were no judgment, the overall good done by humans would be inconsiderately overlooked.

God's Role as Judge

Numerous Scriptures depict God in the role of judge, even though it is His "strange work." "The Lord will rise up . . . to do his work, his strange work, and perform his task, his alien task" (Isa. 28:21). Abraham knew God as "the Judge of all the earth" (Gen. 18:25); Moses declared, "The Lord will judge his people" (Deut. 32:36); and in her prayer Hannah testified, "the Lord will judge the ends of the earth" (1 Sam. 2:10).

God's role in judging through Christ "the living and the dead" is a repeated theme in the New Testament (cf. Acts 10:42; 2 Tim. 4:1; 1 Pet. 4:5). Hebrews describes God as "the judge of all men" (Heb. 12:23), and James noted, "The Judge is standing at the door!" (James 5:9) John describes heaven's response to God's impending judgmental process. The twenty-four elders "fell on their faces and worshiped God, saying . . . 'The time has come for judging the dead, and for rewarding your servants the prophets and your saints and those who reverence your name, both small and great—and for destroying those who destroy the earth'" (Rev. 11:16, 18).

The nature of God's judgments

God's judgments will provide a fair and impartial hearing to all moral intelligences before He assigns them to their eternal state. As it were, each creature will be allowed his or her "day in court." God's judgments will: 1) present all relevant facts, 2) evaluate these facts, 3) bestow appropriate recompense. The omniscient God holds the exclusive right of judgment, because He alone possesses all the facts. Paul spoke of "the day when God will judge men's secrets through Jesus Christ" (Rom. 2:16), and he declared that God "will bring to light what is hidden in darkness and will expose the motives of men's hearts" (1 Cor. 4:5). Jesus taught, "There is nothing concealed that will not be disclosed, or hidden that will not be made known" (Matt. 10:26).

In judging His creatures, God will weigh evidence, and evaluate, and arrive at an opinion that will determine the destiny that each creature deserves. He has promised, "I will judge each of you according to his own ways" (Ezek. 33:20). A scrupulous adherence to righteousness and justice will guide His decisions. "He will judge the world in righteousness and the peoples in his truth" (Psa. 96:13; cf. Psa. 9:8); "He has set a day when he will judge the world with justice" (Acts 17:31).

Paul spoke of "the Lord, the righteous Judge" (2 Tim. 4:8). Peter, in describing Jesus' submission in His passion, declared, "He entrusted himself to him who judges justly" (1 Pet. 2:23). John reported the heavenly voice, "Yes, Lord God Almighty, true and just are your judgments" (Rev. 16:7). Though the reference is primarily to God's "bowl" (or vial) judgments, these words apply to God's judgments in general.

The purpose of God's judgments

God's judgments do not determine character; they simply manifest it. He evaluates evidences of moral responsibility, He confirms His creatures in their status, and on this basis He prescribes their destiny. Paul explains that God's judgments are not capricious, but according to His revealed standards which, in the case of the Jews, was the Old Testament law. Thus, "whatever the law says, it says to those who are under the law, so that every mouth may be silenced and the whole world held accountable to God" (Rom. 3:19).

The application of God's judgment assures that each moral intelligence is identified and classified for what he or she actually is. Paul encouraged the suffering believers in Thessalonica by pointing out, "God's judgment is right, and as a result you will be counted worthy of the kingdom of God" (2 Thess. 1:5).

God judges according to His moral attributes and in vindication of His personal integrity and sovereign government. Each moral intelligence who appears before His judgment bar will receive the benefit of all relevant evidence, including pleas of extenuating circumstances and special situations. God will temper judgment with fairness and mercy, but He will always maintain

His justice and never compromise. Jesus' pronouncement of "Woe" upon the unrepentant cities clearly taught this fact.

Jesus began to denounce the cities in which most of his miracles had been performed, because they did not repent. Woe to you, Korazin! Woe to you, Bethsaida! If the miracles that were performed in you had been performed in Tyre and Sidon, they would have repented long ago in sackcloth and ashes. But I tell you, it will be more bearable for Tyre and Sidon on the day of judgment than for you (Matt. 11:20-22).

The writer to the Hebrews spoke of God's justice in the judgment of angels. "Every violation and disobedience received its just punishment" (Heb. 2:2). Later, this writer quoted God: "It is mine to avenge; I will repay" (Heb. 10:30). In his prayer, Daniel confessed, "The Lord did not hesitate to bring the disaster [Babylonian captivity] upon us, for the Lord our God is righteous in everything he does" (Dan. 9:14).

God demonstrates His attributes of righteousness, holiness, and justice equally when He forgives the penitent, rewards His faithful servant, or condemns the impenitent. "God presented [Jesus] as a sacrifice of atonement . . . to demonstrate his justice . . . so as to be just and the one who justifies those who have faith in Jesus" (Rom. 3:25-26).

Past and Present Judgments

The first judgment that affects the believer took place at Calvary, and the second is ongoing in the present.

The judgment of the believer's sins

God's judgment was imposed upon Jesus Christ on the cross. "The Son of Man [came] . . . to give his life as a ransom for many" (Matt. 20:28). Jesus Christ bore the sins of all humans, and He suffered the stroke of God's judgment as a condemned man. "Our Lord Jesus Christ . . . died for us" (1 Thess. 5:9-10); "The Lord has laid on him the iniquity of us all" (Isa. 53:6). God fulfilled the death penalty upon Him who had become a sinner.

The foregoing Scriptures establish that God's judgment upon sin was exhausted at Calvary. Thus, He has legal basis to forgive the penitent sinner. (See Rom. 3:25-26 quoted above). At Calvary, God judged all the sins of every believer. "Whoever hears . . . and believes . . . has eternal life and will not be condemned; he has crossed over from death to life" (John 5:24); "The result of one act of righteousness was justification that brings life for all men" (Rom. 5:18); "Therefore, there is now no condemnation for those who are in Christ Jesus" (Rom. 8:1).

Scripture teaches that since His ascension, the next event in Christ's program is His appearance to those awaiting Him. "Christ was sacrificed once to take away the sins of many people;

and he will appear a second time, not to bear sin, but to bring salvation to those who are waiting for him" (Heb. 9:28). This and similar Scriptures convince the majority of Christians to reject the doctrine that teaches that beginning in 1844[1] God launched an "investigative" judgment upon earthlings. The Scripture that is used to support the investigative judgment doctrine, Daniel 7:9-10, concerns God's tribulation judgments on earth. The judgments of the tribulation era will be retributive and disciplinary (God's wrath upon rebels that they may repent), not investigative (an examining process to determine who will be saved and who will be lost).

The believer's self-judgment

Each believer, who seeks to live a Christian life on earth, is expected to undergo this judgment. We are to judge ourselves according to the standards of one who is God's child. Numerous supporting Scriptures may be cited. "If we judged ourselves, we would not come under judgment" (1 Cor. 11:31); "Examine yourselves to see whether you are in the faith; test yourselves. Do you not realize that Christ Jesus is in you—unless, of course, you fail the test?" (2 Cor. 13:5); "It is time for judgment to begin with the family of God; and if it begins with us, what will the outcome be for those who do not obey the gospel of God?" (1 Pet. 4:17); "In the same way you judge others, you will be judged, and with the measure you use, it will be measured to you" (Matt. 7:2).

The believer's self-judgment involves putting away sin and systematically modeling his or her life upon Jesus Christ with the goal of "attaining to the whole measure of the fullness of Christ" (Eph. 4:13). Conscientious self-judgment is a wise assurance against painful discipline. "God disciplines us for our good, that we may share in his holiness" (Heb. 12:10).

Scripture teaches that even when a fellow Christian fails, the only valid judgmental action by the believer is toward himself. "Brothers, if someone is caught in a sin, you who are spiritual should restore him gently. But watch [Gk. *skopeo*] yourself, or you also may be tempted" (Gal. 6:1). (*skopeo* [scop-EH-oh]: consider, take heed, look at, mark, keep one's eye on). Self-judgment

---

1   The date 1844 was calculated to be 2,300 years from 457 B.C. when the command to restore Jerusalem was given (cf. Dan. 9:25). The 2,300 years was based on Daniel 8:14—because the biblical "days" were prophetic, they were thought of as years. This exegesis led many Christians, particularly in North America, to believe that they would see the return of Christ in 1844. When He did not return visibly in that year, the doctrine of an investigative judgment was proposed. This judgment was seen as Christ's activity in the heavenly sanctuary since 1844. Christ is considered now to be at work, investigating records and sifting true believers from false, and confirming the former in their status in preparation for His advent.

should be rigorous and ongoing, and not subject to being diverted by focusing upon another's shortcomings.

The believer's bema judgment

Paul wrote, "We must all appear before the judgment seat (Gk. *bema*) of Christ, that each one may receive what is due him for the things done while in the body, whether good or bad [Gk. *phaulos*]" (2 Cor. 5:10). (*bema* [BAY-ma]: a rostrum, tribunal, judgment seat, throne {but note discussion of next paragraph}; *phaulos* [FOWL-os]: worthless, rotten, evil, base, of no account). Jesus said, "The Son of Man is going to come in his Father's glory with his angels, and then he will reward each person according to what he has done" (Matt. 16:27; cf. Luke 14:14). In this judgment, the believer is judged for his achievements as a servant. The bema judgment concerns rewards, and its subjects are already in heaven.

1. The nature of the bema judgment

The judgment of believers' works takes place at "the judgment seat of Christ" (or "the Bar of Christ" or "the tribunal of Christ.") In its secular context in New Testament times, the word *bema* denoted a raised platform or dais upon which a judge, official, or adjudicator could sit to review, evaluate, and bestow an award upon observed participants. In Greek Olympic games, the successful athletes were called to present themselves before the *bema* to receive their laurel leaf crown. Paul's readers would no doubt have associated the word *bema* with events involving rewards upon participating contestants.

For the believer, the bema will be a time of giving account. It has been called "The coming parade day of the army of the living God." Paul wrote, "We will all stand before God's judgment seat [*bema*] . . . each of us will give an account of himself to God" (Rom. 14:10, 12). (This verse is taken as an illustration of Scripture's common interchange of divine Judges; however, it should also be noted that a major family of manuscripts render this passage "Christ's judgment seat.") The true quality of one's works will be revealed. "His work will be shown for what it is, because the Day will bring it to light. It will be revealed with fire, and the fire will test the quality of each man's work" (1 Cor. 3:13).

Paul likens the Christian's works to six substances: gold, silver, costly stones, or wood, hay, or straw. He sees Christ's judgment as the application of fire, so that only nonflammable substances survive. "Fire will test the quality of each man's work. If what he has built survives, he will receive his reward. If it is burned up, he will suffer loss" (1 Cor. 3:13-14). Those works that are burned up and judged to be bad are evidently those that are of no relevance in Christian service or those done with wrong motives. The problem may not be in the works themselves, but in the reasons for which they were done. Paul wrote of those who were responding to his imprisonment by coming forth to preach Christ "out of envy and rivalry . . . out of selfish ambition, not sincerely, supposing that they can stir up trouble for me while I am in chains" (Phil. 1:15, 17).

Since the bema is primarily an awards session, it will reward positive achievements rather than punish shortcomings. "You know that the Lord will reward everyone for whatever good he does" (Eph. 6:8). The focus is not on what is done in the line of duty, but what is done beyond it. In His parable of the unworthy servants, Jesus taught: "Would [the master] thank the servant because he did what he was told to do? So you also, when you have done everything you were told to do, should say, 'We are unworthy servants; we have only done our duty'" (Luke 17:9-10).

To be recognized in a special way at the bema the believer must excel. "Do you not know that in a race all the runners run, but only one gets a prize? Run in such a way as to get the prize. (1 Cor. 9:24). Nevertheless, all who participate will be rewarded. "Behold, I am coming soon! My reward is with me, and I will give to everyone according to what he has done" (Rev. 22:12).

2. The issues and standards at the bema judgment

Many Scriptures instruct and challenge the believer to prepare for that future day. The values that will be relevant at the judgment seat of Christ include at least some of the following:

1) **Faithfulness in service.** "Each one should use whatever gift he has received to serve others, faithfully administering God's grace in its various forms" (1 Pet. 4:10). "It is required that those who have been given a trust must prove faithful" (1 Cor. 4:2). In the parable of the talents, the master used familiar words to commend, "Well done, good and faithful servant" (Matt. 25:23).

2) **Wholeheartedness in service.** Believers must be faithful, and serve with their whole being. "Whatever you do, work at it with all your heart . . . since you know that you will receive an inheritance from the Lord as a reward" (Col. 3:23-24). Paul testified to the Ephesian elders, "I have not hesitated to proclaim to you the whole will of God" (Acts 20:27).

3) **Souls won to Christ.** In his message to the Thessalonian believers, Paul wrote the following: "What is our hope, our joy, or the crown in which we will glory in the presence of our Lord Jesus when he comes? Is it not you? Indeed, you are our glory and joy" (1 Thess. 2:19-20).

4) **The endurance of trials.** Paul was at the midpoint of his ministry when he wrote to the Corinthians, "For our light and momentary troubles are achieving for us an eternal glory that far outweighs them all" (2 Cor. 4:17). A decade or so later, Paul wrote from a Roman prison, "I am suffering even to the point of being chained," but he added, "If we endure we will also reign with him" (2 Tim. 2:9, 12). Jesus taught, "Blessed are you when people insult you, persecute you and falsely say all kinds of evil against you because of me. Rejoice and be glad, because great is your reward in heaven" (Matt. 5:11-12). Peter wrote, "Now for a little while you may have had to suffer grief in all kinds of trials. These . . . may result in praise, glory and honor when Jesus Christ is revealed" (1 Pet. 1:6-7).

5) **Personal conduct.** Paul uses the analogy of a trained athlete who wins. "Therefore I do not run like a man running aimlessly; I do not fight like a man beating the air. No, I beat my body and make it my slave so that after I have preached to others, I myself will not be disqualified for the prize" (1 Cor. 9:26-27). In another context Paul wrote, "You know that the Lord will reward everyone for whatever good he does" (Eph. 6:7). The manner in which believers spend their time and use their resources is certainly of concern to God.

6) **Treatment of other believers.** Jesus has special interest in those favoring His workers and His "little ones." "Anyone who receives a prophet because he is a prophet will receive a prophet's reward, and anyone who receives a righteous man because he is a righteous man will receive a righteous man's reward. And if anyone gives even a cup of cold water to one of these little ones because he is my disciple . . . he will certainly not lose his reward" (Matt. 10:41-42). The writer to the Hebrews reminded them, "God is not unjust; he will not forget your work and the love you have shown him as you have helped his people and continue to help them" (Heb. 6:10).

7) **Readiness for His return.** "There is in store for me the crown of righteousness, which the Lord, the righteous Judge, will award to me on that day—and not only to me, but also to all who have longed for his appearing" (2 Tim. 4:8).

Perfect fairness and His personal understanding will characterize Christ's bema judgment. The gifted person will enjoy no special advantage. "For who makes you different from anyone else? What do you have that you did not receive? And if you did receive it, why do you boast as though you did not?" (1 Cor. 4:7) The motives and intentions of the heart will be taken into account. "Judge nothing before the appointed time; wait till the Lord comes. He will bring to light what is hidden in darkness and will expose the motives of men's hearts" (1 Cor. 4:5).

In the *bema* judgment, many factors that result in special status and reward on earth will be irrelevant. "Neither he who plants nor he who waters is anything, but only God, who makes things grow. The man who plants and the man who waters have one purpose, and each will be rewarded according to his own labor" (1 Cor. 3:7-8).

3. The bema judgment crowns

Scripture depicts the believer's rewards at the bema judgment under the figure of five crowns:

1) **the crown that will last forever** (unfading, imperishable, incorruptible). Paul contrasts competitors in a game who "do it to get a crown that will not last" with those who run the Christian race who "do it to get a crown that will last forever" (1 Cor. 9:25). In context, this crown is sometimes called "the runner's crown." Paul, however, gives an important criterion: "I do not fight like a man beating the air. No, I beat my body and make it my slave" (vv. 26-27). A vital factor in qualifying for this crown is personal self-control.

2) **the crown of righteousness.** The key Scripture, 2 Timothy 4:8, which is quoted above, promises this crown "to all who have longed for his appearing." In this context, this crown is spoken of as "the watcher's crown." It will be awarded to people whose lifestyle was marked by constant readiness for Jesus' return.

3) **the crown of life.** "Blessed is the man who perseveres under trial, because when he has stood the test, he will receive the crown of life that God has promised to those who love him" (James 1:12); "Be faithful, even to the point of death, and I will give you the crown of life" (Rev. 2:10). This crown is considered to be the sufferer or martyr's crown, and it is given to those who love God more than earthly life.

4) **the crown of glory** (glorious crown, or the shepherd's [pastor's] crown). Peter challenges the church elders to be shepherds of God's flock. In turn he promises, "When the Chief Shepherd appears, you will receive the crown of glory that will never fade away" (1 Pet. 5:4). This crown will be awarded pastors who have faithfully tended their spiritual flocks.

5) **the crown of rejoicing** (crown in which we will glory, crown of glorying, boasting). Paul identifies this crown as he speaks of the Thessalonians as his converts. (See 1 Thess. 2:19-20 quoted above). It is considered the soul-winner's crown.

Jesus exhorted those in authority in the church in Philadelphia: "Hold on to what you have, so that no one will take your crown" (Rev. 3:11). In the later scene in heaven, however, John describes the worshipful self-abandonment of the twenty-four elders, the representatives of the church. "[They] fall down before him who sits on the throne, and worship him. . . . They lay their crowns before the throne and say: 'You are worthy, our Lord and God'" (Rev. 4:10-11).

The wedding supper of the Lamb

The wedding supper (marriage supper —KJV) of the Lamb is apart from the bema judgment, but it is an aspect of the believers' rewards. John locates this event in heaven, just prior to the second coming. God the Father is host, and Jesus, the Lamb, is the bridegroom. "The wedding [*gamos*] of the Lamb has come, and his bride has made herself ready. . . . Blessed are those who are invited to the wedding [*gamos*] supper [*deipnon*] of the Lamb!" (Rev. 19:7, 9) The rapture has presented the Bride to the Groom, and now at the supper, their union is celebrated. (*gamos* [GA-mos]: wedding, wedding celebration, marriage, events associated with a wedding; *deipnon* [DIPE-non]: evening dinner, supper, feast).

The marriage figure in the New Testament is according to Oriental culture of that era, and it differs from modern western customs. The first step in an Oriental marriage was the betrothal (KJV) or promise (NIV) (cf. 2 Cor. 11:2) that was a contract to marry and that was legally binding—to break it required a divorce. The marriage itself began with servants arriving at the bride's house and requesting the bride to accompany them to meet the groom. Thus, she would be escorted to the groom's home and there presented with her new husband. At that point the couple were considered legally married, and they began living together as husband and wife.

The church as the Bride of Christ is a recurring New Testament theme—some speak of "nuptial theology." The church's union with Christ is depicted as a wedding: "I promised you to one husband, to Christ, so that I might present you as a pure virgin to him" (2 Cor. 11:2). In the parable on His last day of public ministry, Jesus taught, "The kingdom of heaven is like a king who prepared a wedding banquet for his son. He sent his servant to those who had been invited" (Matt. 22:2-3).

The future role of the church is that of a favored bride, for Jesus will share His millennial kingship with the church. "To him who overcomes, I will give the right to sit with me on my throne" (Rev. 3:21, cf. 2 Tim. 2:12); and His shared glory will be manifested, "I have given them the glory that you gave me" (John 17:22). Similarly, the church will share His name (cf. Rev. 22:4), the characteristics of His resurrection body (Phil. 3:21), and even His personal traits. "We know that when he appears, we shall be like him" (1 John 3:2).

Judgments During the Tribulation Period

The great tribulation is God's time of judgment upon rebellious and unbelieving humans, including both Jews and Gentiles. These judgmental activities are described under the figures of the seals, trumpets, and bowls which have already been discussed In addition to these judgmental processes, however, there are three tribulation judgments that are individually identified. These are as follows:

The judgment upon Israel

The Old Testament describes a comprehensive end time judgment upon Israel that will purge out the nation's rebels.

"I will bring you from the nations and gather you from the countries where you have been scattered—with a mighty hand and an outstretched arm. . . . I will bring you into the desert of the nations [judgment hall—Taylor] and there, face to face, I will execute judgment upon you. . . . I will take note of you as you pass under my rod, and I will bring you into the bond of the covenant. I will purge you of those who revolt and rebel against me. . . . Then you will know that I am the LORD" (Ezek. 20:34-35, 37-38).

The phrase "desert of the nations" in verse 35 is literally "wilderness of the peoples." As we note, in the *Living Bible* Taylor interpretively renders it "judgment hall." Commentators see this place of judgment as an area, probably with specific boundaries, such as the Sinaitic peninsula. At this designated site, wherever it may be, the nation will be purged of rebels, and the survivors will proceed to the land of Israel. Malachi describes similar events under another image. "Who can endure the day of his coming? . . . He will sit as a refiner and purifier of silver; he will purify the Levites and refine them like gold and silver. Then . . . the offerings of Judah and Jerusalem will be acceptable to the LORD" (Mal. 3:2-4).

Generally speaking, Israel's judgment coincides with the destruction and persecution suffered under Antichrist and at Armageddon. Antichrist will be God's instrument of judgment, and his tribulation persecution and warfare will serve judgmentally to purge the nation. In God's providence, those who survive will have willingly accepted Jesus Christ as their conquering Messiah, and they will enter the millennial kingdom in their earthly bodies. Those Israelites who fail to accept their Messiah will be cut off from both millennial and eternal life.

The judgment of the Babylons

We have seen that the Book of Revelation describes the destruction of both ecclesiastical Babylon (cf. Rev. 17), and commercial Babylon (cf. Rev. 18). Each Babylon represents aspects of hostile resistance to the fulfillment of God's earthly plan and the inauguration of the millennium. The name "Babylon" identifies with "Babel," the site of the infamous tower built by self-willed rebellious humans (cf. Gen. 11:1-9). Someone has said, "Where there are humans in rebellion, there is a Babylon." Those human philosophies that construct religious beliefs and economic policies on the basis of secular humanism, when embraced by a colony of humans, become a Babylon in God's sight. The judgment of the Babylons achieves the destruction of humanity's satanically inspired counterfeit religion, and its vain and misleading pursuit of transient earthly wealth.

Ecclesiastical Babylon in Revelation 17 is depicted as the gaudy prostitute representing ecumenical religion and probably embodying apostate Christianity (see p. 149). God in His sovereignty directs her destruction, but Antichrist and his coalition of nations are the actual agents who bring it to pass. "They will bring her to ruin and leave her naked; they will eat her flesh and burn her with fire. For God has put it into their hearts to accomplish his purpose" (Rev. 17:16-17). Religion will likely be an important factor in Antichrist's rise, and in his climb to power he will freely capitalize upon the favor of various religious leaders. Once entrenched, he will fiercely resent their effort to control him. At that time he will act to destroy existing religious systems and replace them with his own.

Commercial Babylon (Rev. 18) is seen as a great city that is the world's trading center (see p. 172). Its citizens are motivated by the persistent human greed for money and the possessions and privileges it obtains. Paul wrote, "The love of money is a root of all kinds of evil" (1 Tim. 6:10). In His judgmental destruction of the city, God appears to act directly rather than through an agent. "God has remembered her crimes . . . in one day her plagues will overtake her. . . . She will be consumed by fire, for mighty is the Lord God who judges her" (Rev. 18:5, 8); "Rejoice, saints and apostles and prophets! God has judged her for the way she treated you" (Rev. 18:20).

The judgment of the Beast, the False Prophet, and their armies

Christ's victory at Armageddon achieves this judgment. "The beast [i.e., Antichrist] was captured, and with him the false prophet . . . the two of them were thrown alive into the fiery lake of burning sulfur. The rest of them were killed with the sword that came out of the mouth of the rider on the horse, and all the birds gorged themselves on their flesh" (Rev. 19:20-21). As a result of this judgment, the Beast and False Prophet remain in the fiery lake (cf. Rev. 20:10), and Antichrist's armies suffer physical death. Presumably, those who comprised Antichrist's armies will be resurrected and judged on an individual basis at the great white throne judgment.

The Judgment of The Nations

This judgment takes place at the close of the tribulation and before the millennium begins. It was described by Jesus in Matthew 25:31-34, 41:

> "When the Son of Man comes in his glory . . . all the nations will be gathered before him, and he will separate the people one from another as a shepherd separates the sheep from the goats. He will put the sheep on his right and the goats on his left. Then the King

JUDGMENT	PLACE	SUBJECT	JUDGE	OUTCOME
Believer's sins	Calvary	Christ	God	Sins atoned for
Believer's self	Here	Believer	Believer	Christian victory
Bema	Bema	Believers	Christ	Rewarded for works
Israel	Wilderness	Jews	God	Penitent remnant spared
Babylons	Each Babylon	Babylons	God	Destruction
Beast Prophet Armies	Armageddon	Beast Prophet Armies	Christ	Destruction
Nations	Armageddon	Nations	Christ	Sheep & goats separated
Satan	Earth	Satan	God	Cast into lake of fire
Great White Throne	Great White Throne	Sinful dead	(God) or Christ	Sinners to lake of fire

Fig. 13: A summary of the judgments described in Scripture. A total of nine are shown. Two have been completed, five will occur during and at the close of the tribulation, and two will occur at the close of the millennium.

will say to those on his right, 'Come . . . take your inheritance, the
kingdom prepared for you.' Then he will say to those on his left,
'Depart from me, you who are cursed, into the eternal fire prepared for the devil and his angels.'"

Joel records God's statement of His plan for this judgment.
"When I restore the fortunes of Judah and Jerusalem [i.e., as the
millennium is launched], I will gather all nations and bring them
down to the Valley of Jehoshaphat [i.e., valley where Jehovah
{Yahweh} judges]. There I will enter into judgment against them
concerning my inheritance, my people Israel" (Joel 3:1-2).

From Matthew's account of the role of the Son of Man (cf.
Matt. 25:31), and Jesus' declaration, "The Father judges no one,
but has entrusted all judgment to the Son" (John 5:22), it is concluded that at this judgment Jesus Christ is the presiding Judge.

a. The Subjects of this Judgment. The word "nations" in
this context is the Greek *ethne* (ETH-nay) which denotes "Gentiles" or "peoples who are non-Jewish" as well as "nations." The
singular is *ethnos* (ETH-nos). The grammar of the original and
the rendering in modern versions indicate that people rather
than nations are set apart (separated), and the fate of the condemned supports this interpretation. Those who are judged are
judged as individuals, not collectively as nations. Whereas the armies of the nations are judged at Armageddon, this judgment
concerns the civilians and noncombatants of those nations. Only
living Gentile humans are judged at this time.

b. The Standards of the Judgment. In teaching concerning this judgment, Jesus stressed that the determining standard
will be the specific attitude toward the Jews. "Whatever you did
for one of the least of these brothers of mine, you did for me . . .
whatever you did not do for one of the least of these, you did not
do for me" (Matt. 25:40, 45). Christ's "brothers" are taken to be
the Jews to whom He is indeed a brother in the flesh. At Nazareth the people asked, "Isn't his mother's name Mary, and aren't
his brothers James, Joseph, Simon, and Judas?" (Matt. 13:55)
Since both the sheep and goats among the Gentiles are judged by
their treatment of these "brothers," they must be a non-Gentile
people. As we have noted, God's family relationship with Israel is
taught elsewhere when He speaks of "my inheritance, my people
Israel" (Joel 3:2).

In the tribulation, a Gentile who befriends a Jew will risk his
life. Likely, those who offer sanctuary to a Jew will be Gentiles
with a personal experience of salvation. In Ryrie's words, "No
one will do this merely out of a beneficent attitude, but only out
of a redeemed heart."[2] Thus, the response of Gentiles to the

---

2 Charles Ryrie, *Basic Theology*. Wheaton: Scripture Press, 1986, p. 514.

plight of the tribulation Jews is no mere capricious test. Nevertheless, all who are judged, whether sheep or goats, are surprised to learn that in relating to the persecuted and deprived Jews they were considered to be dealing with the Lord Himself. God's identity with Israel began with His call of Abram, "I will bless those who bless you, and whoever curses you I will curse" (Gen. 12:3).

c. The Outcome of the Judgment. Scholars debate this matter and two possibilities are suggested:

Possibility 1): This judgment concerns the eternal destiny of its subjects. Jesus' concluding statement is considered basic to the account. "Then they [the ones who did nothing for Christ's brothers] will go away to eternal punishment, but the righteous to eternal life" (Matt. 25:46). This outcome would conclude that the righteous had been kind to Christ's brethren because they had become believers in Christ. Their treatment of the Jews was an indication of their spiritual condition. Their eternal destiny was based on their faith in Christ, but the immediate privilege of remaining on earth to enjoy Christ's millennial kingdom was a reward for their works on behalf of the Jews.

Possibility 2): This judgment is not primarily concerned with eternity, but rather to select the "sheep" who are the people who enter the millennium in their natural bodies. They become the founding fathers of the millennial population. In this view, the concluding verse is considered a statement of an overall principle of eternal destinies. It is indeed the case that there are just two eternal destinies, but a prior earthly judgment may determine an intervening earthly destiny—i.e., survival into the millennium.

Those who suffer physical destruction at this time will still face the great white throne judgment and only then will they be assigned to their eternal state. Tragically, however, their final doom is assured and it may now be predicted (cf. Matt. 25:46). God never compromises His requirements for eternal life in His presence and the essential role of a human's life on earth.

Jesus described this judgment in His Olivet Discourse. "At the coming of the Son of Man . . . two men will be in the field; one will be taken and the other left. Two women will be grinding with a hand mill; one will be taken and the other left" (Matt. 24:39-41, cf. Luke 17:30-37). Since this event is a judgment, outcomes are the reverse of the rapture. Those who are taken, are taken in destructive judgment; those who are left, are spared alive to enter the millennium. These events compare to Noah's flood when humans who were living carelessly were taken away, and only the family of Noah was left (cf. Matt. 24:39).

The Judgment of Satan

Satan's judgment is actually threefold: 1) cast from the heavenlies to the earth (Rev. 12:12)—this judgment has already been discussed as an aspect of mid-tribulation events; 2) cast from earth to the Abyss (Rev. 20:1-3); and 3) cast from the Abyss to the lake of burning sulfur (Rev. 20:10). Scripture describes Satan's fate in detail.

> **An angel ... seized the dragon, that ancient serpent, who is the devil, or Satan, and bound him for a thousand years. He threw him into the Abyss, and locked and sealed it over him, to keep him from deceiving the nations anymore until the thousand years were ended. After that, he must be set free for a short time. . . . When the thousand years are over, Satan will be released from his prison and will go out to deceive the nations. . . . But fire came down from heaven and devoured them. And the devil, who deceived them, was thrown into the lake of burning sulfur, where the beast and the false prophet were thrown. They will be tormented day and night for ever and ever (Rev. 20:1-3, 7, 9-10).**

Because Satan's time had now come, an ordinary angel was able to bind and imprison him. God assigned him temporarily to the Abyss, since the citizens of the millennium were still to be subject to a probation time. Satan has always been the source of the spirit of rebellion against God, and even at the close of the millennium his followers must be excluded from God's people. Scripture provides no grounds for a doctrine of the final conversion of Satan. In return for the terrible pain he has caused generations of humans he will undergo eternal torment.

The Great White Throne Judgment

Scripture reports: "I saw a great white throne and him who was seated on it. . . . I saw the dead, great and small, standing before the throne, and books were opened. Another book was opened, which is the book of life. The dead were judged according to what they had done as recorded in the books" (Rev. 20:11-12). Notably, those who died as sinners are called simply "the dead." Believers are called "the dead in Christ" (1 Thess. 4:16).

a. The time, place, and manner of the judgment. This judgment does not take place until the 1,000 year millennium has ended (cf. Rev. 20:5), and the Battle of Gog and Magog, with its vast destruction of human life, has occurred (cf. Rev. 20:8-9). It is indeed the final end time judgment at the conclusion of all of earth's history. Since earth and sky have fled from before God (cf. Rev. 20:11), this judgment event evidently will take place before God's heavenly throne. By this time, the divine attitude toward the sinner will no longer be mercy, but judgment.

This judgment marks the day of which Paul wrote: "Because of your stubbornness and your unrepentant heart, you are storing up wrath against yourself for the day of God's wrath, when his righteous judgment will be revealed" (Rom. 2:5). Though many sins are committed against people, at the great white throne judgment individuals are arraigned against deity. Humans may not recognize it, but in every case of sin and exploitation, God and His Son are ultimately the ones offended.

b. The subjects and terms of the judgment. In what we choose to call the second resurrection (cf. Rev. 20:5), all humans still dead will be resurrected. John wrote, "I saw the dead, great and small, standing before the throne. . . . The sea gave up the dead that were in it, and death and Hades gave up the dead that were in them, and each person was judged according to what he had done" (Rev. 20:12-13). Scripture gives the terms of the judgment that the resurrected will undergo: "[E]ach person was judged according to what he had done" (Rev. 20:13). Unfortunately for the sinner, the standard of works that is applied is not that of secular society, but of the righteous life of Jesus Christ.

When they are compared to the record of Christ's life, the sinner's works will, inevitably, be pronounced inadequate. The sinner's one hope is to have his or her name inscribed in the Lamb's book of life (cf. Rev. 21:27). Either none, or at most, a few, of those at the great white throne judgment will be thus listed. Apparently, the book of life is made available mainly or entirely as a negative exhibit for the one who insists that it contains his or her name.[3] John reports the tragic outcome, "If anyone's name was not found written in the book of life, he was thrown into the lake of fire" (Rev. 20:15). God declares that being cast into the fiery lake is the "second death" (cf. Rev. 20:14, 21:8).

The great white throne judgment will concern primarily the wicked dead, since all the righteous up to that time have been caught up in the first resurrection. Daniel predicted this occasion, "Multitudes who sleep in the dust of the earth will awake: some to everlasting life, others to shame and everlasting contempt" (Dan. 12:2). Jesus taught, "A time is coming when all who are in their graves will hear his voice and come out—those who have done good will rise to live, and those who have done evil will rise to be condemned" (John 5:28-29). Both Daniel and Jesus passed over the one-thousand-year time separation between the judgment of the righteous and the judgment of sinners.

Jesus' parable of the wheat and the weeds (Matt. 13:24-30, 36-43) relates to this judgment. In the parable, the harvesters

---

3 Scripture gives no information about the judgment of the righteous dead of the millennium. It is possible that they will be included at thegreat white throne, and if so, they would be listed in the book of life. The possibility is strictly speculative, however.

are instructed, "First collect the weeds and tie them in bundles
to be burned; then gather the wheat and bring it into my barn"
(Matt. 13:30). Jesus interpreted the parable, "As the weeds are
pulled up and burned in the fire, so it will be at the end of the
age" (Matt. 13:40). The parable depicts the prior harvesting of
the weeds (the wicked at Armageddon), and their detention until
the great white throne judgment.

The great white throne judgment is the final event that determines the sinner's eternal destiny. On this solemn occasion,
the sinner's fate in being committed to the lake of fire is announced and the reason for it is given. Ed Hindson comments,
"Both death (*thanatos*) and hell (*hades*) are pictured as though
they were the city jail, whereas the lake of fire is the peniten-
tiary."[4] Some consider that this judgment will determine the degree of the believer's punishment in the lake of fire. As we have
noted, Jesus hinted at this outcome. He declared to the people of
the local Jewish town in which He had performed miracles, "I tell
you, it will be more bearable for Tyre and Sidon on the day of
judgment than for you" (Matt. 11:22). Apparently, some destinies in the lake of fire will be more bearable than others.

Scripture appears to be silent on the matter of the judgment
of the righteous millennial citizens. Although Satan will win followers numbered "like the sand on the seashore" (Rev. 20:8), it
can be expected that there also will be multitudes of millennial
citizens who reject Satan and maintain their allegiance to the
rule of Jesus Christ. As we have noted, it is possible that one of
the purposes of the book of life (Rev. 20:12) at the great white
throne judgment will be to identify the millennial saints who by
their faith and obedience qualify for eternity with the Lord.

There is no further information about the judgment of the
fallen angels. "The angels who . . . abandoned their own home—
these he has kept in darkness, bound with everlasting chains for
judgment on the great Day" (Jude 6). It would be plausible to assign these two companies to the great white throne judgment,
though the view is preferably seen as an assumption, rather than
a Biblical doctrine.

c. The identity of the Judge. The presiding Judge at the
great white throne has traditionally been identified as God (implying God the Father), but modern versions leave the matter
ambiguous. The text that formerly read "stand[ing] before God"
(Rev. 20:12 KJV), in current versions now reads "standing before
the throne" (cf. NIV, NASB, NRSV).

---

4 Ed Hindson, *Earth's Final Hour.* Eugene: Harvest House Publishers, 1999,
p. 160.

In fact, it is warranted to identify Christ as the Judge at this time. Jesus declared, "The Father judges no one, but has entrusted all judgment to the Son, that all may honor the Son just as they honor the Father" (John 5:22). Paul, however, makes judgment a joint project, "It is those who obey the law who will be declared righteous. . . . This will take place on the day when God will judge men's secrets through Jesus Christ" (Rom. 2:13, 16). This latter verse implies that in administering judgment God directs overall, but He works through the agency of Christ.

Although for study purposes it is helpful to assign a particular divine Person to each judgment, we should not lose sight of unity in the trinity. Daniel spoke of the one with white clothing and white hair in whose presence "the court was seated, and the books were opened" (Dan. 7:10), and he calls Him reverently "the Ancient of Days" (Dan. 7:9).

It can be suggested that the great white throne judgment would be an appropriate occasion to fulfill Paul's prophecy concerning Jesus. "At the name of Jesus every knee should bow . . . and every tongue confess that Jesus Christ is Lord, to the glory of God the Father" (Phil. 2:10-11). Jesus will receive the ongoing willing worship of the redeemed throughout eternity, but the one occasion when "every knee should bow" would be the judgment of sinners at the great white throne. How tragically ironic that if only rebel humans had done sooner what they are eventually forced to do, they would have been spared destruction!

TWELVE

The Millennium: Part 1

The term "millennium" denotes the kingdom age when Christ the king will rule on earth. The word is not biblical, but it is from Latin roots which mean "one thousand years." This combination of words occurs six times in the first seven verses of Revelation 20. Futurists hold that the thousand years is a literal time span counted on the same basis as God's original establishment of years (cf. Gen. 1:14). Since the term "kingdom" may be ambiguous, the term "millennium" is preferred because it indicates the actual time span. We note that the millennium is only the earthly aspect of God's kingdom. His kingdom in the ultimate sense, is eternal.

Traditionally, belief in the millennium, or millennialism, is known as "chiliasm" ("ch" is pronounced as "k") from the Greek *chilioi* (KHIL-ee-oy) which means a thousand. In the English language, millennialism is sometimes referred to as "millenarianism"—note that this word does not double the "n."

The Nature of the Millennial Doctrine

Students of millennialism find approximately 225 Scripture references that depict a day when earthly kingdoms will be set aside in favor of God's appointed Messiah. The premillennialist expects these predictions and promises to be fulfilled on earth as Jesus Christ assumes the throne of David and becomes the absolute ruler of all humans. As Jesus reigns on earth, He will restore nature to the pristine state that prevailed before the fall. He will thus implement His victory in the physical universe. Paul described matters, "The creation itself will be liberated from its bondage to decay and brought into the glorious freedom of the children of God" (Rom. 8:21). Humans will enjoy unprecedented blessings as their age-long dreams are fulfilled.

The fact of a future golden age on earth is taught throughout the Bible. The manner of the launching of the age by Jesus' violent conquest is repeatedly described. As we have noted, we learn from Revelation 20:1-8 that the duration of the golden age will be a thousand years. The sixfold repetition of the thousand-year duration pointedly provides the name "millennium" to this prophesied era. Even those who deny this literal Biblical measure of time are usually identified by their relationship to it (cf. postmillennialism, amillennialism). An alternate approach is to use the expression "transitional kingdom." This designation would allow for Christ's earthly kingdom prior to the eternal age to be of undetermined length.

The Old Testament promises

God's promises to Israel have been systematized under three covenants. The Abrahamic covenant (Gen. 15:4-21) promised him a posterity that would become a nation that would possess a land. The Palestinian covenant (Deut. 29:1-30:10) promised the desolation of the land and the deportation of the Jews for disobedience, but forgiveness and restoration to the land upon their repentance. The Davidic covenant (2 Sam. 7:11-16) promised an eternal royal dynasty and an eternal kingdom.

Since the millennium thus focuses upon Israel, many key Scriptures are found in the Old Testament.

> Psa. 22:27-28 "All the families of the nations will bow down before him, for dominion belongs to the LORD and he rules over the nations." In that day, deity Himself will rule upon earth.
>
> Isa. 2:3 "The law will go out from Zion, the word of the LORD from Jerusalem." Deity will rule by His law and by His word.
>
> Isa. 11:12 "He will . . . gather the exiles of Israel; he will assemble the scattered people of Judah from the four quarters of the earth."
>
> Isa. 24:23 "The LORD Almighty will reign on Mount Zion and in Jerusalem."
>
> Isa. 32. 18 "My people will live in peaceful dwelling places, in secure homes, in undisturbed places of rest."
>
> Isa. 35:10 "The ransomed of the LORD will return. They will enter Zion with singing; everlasting joy will crown their heads."
>
> Jer. 31:33 "This is the covenant I will make with the house of Israel. . . . I will put my law in their minds and write it on their hearts. I will be their God, and they will be my people."
>
> Dan. 2:44 "In the time of those kings, the God of heaven will set up a kingdom that will never be destroyed. . . . It will crush all those kingdoms and bring them to an end, but it will itself endure forever." Daniel is here interpreting Nebuchadnezzar's dream image of a final world empire dividing into ten kingdoms.
>
> Zech. 2:10, 12 "'Shout and be glad, O Daughter of Zion. For I am coming, and I will live among you,' declares the LORD. . . . The LORD will inherit Judah as his portion in the holy land and will again choose Jerusalem."
>
> Zech. 14:9 "The LORD will be king over the whole earth. On that day there will be one LORD, and his name the only name" (Zech. 14:9).

The kingdom will install the Jews in their ancient national territory, "The whole land of Canaan . . . I will give as an everlasting possession to you and your descendants after you" (Gen. 17:8). The promises to Abraham and David will be fulfilled.

Your house and your kingdom will endure forever before me; your throne will be established forever (2 Sam. 7:16). "The days are coming," declares the LORD, "when I will raise up to David . . . a King who will reign wisely and do what is just and right in the land" (Jer. 23:5); "This is what the LORD says: 'David will never fail to have a man to sit on the throne of the house of Israel'" (Jer. 33:17).

The promises both of the inheritance of the land, and of the rulership of a Davidic king, come together in Ezekiel 37:25 "They will live in the land I gave to my servant Jacob. . . . They and their children and their children's children will live there forever, and David my servant will be their prince forever."

The New Testament portrayal of the kingdom

The New Testament confirms and expands the Old Testament kingdom promises. Both John the Baptist and Jesus began their ministry by proclaiming "the kingdom . . . is near." (cf. Matt. 3:1; 4:17). We have noted, however, (see Chapter two) that the kingdom launched by Jesus was in mystery form and only visible to those who voluntarily submitted to His rule.

In contrast with this present mystery kingdom, Scripture describes the dramatic launching of the literal millennial kingdom. "I saw heaven standing open and there before me was a white horse, whose rider is called Faithful and True. . . . The armies of heaven were following him, riding on white horses. . . . Out of his mouth comes a sharp sword with which to strike down the nations. He will rule them with an iron scepter" (Rev. 19:11, 14-15). Jesus declared, "At that time the sign of the Son of Man will appear in the sky, and all the nations of the earth will mourn. They will see the Son of Man coming on the clouds of the sky, with power and great glory" (Matt. 24:30).

The New Testament associates Jesus with the messianic promises to Abraham and David. Gabriel declared of Mary's Child, "The Lord God will give him the throne of his father David, and he will reign over the house of Jacob forever" (Luke 1:32-33). Paul linked Christ to David and associated His rule with God's promises to David. "Remember Jesus Christ . . . descended from David" (2 Tim. 2:8, cf. Rom. 1:3). Jesus declared, "I, Jesus . . . am the Root and the Offspring of David" (Rev. 22:16). Peter saw the millennial rule as the restoration of the earth to its state prior to the fall. "Jesus . . . must remain in heaven until the time comes for God to restore everything, as he promised long ago through his holy prophets" (Acts 3:21). These passages clearly show that the millennium will fulfill the Old Testament kingdom promises.

Just prior to the ascension of Christ, the disciples asked, "'Lord, are you at this time going to restore the kingdom to

Israel?' He said to them, 'It is not for you to know the times or dates the Father has set by his own authority'" (Acts 1:6-7). Jesus did not deny the future restoration of the kingdom, but He declared that the time schedule was solely in God's hands. He then proceeded to affirm their commission to minister in the interim as witnesses (cf. Acts 1:8).

God's purposes in the millennium

God's indicated purposes in scheduling the millennium would no doubt include the following:

To recover creation from the curse. When humans fell the only home that subsequent humans have known was cursed. The millennial earth will be restored to the beauty and harmony of the garden of Eden. The deliverance of nature from its curse was included in Christ's victory on Calvary. In this final earthly age, God will implement this victory. Paul personified creation's state and its expectation when he wrote, "The creation itself will be liberated from the bondage to decay. . . . The whole creation has been groaning as in the pains of childbirth right up to the present time" (Rom. 3:22).

To fulfill His promises to Israel. The foregoing section cited a number of Old Testament promises to Israel. Not only are there numerous promises, but as we have seen, God extended formal covenants to Abraham, to the nation as a whole, and to David to confirm the certainty of future national blessings to Israel. They would be a people with a land and a very special Ruler of David's royal line. Only the millennium will be adequate to see these covenants fulfilled along with their accompanying promises.

To win a final company of humans to Himself. The vast population upon earth at the close of the millennium will have known only Eden-like conditions upon earth. They will be a people to whom God has sent blessing and unending good. As it were, the profusion of blessings is God's evangelistic strategy by which He wins the final company of converts. (cf. He previously used: works [Old Testament era], grace [New Testament era], and suffering [tribulation period]). The release of Satan and the final war (Gog and Magog) sets apart rebels from those He has won.

To reward faithful believers. As we will discuss in the next chapter, the millennium will involve glorified Christians in honored roles as Christ's deputies, agents, and assistants in ruling the people of earth. "Jesus said . . . 'At the renewal of all things, when the Son of Man sits on his glorious throne, you who have followed me will also sit on twelve thrones, judging the twelve tribes of Israel" (Matt. 19:28). Paul wrote, "If we died with him [i.e., Christ], we will also live with him; if we endure, we will also reign with him" (2 Tim. 2:11). The parable of the minas (pounds) (Luke 19:11-27) teaches that our Lord's faithful servants will be assigned the administration of cities in proportion to their faithfulness.

Christ's Rulership During the Millennium

The primary fact about the millennium is that Jesus Christ Himself will be supreme ruler upon earth. In Him, and in His rule, the ancient promises of an earthly kingdom and kingship will be fulfilled. That which through the centuries has appeared hopeless and impossible will suddenly become a reality.

The inauguration of the millennium

The millennium is not the gentle infiltration of earthly kingdoms; it is their violent overthrow and total replacement. Christ comes in judgment as a smiting rock, and suddenly in a drastic stroke He establishes His kingdom.

Daniel described Nebuchadnezzar's dream image. "A rock was cut out, but not by human hands. It struck the statue. . . . Then the iron, the clay, the bronze, the silver and the gold were broken to pieces . . . and became like chaff on a threshing floor in the summer. The wind swept them away without leaving a trace. But the rock that struck the statue became a huge mountain and filled the whole earth" (Dan. 2:34-35).

In Psalm 2 the LORD installs His King by decree and declares, "You are my Son . . . I will make the nations your inheritance. . . . You will rule them with an iron scepter; you will dash them to pieces like pottery" (Psa. 2:7, 9).

Isaiah predicted the emergence of "A shoot . . . from the stump of Jesse" and he declared that "He will strike the earth with the rod of his mouth; with the breath of his lips he will slay the wicked" (Isa. 11:4).

Jesus described His own triumphal return. "At that time the sign of the Son of Man will appear in the sky, and all the nations of the earth will mourn. They will see the Son of Man coming on the clouds of the sky with power and great glory" (Matt. 24:30).

John saw the end time events. "There before me was a white horse, whose rider is called Faithful and True. With justice he judges and makes war. . . . Out of his mouth comes a sharp sword with which to strike down the nations. 'He will rule them with an iron scepter'" (Rev. 19:11, 15).

Christ's role in millennial rulership

Christ's millennial rule will be a theocracy administered by His personal and visible presence. He will rule as a benevolent despot without the benefit of parliament, committees, or advisors, and without particular reference to public opinion. It is not that the Lord Jesus covets power, or that He is insensitive to human desires, but He cannot permit the prosperity and blessing of His rule to be marred by the interference of human rebels.

"In the time of those kings, the God of heaven will set up a kingdom that will never be destroyed, nor will it be left to another people. It will crush all those kingdoms and bring them to an end" (Dan. 2:44); **So great is your power that your enemies cringe before you (Psa. 66:3); In that day the Root of Jesse will stand as a banner for the peoples; the nations will rally to him (Isa. 11:10); [The Ancient of Days] was given authority, glory and sovereign power; all peoples, nations and men of every language worshiped him. His dominion is an everlasting dominion (Dan. 7:14); The root of Jesse will spring up, one who will arise to rule over the nations; the Gentiles will hope in him (Rom. 15:12).**

Psalm 110 depicts God the Father speaking to God the Son. "The Lord says to my Lord: 'Sit at my right hand until I make your enemies a footstool for your feet'" (Psa. 110:1). This verse is so much a biblical theme that it is quoted or paraphrased a total of sixteen times in the New Testament.

Such stern rulership will inevitably engender resentment within some humans, and it is likely that some will only feign submission. Such people will be prime candidates to become Satan's followers at the close of the millennium. But in spite of His autonomous dictatorial rule, Jesus will exploit no one, nor in any way commit any unjust actions.

"I will raise up to David a righteous Branch, a King who will reign wisely and do what is just and right in the land" (Jer. 23:5); With righteousness he will judge the needy, with justice he will give decisions for the poor of the earth. . . . Righteousness will be his belt and faithfulness the sash around his waist (Isa. 11:4-5).

Christ's millennial rule on earth will be limited to 1,000 years, but the quality of rulership that He establishes will be eternal. In the millennium, Christ will achieve a mandate to rule that will prevail eternally. "He was given authority, glory and sovereign power; all peoples, nations and men of every language worshiped him. His dominion is an everlasting dominion that will not pass away, and his kingdom is one that will never be destroyed" (Dan. 7:14). When the millennium ends, Jesus' rulership will be transferred to the eternal realm in order to maintain millennial relationships forever. God promised, "David my servant will be their [i.e., Israel's] prince forever" (Ezek. 37:25).[1]

---

1 Because David is named as the millennial administrative ruler in this and other Scriptures (cf. Ezek. 34:23-24; Jer. 30:9, 33:15-17) some suggest that King David in a resurrected body will literally rule. If so, David will, of course, rule under the authority of Jesus. Most scholars prefer to hold, however, that Jesus is the sole ruler, and thus the name David is applied to Him as the greater David and in recognition of His role in fulfilling God's promises to David.

The geography of the kingdom

Certain descriptions of Israel's geographical boundaries await the millennium for their fulfillment. God promised: "I will establish your borders from the Red Sea to the Sea of the Philistines, and from the desert to the River" (Exod. 23:31), and "On the east side the boundary will run . . . to the eastern sea" (Ezek. 47:18). The expression "eastern sea" could imply the Persian Gulf, but most scholars see it as the Dead Sea.

Israel's neighbors during the millennium are identified. "In that day there will be a highway from Egypt to Assyria. . . . The Egyptians and Assyrians will worship together. In that day Israel will be the third, along with Egypt and Assyria" (Isa. 19:23-24). Israel will thus include the entire Arabian peninsula with the River Euphrates as the northern boundary. Geologists speak of this region as the Arabian plate, since it is bounded by a geologic fault line or fracture zone that distinctively marks it out. Its area is about one-third that of continental United States.

Israel During the Millennium

In the millennium, at last, God's unconditional covenants to the Israelites will be fulfilled. He promised: 1) a land—"To your descendants I give this land" (Gen. 15:18); 2) a king and a kingdom—"Your house and your kingdom will endure forever" (2 Sam. 7:16); and 3) a nation—"I will make them one nation in the land, on the mountains of Israel" (Ezek. 37:22).

The regathering of Israel

The twentieth century regathering of the Jews in Israel that attracted about one Jew in five, was a harbinger of the total millennial return. Jesus revealed His plan: "The Son of Man . . . will send his angels and gather his elect from the four winds, from the ends of the earth to the heavens" (Mark 13:26-27). The Old Testament prophets described that future time:

> In that day the Lord will reach out his hand a second time to reclaim the remnant that is left of his people. . . . [He] will assemble the scattered people of Judah from the four quarters of the earth (Isa. 11:11-12); "He who scattered Israel will gather them and will watch over his flock like a shepherd" (Jer. 31:10); "This is what the Sovereign LORD says: I will gather you from the nations and bring you back from the countries where you have been scattered, and I will give you back the land of Israel again" (Ezek. 11:17); "I will surely gather all of you, O Jacob; I will surely bring together the remnant of Israel. I will bring them together like sheep in a pen, like a flock in its pasture; the place will throng with people" (Mic. 2:12).

The establishment of the kingdom

The nation of Israel will be established in a single day. "Who has ever heard of such a thing? . . . Can a country be born in a day? . . . Yet no sooner is Zion in labor than she gives birth to her children" (Isa. 66:8). This sudden new unity and identity will be neither political nor national, but a fundamental spiritual conversion to love and serve Jesus Christ. "For on my holy mountain . . . the entire house of Israel will serve me, and there I will accept them. There I will require your offerings and your choice gifts. . . . I will accept you as fragrant incense when I bring you out from the nations . . . where you have been scattered" (Ezek. 20:40-41). "I will put my Spirit in you and you will live, and I will settle you in your own land" (Ezek. 37:14). At last the Israelites' homeland will be a place of refuge, and completely their own possession. "On Mount Zion will be deliverance; it will be holy, and the house of Jacob will possess its inheritance" (Obad. 17).

The regathering of Israel will be not only a commitment to a place, but also a commitment to God's theocratic rule. "I will surely gather them from all the lands where I banish them . . . I will bring them back to this place and let them live in safety. They will be my people, and I will be their God" (Jer. 32:37-38). Israel will discover a gratifying stability and permanence. "I will plant Israel in their own land, never again to be uprooted from the land I have given them, says the LORD your God" (Amos 9:15).

At this time, the nation will relate to God not merely politically, but spiritually as well. "All Israel will be saved, as it is written: 'The deliverer will come from Zion; he will turn godlessness away from Jacob. And this is my covenant with them when I take away their sins'" (Rom. 12:26-27). "I will raise up to David a righteous Branch, a King who will reign wisely. . . . In his days Judah will be saved and Israel will live in safety" (Jer. 23:5-6).

Israel's spiritual life in the millennium

God had extended His millennial covenant:

"I will make an everlasting covenant with them: I will never stop doing good to them, and I will inspire them to fear me, so that they will never turn away from me" (Jer. 32:40); "My dwelling place will be with them; I will be their God, and they will be my people. Then the nations will know that I the LORD make Israel holy, when my sanctuary is among them forever" (Ezek. 37:27-28); "The time is coming . . . when I will make a new covenant with the house of Israel and with the house of Judah. . . . I will put my law in their minds and write it on their hearts. I will be their God, and they will be my people. . . . I will forgive their wickedness and will remember their sins no more" (Jer. 31:31, 33-34; cf. Heb. 8:8-12).

Joel's vision includes many details of the life of millennial Israel. He declared: 1) all the nation would enjoy the Spirit's outpouring (2:28); 2) prophecies, dreams, and visions would be commonplace (2:28); 3) the outpouring would include servants and not be limited to leaders (2:29); 4) the millennial era would be preceded by dramatic cosmic upheavals (2:30-31); 5) salvation would be readily available to everyone (2:32); and 6) the spiritual headquarters would be Mt. Zion and Jerusalem (2:32).

At Pentecost, Peter cited Joel's prophecy to explain the spectacular events that were occurring (cf. Acts 2:17-21). The day of Pentecost, however, exhibited only some aspects of the spiritual promises; the cosmic upheavals remained future. The millennium will see the Israelites brought into the realm of the gospel. In experiences paralleling those of today's Christians, they will be born again, and indwelt by the Holy Spirit.

Various biblical promises will be fulfilled during this era.

> "My dwelling place will be with them; I will be their God, and they will be my people. Then the nations will know that I the LORD make Israel holy when my sanctuary is among them" (Ezek. 37:27-28); "I will gather them to their own land, not leaving any behind. . . . I will pour out my Spirit on the house of Israel" (Ezek. 39:28-29); "On that day a fountain will be opened to the house of David and the inhabitants of Jerusalem, to cleanse them from sin and impurity" (Zech. 13:1); On that day HOLY TO THE LORD will be inscribed on the bells of the horses, and . . . every pot in Jerusalem and Judah will be holy to the LORD Almighty (Zech. 14:20-21).

Israel's leadership during the millennium

At this time, the Jews will fulfill the role for which God chose them. They will be His channels to teach His truth and His ways to the millennial Gentile citizens. Having accepted their Messiah, the Jews now will serve as His ministers. "I will send some of those who survive to the nations. . . . They will proclaim my glory among the nations. And they will bring all your brothers, from all the nations, to my holy mountain in Jerusalem as an offering to the LORD" (Isa. 66:19-20). Both their own people and the Gentile nations will enjoy their ministry. "In those days ten men from all languages and nations will take firm hold of one Jew by the hem of his robe and say, 'Let us go with you, because we have heard that God is with you'" (Zech. 8:23).

As they take their place in leadership, the Jews will become the head of nations and through them God will bless all humans. "You will lend to many nations but will borrow from none. The LORD will make you the head, not the tail. If you pay attention to the commands of the LORD . . . and carefully follow them, you will always be at the top, never at the bottom" (Deut. 28:12-13). God's blessings will provide Jews with a strikingly favorable reputation. "I will give you honor and praise among all the peoples of the earth when I restore your fortunes before your very eyes, says the LORD" (Zeph. 3:20).

The millennial city of Jerusalem

At the outset of the millennium Jerusalem will undergo major geographic and topographic changes from today's city. Its basic location will be unchanged, nevertheless, and it will continue to relate to humans as an earthly city and the world's capital. "Many peoples will come and say, 'Come, let us go up to the mountain of the LORD, to the house of the God of Jacob. He will teach us his ways, so that we may walk in his paths.' The law will go out from Zion, the word of the LORD from Jerusalem" (Isa. 2:3). The city will be the world center of government. "The LORD Almighty will reign on Mount Zion and in Jerusalem, and before its elders, gloriously" (Isa. 24:23).

The security and the impregnability of the city will be assured: "Jerusalem will be raised up and remain in its place. . . . It will be inhabited; never again will it be destroyed. Jerusalem will be secure" (Zech. 14:10-11). Gentile domination of Jerusalem will have ended, for Jesus taught, "Jerusalem will be trampled on by the Gentiles until the times of the Gentiles are fulfilled" (Luke 21:24). Joel had seen that day, "Then you will know that I, the LORD your God, dwell in Zion, my holy hill. Jerusalem will be holy; never again will foreigners invade her" (Joel 3:17).

The city will provide spiritual leadership to all humans. "Nations will come; to your light, and kings to the brightness of your dawn" (Isa. 60:3); "The name of the LORD will be declared in Zion and his praise in Jerusalem when the peoples and the kingdoms assemble to worship the LORD" (Psa. 102:21-22). Because Jerusalem is the LORD's chosen city His presence will be especially manifested there. "The LORD has chosen Zion, he has desired it for his dwelling " (Psa. 132:13). During the millennium, God's personal presence will impart a unique sanctity in which the prophet exalted, "Put on your garments of splendor, O Jerusalem, the holy city. The uncircumcised and defiled will not enter you again" (Isa. 52:1).

Israel's millennial temple

Restored Israel in the land will construct the millennial temple and use its facilities to revive temple worship (cf. Ezek. Chs. 40-48). God commanded, "Make known to [the people of Israel] the design of the temple—its arrangement, its exits and entrances—its whole design and all its regulations and laws. Write these down before them so that they may be faithful to its design and follow all its regulations" (Ezek. 43:11). As Israel's fourth temple[2] its plans are literal and detailed. References in Isaiah 2:3, 60:13, Joel 3:18, and Haggai 2:7-9 expand Ezekiel's account. The structure will apparently be built north of the city of

---

2 Previously there will have been: Solomon's (destroyed c. 586 BC), Zerubbabel's (destroyed c. 20 BC), Herod's (destroyed A.D. c. 70), and the tribulation temple desecrated by Antichrist. It is usually held that since Herod's temple was a reconstruction of Zerubbabel's it should also be counted the second temple.

Jerusalem in the land portion dedicated to the LORD. The temple courtyard alone will be larger than the present city of Jerusalem.

Israel's millennial system of worship

The millennial system of sacrifices is primarily described in Ezekiel (but cf. Isa. 56:6-7; 60:7; Jer. 33:15-18; and Zech. 14:16-21). Ezekiel names the five restored ceremonial offerings: sin offerings, guilt offerings, grain offerings, burnt offerings, and fellowship offerings (cf. Ezek. 42:13; 43:27). These offerings will apparently look backward to Calvary, and thus contrast with Old Testament times when they looked forward. Christians use the bread and cup of the communion service to remind them of Calvary and to be an occasion of self-examination and confession of sin. The broken bread and the poured out cup are symbols of Christ's broken body and shed blood, but in no sense are they the repeated crucifixion of Christ. Similarly, millennial Jews will use their own visible reminders of Christ's atoning death.

All of the Old Testament laws and ceremonies were fulfilled in Jesus Christ. At no time were Old Testament sacrifices efficacious to atone for sin, for had they been, there would have been no necessity for the cross of Christ. The writer to the Hebrews states, "It is impossible for the blood of bulls and goats to take away sins. Therefore, when Christ came into the world, he said . . . 'I have come to do your will, O God.' . . . And by that will, we have been made holy through the sacrifice of the body of Jesus Christ once for all" (Heb. 10:4, 5, 7, 10).

The millennial sacrifices cannot negate the eternal victory of the cross. They are a response to God's theocratic rule, and a way of worshiping God in a prosperous and affluent earth where offerings of money or goods would be superfluous, and even the offering of oneself in service is not a vocational choice. Ezekiel describes these sacrifices, "One sheep is to be taken . . . to make atonement for the people, declares the Sovereign LORD. . . . You are to take a young bull without defect. . . . The priest is to take some of the blood . . . and put it on the doorposts of the temple. . . . So you are to make atonement for the temple" (Ezek. 45:15, 18-20). The atonement of which Ezekiel speaks is efficacious only because of and through the shed blood of Christ.

The millennial sacrifices will reveal their ultimate purpose—to point mankind to the atoning death of the Messiah and His atonement for sin. In every age, God's only formula to pardon the penitent has been the shed blood of Jesus. Over the centuries, however, God has revised the pattern for the expression of faith. In Old Testament times, faith required the practice of the ceremonial law; in the church age the believer accepts the gospel and Lordship of Christ; in the millennial age, believers will

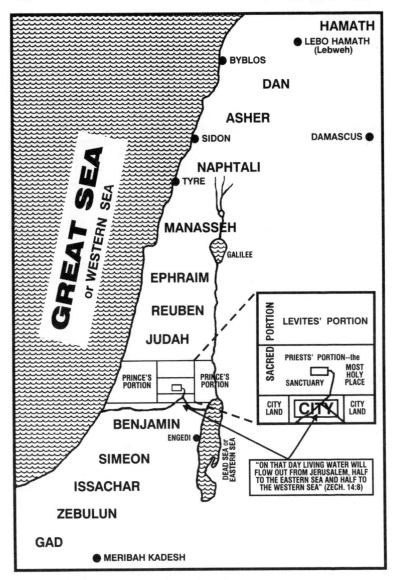

Fig. 14: Ezekiel's vision of the distribution of the promised land in the millennial age. The prophet names known geographic sites as the boundaries of a literal kingdom. The dimensions of the Sacred Portion are uncertain, since the original omits the unit of measure. Earlier versions of the Sacred Portion [Holy Oblation —KJV] projected a square eighty kilometers (50 miles) to the side; currently eleven kilometers (7 miles) each side is suggested.

participate in temple worship. We have noted that during the millennium, even routine living will qualify for devout acts of worship. The cooking pots in the believer's family kitchen will be as holy as those of the sanctuary (cf. Zech. 14:20-21 cited above).

In the descriptions of the millennial temple, one looks in vain for the ark of the covenant, the lampstand, the holy of holies, the separating veil, the bread of the Presence, the evening sacrifice, or the Day of Atonement. Only two feasts are reported: 1) the feast of the Passover is named and its revival indicated (cf. Ezek. 45:21), and 2) the feast of Tabernacles is described in Ezekiel 45:25 and named in Zechariah 14:16.

The sons of Zadok are designated as God's only temple ministers (cf. Ezek. 40:46; 43:19; 44:15; 48:11). Most commentators consider the prince, who is spoken of repeatedly by Ezekiel, to be a flesh and blood Jew who is in the royal Davidic line and a true representative of Christ. The prince is an ordinary human since he offers sacrifices, fathers children, and suffers rebuke. He provides leadership to the people as they serve and worship their divine Messiah.

The millennial worship system will have much in common with the Mosaic system, but also much that is unique to itself. The millennial temple will provide a worship structure appropriate for humans who have been saved from the results of mankind's fall. The system will provide for the personal presence of deity upon earth. Ezekiel notes, "The name of the city from that time on will be: THE LORD IS THERE" (Ezek. 48:35).

The implementation of the worship system of this era will provide that God's promises will be fulfilled. "David will never fail to have a man to sit on the throne of the house of Israel, nor will the priests, who are Levites, ever fail to have a man to stand before me continually to offer burnt offerings, to burn grain offerings and to present sacrifices" (Jer. 33:17-18). It is evident that during the millennium, Israel will develop and maintain the greatest system of worship, praise, and adoration of God that this world has ever seen.

The Gentile Nations During the Millennium

Though the millennium emerges out of God's promises to Israel, it constitutes the golden age for all mankind. It is God's program to fulfill His promise to Abram, "All peoples on earth will be blessed through you" (Gen. 12:3).

The Gentile millennial citizens

Humans who are approved to enter the millennium will be those who were spared judgment at Armageddon, and those whom Jesus classified as sheep (cf. Matt. 25:33-40). All rebels will have been destroyed by events at Armageddon. Jesus explained the parable, "The Son of Man will send out his angels, and they will weed out of his kingdom everything that causes sin and all who do evil. They will throw them into the fiery furnace. . . . Then the righteous will shine like the sun in the kingdom of their Father" (Matt. 13:40-43).

At long last in the history of earth's peoples, rebellious hostility against God and His Son will cease. "At that time they will call Jerusalem The Throne of the LORD, and all nations will gather in Jerusalem to honor the name of the LORD. No longer will they follow the stubbornness of their evil hearts" (Jer. 3:17). In millennial times, believers will be genuinely transformed in their attitudes and actions, just as believers who are in Christ today have the potential to be changed.

Scripture stresses that Gentile millennial citizens will be devout worshipers of Jehovah. "My name will be great among the nations, from the rising to the setting of the sun. In every place incense and pure offerings will be brought to my name, because my name will be great among the nations, says the LORD Almighty" (Mal. 1:11); "All the nations you have made will come and worship before you, O LORD; they will bring glory to your name" (Psa. 86:9). Even nations who have traditionally rejected God and opposed His people will undergo a total turnaround. "The LORD will make himself known to the Egyptians, and in that day they will acknowledge the LORD. They will worship with sacrifices and grain offerings; they will make vows to the LORD and keep them" (Isa. 19:21).

In the millennium, all humans will be united in worship and even in language. "Then will I purify the lips of the peoples [or "I will restore to the peoples a pure language—NKJV], that all of them may call on the name of the LORD to serve him shoulder to shoulder [or "with one accord"—NKJV]" (Zeph. 3:9). Worship customs will call for annual pilgrimages to Jerusalem. "The survivors from all the nations that have attacked Jerusalem will go up year after year to worship the King, the LORD Almighty, and to celebrate the Feast of Tabernacles" (Zech. 14:16).

We have noted that Gentiles will look to Jews for leadership in spiritual matters (see p. 217). Zechariah 8:23 which was cited speaks of ten Gentiles attaching themselves to one Jew to join him as he goes to "seek the Lord Almighty." In speaking of these times through Isaiah, God addressed His "servant": "It is too small a thing for you to be my servant to restore the tribes of Jacob and bring back those of Israel I have kept. I will also make you a light for the Gentiles, that you may bring my salvation to the ends of the earth" (Isa. 49:6). Paul quoted the second clause of this verse to justify his ministry to the Gentiles (cf. Acts 13:4). Paul did not restore the tribes, however, and his ministry to Gentiles was only a preview of millennial events.

Scripture does not specify the degree to which the Gentiles will be required to become proselytes to Judaism.[3] Gentiles could not so completely embrace Judaism, however, that they would threaten the unique status of the Jews. If, as some believe, circumcision will be required of Gentiles, that action will not include them in the Jewish covenant seal, but simply qualify them to participate in the sacred temple ceremonies. Traditionally, God had said, "No foreigner uncircumcised in heart and flesh is to enter my sanctuary" (Ezek. 44:9). In contrast, however, "In the last days . . . all nations will stream to [the LORD's temple]. . . . Many peoples will come and say 'Let us go up to . . . the house of the God of Jacob'" (Isa. 2:2-3). We are reminded that when God included Gentiles in the church, He fully exempted them from Jewish ceremonial law (cf. Acts 15:5-29).

Personal lifestyle in this era

Some aspects of millennial life on earth will parallel those of the present. There will be the usual span of ages: "Once again men and women of ripe old age will sit in the streets of Jerusalem, each with cane in hand because of his age. The city streets will be filled with boys and girls playing there" (Zech. 8:4-5). Marriages will be joyfully celebrated. "In . . . the streets of Jerusalem . . . there will be heard once more the sounds of joy and gladness, the voices of bride and bridegroom" (Jer. 33:10-11).

The millennium will be an era of unexcelled physical health. Neither infant mortality nor premature death will threaten. "Never again will there be in [Jerusalem] an infant who lives but a few days, or an old man who does not live out his years; he who dies at a hundred will be thought a mere youth" (Isa. 65:20); "Then will the eyes of the blind be opened and the ears of the deaf unstopped. Then will the lame leap like a deer, and the mute tongue shout for joy. Water will gush forth in the wilderness and streams in the desert" (Isa. 35:5-6).

Under millennial rule, humans will no longer exploit one another, and people will enjoy the fruits of their labor. "No longer will they build houses and others live in them, or plant and others eat. . . . My chosen ones will long enjoy the works of their hands. They will not toil in vain or bear children doomed to

---

3 Note that the people who make annual pilgrimages and "celebrate the feast of Tabernacles" (Zech. 14:16 cited above), are "survivors from . . . the nations that have attacked Jerusalem." They clearly are Gentiles, but they choose to practice Jewish religious customs.

misfortune; for they will be a people blessed by the Lord" (Isa. 65:22-23). A spirit of joyfulness and peace will characterize every life. "You will go out in joy and be led forth in peace" (Isa. 55:12). People will respond to one another and to God in understanding and empathy. "I will remove from them their heart of stone and give them a heart of flesh" (Ezek. 11:19). It is in this era, of course, that wars will cease. "They will beat their swords into plowshares and their spears into pruning hooks. Nation will not take up sword against nation, nor will they train for war anymore" (Mic. 4:3); "I will take away the chariots . . . and the war-horses . . . and the battle bow will be broken" (Zech. 9:10).

With Satan rendered inactive, nature freed from the curse, and only believers—whether Jews or Gentiles—surviving to become the initial millennial citizens, universal joyfulness will prevail on earth. "The ransomed of the Lord . . . will enter Zion with singing; everlasting joy will crown their heads. Gladness and joy will overtake them, and sorrow and sighing will flee away" (Isa. 35:10). The lifestyle standards of the Sermon on the Mount will prevail. Righteousness will become the basic human standard.

Remarkably, however, even this beautiful environment will not guarantee generations of committed believers. Just as Adam and Eve in Eden, so the millennial citizens will be responsible for choosing or rejecting the standards that God imposes. The open rebellion of humans against God's standards, however, will occur only when the millennium has run its course.

The millennial government of the Gentile nations

All nations on earth will be totally subject to Messiah's rule. "The Lord will be king over the whole earth. On that day there will be one LORD, and his name the only name" (Zech. 14:9); "He was given authority, glory and sovereign power; all peoples, nations and men or every language worshiped him" (Dan. 7:14). Christ's absolute rule will be justified by His impeccably righteous integrity. "A king will reign in righteousness and rulers will rule with justice" (Isa. 32:1).

Jesus Christ will be both the One who rules and also the divine Object of worship. "All the families of the nations will bow down before him, for dominion belongs to the LORD and he rules over the nations" (Psa. 22:27-28). This knowledge of the Lordship of Christ will be universal. "The earth will be full of the knowledge of the LORD as the waters cover the sea" (Isa. 11:9). The Gentiles will have cause to react to their absolute Ruler with genuine joy. "May the nations be glad and sing for joy, for you rule the peoples justly and guide the nations of the earth" (Psa. 67:4, cf. Isa. 35:10 cited above).

Millennial Conditions on Earth

Jesus spoke of a greatly changed physical earth and order of nature. "At the renewal (Gk. *paliggenesia*) of all things, when the Son of Man sits on his glorious throne, you who have followed me will also sit on twelve thrones" (Matt. 19:28). (*paliggenesia* [pal-ing-ghen-es-EE-ah]: rebirth, renovation, restoration, regeneration, renewal of the world). The same word identifies both God's renewal of the world, and also His regeneration of a life. (e.g., "He saved us through the washing of rebirth [*paliggenesia*]" [Tit. 3:5]). Thus, that which God plans for the physical earth and nature is totally transforming. Though the earth will have been severely damaged by the judgments of the tribulation, it will be gloriously restored and renewed.

Notable changes in the earth

Christ's second coming will result in major topographical changes upon earth. "Then the LORD will go out and fight against those nations. . . . On that day his feet will stand on the Mount of Olives, east of Jerusalem, and the Mount of Olives will be split in two from east to west, forming a great valley, with half of the mountain moving north and half moving south" (Zech. 14:3-4). A major river will flow from the temple, with a branch flowing into the Dead Sea. As a result, the lifeless Dead Sea, six times saltier than the oceans, will become ecologically purified, and it will swarm with living creatures (cf. Ezek. 47:1-9; Zech. 14:8).

Ezekiel's detailed description of millennial Palestine (Chs. 47-48) applies only loosely to the present land. The sites and dimensions he describes will require the rearrangement of the earth's surface. Perhaps Jerusalem will become a world class seaport standing on a great canal that unites the Mediterranean and Dead Sea. The latter will have enlarged to connect with the Gulf of Aqaba, and thence to the world's oceans of the eastern hemisphere. Such dramatic changes are all part of the world-shaking events associated with Christ's second coming. Even the stars and planets will be affected: "The sun will be darkened . . . the stars will fall from the sky, and the heavenly bodies will be shaken" (Mark 13:24-25).

The millennial earth, in contrast with the present earth, will be prolifically productive, requiring little human effort to yield its bounties. "The reaper will be overtaken by the plowman and the planter by the one treading grapes" (Amos 9:13); "I will send down showers in season. . . . The trees of the field will yield their fruit and the ground will yield its crops" (Ezek. 34:26-27); "He will also send you rain for the seed you sow in the ground, and the food that comes from the land will be rich and plentiful. In that day your cattle will graze in broad meadows" (Isa. 30:23); "Every man will sit under his own vine and under his own fig tree" (Mic. 4:4). With adequate rainfall, the deserts will be reclaimed to be inviting and productive. "I will make rivers flow on barren heights, and springs within the valleys. I will turn the desert into pools of water. . . . I will put in the desert the cedar and the acacia, the myrtle and the olive. I will set pines in the wasteland, the fir and the cypress together" (Isa. 41:18-19).

Notable changes in nature

Christ's victory over sin will restore millennial nature to its Edenic paradise. Vegetation will appear in former deserts, and all that grows will please and serve humans. "The LORD will surely comfort Zion . . . he will make her deserts like Eden, her wastelands like the garden of the LORD" (Isa. 51:3); "Instead of the thornbush will grow the pine tree, and instead of briers the myrtle will grow" (Isa. 55:13). The nature of animals and reptiles will be changed: "The wolf will live with the lamb, the leopard will lie down with the goat, the calf and the lion and the yearling together; and a little child will lead them. The cow will feed with the bear, their young will lie down together, and the lion will eat straw like the ox. The infant will play near the hole of the cobra, and the young child put his hand into the viper's nest. They will neither harm nor destroy on all my holy mountain" (Isa. 11:6-9).

As we have noted, Jesus appropriately likened earth's millennial changes to a rebirth, and Paul personified creation and interwove creation's desire for rebirth with the believer's desire for a glorified body (cf. Rom. 8:20-23). In view of God's promises for the millennium that He has planned, both humans and nature await an awesomely glorious future!

THIRTEEN

The Millennium: Part 2

Virtually all moral intelligences, except for the unsaved dead, will be affected in some way by the millennium. In this chapter we will consider the role of the church and its people and the destiny of Satan during this era. Also, we will trace the historical development of the millennial doctrine, and the divergent views of postmillennialism and amillennialism.

The Church During the Millennium

In worshiping the Lamb, the twenty-four elders sang, "With your blood you purchased men for God from every tribe and language and people and nation . . . and they will reign on the earth" (Rev. 5:9-10). The career of the blood-washed church in sharing Christ's earthly reign is a major theme of heaven. The church will have just been united with Christ at the rapture, so that her millennial role can be called "her 1,000 year honeymoon."

The church's millennial leadership role

Since millennial citizens will be flesh and blood humans, resurrected believers will not be part of their society. Rather, these believers will serve as Christ's deputies, agents, and assistants in ruling the people of earth. "Jesus said . . . at the renewal of all things, when the Son of Man sits on his glorious throne, you who have followed me will also sit on twelve thrones, judging the twelve tribes of Israel" (Matt. 19:28). Keith Bailey commented concerning God's plan, "The purpose of God is to make all His sons crown princes able to rule with Christ in that day."[1]

In the upper room following the last supper, Jesus responded to the dispute between the disciples concerning which one was greatest. "You are those who have stood by me in my trials. And I confer on you a kingdom, just as my Father conferred one on me, so that you may eat and drink at my table in my kingdom and sit on thrones, judging the twelve tribes of Israel" (Luke 22:28-30). The reward promised the twelve apostles is representative of the reward anticipated for all who comprise Christ's church.

---

[1] Keith M. Bailey, *Christ's Coming and His Kingdom*. Harrisburg: Christian Publications, 1981, p. 153.

Paul reminded the disputing Corinthians, "Do you not know that the saints will judge the world?" (1 Cor. 6:2); and he encouraged himself in his sufferings, "If we endure, we will also reign with him" (2 Tim. 2:12). In Scripture, the verbs "judge" and "reign" are often interchangeable; the Old Testament judge was actually a regional ruler. Daniel described the future Kingdom, "Then the sovereignty, power and greatness of the kingdoms under the whole heaven will be handed over to the saints, the people of the Most High. His kingdom will be an everlasting kingdom, and all rulers will worship and obey him" (Dan. 7:27).

The church, as the bride of Christ, will be especially favored in its millennial role by being seated at the King's right hand. In sharing Christ's rule, however, the church will not be the only company that is honored. All saints who are part of the first resurrection will also participate in this millennial rulership, including Old Testament saints and tribulation saints. "Blessed and holy are those who have part in the first resurrection . . . they will be priests of God and of Christ and will reign with him for a thousand years" (Rev. 20:6). The parable of the talents (Matt. 25:14-30), and the parable of the minas (pounds) (Luke 19:11-26) indicate that appointments and recognitions of the future age will be based upon faithfulness and achievements in service in this life. The tasks of resurrected believers in the millennium will be considered rewards rather than burdens.

The status of church saints in the millennial era

The resurrected bodies of church saints during this era will conform to the model of the resurrected Christ. They will travel with the speed of thought, and be just as independent of physical environment. Being without physical limitations, they will be adequate for whatever role God has planned. The relationship of such resurrected beings to earthly millennial citizens compares with the relationship of angels to Christians on earth in this present day. Angels are "ministering spirits" (Heb. 1:14), however, but resurrected believers will be deputy rulers.

The basic millennial home of church saints will be the new Jerusalem, even while they fulfill their duties on earth. The rapture provides that "We will be with the Lord forever" (1 Thess. 4:17). The spiritual nature of believers' bodies assures that the location of the new Jerusalem is not a problem, though it remains in God's third heaven. Some scholars hold that during the millennium the new Jerusalem descends within view of the earth, and it becomes a "satellite city" or "heavenly chandelier." Such texts as Revelation 21:22-27 appear to hint at this view. But as Walvoord points out, "The possibility of Jerusalem being a satellite city over the earth during the millennium is not specifically taught in any Scripture and at best is an inference."[2] Most scholars prefer to see only one descent of the new Jerusalem—that which occurs as the eternal age is launched.

Satan During the Millennium

The removal of Satan from the scene will assure that earth enjoys a true golden age under the rulership of Jesus Christ. Satan's release at the end of the millennium provides an occasion for all those born during the millennium to make their own choice. As it were, every human will have an opportunity to replay the choice of the Garden of Eden. Apparently, most humans will have learned nothing, for multitudes of millennial citizens will once again fail their moral test.

Satan's imprisonment and release

John wrote: "I saw an angel coming down out of heaven. . . . He seized the dragon, that ancient serpent, who is the devil, or Satan, and bound him for a thousand years. He threw him into the Abyss, and locked and sealed it over him, to keep him from deceiving the nations anymore until the thousand years were ended" (Rev. 20:1-3). To assure that Satan does not interfere with Christ's Kingdom, and that during this period he has absolutely no influence on earth, he is both bound and imprisoned. Isaiah wrote: "In that day the Lord will punish the powers in the heavens above. . . . They will be herded together like prisoners bound in a dungeon; they will be shut up in prison and be punished after many days" (Isa. 24:21-22). This view of Satan accords with Paul's identification of him as "the ruler [or prince] of the kingdom of the air" (Eph. 2:2). In this present age, Satan is intensely active.

John told of Satan's release from his millennial imprisonment, "When the thousand years are over, Satan will be released from his prison and will go out to deceive the nations in the four corners of the earth" (Rev. 20:7-8). Presumably, with the unlimited prosperity, universal peace, and near perfect health on earth, a vast population will have been born during the millennium, and almost all of them will be alive at the end. These enormous multitudes will be susceptible to Satan's deception, and he will win a substantial following. Just as in Eden, he will win followers both by outright deception, and also by emotional persuasion. "Adam was not the one deceived; it was the woman who was deceived and became a sinner" (1 Tim. 2:14).

God's release of Satan will become an occasion for millennial citizens to make a moral choice. Multitudes of humans born

---

2 John F. Walvoord, *The Revelation of Jesus Christ.* Chicago: Moody Press, 1966, p. 313.

during the millennium will have simply conformed to the prevailing behavior patterns without ever having made a conscious choice to submit their wills to God and His saving grace. Heaven's citizens can only be those who have chosen to be there. The response to Satan's call for followers will become for each human the choice of his or her eternal destiny.

Gog and Magog and its aftermath

Satan's story continues as the millennium ends. "[He] will go out to deceive the nations in the four corners of the earth—Gog and Magog—to gather them for battle. In number they are like the sand of the seashore. They marched across the breadth of the earth and surrounded the camp of God's people, the city he loves. But fire came down from heaven and devoured them" (Rev. 20:8-9). Tragically, the millennium, the most beautiful era since Eden, will end in fire and smoke and total destruction. In spite of the privileges and blessings of the millennium, humans will respond in rebellion and hostility to their benevolent King. They will hail Satan as their leader and deliverer, and his followers will become a vast military force that attacks the millennial Jerusalem.

In this usage "Gog and Magog" is a collective title for all nations at all points of the compass. There is no battle, but God's judgment fire responds to their preparations for war, or at least their mass objection to the rule of Jesus Christ. The city of Jerusalem, to which they direct their protests, will be the earthly counterpart of the new Jerusalem in the heavenlies. God's fiery judgment stroke will immediately end all hostilities.

The judgment fire of God at this time will likely continue its work in order to achieve the total renovation that prepares the new earth. Peter had prophesied, "The day of the Lord will come like a thief. The heavens will disappear with a roar; the elements will be destroyed by fire, and the earth and everything in it will be laid bare" (2 Pet. 3:10). Isaiah wrote repeatedly of this day:

> The earth will be completely laid waste and totally plundered (Isa. 24:3); The LORD is angry with all nations; his wrath is upon all their armies. He will totally destroy them, he will give them over to slaughter.... All the stars of the heavens will be dissolved and the sky rolled up like a scroll; all the starry host will fall like withered leaves from the vine (Isa. 34:2, 4); The heavens will vanish like smoke, the earth will wear out like a garment and its inhabitants die like flies (Isa. 51:6).

Scripture does not describe the deliverance of the millennial saints from this end time holocaust, but God will surely provide whatever escape is needed. The catching away of the church saints before the tribulation may be the model of what He plans.

John described later events: "And the devil, who deceived them, was thrown into the lake of burning sulphur, where the beast and the false prophet had been thrown. They will be tormented day and night for ever and ever" (Rev. 20:10). This stroke of divine judgment reunites Satan with Antichrist and the False Prophet so that the satanic triad eternally share their doom.

The variant expressions: "lake of burning sulphur [lit. lake of fire and sulphur]" (Rev. 20:10), "lake of fire" (20:14-15), and "fiery lake of burning sulphur [lit. burning lake of fire and sulphur]" (21:8), all identify the same place. It is described as a place of eternal torment for the satanic triad (20:10), and the place of second death for unrepentant sinners (21:8). In this fiery lake, Satan will be forever cut off from associations with righteous humans, or with God. There, at last, his leadership role will be everlastingly terminated, and he will become simply a common prisoner.

The Historical Development of Millennialism

Although, currently, millennialism may not be a majority opinion in Christendom as a whole, there was a time when it was. Over the centuries, the doctrine has experienced a checkered career, but even prior to the Christian era, some in Judaism taught a one-thousand year golden age. As we have noted (p. 209), references to the early church version of millennialism are likely to use the designation chiliasm.

Within the early church, chiliasm was popular during the years of persecution prior to 313. In that period, however, many portrayals of millennial glories imaginatively emphasized the human bias of their originators. Christianity's triumph over the secular Roman world in 313, together with the excesses of some of the descriptions, led to the widespread demise of chiliastic beliefs. It is said that Augustine's reaction to "the wild exaggerations and crude ideas of the chiliasts" in their descriptions of the millennium was his basic motivation for rejecting a future earthly kingdom.

The doctrine in the patristic era

In his volume, *The Theocratic Kingdom*, George N.H. Peters lists fifteen supporters of the millennial doctrine among first century church fathers, and many others in succeeding centuries. He notes that through the first two centuries no known patristic writing opposes millennialism. On the other hand, some clear statements favoring millennialism have survived:

Clement of Rome (A.D. c. 96): "Speedily will He come, and will not tarry. . . . The Lord shall suddenly come to His temple" (*To the Corinthians*).

Justin Martyr (c. 100-165): "There will be a resurrection of the dead and a thousand years in Jerusalem, which will then be built, adorned and enlarged" (*Dialogue with Tryphone*). He taught the reality of a new earthly Jerusalem, the reign of Christ on earth, and the future glory of the chosen people.

Irenaeus (c. 120-202): "When this Antichrist shall have devastated all things in this world . . . then the Lord will come from heaven in the clouds . . . bringing in for the righteous the times of the kingdom" (*Against Heresies*). He taught that the millennium would consummate Christ's victory on earth, and provide opportunity for humans to prepare for eternity.

Tertullian (c. 155-220): His views changed during his lifetime, but in his later years he endorsed the millennial viewpoint. "A kingdom is promised to us upon the earth, although before heaven, only in another state of existence; inasmuch as it will be after the resurrection for a thousand years in the divinely built city of Jerusalem" (*Against Marcion*).

In contrast with the foregoing, Origen (c. 185-254) and his followers rejected all claims of a literal millennium. Origen adopted his position because he saw Scripture as nonliteral allegory. Eusebius of Caesarea (260-340), in his earlier writings (e.g., *Proof of the Gospel),* taught the literal return of Christ and the establishing of His kingdom on earth. In later life, however, when Eusebius wrote his classic *Ecclesiastical History,* he declared that the kingdom had already come. Between these publications, Emperor Constantine had been converted and Christianity had become the popular religion. Eusebius felt that these events had established the kingdom, and as the fourth century progressed, this viewpoint became virtually unanimous. In A.D. 373 the Council of Rome condemned millennialism as heretical, for the church now saw itself as the kingdom of Christ.

As Augustine developed his rejection of millennialism, in his *City of God* he argued that the promise of the kingdom was being fulfilled in the church's rule on earth. The apocalyptic texts were an allegorical account of the eternal struggle between good and evil. To Augustine, the term "church" was synonymous with such Bible terms as: Zion, Judah, Israel, Jerusalem, Jacob, the bride, and the kingdom of Christ.

Millennialism in the medieval period

During the middle ages those who supported millennialism were usually outside of the Catholic church. Versions of millennialism were taught by the Catharians, the Waldenses, the Huguenots, and the Paulicians, all of whom the Catholic church considered to be heretics. Bernard McGinn writes concerning these "medieval millenarianists":

> The social type to which most medieval apocalyptic propagandists conform was . . . the well-educated and well-situated clerical intelligentsia. . . . Christian apocalypticism . . . was, for the most part, an attempt by a group of educated religious *literati* to interpret the times, to support their patrons, to console their supporters, and to move men to pursue specified aims at once political and religious in nature.[3]

Notwithstanding their efforts, the medieval dissenters did little to modify the prevailing views of the Catholic church.

Millennialism in the modern period

At the outset of the Reformation, the Protestant reformers, including Martin Luther (1483-1546), Philipp Melanchthon (1497-1560), and John Calvin (1509-1564), looked with favor upon millennialism. They became disillusioned, however, with the excesses of some millennialists, and in their later conclusions they were firmly opposed. Luther rejected both millennialism and the canonicity of the Book of Revelation. The *Augsburg Confession* (1530), of which Melanchthon was a key author, and which Luther personally approved, declared that millennialism was a "Jewish opinion." Calvin wrote of the millenarians: "Their fiction is too puerile to require or deserve refutation." Out of this heritage, Church of England Protestants in 1553 declared officially in a document which later was condensed to become the *Thirty-Nine Articles*: "Those who attempt to revive the fable of the millenarians oppose the sacred Scriptures and throw themselves headlong into Jewish absurdities."

Not surprisingly, the Anabaptists who emerged from the Reformation were millennialists. Those who settled in England produced in 1660 *The Baptist Confession* which was endorsed by 20,000 followers. This document plainly declared that Christ and His people would return and reign on earth. Although the Church of England's *Thirty-Nine Articles* were amillennial, some within that body supported millennialism. Thus, when in 1555 the country briefly returned to Catholicism, the two martyred Protestant leaders, Nicholas Ridley (c. 1503-1555) and Hugh Latimer (1485-1555), both identified with millennialism. In the next century in England, Joseph Mede's presentation of millennialism, *Clavis Apocalyptic* (1627), was translated and widely circulated, virtually under government auspices.

In the early nineteenth century, when J.N. Darby began teaching his literalist futurist eschatology in the British Isles, his doctrines won wide acceptance. Since his time, the development of the doctrine of millennialism has largely merged with premillennialism and the overall study of Bible prophecy.

---

3   Bernard McGinn, *Visions of the End*. New York: Columbia University Press, 1979, pp. 31-32.

The Doctrine of Postmillennialism

Postmillennialism teaches that Christ will return to earth at the close of one thousand years (or a very long period of time) during which the church has triumphed in achieving peace, harmony, prosperity and blessing upon earth. In this coming, Christ will resurrect the dead and He will launch the great end-time judgment. As we will note, evangelical postmillennialists usually hold that this dramatic transformation of human lifestyles will be achieved by the preaching of the Christian gospel. The church's successes will thus launch Christ's millennial kingdom and this kingdom will continue on earth for an extended period prior to His return.

Postmillennial antecedents

The emerging Protestant denominations in the sixteenth century sooner or later subjected Roman Catholic eschatology to a critical review. They particularly rejected the view that held that the Catholic Church was Christ's kingdom on earth, ruled by the Pope who was the Vicar (i.e., substitute) of Christ. As they read their Bibles, they saw a future day of great blessing for Israel and a future glorious kingdom of Christ. They tended to see these events, however, as spiritual and heavenly. In the uncertainties of their interpretation they tended to settle for only fragmentary statements concerning eschatology.

Out of their background, most Reformers identified Israel as the church, and thus they applied the promised golden future to the church. They counted the Reformation as a notable advance of the church, and many concluded that the end time revival had begun. Though they may not have adopted a rigorous one-thousand year millennium, in effect there was a swing from traditional amillennialism to postmillennialism. These changes were not immediate, and some adopted ambiguous views, but in the overall, postmillennialism mostly prevailed. Erickson comments:

> **Many major denominations eventually incorporated post-millennialism into their creeds. The Augsburg and Westminster Confessions are basically postmillennial. Lutheran, Presbyterian and Reformed groups have tended to follow this position. The great Princeton school of theology . . . represented by the Hodges and Benjamin B. Warfield staunchly presented this system.**[4]

By the eighteenth and nineteenth centuries, among Protestants, postmillennialism was the leading eschatological doctrine. Postmillennialism's emphasis upon reforming the world motivated the nineteenth century missionary thrust, along with social reforms, concern for the poor, the provision of public

---

4   Millard J. Erickson, *Contemporary Options in Eschatology*. Grand Rapids: Baker Book House, 1977, p. 61.

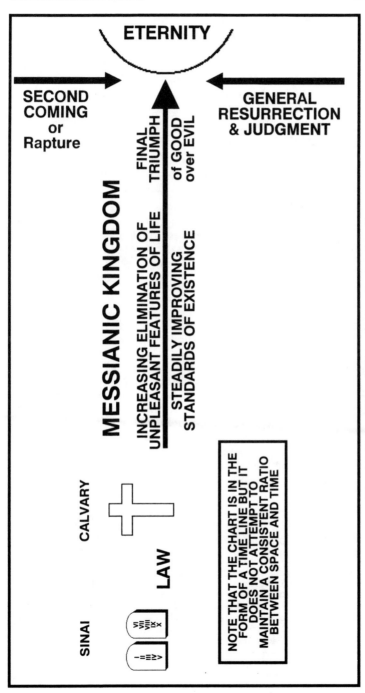

Fig. 15: Postmillennialism depicted as a time line.

education, and the abolition of slavery. The triumphs in these areas encouraged postmillennialists to interpret the ongoing scene to support their claim of the progressive improvement of conditions on earth. Though World War I appeared as a setback, there was widespread acceptance of the message of James H. Snowden. In his book, *The Coming of the Lord* (1919), Snowden taught that World War I had "ended militarism forever" and that the world was now rapidly moving toward the millennium.

Postmillennial viewpoints

Specific viewpoints, some or all of which are likely to be held by the typical postmillennialist, include the following:

1) In the present day, Christian teaching and preaching are steadily extending the kingdom, and it is undergoing a "gradualistic, developmental, incremental expansion." Converts become kingdom-subjects whom Christ now rules from heaven. Eventually, the world will become Christianized, and then Christ will return. In that day the great commission will have been fulfilled, and all nations discipled and baptized. Christ's coming primarily will announce the millennium rather than assume power.

2) Biblical backgrounds that teach postmillennialism are the parables of Matthew 13, particularly the parable of the yeast in the dough. "The kingdom of heaven is like yeast [or leaven] that a woman took and mixed into a large amount of flour until it worked all through the dough" (Matt. 13:33). The yeast is Christian influence and the dough is human society. The emphasis is upon growth. Christ's return is not the cataclysmic replacement of earth's kingdoms, but His assumption of authority that converted humans gladly extend to Him. The kingdom age will emerge out of the church age just as imperceptibly as the modern age emerged out of medievalism.

3) Most postmillennialists do not demand total perfection for their kingdom, though they see it as a time when primarily the will of God will be done on earth. Postmillennialist Loraine Boettner taught that his difference with premillennialism was not just a matter of timing, but rather a matter of the overall manner of Christ's control:

> **The postmillennialist looks for a golden age that will not be essentially different from our own. . . . This age gradually merges with the millennial age as an increasing proportion of the world inhabitants are converted to Christianity. . . . Life during the millennium will compare with life in the world today in much the same way that life in a Christian community compares with that in a pagan or irreligious community.**[5]

5   Loraine Boettner, "Postmillennialism." in *The Meaning of the Millennium*. Robert G. Clouse, editor. Downers Grove: Inter-Varsity Press, 1977, pp. 120-121.

4) The millennium will consist of extended prosperity and peace upon earth, though not necessarily 1,000 years. This time period is considered symbolic rather than literal. Revelation 20 is not a basic millennial text and, therefore, it is to be interpreted, not by what it says, but by postmillennialism's overall view. Whatever the duration of these passing centuries, the generations of living humans will enjoy an increasingly secure peace and prosperity. Many will be converted, including large numbers of ethnic Jews.

5) Some postmillennialists, who are committed to the literal Biblical text, see this era ending in apostasy and evil through the coming of Antichrist. They accept that the millennium (and the world) will end with Christ's personal bodily return. He will then bring about a general resurrection and judgment.

Postmillennialism tends to be formulated in one of two versions: evangelical or liberal. The evangelical school stresses a "gospel victory" theme that sees the kingdom now being extended as it adds converted penitents who respond to the Holy Spirit under the preaching of the gospel. Most versions expect that someday these Christian converts will become the majority of earth's people. Some, however, hold that it is more a matter of coexistence with secular society, while God's people as a major body enter into the fulfillment of the Old Testament prophecies.

The liberal school of postmillennialism holds that the necessary human improvement will be achieved through natural human progress which the church is expected to support. Scientific discovery, expanded popular education, upgraded medical institutions, improved management of natural resources, a higher level of human productivity, peace between nations and individuals, and liberty and justice for every human would be among the desired goals. The working tool of the liberal postmillennialist is often social and political action.

Shortcomings of the postmillennial doctrine

The literalist holds that postmillennialism either ignores or spiritualizes numerous relevant Scriptures, its interpretations are sometimes arbitrary, and it is neither a complete nor adequate system of eschatology. Some specific objections against postmillennialism would likely be as follows:

1) There is no convincing evidence in Scripture that the world will increase in righteousness up to the time that Jesus returns. "When the Son of Man comes, will he find faith on the earth?" (Luke 18:8); "There will be terrible times in the last days" (2 Tim. 3:1 et al.).

2) Scripture does not teach the virtual mass conversion of the world. Jesus taught, "Many are invited, but few are chosen"

(Matt. 22:14). Scripture does teach that in the end time there will be multitudes of rebellious unbelievers. "In number they are like the sand on the seashore" (Rev. 20:8).

3) Since the Old Testament rituals required the purging of yeast as an emblem of sin, a more plausible interpretation of Matthew 13:33 would identify the yeast as falsehood and heresy, and the dough as the church on earth.

4) There is warrant to take seriously and literally the account of the fulfillment of the promises to national Israel, the reign of Antichrist, the timed and measured tribulation, the 1,000 years, the actual personal reign of the Messiah upon earth, the distinctive judgments upon various moral entities, the binding and loosing of Satan, and more than one resurrection. All of these concepts, postmillennialism either spiritualizes into events in the present or the expanding future, or it coalesces into a general resurrection and a general judgment. The literalist would deny that the binding of Satan is an image of achieving a majority of gospel converts, that what Scripture calls the first resurrection is a synonym for the new birth, or that the church is the true Israel and that the people who dwell in the State of Israel are just another nation.

5) Much of postmillennialism's optimism in regard to human progress and its institutions is now seen to be misplaced. Observers of the human scene generally reject the postmillennialists' claims of a better world, including their sometimes optimistic view of church victories.

6) In the postmillennial view, Scripture's description of Christ at the right hand of the Father (Psa. 110:1) adequately fulfills the promise of His latter day reign. They thus spiritualize all the further details of the personally reigning Christ which premillennialists consider will require His personal literal presence on earth.

7) Postmillennialism sees itself as "An eschatology of hope" or "the theology of the latter-day glory." It points out that it believes in the triumph of the gospel and the conversion of the world—or at least a majority. This message is considered a comfort and encouragement to all who believe in soul winning. The futurist responds that the expectation of Christ's conquering return at the second coming (preceded by the rapture which is the Christian's "blessed hope") will immediately accomplish the total Christianization of the world. Thus, the futurist possesses hope equal to or greater than that of the postmillennialist.

The historical development of postmillennialism

Some supporters of postmillennialism find its roots in Eusebius (c. 260-340), Athanasius (c. 297-373), and Augustine

(354-430). They hold that the view has prevailed since the fourth century. In fact, however, most older statements are too fragmentary to be definitive. Some see postmillennialism in the views of Joachim of Floris (1132-1202) who taught a future worldwide outpouring of the Holy Spirit. The radical German Anabaptists, who in 1535 designated the city of Münster (or Münzer) as the new Jerusalem, exemplified a misguided application of postmillennialism. The British Presbyterian, Thomas Brightman (1562-1607), in his posthumous work, *A Revelation of the Revelation,* is considered to have definitively systematized postmillennial views. Brightman used the term "postmillennialism" to identify his position, and he taught a future "latter-day glory" when the world would be blessed and Christ would return to judge all humans.

A well-developed statement of postmillennialism, however, awaited the seventeenth century. By that time the doctrine had won its own company of supporters. A notable sermon by John Owen in 1651 set forth a defense of postmillennialism, and the *Savoy Declaration* of 1658 gave it an official doctrinal status. This Declaration was a statement of faith associated with England's independent Congregational churches, and a leading spokesperson among them was Thomas Goodwin (1600-1679) who wrote of a glorious future time on earth.

Many associate the doctrine of postmillennialism with Unitarian Daniel Whitby (1638-1726) who is credited with popularizing selected views from what he described as "the best commentators." Major works by Whitby were *Treatise of the True Millennium* (1700), and *Paraphrase and Commentary on the New Testament* (1703). Whitby taught that the world would be converted, the Jews would be restored to the Holy Land and they would defeat both the Pope and the Turks resulting in peace on earth for 1,000 years, and then Christ would return. Christ's victory at Armageddon would be a spiritual victory, and the release of Satan would be the manifestation of the spirit of unbelief. These views were widely accepted during the eighteenth and nineteenth centuries.

Notable promoters of the postmillennial position in past centuries were Jonathan Edwards (1703-1758), Charles G. Finney (1792-1875), and Charles Hodge (1797-1878). Those in the twentieth century included: A.H. Strong (1836-1921), Lyman Abbott (1835-1922) and Oswald T. Allis (1878-1973). Both Edwards and Finney wrote monographs supporting a postmillennial view of eschatology. Edwards taught that the millennium would arrive through the overthrow of Islam and the conversion of the Jews. Finney associated his belief in the doctrine with his zeal for winning souls. A nineteenth century work by Presbyterian David Brown, *The Second Advent* (1846, 1849), for many years was recognized as the standard work on the subject of postmillennialism. Two notable works in the twentieth century were *The Coming of the Lord* by James H. Snowden (1919) which has already been mentioned, and *The Millennium* by Loraine Boettner (1957).

The status of the doctrine of postmillennialism

As the twentieth century advanced, postmillennialism's following rapidly declined. The fact of a worldwide depression of the 1930's, a second World War, numerous local wars, and the cruel exploitation of millions in totalitarian states largely silenced claims of cultural progress. By mid-century postmillennialism was probably at its lowest ebb. Not only did current events appear to refute the doctrine, but the immensely popular Scofield Bible provided Christians with an alternate premillennial, pretribulational outlook. Also, by this time there was a reaction against the older liberalism (higher criticism) with which many postmillennialists of that era identified.

Beginning in the late 1960s, postmillennialism began a modest revival. Since this view was embodied in many historic confessions and creeds, a new generation emerged out of these backgrounds. Typically, these theologians were committed evangelicals who dissociated postmillennialism from the unwarranted optimism of liberal theology. They attempted, rather, to defend their views on the basis of literal Scripture, and in this form the doctrine was much more palatable to Bible-believers. Greg Bahnsen explained the postmillennial viewpoint:

> Postmillennialism . . . expects the gradual, developmental expansion of the kingdom of Christ in time and on earth. This expansion will proceed by means of the full-orbed ministry of the Word, fervent and believing prayer, and the consecrated labors of His Spirit-filled people. . . . It confidently anticipates a time in earth history (which is continuous with the present) in which the very gospel already operative in the world will have won the victory throughout the earth in fulfillment of the Great Commission. During that time, the overwhelming majority of men and nations will be Christianized, righteousness will abound, wars will cease, and prosperity and safety will flourish. After an extended period of gospel prosperity, earth history will be drawn to a close by the personal, visible, bodily return of Jesus Christ.[6]

At the outset of the twenty-first century, voices in support of postmillennialism were increasingly being heard. Currently, however, the size and strength of the body of supporters of postmillennialism appear to be a matter of conjecture. Some

---

6 Greg L. Bahnsen and Kenneth L. Gentry Jr., *House Divided*. Tyler: Institute for Christian Economics, 1989, p. 141.

scholars hold postmillennialism as a well-developed system. Others have adopted the view chiefly by default, choosing it as a preferred alternative to what they classify as either dispensationalism or amillennialism. The excessive optimism of older postmillennialism may no longer be fashionable, but present supporters continue to find evidences that the quality of human existence today is improved over that of the past centuries.

Whatever their differences, the premillennial futurist notes with approval that the postmillennialist supports a commitment to a doctrine of the second coming of Christ. Though for the postmillennialist, this return is the end of the world, at least it is a return of the Savior. In many situations, this common expectation permits premillennialists and post millennialists comfortably to worship together.

Reconstructionism and Theonomy

Christian Reconstructionism is a form of postmillennialism that appeared in the closing decades of the twentieth century, particularly in some Reformed Church and Presbyterian circles. It holds that the church's task is the restructuring of society according to the standards of the whole Bible. All, or virtually all, aspects of God's Old Testament law are valid today, and society should be ruled by this law of God—whence "theonomy" (which means "God's law). Reconstructionists blend: 1) an emphasis upon personal regeneration, 2) the application of biblical law to all human life, 3) the extension of Christ's kingdom by examples of Christian living before a fallen world, 4) the responsibility of the church to convince society to think in these terms.

Reconstructionists hold that Christians should actively oppose the shaping of their culture by secularism, and they should pressure civil government to agree to be guided in legislative decisions by the laws of the Old Testament. Greg Bahnsen explains this viewpoint:

> **Reconstructionists are committed to the transformation (re- construction) of every area of life including the institutions and affairs of the socio-political realm, according to the holy principles revealed throughout God's inspired word (theonomy).[7]**

It is evident that reconstructionists attempt to achieve the redemption of institutions as well as the redemption of people. It is on this basis that they see their role in achieving the millennium and setting the stage for Christ's return.

While futurists are grateful for the moral, social, and political victories achieved by Reconstructionists, they deny that restructuring society is the church's basic task. The futurist holds

---

7   ibid., p. 43.

that righteousness in human society can be achieved only by a divine work as He changes hearts, not by human legislative action. The theocratic pattern of God's Old Testament law was not intended as a system of governance for Gentiles in this age on earth. Jesus distinguished the secular state from His own kingdom: "Give to Caesar what is Caesar's, and to God what is God's" (Matt. 22:21). The futurist sees Reconstructionism as a postmillennial system that seeks through human effort to do what Christ will do by a single stroke.

Kingdom Now and the Manifested Sons of God

These concepts of postmillennialism, particularly the manifested (or manifest) sons of God aspect, have survived for several decades. They associate chiefly with independent charismatic groups. In the 1980s the Kingdom Now doctrine substantially extended its following, and it embraced the Manifest Sons of God doctrine as an aspect of its teaching. The movement is also known as: Restorationism, Restoration of the Tabernacle of David, the Kingdom Movement, or Dominion Theology.

Teaching concerning the manifest sons of God takes its name from Romans 8:19 "For the earnest expectation of the creature waiteth for the manifestation of the sons of God" (—KJV). In the NIV this verse is rendered, "The creation waits in eager expectation for the sons of God to be revealed." This doctrine holds that God's destiny for creation, which in the millennium involves revoking the curse, depends upon believers (i.e., sons of God) possessing their potential in Christ. In this day, believers are challenged to manifest miracle-working faith to achieve Christ's kingdom on earth and prepare for His return.

Kingdom Now teaches that Christians are to take over the dominion of the earth from Satan and thus confirm the reality of Christ's millennial kingdom. God expects that an earthly army of Christian overcomers will establish the kingdom. Christ postpones His return until Christians as sons of God become manifest and convert this world into His footstool. This manifestation will result when the true church, Christ's body, becomes mature. In that day, Christians will have so taken dominion over the earth that even physical death will be conquered.

Kingdom Now supporters look for today's church to be divinely indwelt as David's tabernacle. (cf. "After this I will return, and will build again the tabernacle of David, which is fallen down" [Acts 15:16 —KJV.]). Frequently, they promote a demonstrative worship style including pageantry and dance, and they pursue in this present life the perfections associated with the millennium. A spokesperson for this position wrote:

A new creation and a new order which Isaiah foresaw as the millennium is now possible, which reestablishes a perfect order. The essence of the millennium is within us now because of the promises in Isaiah that we can begin to claim by faith. The millennial attributes are already available to us.[8]

Futurists agree that the millennium will free nature from the curse, and give new status to God's people—i.e., the sons of God. (cf."You are all sons of God" Gal. 3:26). They deny, however, that human faith or energy are the instruments to bring these changes. In His time, God will launch the millennium. Until the rapture, there will be no change in God's provisions for humans, nor in the order of nature. John instructs, "Now, dear children, continue in him, so that when he appears we may be confident and unashamed before him" (1 John 2:28).

As futurists see matters, Christians prepare for the rapture by being faithful in Christ, not by attempting to be super saints. Scoffers in the last days will reject the message of the second coming on the grounds that "everything goes on as it has since the beginning of creation" (2 Pet. 3:4). The conquest of nature's curse awaits Christ's inauguration of the millennium.

The Doctrine of Amillennialism

Though the prefix "a" means "not" or "no," the amillennial view does not really deny the fact of the millennium, but only the version given by literalist Bible scholars. Amillennialists deny an interpretation, but not necessarily the total concept. For this reason, some amillennialists prefer to identify their view as "realized millennialism," but this usage is not widespread.

Statements of the amillennial viewpoint

According to amillennialism, the present life of the believer in the church and in the world is as much of the millennium as will ever be known. The Christian's everyday experiences constitute millennial living. The Bible accounts of a one-thousand year idyllic age are not meant to be taken literally; rather, they are picture images of an otherwise indescribable realm. Random statements from an amillennial interpretation of Scripture illustrate this viewpoint:

> "The Son of man coming on the clouds of heaven" . . . indicates that the advent is not a physical one of the Son of man but a witness to the Son of man who is in heaven. That is, the coming is to occur through historical events. . . . The binding of Satan, the resurrection of the saints, and the thousand-year reign are metaphors for the present situation of Christians.[9]

---

8 Earl Paulk, *Ultimate Kingdom*. Atlanta: K Dimension Publications, 1984, p. 289.

9 William J. Dumbrell, *The Search for Order: Biblical Eschatology in Focus.* Grand Rapids: Baker Books, 1994, pp. 176, 342.

To the amillennialist, the millennium is an ongoing event that the professing Christian enters here and now by religious commitment or the new birth.

Although it can be said that the denial of a thousand-year reign of Christ on earth is the chief or only belief uniting amillennialists, the following are among the teachings, attitudes, and emphases commonly supported by most amillennialists:

1. **There is no future for national Israel.** National Israel's role in the history of redemption has ended and "God has finished with Judaism forever." Jews share the option of other humans in the offer of the gospel of Jesus Christ, but they no longer possess special privileges.

2. **There is only one people of God.** The body of believers that was Israel in Old Testament times is now the church. Because of Israel's failures, God's covenants extended to Israel have now been transferred from the Jews as the people of God to the church as the people of God. Today's church is Israel, and it is an error to identify Israel of the Old Testament with the people of the modern State of Israel.

3. **There is no specific future tribulation.** The Biblical expression "great tribulation" does not denote a tribulation for a set period before the world ends, but these words are a way of stressing the acuteness of the believer's oppression in this life on earth. Antichrist is not a specific short-lived individual but a prevailing spirit, and so also is the False Prophet. Each generation may experience antichrists and false prophets.

4. **Bible numbers are not to be taken literally.** "Literalism is the most stupid and dangerous scheme ever advocated." The "1,000 years" of Revelation 20 is symbolic. The expression simply denotes the time period of the church age. Anthony Hoekema commented on Scripture's thousand years, "Since the number ten signifies completeness, and since a thousand is ten to the third power, we may think of the expression 'a thousand years' as standing for a complete period, a very long period of indeterminate length."[10]

5. **The only rule of Christ is heavenly.** All promises of Christ's future rule were fulfilled at His ascension when, "He sat down at the right hand of the Majesty in heaven" (Heb. 1:3). Christ now reigns in heaven as the Father's co-ruler. The kingdom promises are all fulfilled in the blessedness of the saints in heaven. A literal concept of the rule of Christ is a "hybrid doctrine of half-Jewish, half-Christian political messianism." The second coming will be followed by the

---

10 Anthony A. Hoekema, "Amillennialism." *The Meaning of the Millennium.* Robert G. Clouse, editor. Downers Grove: InterVarsity Press, 1977, p. 161.

Fig. 16: Amillennialism depicted as a time line.

general resurrection and judgment, and the eternal age. The amillennialist is committed to Christ's imminent return, but he is likely not preoccupied with "the blessed hope."

6. **Prophecy applies now, not in the future.** Prophetic passages, such as much of the content of the Book of Revelation, are nonchronological. They are pictorial or symbolic images depicting events that could occur at any time. The "first resurrection" simply is a way of describing the "new birth." William Hendriksen sees the content of Revelation as "progressively parallel." There is no overall chronological progress in the Book, but the parallel sections each portray aspects of today's life.

7. **The first resurrection is spiritual.** The account in Revelation 20:4-5 is not of two physical resurrections separated by 1,000 years, but a symbolic description of the victory of Christian martyrs.[11] Amillennialists hold that the first resurrection is spiritual, and some (e.g., James A. Hughes) consider that the second is also. The majority, however, accept that the second resurrection is physical and they see it as a general resurrection that ushers in the eternal age.

8. **To bind Satan is to restrain his power.** The account of the binding of Satan (Revelation chapter 20) is a way of describing God's restraint that is imposed upon him in this age. God's restrictions mean that Satan cannot prevent the spread of the gospel, nor can he destroy the entire church. Though Satan is bound, he has been given a long chain!

Two distinctive versions of amillennialism are popularly identified. The Augustinian version stresses the present life on earth and considers that, in our spiritual riches and blessings, the millennium is now underway. As much millennium as we will ever know, we now have. A different view, known as Warfield's version[12], holds that the millennial prophecies are now being fulfilled in the lives and experience of the saints in heaven. In that spiritual realm they are enjoying all that they hoped for and that God has promised. This latter version is said to have been particularly popular since the mid twentieth century.

In the foregoing evaluations and those that follow a qualifying caution should be noted: Not every document that is labeled amillennial may actually be so. We are wise to pay heed to Millard Erickson's comment:

---

11 An informative review of amillennial arguments on this issue is found in Millard Erickson's *Contemporary Options in Eschatology.*, pp. 76-89.

12 Ironically, Benjamin Warfield mostly associates with a postmillennial view, but his interpretation of the nature of the millennium proved attractive to many amillennialists.

Amillennialism has often been difficult to distinguish from postmillennialism. Such men as Augustine ... John Calvin ... and Benjamin B. Warfield ... have been claimed by both groups. Unless a man addresses the specific issues that separate the two positions, he may not clearly enunciate his stand. This has led to confusion.[13]

Shortcomings of the amillennial viewpoint

Amillennialists generally interpret the Bible from a nonliteral viewpoint, and they typically use a spiritualizing hermeneutic. Their eschatological system is likely to be an interpretative commitment rather than the voice of the literal written Word. As we noted in Chapter 1, the valid development of eschatology involves grammatico-historical techniques—vocabulary, grammar, context, historical interpretations and usage are all relevant in determining the meaning of the text. A spiritualizing technique will produce a different eschatology. For the literalist, the unadorned statement of amillennial viewpoints are their own Scriptural refutation. Amillennialism, in the opinion of most literalists, is not a Scriptural statement, but a statement of what the amillennialist has chosen to believe.

The literalist freely admits that given the Bible's many prophetic visions, particularly in the Book of Revelation, spiritualization is one of the necessary tools for interpreting eschatology. The scholar needs to know how to interpret spiritually and how to interpret literally, and he especially needs the wisdom to know when to choose between them. It is the opinion of the literalist, however, that the amillennialist errs because he exceeds the legitimate occasions for interpreting by spiritualizing.

The status of the doctrine of amillennialism

In its backgrounds, amillennialism is rooted in the Alexandrian school of Biblical interpretation which included Origen (c. 185-254) and Clement of Alexandria (c. 150-215). Augustine (354-430) has been described, however, as "the first theologian of solid influence to adopt amillennial eschatology." The fact that Augustine's brief sketches allow postmillennial interpretations apparently did not deter his successors from adopting his writings as an authorative statement proclaiming amillennialism.

For several centuries, from Augustine's time, amillennialism has largely dominated both Roman Catholic and Reformation Protestant mainstream Christian theology. The occasional alternate view that emerged likely was limited to minority Protestant groups. Conservatives in the historic Reformed groups—denominations such as the Reformed Church of America, as well as many Presbyterian bodies—are chiefly amillennial. Some of the

---

13 Erickson, op. cit. p. 73.

better-known writers who support amillennialism include Herman Bavinck, Geerhardus Vos, William J. Grier, Albertus Pieters, Louis Berkhof, Floyd E. Hamilton, George L. Murray, Abraham Kuyper, William Hendriksen, Anthony A. Hoekema, and Ray Summers.

Amillennialism experienced some setbacks in the eighteenth and nineteenth centuries, but it was by no means eclipsed. In the eighteenth century the influence of Daniel Whitby (1638-1727) led to postmillennialism supplanting amillennialism as the most popular view. In the nineteenth century, J.N. Darby's literal futurism that led to his premillennialism won a wide following. These divergent views carried over to the twentieth century and they continue to compete.

Currently, amillennialism tends to be increasingly active and aggressive in its contacts with literalism. Its spokespersons bring the skills and resources of scholarship to critique what is weak and vulnerable in some presentations of literalist eschatology. Social trends, which in many parts of the world see the expansion of post secondary education, result in increasing interaction between the levels of education. Thus, the graduate school, whose amillennial beliefs were formerly mostly restricted to professional theological academics, now is training lay persons, Bible college and undergraduate teachers of theology, and popularizers of theological truth. It can be hoped that this substantial interaction will result in the eschatological insights that the Holy Spirit intended that Scripture should reveal.

FOURTEEN

The Final State

With the conclusion of the millennium and the final judgments, the eternal state begins. The permanent final status has been determined for all moral intelligences—redeemed humans and those who have died as sinners, along with angels, and Satan and his demons. In each case, each moral being is unalterably confirmed in whatever state he or she has chosen. Stanley Horton wrote,

> Believers go to a place prepared for them. The lost go to a place never meant for them, a place prepared for the devil and his angels, a place that is Satan's final doom, his final prison.[1]

The Final Destiny of the Righteous

Even Scripture appears to be at a loss to describe the glories that await the believer in the life to come. Paul quotes Isaiah, "No eye has seen, no ear has heard, no mind has conceived what God has prepared for those who love him" (1 Cor. 2:9). One index of the anticipated blessing is the measure of His grace. Paul wrote that "God raised us up with Christ . . . in order that in the coming ages he might show the incomparable riches of his grace, expressed in his kindness to us in Christ Jesus" (Eph. 2:7).

The expectation of heaven

The words "heaven" and "heavens" occur a total of 595 times in our Bibles (NIV), with 344 occurrences in the Old Testament and 251 in the New. The usual denotation of "heaven" (or "heavens") is simply the realm beyond the earth. Thus, "In the beginning God created the heavens [Heb. *shamayim*] and the earth" (Gen. 1:1). (*shamayim* [shaw-MAH-yim]: the heights, that which is lofty, the heavens). Other denotations of "heaven" include the dwelling place of God (cf. 1 Kings 8:30), the realm of angels and spirit beings (cf. Zech. 6:5), the realm of the stars (cf. Isa. 13:10), and the atmosphere (cf. Isa. 55:10).

Popular usage identifies "heaven" with the destiny of the righteous, although Scriptural references are limited. Among

---

1 Stanley Horton, *Our Destiny.* Springfield: Logion Press, 1996, p. 240.

those that implicitly, if not explicitly, depict heaven as the believer's future home are the following:

"As they were walking along . . . suddenly a chariot of fire and horses of fire appeared and separated the two of them, and Elijah went up to heaven [Heb. *shamayim*] in a whirlwind" (2 Kings 2:11).

"Blessed are you when people insult you. . . . Rejoice and be glad, because great is your reward in heaven" (Matt. 5:11-12).

"Store up for yourselves treasures in heaven, where moth and rust do not destroy" (Matt. 6:20).

"Now we know that if the earthly tent we live in is destroyed, we have a building from God, an eternal house in heaven" (2 Cor. 5:1).

"We have heard of your faith . . . the faith and love that spring from the hope that is stored up for you in heaven" (Col. 1:4-5).

"The Lord will rescue me from every evil attack and will bring me safely to his heavenly kingdom" (2 Tim. 4:18).

"Therefore, holy brothers, who share in the heavenly calling, fix your thoughts on Jesus" (Heb. 3:1).

"He has given us new birth into a living hope . . . and into an inheritance that can never perish, spoil or fade—kept in heaven for you" (1 Pet. 1:3-4).

Scripture definitively establishes that the future destiny of the believer will be in the Lord's presence.

"In righteousness I will see your face; when I awake, I will be satisfied with seeing your likeness" (Psa. 17:15).

"You will fill me with joy in your presence, with eternal pleasures at your right hand" (Psa. 16:11)

"If I go and prepare a place for you, I will come back and take you to be with me that you also may be where I am" (John 14:3).

"Father, I want those you have given me to be with me where I am, and to see my glory" (John 17:24).

"We are confident, I say, and would prefer to be away from the body and at home with the Lord" (2 Cor. 5:8).

"We who are still alive and are left will be caught up . . . in the clouds to meet the Lord in the air. And so we will be with the Lord forever" (1 Thess. 4:17).

"[He] is able to keep you from falling and to present you before his glorious presence without fault and with great joy" (Jude 1:24).

"Now the dwelling of God is with men, and he will live with them" (Rev. 21:3).

Heaven as the new Jerusalem

Though the foregoing Scriptures appear to indicate that the believer's immediate destiny in the after life is heaven, other insights reveal that in eternity the believer's heaven is actually the new Jerusalem. To be told that the believer's heaven is the new Jerusalem is not to be given different information, but simply to have prior information made more specific.

In the eternal state the triune God will establish His residence in the new Jerusalem, and there He will be united with the redeemed. John wrote, "I did not see a temple in the city, because the Lord God Almighty and the Lamb are its temple" (Rev. 21:22); and "The throne of God and of the Lamb will be in the city" (Rev. 22:3). The Psalmist wrote, "There is a river whose streams make glad the city of God, the holy place where the Most High dwells" (Psa. 46:4).

Scripture speaks of the pilgrim heroes of faith who were looking for a country other than the one that they had left. "Instead, they were longing for a better country—a heavenly one. Therefore God is not ashamed to be called their God, for he has prepared a city for them" (Heb. 11:16). Abraham anticipated a remarkable future city home, "For he was looking forward to the city with foundations, whose architect and builder is God" (Heb. 11:10). In the following chapters, the author of Hebrews states, "You have come to Mount Zion, to the heavenly Jerusalem, the city of the living God. You have come . . . to the church of the firstborn, whose names are written in heaven" (Heb. 12:22-23); and again, "Here we do not have an enduring city, but we are looking for the city that is to come" (Heb. 13:14). New Jerusalem's citizens will be a special company "handpicked by God."

Scripture describes the beauty of the new Jerusalem in a figure. It is "prepared as a bride beautifully dressed for her husband" (Rev. 21:2; cf. 2 Cor. 11:2, cf. Eph. 5:23-32). The figure of the bride-city speaks of the special personal relationship between Christ and the redeemed. It also underscores the glorious wonder of their shared home.

Prior to the appearance of the new Jerusalem, heaven enjoys an exciting event: "The wedding of the Lamb has come, and his bride has made herself ready. Fine linen, bright and clean, was given her to wear. (Fine linen stands for the righteous acts of the saints.)" (Rev. 19:7-8) Though the figure of a bride describes the new Jerusalem, Christ's bride is not the city, but the body of saints who comprise the church. Christ brings His bride home to the new Jerusalem to live, and her beauty complements the beauty of her home. When the angel promised John, "I will show you the bride, the wife of the Lamb" (Rev. 21:9), since John had already seen the bride, what he now saw was the bride's home.

Life in the new Jerusalem

The new Jerusalem has been described as "the saints' everlasting rest" and "the perfect answer for every holy desire." In part, the city's blessedness will result because of what is missing from it. No longer will there be the pains and hurts of earthly life. "[God] will wipe every tear from their eyes. There will be no more death or mourning or crying or pain, for the old order of things has passed away" (Rev. 21:4). Also, in the new Jerusalem there will be no temple (cf. Rev. 21:22), sun, moon or lamp (cf. 21:23; 22:5), night (21:25); 22:5), impurity shame or deceit (cf. 21:27), or curse (cf. Rev. 22:3).

One reason for the blessedness of heaven is the careful selection of its inhabitants. "Nothing impure will ever enter it, nor will anyone who does what is shameful or deceitful, but only those whose names are written in the Lamb's book of life" (Rev. 21:27). Humans will be in the immediate presence of deity, and the temple will no longer be needed as a meeting place (cf. Rev. 21:22 previously cited). Everything in the new Jerusalem is bright and beautiful. "The city does not need the sun or the moon to shine on it, for the glory of God gives it light, and the Lamb is its lamp" (Rev. 21:23). Here is the fulfillment of Jesus' promise, "I am going . . . to prepare a place for you" (John 14:2).

Scripture describes various notable aspects of life that are promised the believer in his or her eternal existence in the new Jerusalem.

1. There will be opportunity to serve. "The throne of God and of the Lamb will be in the city, and His servants will serve him" (Rev. 22:3); "Do you not know that the saints will judge the world? . . . Do you not know that we will judge angels?" (1 Cor. 6:2-3) "They have washed their robes and made them white in the blood of the Lamb. Therefore, they are before the throne of God and serve him day and night in his temple" (Rev. 7:14-15). The believer has been described as "delightfully busy" in service forever and ever. Many present earthly vocations will become irrelevant—policemen, funeral directors, doctors, dentists, etc.—but appealing alternatives will replace them.

2. There will be meetings and reunions. "Many will come from the east and the west, and will take their places at the feast with Abraham, Isaac and Jacob in the kingdom of heaven" (Matt. 8:11). Evidently, people will be recognizable. David said of his dead child, "I will go to him, but he will not return to me" (2 Sam. 12:23). God's servants "will see his face" (Rev. 22:4), for as the beatitude promised: "the pure in heart . . . will see God" (Matt. 5:8). Jesus also will be present: "Your eyes will see the king in his beauty" (Isa. 33:17).

3. There will be unrestrained joy. "He will wipe every tear from their eyes" (Rev. 21:4); "The ransomed of the Lord . . . will enter Zion with singing; everlasting joy will crown their heads. Gladness and joy will overtake them, and sorrow and sighing will flee away" (Isa. 35:10). The great multitude cry, "Let us rejoice and be glad and give him glory" (Rev. 19:7).

4. There will be opportunity to rule. "The Lord God will give them light. And they will reign for ever and ever" (Rev. 22:5); "To him who overcomes, I will give the right to sit with me on my throne" (Rev. 3:21). Not only do believers share in the millennial rule, but Scripture indicates that in some way their ruling authority will continue throughout eternity.

5. There will be opportunity to rest. "Blessed are the dead who die in the Lord from now on . . . 'they will rest from their labor [They will enjoy rest from their hard work—TEV], for their deeds will follow them'" (Rev. 14:13). "There remains, then, a Sabbath-rest for the people of God; for anyone who enters God's rest also rests from his own work" (Heb. 4:9-10). Jesus promised, "In my Father's house are many rooms [Gk. *mone*]; if it were not so, I would have told you. I am going there to prepare a place for you" (John 14:2). (*mone* [mon-EH]: dwelling place, room, abode, home, resting place).

6. Worship will be the major activity. It has often been noted that "Worship is the serious business of heaven." The twenty-four elders "lay their crowns before the throne and say: 'You are worthy, our Lord and God, to receive glory and honor and power'" (Rev. 4:10-11); "The twenty-four elders fell down before the Lamb . . . [a]nd they sang a new song: 'You are worthy'" (Rev. 5:8-9). John reports the spontaneous response of those "who had been victorious over the beast and his image": "They held harps given them by God and sang . . . 'Great and marvelous are your deeds, Lord God Almighty. . . . All nations will come and worship before you, for your righteous acts have been revealed'" (Rev. 15:2-4). John Gilmore comments, "Get ready. Everybody in heaven seems to sing."[2]

7. Christlikeness will have been achieved. "We shall be like him, for we shall see him as he is" (1 John 3:2); "Now we see but a poor reflection as in a mirror; then we shall see face to face. Now I know in part; then I shall know fully, even as I am fully

---

2 John Gilmore, *Probing Heaven*. Grand Rapids: Baker Book House, 1989, p. 167.

known" (1 Cor. 13:12); "You have come to God, the judge of all men, to the spirits of righteous men made perfect" (Heb. 12:23). In the personal presence of Father and Son, the believer will enjoy access to unlimited spiritual insight and Christlikeness. All of the redeemed are equally redeemed, and each one has the prospect of being like Christ.

8. Those who qualify will enjoy rewards. "For our light and momentary troubles are achieving for us an eternal glory that far outweighs them all" (2 Cor. 4:17). Believers will be rewarded at the judgment seat of Christ (cf. Chapter 11). As Jesus began His final scriptural message, He reminded His readers, "Behold, I am coming soon! My reward is with me, and I will give to everyone according to what he has done" (Rev. 22:12). When believers enter into their permanent life in the new Jerusalem, Jesus will implement within the life of each one his or her deserved rewards.

The Biblical model for the life to come. The foregoing Biblical insights establish that in their eternal existence redeemed humans will participate in activities and events that dramatically expand the patterns of human life on earth. The believer can anticipate an active productive lifestyle that will provide personal gratification and rewards even in the celestial realm. Craig Blaising[3] speaks of this view as the **New Creation Model** of life in eternity. In this interpretation, redeemed humans will live active lives that compare with life on earth, but in glorified bodies and in the new creation realm of sinless perfection. These celestial humans will take their place as citizens in God's eternal Kingdom and in a never-ending sequence they will continue the experiences of that life.

This New Creation model of life to come contrasts with the traditional view that over the centuries has been favored by the majority. Blaising labels this traditional view the **Spiritual Vision Model**. In this view, the saved are destined to a heaven where they will be engaged in an unchanging beatific contemplation of God in His infinite reality. This heaven will be the highest realm of spiritual existence, free of all change, and outside of time and history. In this view eternal life is linked with third century Origen's allegorical interpretations of Scripture. This Spiritual Vision Model was not widely evaluated or challenged until the nineteenth century when the literal interpretation of eschatological texts started to become popular. Secular caricatures of

---

3 See Craig A. Blaising "Premillennialism." In *Three Views on the Millennium and Beyond*, edited by Darrell L. Bock, pp. 157-227. Grand Rapids: Zondervan Publishing House, 1999.

this view depict the redeemed in flowing robes seated on clouds and playing harps.

The Biblical portrayal of the city

The new Jerusalem will be made "in the workshop of heaven" and it will be "a divinely constructed space colony." It will shine with the glory of God (Rev. 21:11) as probably its most dominant characteristic. The city was seen by John (cf. Rev. 21:1-2, 10) in its descent from heaven to the new earth. This event, following the creation of the new earth, will be one of the phenomena launching the eternal age. The new Jerusalem relating to the new earth compares with the earthly city of Jerusalem on the millennial earth. Scriptural expressions identifying the new Jerusalem include "the Jerusalem that is above" (Gal. 4:26); "the city with foundations" (Heb. 11:10); "a city" (Heb. 11:16); "Mount Zion," "the heavenly Jerusalem," "the city of the living God" (Heb. 12:22); "the Holy City," "the new Jerusalem (Rev. 21:2); and "the Holy City, Jerusalem" (Rev. 21:10).

The born again of the church and the righteous of Israel will be eternally united in the new Jerusalem. The names of the twelve tribes of Israel will be inscribed on the twelve gates of the city. On the twelve foundations there will be the names of the twelve apostles of the Lamb. The new Jerusalem is the long-looked for home both of the church, and of Old Testament believers as well. Abraham sought this city: "For he was looking forward to the city with foundations, whose architect and builder is God" (Heb. 11:10).

We have noted that in speaking of the citizens of the new Jerusalem, Scripture identifies them as "the church of the first-born" and as "the spirits of righteous men made perfect" (cf. Heb. 12:22-23). The perfection that humans seek on earth in vain, is at last attained. The writer to the Hebrews concluded his review of the Old Testament heroes of faith: "God had planned something better for us so that only together with us would they be made perfect" (Heb. 11:40). In contrast, Scripture lists those who are excluded from the new Jerusalem. "But the cowardly [fearful], the unbelieving [faithless], the vile [abominable, polluted], the murderers, the sexually immoral, those who practice magic arts [sorcerers], the idolaters and all liars—their place will be in the fiery lake of burning sulfur" (Rev. 21:8).

Scripture provides so much detail concerning the new Jerusalem that one is encouraged to construct a diagram. Most versions see it as a vast cube more than 2,200 kilometers (1,400 miles) in each dimension (cf. Rev. 21:16), though some have suggested that its shape could be a pyramid, or even a sphere. A cube would conform to the proportions of the Most Holy Place of the tabernacle. It was in the Most Holy Place that the LORD's presence was especially manifested. It is suggested that the entire new Jerusalem will be the LORD's sanctuary, and for this reason there is no temple in the city (cf. Rev. 21:22).

John heard the loud voice proclaiming, "Now the dwelling of God is with men, and he will live with them. They will be his people, and God himself will be with them and be their God" (Rev. 21:3). With God's personal presence, and the assembled multitude of the saints of earth from all ages, the new Jerusalem will be the spiritual headquarters and the capital city of the entire universe. Its gates will allow its dwellers to come and go, and presumably to visit or perform errands either on the new earth or in any celestial realm.

If our present concepts of human living space are applied, a city the size of the new Jerusalem could easily house 100 billion people. Scripture's thorough description of the walls, gates and foundations suggest that the city will be set off from its surroundings. Although some aspects of what is portrayed transcend present human experience (e.g., "each gate was made of a single pearl" or "pure gold, like transparent glass"), the city is described in literal terms as: foundations, gates, walls, and streets. Its materials are known substances which now occur in extremely small quantities as precious stones and metals.

The tree of life. John reported, "On each side of the river stood the tree of life, bearing twelve crops of fruit, yielding its fruit every month. And the leaves of the tree are for the healing [*therapeia*] of the nations" (Rev. 22:2). (*therapeia* [ther-ah-PIE-ah]: healing, the achievement of total well being, the communication of total health). The tree of life, with its monthly harvest of fruit and its healing leaves, will be an important feature of the new Jerusalem. As the tree of life in Eden was the secret of immortality (cf. Gen. 3:22), so the tree of life may be in the new Jerusalem. God promised the Ephesians, "To him who overcomes, I will give the right to eat from the tree of life, which is in the paradise of God" (Rev. 2:7).

Commentators tend to agree that the word "nations" is equivalent to "people(s)," and that a specific national body is not necessarily intended. The sense in which the citizens of the new Jerusalem would need healing, however, is likely to be debated. One possibility would be that the residents of the city may need healing from painful prior memories. This healing will be accomplished upon their arrival when God Himself "will wipe every tear from their eyes" (Rev. 21:4). An alternate possibility is that the healing is provided for the inhabitants of the new earth who have access to the new Jerusalem through the gates that are

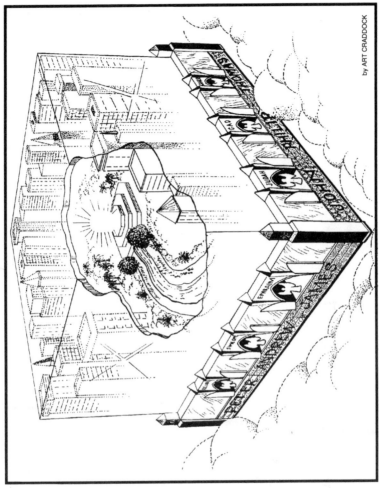

by ART CRADDOCK

Fig. 17: An artist's concept of the new Jerusalem. Bible scholars agree that no human visualization could begin to do justice to the celestial city. Nevertheless, a sketch provides a beginning tangible basis for the believer's expectation. Scriptural facts about the city include: its length is 2,300 kilometers (1,400 mi.) and it is equally wide and high and long; the city has twelve gates which are never closed, each a pearl and with a presiding angel, and each inscribed with the name of a tribe of Israel; the city has a great high crystal-clear jasper wall with twelve foundations each named for one of the twelve apostles; a stream flows down the great street, and the tree of life grows on both sides; the glory of God provides light to the city and it shines with His glory.

always open. This matter will be mentioned again in the discussion of the inhabitants of the new earth.

The New Heaven and New Earth

John reports, "Then I saw a new [Gk. *kainos*] heaven and a new [Gk. *kainos*] earth, for the first heaven and the first earth had passed away, and there was no longer any sea" (Rev. 21:1). (*kainos* [kine-NOS]: unused, not previously present, unknown, strange, remarkable, a superior replacement for the old). Clearly, the new heaven and new earth are observably and functionally new as designated by the expression, "brand new." God declared, "I am making everything new!" (Rev. 21:5). Peter wrote of God's promise for the future, "In keeping with his promise we are looking forward to a new heaven and a new earth, the home of righteousness" (2 Pet. 3:13).

Isaiah twice wrote of a future new heavens and new earth. In the second of these texts the future creation serves simply as a measure of time. "As the new heavens and the new earth that I will make will endure before me . . . so will [Israel's] name and descendants endure" (Isa. 66:22). The first reference is more specific. "Behold, I will create new heavens and a new earth" (Isa. 65:17). This promise is followed by a description of future events (cf. 65:17-25).

Portions of Isaiah's description of the events that will follow the creation of the new heaven and earth closely parallel or are identical with his prior description of the millennial age (cf. "the lion will eat straw like the ox" [Isa. 11:17], and "the lion will eat straw like the ox" [Isa. 65:25]). Some scholars therefore conclude that Isaiah believed that on the new earth in the eternal age there would be humans who would enjoy a lifestyle similar to that of earthlings in the millennial age.

Another possibility can be suggested. In commenting on Isaiah 65:17-25 John Martin writes,

> In these verses the Lord described the millennial kingdom, which is seemingly identified here with the eternal state (new heavens and a new earth). In Revelation, however, the new heavens and new earth (Rev. 21:1) follow the Millennium (Rev. 20:4). Most likely Isaiah did not distinguish between these two aspects of God's rule; he saw them together as one.[4]

The new heaven

The present heaven is marked for demolition. Isaiah wrote, "All the stars of the heavens will be dissolved and the sky rolled up like a scroll; all the starry host will fall like withered leaves

---

4 John A. Martin, "Isaiah." In *The Bible Knowledge Commentary*, John F. Walvoord and Roy B. Zuck, editors. Wheaton: Victor Books, 1985, p. 1120.

from the vine, like shriveled figs from the fig tree" (Isa. 34:4). Jeremiah reported God's view of the future, "I looked at . . . the heavens, and their light was gone" (Jer. 4:23). Apparently the destruction of the present second heaven, the realm of the planets and stars, is being described. The Psalmist wrote, "In the beginning you laid the foundations of the earth, and the heavens are the work of your hands. They will perish, but you remain; they will all wear out like a garment. Like clothing you will change them and they will be discarded" (Psa. 102:25-26). Jesus said, "Heaven and earth will pass away" (Matt. 24:35); Peter wrote, "The heavens will disappear with a roar" (2 Pet. 3:10).

Scripture distinguishes the first or atmospheric heaven— "the birds of heaven"; the second or planetary and sidereal heaven—cf. Isa. 34:4 above; and the third heaven which is the dwelling place of God. Paul wrote, "I know a man in Christ who . . . was caught up to the third heaven. . . . —was caught up to paradise. He heard inexpressible things, things that man is not permitted to tell" (2 Cor. 12:2, 4).

It is evident that the earth's atmosphere has been polluted by humans, and even the planetary and sidereal heaven has been invaded by mankind's rockets. Also, the sidereal heaven is thought of as the realm of Satan. "For our struggle is not against flesh and blood, but against . . . the spiritual forces of evil in the heavenly realms" (Eph. 6:12).

Though it is warranted that the first and second heaven be replaced, it appears that the third heaven, God's dwelling place, may be unchanged. God may maintain it as a component in the new heaven. On the other hand, it is possible that God will transfer His throne to the new Jerusalem. Should He do so, it would appear that He would discontinue maintaining the former place as the center of His primary manifestation.

The new earth

As we have noted, most Scriptures that promise a new heaven also promise a new earth. These changes will occur before the great white throne judgment. "Then I saw a great white throne and him who was seated on it. Earth and sky fled from his presence, and there was no place for them" (Rev. 20:11). After his comment about the disappearance of the heavens (2 Pet. 3:10 cited above), Peter continued by explaining, "the elements will be destroyed [*luo*] by fire, and the earth and everything in it will be laid bare [burned up —NASB]. . . . That day will bring about the destruction of the heavens by fire, and the elements will melt in the heat. But in keeping with his promise we are looking forward to a new heaven and a new earth, the home of righteousness" (2 Pet. 3:10, 12-13). (*luo* [LU-oh]: to set free, loose, break up into its component parts, destroy, demolish). Stanley Horton comments, "[This verb] would be the New Testament word most likely to be used to describe atomic disintegration."[5]

Scripture portrays the new earth in only the briefest of sketches, and much basic data is lacking. John notes that in the new earth "there was no longer any sea" (Rev. 21:1). In this present fallen world the seas are often used for the disposal of refuse, and they serve to isolate the nations. By covering the earth's surface, they render about three-fourths of the earth uninhabitable, though humans are dependent upon the seas for, among other things, the renewal of the atmosphere. Evidently, God has determined that an earth without a sea would be the preferred habitat for His creatures.

The inhabitants of the new earth. Whether the nations and kings who relate to the new Jerusalem are residents of the city or of the new earth is a matter of debate. (cf. "The nations will walk by [the new Jerusalem's] light, and the kings of the earth will bring their splendor into it" [Rev. 21:24]). Two viewpoints prevail:

Viewpoint 1): The nations and kings reside in the new Jerusalem rather than on the new earth. Current commentaries on the book of Revelation prefer this view. Thus, John Walvoord writes,

> The meaning is not that political entities will enter into the new Jerusalem but rather that those who are saved Gentiles . . . will be in the city. . . . That the kings of the earth bring their glory and honor into the city means that those among the saved who have honored positions on earth will ascribe the glory and honor that once were theirs to the Lord.[6]

In a similar vein, Stanley Horton writes,

> The meaning here is . . . that the nations, or peoples, who are saved are the same ones who are resident in the city. . . . They will all be brought together, whether ordinary people or kings, and whatever glory or honor they had, they will bring into the city and present it all to God, to whom it is due.[7]

This viewpoint would imply that Scripture does not provide insights into the inhabitants of the new earth. It holds that in these references the term "nations" is equivalent to "people." The kings who are spoken of are resurrected former earthly kings who are now citizens of the new Jerusalem.

Viewpoint 2): The nations and kings are citizens of the new earth who live under the spiritual and political guardianship

---

5   Stanley M. Horton, op.cit., p. 249.
6   John F. Walvoord, *The Revelation of Jesus Christ*. Chicago: Moody Press, 1966, p. 327.
7   Stanley M. Horton, *The Ultimate Victory*. Springfield: Gospel Publishing House, 1991, p. 324.

of the new Jerusalem. John's words seem to imply that these people dwell on the new earth rather than in the new Jerusalem. "The nations will walk by its light, and the kings of the earth will bring their splendor into it. On no day will its gates by shut" (Rev. 21:24-25). The continuously open gates will permit visits by the citizens of the new earth. The fact that the new earth is described as "the home of righteousness" (2 Pet. 3:13), can be understood to mean that it will be a dwelling place of humans who have made the choice to live for God. Presumably, life on the new earth will be an extension of the idyllic life of the millennium.

As suggested above, people on the new earth may logically be those who are candidates for healing by the leaves of the tree of life. If in that age there are those who require healing it would likely be new-earth humans. Though there is no more curse, dwellers on the new earth might still suffer accidents or experience chronic medical conditions. Thus, the promise of healing to the nations may be taken as added support for the claims of Viewpoint 2. The place to find people needing healing would be the new earth.

The Final Destiny of the Wicked

Though the new earth, the new Jerusalem, and possibly the new heaven are each the home of particular moral intelligences, there are those who are excluded from all three of these realms. "Outside are the dogs [shameless unclean persons, see Phil. 3:2], those who practice magic arts, the sexually immoral, the murderers, the idolaters and everyone who loves and practices falsehood" (Rev. 22:15). But even in the realm of those excluded from the righteous, God reigns. Nothing happens even there except it is in accord with His strict justice.

The sinner's destiny in Gehenna

Jesus used the term *geenna* [GHEH-en-nah], (better known in its Latin form as *gehenna*) which is translated "hell," to denote the destiny of the wicked. "It is better for you to enter life crippled than to have two feet and be thrown into hell [Gk. *geenna*]" (Mark 9:45). Out of twelve occurrences of *geenna* in the New Testament, eleven were spoken by Jesus (cf. Matt. 5:22, 5:29, 5:30, 10:28, 18:9, 23:15, 23:33; Mark 9:43, 9:45, 9:47; Luke 12:5; and James 3:6). Two references combine *geenna* and fire. "Anyone who says, You fool! will be in danger of the fire of hell ["fiery gehenna"—Rotherham]" (Matt. 5:22, cf. 18:9).

Mark 9:43 refers to "hell, where the fire never goes out [Gk. *geennan, eis to pyr to asbeston*: literally—hell, to the fire the unquenchable]." The Greek *asbestos* [AS-bes-tos] has been brought into English to name the substance that does not disintegrate in flame but which was believed to be inextinguishable when finally set on fire. In the sole New Testament mention of Gehenna not spoken by Jesus, the reference is to the tongue: "[It] is itself set on fire [Gk. *phlogidzo*] by hell [*geenna*]" (James 3:6). (*phlogidzo* [flog-ID-zo]: to set on fire, enflame, ignite, set ablaze). Gehenna clearly identifies with fire.

The New Testament *geenna* (or *gehenna*) is the Greek form of the Hebrew *gay hinnom* [GAH-ee hin-NOME] meaning "Valley of Hinnom." Though the location of this valley is disputed by scholars, from time to time it was the site of Old Testament events. At times it is given the expanded name of "Valley of Ben Hinnom [i.e., the son of Hinnom]. " Thus: "[Ahaz] burned sacrifices in the Valley of Ben Hinnom and sacrificed his sons in the fire, following the detestable ways of the nations the Lord had driven out before the Israelites" (2 Chron. 28:3, cf. Jer. 7:31). The reforming king, Josiah, abolished Molech worship in the Valley of Hinnom (cf. 2 Kings 23:8-11), and there is no evidence that the Jews ever revived it.

Tradition—by some accounts no older than A.D. 1200—holds that after Josiah, the Valley of Hinnom was used as a place to dispose of the bodies of animals by burning, and later it became a general garbage dump where fire always burned and flesh-eating maggots and worms were active. The continuously burning garbage would certainly support Jesus' use of the Valley of Hinnom (*gehenna*) as synonymous with the place of eternal torment. Even if the tradition is not validated, however, the ancient use of the Valley for the sacrifice of children to Molech would adequately justify Jesus' usage.

Gehenna, the lake of fire, and Topheth

Scripture uses the expressions "lake of fire" or "fiery lake of burning sulfur" as alternates for *gehenna*. "If anyone's name was not found written in the book of life, he was thrown into the lake of fire" (Rev. 20:15); "The cowardly, the unbelieving, the vile, the murderers, the sexually immoral, those who practice magic arts, the idolaters and all liars—their place will be the fiery lake of burning sulfur. This is the second death" (Rev. 21:8).

In a single instance in Scripture, Isaiah applied the name *Topheth* (or *Tophet* —KJV), apparently as a synonym for Gehenna, to the place of the wicked king's future judgment. "Topheth has long been prepared; it has been made ready for the king . . . the breath of the LORD, like a stream of burning sulfur, sets it ablaze" (Isa. 30:33). Topheth's association with Molech worship in the Valley of Hinnom further identifies it with *gehenna*.

Scripture depicts the fire of *gehenna* as perpetual (cf. Mark 9:43 discussed above). In speaking of the destiny of the sinner in *geenna* Jesus quoted Isaiah 66:24, "where their worm does not die, and the fire is not quenched" (Mark 9:48).

The fate of the wicked is repeatedly associated with fire. "The angels will come and separate the wicked . . . and throw them into the fiery furnace" (Matt. 13:49-50); "They serve as an example of those who suffer the punishment of eternal fire" (Jude 7); "If anyone worships the beast . . . he will be tormented with burning sulfur. . . . And the smoke of their torment rises for ever and ever" (Rev. 14:9-11); "The King will reply . . . 'Depart from me, you who are cursed, into the eternal fire prepared for the devil and his angels'" (Matt. 25:40-41). This latter verse not only declares the fire to be eternal (or everlasting), but it also explains Gehenna's real purpose—"for the devil and his angels." Tragically, those who choose to follow Satan must share his doom in the fire of *gehenna*.

When this realm of the after life is identified, it would be less confusing to retain the Greek name *geenna*, or at least its Latin form *gehenna*. The English word "hell" comes from roots that imply "that which is concealed or buried," and thus it associates with the grave rather than with a place of fiery punishment.

The state of the sinner in eternity

Those who die in their sins proceed to darkness and misery. "Throw that worthless servant outside, into the darkness, where there will be weeping and gnashing of teeth" (Matt. 25:30). Darkness results from the sinner's separation from God's light. Jude wrote of hypocrites, "These men are blemishes at your love feasts . . . twice dead. They are wild waves of the sea . . . for whom blackest darkness has been reserved forever" (Jude 12-13). Paul wrote, "When the Lord Jesus is revealed from heaven in blazing fire with his powerful angels He will punish those who do not know God and do not obey the gospel of our Lord Jesus. They will be punished with everlasting destruction [Gk. *olethros*] and shut out from the presence of the Lord and from the majesty of his power" ["eternal exclusion from the radiance of the face of the Lord"—Phillips] (2 Thess. 1:7-9). (*olethros* [OL-eth-ros]: destruction, ruin, death).

The second death of the sinner is spiritual, and it entails eternal separation from God. As the just consequence of his own foolish choice, the sinner will be forever cut off from the grace and love of God. The second death finally and eternally separates from God's new creation, just as physical death separates from this world. The sinner's separation from God in the life to come parallels that of a living sinner who is "dead in . . . transgressions and sins" (Eph. 2:1). Paul Althaus commented, "Eternal death is inescapable godlessness in an inescapable God relationship." The perpetual human thirst for God will find no relief.

The sinner's mode of existence in *gehenna* will evidently be appropriate for his fate. Scripture does not describe the sinner's form of being, but apparently his outward being and person will correspond to that which is within him. "Let him who does wrong continue to do wrong; let him who is vile continue to be vile" (Rev. 22:11). Jesus' parables indicate that there are degrees of punishment in *gehenna*. "That servant who knows his master's will and does not get ready or does not do what his master wants will be beaten with many blows. But the one who does not know and does things deserving punishment will be beaten with few blows" (Luke 12:47-48). Jesus said of the hypocritical teachers of the law, "They devour widows' houses . . . [s]uch men will be punished most severely" (Luke 20:47). Eternal punishment, nevertheless, is not a remedial program to change the sinner; rather, it is God's vindication of His holiness, righteousness, and justice. "The face of the Lord is against those who do evil, to cut off the memory of them from the earth" (Psa. 34:16). The sinner must be removed from the realm of God's people, and God must vindicate in him His eternal moral standards.

Variant Theories of the Eternal State

Through the centuries, the prospect of the eternal punishment of the sinner in the afterlife has periodically generated protests from those to whom the idea is repugnant. In the opinion of most biblical literalists, however, denials of eternal punishment must deliberately reject Scripture. It has been noted that there is a total of thirty-seven biblical Hebrew and Greek words that are used to describe the final state of the wicked, all of them indicating some aspect or phase of the destruction that awaits the sinner. God's Word teaches eternal punishment in spite of human efforts to defend other possibilities.

The claims of universalism

According to universalism (also known as "reconciliationism" or "restorationism," or referred to as the "doctrine of *apokatastasis* [ap-ok-at-AS-tas-is]" if the Greek form is used), all moral intelligences, including sinners, Satan, and Satan's demons, will be reconciled to God and share eternity with Him. One of the first proponents of universalism was Origen (c. 185-254) who taught that the renovation of the earth would achieve the purification of humans and all created beings. Following a brief period of punishment, they would all be restored to the original unity with God.

Origin's views on this subject earned him the title, "The Father of Universalism." Three centuries later, there were enough supporters of universalism that, in the Second Council of Constantinople (553), the Catholic church pronounced it heresy. In spite of such actions, the doctrine persisted, and in the modern period it was conspicuously defended by Hosea Ballou (1771-1852). Some contemporary liberal theologians find universalism fully acceptable on the grounds of the logic and sentiment upon which they base their theology. Typically, the Bible statements that speak of an eternal hell are explained as "mythical language designed to provoke response to God."

The universalist correctly sees that Scripture depicts God's desire that all humans be saved. "God . . . wants all men to be saved and to come to a knowledge of the truth" (1 Tim. 2:3-4; cf. Acts 3:19-21; Rom. 5:18, 11:32; 1 Cor. 15:22, 25; Eph. 1:9-10; Col. 1:19-20; 1 Tim. 4:10;). These Scriptures, however, do not teach that God's program will achieve the universal salvation of all creatures. His provision assures that all who respond will find salvation, that the gift of eternal life is potentially available to all, that His every enemy is conquered, and that He one day will inaugurate a world that is no longer under a curse.

To fulfill God's desire, the additional element that is always required is His acceptance by the individual being, and the personal appropriation of that provision. The universalist confuses God's provision for the moral universe with the actual outcome of the behavior of free moral creatures, and the two are not the same. Universalism makes a mockery of both the law and the gospel. Someone has said, "If there is no eternal hell, then God is Santa Claus, and life is a parlor game."

Scriptures that clearly contradict the claims of universalism include "Anyone who speaks against the Holy Spirit will not be forgiven, either in this age or in the age to come" (Matt. 12:32); and "Whoever rejects the Son will not see life, for God's wrath remains on him" (John 3:36). The wicked are destined to destruction: "Wide is the gate and broad is the road that leads to destruction [Gk. *apoleia*]" (Matt. 7:13); "Many live as enemies of the cross of Christ. Their destiny is destruction [Gk. *apoleia*" (Phil. 3:18-19). (*apoleia* [ap-OH-lie-ah]: ruin, loss, destruction, waste, perniciousness).

Process theology eschatology

This outlook is adapted from secular philosophy, and it chiefly appeals to liberals who interpret Scripture casually. One of its spokesmen is Walter Wink. Process theology begins with the denial of the personal self or soul as a substantive entity—an idea held by secular psychology. If humans are mere functions of their living bodies, when the body dies there is no "soul" (self) to survive. What survives of an individual human is the memory of his values that are held in the mind of the Cosmic Consciousness or God. The aggregate of that which is immortal in all the lives of all humans cumulate in the progressive reality that we call God.

Though process theology sees individual earthly experiences to be lost, that which can be salvaged is perpetuated in what is called a "concrescence." This concrescence is an "energy-event" commonly called "God" that continues a progressive advance. On one hand it is the realm of heaven and eternity, on the other it is the inner essence of present reality. By identifying with this concrescence, humans will some day be able to come together in a great one-world religion. God and heaven and all living humans achieve eternal status in the perpetuation of the values proved worthy in the lives of those who have lived on earth.

Process theology has no valid Biblical basis. God is a personal entity, and so is each human. The process that matters is the implementation of God's truth by which a believer grows in grace. Paul wrote to the Philippians, "I will continue with all of you for your progress and joy in the faith" (Phil. 1:25). Ongoing process in the sinner's life leads him downward. "Evil men and impostors will go from bad to worse" (2 Tim. 3:13). Future reward or judgment awaits individual humans according to the direction of their growth—which process works in them. From eternity, the supreme God has embodied the totality of all virtue, and in no way does any creature or event add to His being.

The doctrine of annihilationism

The doctrine of annihilationism (also known as conditionalism) has arisen periodically over the centuries, and it has been the belief both of cults, and of otherwise orthodox theologians. Names associated with the view include E.W. Bullinger, Henry Drummond, Pastor C.T. Russell, John H. Pettingell, and F.W. Farrar in the nineteenth century, and David Elton Trueblood, and Oscar Cullmann in the twentieth century.

Annihilationism teaches that the sinner is totally destroyed, or annihilated, by being cast into the lake of fire. Thus, only the righteous will live eternally, and their immortality is granted upon fulfilling the condition of accepting God's gift of eternal life through Jesus Christ. The sinner's destiny in hell is eternal in the sense that there is no further resurrection or return from the destruction that he or she suffers.

To declare the believer's conditional immortality and the sinner's annihilation is to teach contrary to overall Scripture. In the after life, humans are not merely placed in the grave, but they proceed to an actual place. We have previously seen that Scripture depicts the immediate destiny of the departed as either Paradise or *sheol*, and the ultimate destiny as either the new Jerusalem, or *gehenna*.

Jesus provided clear statements in regard to the future life: "They [those who are cursed] will go away to eternal [Gk. *aionios*] punishment, but the righteous to eternal [Gk. *aionios*] life" (Matt. 25:46). (*aionios* [ai-OH-nee-os]: without end, forever, eternal, perpetual). In this statement, He applied the word *aionios* identically to both states of existence. Elsewhere in Scripture, the same word *aionios* is used to denote the duration of the life of God. "[He] who sits on the throne and who lives for ever [Gk. *aionios*] and ever" (Rev. 4:9).

The sinner is not annihilated, but he must undergo punishment in *gehenna* that endures equally with the believer's bliss in the new Jerusalem. In a specific Biblical example, the beast and false prophet were thrown into the lake of fire at the end of the tribulation, and therefore just prior to the launching of the millennium (cf. Rev. 19:20). One thousand years later, Satan also was cast into *gehenna*. Scripture reports, "The devil . . . was thrown into the lake of burning sulfur, where the beast and the false prophet had been thrown [where the beast and the false prophet are also - NASB]. They will be tormented day and night for ever and ever" (Rev. 20:10). Clearly, the Beast and False Prophet survived 1,000 years in *gehenna*, and in fact they, and all the other moral creatures who chose to join them, will continue to survive eternally.

SELECTED BIBLIOGRAPHY

Alderman, Paul B. Jr. *The Unfolding of the Ages*. Grand Rapids: Zondervan Publishing House, 1954.

Allnutt, Frank. *Antichrist After the Omen*. Old Tappan: Fleming H. Revell Company, 1976.

Anderson, Robert. *The Coming Prince*. London: Pickering and Inglis, 1876.☥

Armerding, Carl E., and W. Ward Gasque eds. *handbook of biblical prophec*y. (sic) Grand Rapids: Baker Book House, 1977.

Bahnsen, Greg L., and Kenneth L. Gentry, Jr. *House Divided*. Tyler (TX): Institute for Christian Economics, 1989.◆

Bailey, Keith M. *Christ's Coming and His Kingdom*. Harrisburg: Christian Publications Inc., 1981.☥

Baker, Charles F. *A Dispensational Theology*. Grand Rapids: Grace Bible College Publications, 1972.☥

Bass, Clarence B. *Backgrounds to Dispensationalism*. Grand Rapids: Wm. B. Eerdmans Publishing Co., 1960.

Baxter, Michael Paget. *Forty Prophetic Wonders*. London: Christian Herald, 1923.

Barclay, William. *King and Kingdom*. Edinburgh: St. Andrews Press, 1969.

Beckwith, George D. *God's Prophetic Plan*. Grand Rapids: Zondervan Publishing House, 1942.

Beechick, Allen. *The Pretribulation Rapture*. Denver: Accent Publications, 1980.☥

Beet, Joseph Agar. *The Last Things*. New York: Eaton and Mains, 1898.

Belcher, Richard P. *Dispensationalism and Covenant Theology*. Southbridge (MA): Crowne Publications, 1986.

Biederwolf, William E. *The Second Coming Bible*. Grand Rapids: Baker Book House, 1972.✳

Blackstone, W.E. *Jesus is Coming*. New York: Fleming H. Revell Co., 1908.☥

Bobo, Truett E. *An Evangelical Theology of the Intermediate State*. Pasadena: Fuller Theological Seminary, 1978, unpublished Doctor of Philosophy dissertation.

Bock, Darrell L., gen. ed. *Three Views on the Millennium and Beyond*. Grand Rapids: Zondervan Publishing House, 1999.

Boettner, Loraine. *Immortality*. Grand Rapids: Wm. B. Eerdmans Publishing Co., 1956.

———. *The Millennium*. Philadelphia: Presbyterian and Reformed Publishing Co., 1958.◆

Boersma, T. *Is the Bible a Jigsaw Puzzle? An Evaluation of Hal Lindsey's Writings*.St. Catherines (ON): Paideia Press, 1978.❖

Boice, James Montgomery. *Last and Future World*. Grand Rapids: Zondervan Publishing House, 1974.

Braaten, Carl E. *Eschatology and Ethics*. Minneapolis: Augsburg Press, 1974.

Bradbury, John W. (ed.). *The Sure Word of Prophecy*. New York: Fleming H. Revell Co., 1943.

Bratt, John H. *The Final Curtain*. Grand Rapids: Baker Book House, 1978.

Brown, Hugh D. *Our Happy Dead*. London: Morgan and Scott Ltd., 1916.

Brunner, Emil. *Eternal Hope*. London: Lutterworth Press, 1954.

Bultema, Harry. *Maranatha*. Grand Rapids: Kregel Publications, 1985 (translation of Dutch edition of 1917).☥

Buswell, J. Oliver. *A Systematic Theology of the Christian Religion*. Grand Rapids: Zondervan Publishing House, 1963.✳

Buxton, Clyne W. *What About Tomorrow?* Cleveland: Pathway Press, 1974. ☥

Byers, Marvin, *The Final Victory. The Year 2000*. Shippensburg (PA): Companion Press, 1991.✳

Carver, Everett I. *When Jesus Comes Again*. Phillipsburg: Presbyterian and Reformed Publishing Co., 1979.❖

Case, Shirely. *The Millennial Hope*. Chicago: University of Chicago Press, 1918.

Chader, C.A. *God's Plan Through The Ages*. Grand Rapids: Zondervan Publishing House, 1938.☥

Chafer, Lewis S. *Systematic Theology* (Vol. IV). Dallas: Dallas Seminary Press, 1948. ☥

Chilton, David. *The Great Tribulation*. Fort Worth: Dominion Press, 1987.◆

Clouse, Robert G. (ed.). *The Meaning of the Millennium*. Downers Grove: InterVarsity Press, 1977.

Clouser, G.B.M. *The Age Times*. Harrisburg: Evangelical Publishing House, 1917.

Coder, S. Maxwell. *The Final Chapter*. Wheaton: Tyndale House, 1984.☥

Cox, William E. *Amillennialism Today*. Philadelphia: Presbyterian and Reformed Publishing Co., 1966.❖

Crenshaw, Curtis I., and Grover E. Gunn III, *Dispensationism Today, Yesterday, and Tomorrow*. Memphis: Footstool Publications, 1985. (Implicit ◆)

Crouch, Mal, ed. *Dictionary of Premillennial Theology*. Grand Rapids: Kregel Publications, 1996.

Dahlin, John E. *Prophetic Truth for Today.* Minneapolis: Beacon Publishing, 1961.

Darby, J.N. *Lectures on the Second Coming.* London: G. Morrish, 1909.✝

Davis, John Jefferson. *Christ's Victorious' Kingdom.* Grand Rapids: Baker Book House, 1986.◆

DeHaan, M.R. *The Second Coming of Jesus.* Grand Rapids: Zondervan Publishing House, 1946.✝

DeMar, Gary. *The Debate over Christian Reconstruction.* Fort Worth: Dominion Press, 1988.◆

Dumbrell, William J. *The Search for Order: Biblical Eschatology in Focus.* Grand Rapids: Baker Books, 1994.❖

Duncan, Homer. *The Millennial Reign of Christ.* Lubbock: Missionary Crusader, n.d.

Dunham, T. Richard. *The Great Tribulation.* Hoytville: Fundamental Truth Store, 1933.

Duty, Guy. *Christ's Coming and the World Church.* Minneapolis: Dimension Books, 1971.

Eddleman, H. Leo. *Last Things.* Grand Rapids: Zondervan Publishing House, 1969.

English, Eugene Schuyler. *Re-Thinking the Rapture.* Traveler's Rest: Southern Bible Book House, 1954.✝

Epp, Theodore H. *A Brief Outline of Things to Come.* Chicago: Moody Press, 1952.✝

Erickson, Millard J. *Contemporary Options in Eschatology.* Grand Rapids: Baker Book House, 1977.

Evans, William. *The Coming King.* New York: Fleming H. Revell, 1923.

Feinberg, Charles Lee. *Premillennialism or Amillennialism.* Wheaton: Van Kampen Press, 1954.○

———, ed. *Prophecy and the Seventies.* Chicago: Moody Press, 1971.○

Fereday, W.W. *Coming Events on Earth and in Heaven.* London: Pickering and Inglis, n.d.

Fletcher, George B. *The Millennium.* Swengel: Reiner Publications, 1972.

Forsyth, P.T. *This Life and the Next.* London: Independent Press, 1918.

Fraser, Alexander. *Return of Christ in His Glory.* Pittsburg: Evangelical Fellowship, 1950.

Frodsham, Stanley H. *The Coming Crises and the Coming Christ.* Springfield: Gospel Publishing House, n.d.
✝

———. *Things Which Must Shortly Come to Pass.* Springfield: Gospel Publishing House, 1928. ✝

Gaebelein, Arno C. *The Conflict of the Ages.* New York: Our Hope, 1933.✝

———. *Coming Great Events.* New York: D.T. Bass, n.d.✝

———. *Studies in Prophecy.* New York: Our Hope, 1918.✝

Gentry, Kenneth L., Jr., *The Beast of Revelation.* Tyler (TX): Institute for Christian Economics, 1989. (Implicit ◆)

Gilmore, John. *Probing Heaven.* Grand Rapids: Baker Book House, 1989.❖

Goetz, William R. *Apocalypse Next.* Beaverlodge (Alberta): Horizon House Publishers, 1980.✝

———. *The Economy to Come.* Beaverlodge (Alberta): Horizon House Publishers, 1983.✝

Gordon, S.D. *Quiet Talks About our Lord's Return.* New York: Fleming H. Revell Co., n.d.

Gray, James M. *Prophecy and the Lord's Return.* New York: Fleming H. Revell Co., 1917.✝

Grier, W.J. *The Momentous Advent.* Edinburgh: The Banner of Truth Trust, 1970.❖

Gundry, Robert H. *The Church and the Tribulation.* Grand Rapids: Zondervan Publishing House, 1973.✲

Gundry, Stanley N. series ed. *Three Views on the Rapture.* Grand Rapids: Zondervan Publishing House, 1984, 1996.

Hall, John G. *Prophecy Marches On!* (Vols. 1 and 2). Newcastle (OK), published by the author, 1963,1966.✝

Hamilton, Floyd E. *The Basis of Millennial Faith.* Grand Rapids: Wm. B. Eerdmans Publishing Co., 1942.❖

Hanson, Paul D. *The Dawn of Apocalyptic.* Philadelphia: Fortress Press, 1975.

Harris, Charles. *What's Ahead.* Springfield: Gospel Publishing House, 1981.✝

Harrison, Norman B. *His Coming.* Minneapolis: The Harrison Service, 1946.✹

———. *His Sure Return.* Chicago: Bible Institute Colportage Association, 1926.✹

Harrison, William K. *Hope Triumphant.* Moody Press, 1966.

Haynes, Carlyle B. *The Return of Jesus.* South Bend: Review and Herald Publishing Association, 1926.

Helm, Paul, *The Last Things.* Edinburgh: The Banner of Truth Trust, 1989.

Hendriksen, William. *The Bible on the Life Hereafter.* Grand Rapids: Baker Book House, 1959.❖

———. *Lectures on the Last Things.* Grand Rapids: Baker Book House, 1951.❖

Henry, Carl F.H., ed. *Prophecy in the Making.* Carol Stream: Creation House, 1971.✲

Hewitt, P.E. *Coming Events.* Grand Rapids: Zondervan Publishing House, 1942.

Hicks, Roy H. *Another Look at the Rapture.* Tulsa: Harrison House, 1982.

Hindson, Ed. *Earth's Final Hour.* Eugene: Harvest House Publishers, 1999.⇧

Hitchcock, Mark. *The Complete Book of Bible Prophecy.* Wheaton: Tyndale House Publishers, 1999.⇧

Hodges, Jesse W. *Christ's Kingdom and Coming.* Grand Rapids: Wm. B. Eerdmans Publishing Co., 1957.

Hopkins, Samuel. *A Treatise on the Millennium.* New York: Arno Press, 1972.

Horton, Stanley. *Our Destiny.* Springfield: Logion Press, 1996.⇧

———. *The Promise of His Coming.* Springfield: Gospel Publishing House, 1967.⇧

———. *The Ultimate Victory.* Springfield: Gospel Publishing House, 1991.⇧

Hough, Robert Ervin. *The Christian After Death.* Chicago: Moody Press, 1947.

Hoyt, Herman A. *The End Times.* Chicago: Moody Press, 1969.

Ironside, H.A. *Death and Afterwards.* New York: Loizeaux Brothers, n.d.⇧

———. *The Lamp of Prophecy.* Grand Rapids: Zondervan Publishing House, 1940.⇧

James, William T., ed. *Piercing the Future.* Benton: Nelson Walker Publishers, 2000.⇧

Jeffrey, Grant R. *Armageddon—Appointment With Destiny.* Toronto: Frontier Research Publications, 1988.⇧

Jeffress, Robert. *As Time Runs Out.* Nashville: Broadman & Holman Publishers, 1999.⇧

Jessop, Harry E. *The Day of Wrath.* New York: Fleming H. Revell, 1943.

Jones, R. Bradley. *What, Where, and When is the Millennium?* Grand Rapids: Baker Book House, 1975.

Kaiser, Walter C., Jr. *Back Toward the Future: Hints for Interpreting Biblical Prophecy.* Grand Rapids: Baker Book House, 1989.

Kelley, William. *Lectures on Revelation.* New York: Loizeaux Brothers, n.d.

Kimball, William R. *The Rapture.* Grand Rapids: Baker Book House, 1985. (Implicit ❖)

Kincheloe, Raymond McFarland. *A Personal Adventure in Prophecy.* Wheaton: Tyndale House, 1974.⇧

Kingston, Charles J. *The Coming of Christ and After.* London: Victory Press, 1939.

Kraus, C. Norman. *Dispensationalism in America: Its Rise and Development.* Richmond: John Knox Press, 1958.

Ladd, George Eldon. *Presence of the Future.* Grand Rapids: Wm. B. Eerdmans Publishing Co., 1974.✳

———. *The Last Things.* Grand Rapids: Wm. B. Eerdmans Publishing Co., 1978.✳

LaHaye, Tim. *The Beginning of the End.* Wheaton: Tyndale House Publishers, 1981.⇧

———. *The Coming Peace in the Middle East.* Grand Rapids: Zondervan Publishing House, 1984.⇧

———. *No Fear of the Storm.* (Republished as *Rapture Under Attack*, 1998). Sisters (OR): Multnomah Press, 1992.⇧

Lewis, David Allen. *Signs of His Coming.* Green Forest: New Leaf Press. 1997.⇧

———. *The Ten Lost Tribes.* Springfield: Menorah Press, 1986.⇧

———. *Time for the Temple.* Springfield: Menorah Press, 1986.⇧

Lightner, Robert P. *The Last Days Handbook.* Nashville: Thomas Nelson Publishers, 1990.

Lindsey, Gordon. *Present World Events in the Light of Prophecy.* Shreveport: Voice of Healing, 1951.

Lindsey, Hal. *Planet Earth.* Beverly Hills: Western Front Ltd., 1998.⇧

———. *There's A New World Coming.* Santa Ana: Vision House, 1973.⇧

———. *The Late Great Planet Earth.* Grand Rapids: Zondervan Publishing House, 1970.⇧

———. *The Rapture.* New York: Bantam Books, 1983.⇧

Longley, Arthur. *Israel Tomorrow.* Hull: Yorkshire Expositor, 1971.

Ludwigson, R. *Survey of Bible Prophecy.* Grand Rapids: Zondervan Publishing House, 1973.

MacDonald, Ken and Agnes, *The Second Coming.* Newcomerstown (OH): Berean Publications, 1991. ✳❖

MacNeil, John. *Some One is Coming.* London: Marshall, 1896.

MacPherson, Dave. *The Incredible Cover-Up.* Medford: Omega Publications, 1975.

McBirnie, W.S. *Fifty Progressive Messages on the Second Coming of Christ.* Norfolk: McBirnie Publishing Ass'n., 1944.

McConkey, James H. *The End of the Age.* Pittsburgh: Silver Publishing Society, 1918.

McClain, Alva J. *Greatness of the Kingdom.* Chicago: Moody Press, 1959.○

McCrossan, T.J. *World's Crisis and the Coming Christ.* Seattle: McCrossan, n.d.

McKeating, Henry. *God and the Future.* London: SCM Press, 1974.

McKeever, James. *Christians Will Go Through The Tribulation.* Medford: Alpha Omega Publishing Co., 1978.✳

————. *The Rapture Book*. Medford: Omega Publications, 1987.✳

————. *Claim Your Birthright*. Medford: Omega Publications, 1989.✳

McLeman, James. *Resurrection Now and Then*. Philadelphia: J.B. Lippincott, 1967.

Martin, James P. *The Last Judgment*. Grand Rapids: Wm. B. Eerdmans Publishing Co., 1963.

Mason, Clarence E. Jr. *Prophetic Problems*. Chicago: Moody Press, 1973.

Mauro, Philip. *The Seventy Weeks and the Great Tribulation*. Swengel: Reiner Publications, 1975.

Missen, Alfred F. *Notes on the Second Coming of Christ*. (published by the author, 1945).

Moody, Dale. *The Hope of Glory*. Grand Rapids: Wm. B. Eerdmans Publishing Co., 1964.✳

Morgan, G. Campbell. *Behold, He Cometh!* New York: Fleming H. Revell Co., 1912.✳

Murray, George L. *Millennial Studies*. Grand Rapids: Baker Book House, 1948.

Naish, Reginald T. *Midnight Hour and After*. London: Tynne and Jarvis, 1925.

Ottman, Ford C. *The Coming Day*. Philadelphia: The Sunday School Times Co., 1921.

Pankhurst, Christabel, *Seeing the Future*. New York: Harper and Brothers, 1929.

Paulk, Earl, *Ultimate Kingdom*. Atlanta: K Dimension Publications, 1984.◆

Payne, J. Barton. *Encyclopedia of Biblical Prophecy*. Grand Rapids: Baker Book House, 1973.

Pentecost, J. Dwight. *Prophecy for Today*. Grand Rapids: Zondervan Publishing House, 1961.⊕

————. *Things to Come*. Findlay: Dunham Publishing Co., 1959.⊕

Peters, George N.H. *The Theocratic Kingdom*. Grand Rapids: Kregel Publications, 1957.

Pettingill, William L. *Nearing the End*. Wheaton: Van Kampen Press, 1948.⊕

Phillips, John. *Exploring the Future*. Nashville: Thomas Nelson Publishers, 1983.⊕

Poythress, Vern S. *Understanding Dispensationalists*. Grand Rapids: Zondervan Publishing House, 1987. (Implicit◆)

Price, Walter. *Coming Antichrist*. Chicago: Moody Press, 1974.

Ramm, Bernard. *Them He Glorified*. Grand Rapids: Wm. B. Eerdmans Publishing Co., 1963.✳

Reese, Alexander. *The Approaching Advent of Christ*. Grand Rapids: International Publication, 1975 (reprint of edition of 1937). ✳

Reinhold, Roy A. *The Day of the Lord*. Virginia Beach: Windstar Books, 1986.✴

Richardson, Stanton W. *Studies in Biblical Theology* (Vol. II). St. Paul: St. Paul Bible College, 1969.⊕

Riggs, Ralph M. *The Story of the Future*. Springfield: Gospel Publishing House, 1968.⊕

Rimmer, Harry. *The Coming King*. Grand Rapids: Wm. B. Eerdmans Publishing Co., 1945.✳

Roberts, Oral. *The Drama of the End-Time*. Tulsa: published by the author, 1963.

Robinson, O. Palmer. *Covenants: God's way with his people*. Philadelphia: Great Commission Publications, 1987.

Rose, George L. *Tribulation Till Translation*. Glendale: published by the author, 1943.✳

Rosenthal, Marvin. *The Pre-Wrath Rapture of the Church*. Nashville: Thomas Nelson Publishers, 1990.✴✳

Rowell, Geoffrey. *Hell and the Victorians*. Oxford: Clarendon Press, 1974.

Ryrie, Charles Caldwell. *The Basis of the Premillennial Faith*. New York: Loizeaux Brothers, 1953.⊕

————. *Basic Theology*. Wheaton: Scripture Press, 1986.⊕

Ryrie, Charles, Joe Jordan, and Tom Davis, eds. *Countdown to Armageddon*. Eugene: Harvest House Publishers, 1999.⊕

Sabiers, Karl. *Where Are the Dead?* Los Angeles: Christian Pocket Books, n.d.

Sale-Harrison, L. *The Resurrection of the Old Roman Empire*. New York: Hephzibah House, 1934.

Schwarz, Hans. *On the Way to the Future*. Minneapolis: Augsburg Publishing House, 1972.

Schep, J.A. *The Nature of the Resurrection Body*. Grand Rapids: Wm. B. Eerdmans Publishing Co., 1964.

Schumm, F.C.G. *Does Revelation 20 Teach a Millennium?* St. Louis: Concordia Publishing House, 1962.◆

Scroggie, W. Graham. *The Lord's Return*. London: Pickering and Inglis Ltd., n.d.

Sears, William. *Thief in the Night*. London: George Ronald, 1961.

Seventh-day Adventists Believe. Hagerstown: Review and Herald Publishing Association, 1988.

Shipman, Charles A. *Unfulfilled Prophecy*. London: Samuel E. Roberts, 1908.

Sims, A. *The Coming Golden Age*. Toronto: published by the author, n.d.

Smith, Wilbur M. *The Biblical Doctrine of Heaven*. Chicago: Moody Press, 1968.

————. *You Can Know the Future.* Glendale: Regal Books, 1971.

Sparrow-Simpson, W.J. *The Resurrection and the Christian Faith.* Grand Rapids: Zondervan Publishing House, 1968.

Sproule, John A. *In Defense of Pre-Tribulationism.* Winona Lake: BMH Books, 1980.✝

Stanton, Gerald B. *Why I Am a Premillennialist.* West Palm Beach: Ambassadors International, 1976.✝

Stevens, William Wilson. *The Doctrines of the Christian Religion.* Clinton: Mississippi College, 1965.

Strauss, Lehman. *The End of This Present World.* Grand Rapids: Zondervan Publishing House, 1967.

Strombeck, J.F. *First the Rapture.* (3rd ed.). Moline: Strombeck Agency, 1950.

Stuernagel, A.E. *Christ's Coming Reign of Peace.* Sacramento: World's Best Literature Depot, 1926.

Summers, Ray. *The Life Beyond.* Nashville: Broadman Press, 1959.❖

Synan, J.A. *The Shape of Things to Come.* Franklin Springs: Advocate Press, 1969.

Talbot, Louis T. *God's Plan of the Ages.* Grand Rapids: Wm. B. Eerdmans Publishing Co., 1946.

Tan, Paul Lee. *The Interpretation of Prophecy.* Rockville (MD): Assurance Publishers, 1974.✝

————. *Jesus is Coming.* Rockville (MD): Assurance Publishers, 1982.✝

Tatford, Frederick A. *God's Program of the Ages.* Grand Rapids: Kregel Publications, 1967.✝

Taylor, Charles R. *Watch World Events Relating to the Bible in 1989.* Huntington Beach: Today in Bible Prophecy, n.d.✝

Tedder, H.J. *Prophetic Telescope.* Barberton: published by the author, 1928.

Thomas, Lawrence Rowe. *A Symposium of Prophecy.* Albany (Australia): published by the author, n.d.

Tooley, Dale. *All Things New.* Lower Hutt (New Zealand): Hasten the Light Ministries, 1989.❖

Travis, Arthur E. *Where on Earth is Heaven?* Nashville: Broadman Press, 1974.

Travis, Stephen H. *The Jesus Hope.* Downers Grove: InterVarsity Press, 1974.❖

————. *I Believe in the Second Coming.* Grand Rapids: Wm. B. Eerdmans Publishing Co., 1982. ❖

Tubby, C.S. *The End of the Time.* Stevensville: published by the author, n.d.

Tulga, Chester E. *The Case for the Second Coming of Christ.* Chicago: Conservative Baptist Fellowship, 1951.

Van Impe, Jack. *11:59 . . . and Counting.* Nashville: Thomas Nelson Publishers, 1987.✝

Van Kampen, Robert. *The Sign.* Wheaton: Crossway Books, 1992.✸✳

Vos, Geerhardus. *Pauline Eschatology.* Grand Rapids: Wm. B. Eerdmans Publishing Co., 1972.

Walvoord, John F. *The Church in Prophecy.* Grand Rapids: Zondervan Publishing House, 1964.✝

————. *The Blessed Hope and the Tribulation.* Grand Rapids: Zondervan Publishing House, 1976.✝

————. *The Rapture Question.* Grand Rapids: Zondervan Publishing House, 1979 ✝

————. *The Prophecy Knowledge Handbook.* Wheaton: Victor Books, 1990.✝

————. *The Revelation of Jesus Christ.* Chicago: Moody Press, 1966.✝

Walvoord, John F. and John E. Walvoord. *Armageddon, Oil and the Middle East Crisis.* Grand Rapids: Zondervan Publishing House, 1974.

Ward, William B. *After Death, What?* Richmond: John Knox Press, 1967.

Weber, Timothy P. *The Future Explored.* Wheaton: Victor Books, 1978.

————. *Living in the Shadow of the Second Coming.* Grand Rapids: Academie Books, 1983.

West, Nathaniel. *The Thousand Years.* Fincastle: Scripture Truth Co., reprint of edition of 1889.

Williams, Ernest S. *Systematic Theology* (Vol. III). Springfield: Gospel Publishing House, 1953.✝

Willmington, H.L. *The King is Coming.* Wheaton: Tyndale House Publishers, 1981.

Wilson, Dwight. *Armageddon Now.* Grand Rapids: Baker Book House, 1977✝

———

The symbols attached to certain listings indicate the author's opinion of the perspective of the work according to the key that follows. Only some works are keyed because either: 1) the book's content does not lend itself to such classification, or 2) the book's title clearly indicates its approach, or 3) the author read the book before he kept such records.

✝pretribulationist; ✸midtribulationist; ✳posttribulationist; ◆postmillennialist; ❖amillennialist; ○ premillennialist

INDEX